WITHDRAWN

General Linguistics

AN INTRODUCTORY SURVEY

INDIANA UNIVERSITY STUDIES

IN THE

HISTORY AND THEORY OF LINGUISTICS

General Linguistics

AN INTRODUCTORY SURVEY

by

R. H. Robins

INDIANA UNIVERSITY PRESS

BLOOMINGTON & LONDON

P
121
R6
1965

THIRD PRINTING 1968

Copyright © 1964 by R. H. Robins
First published in the United States 1965
Library of Congress Catalog Card Number 65-21146
Manufactured in the United States of America

Contents

v

CONTENTS

CONTENTS

CONTENTS

Preface

An apology is perhaps desirable for the appearance of a book purporting to survey the whole range of general linguistic studies. In a period of increasing specialization, experts in several branches of linguistics are likely to find that, in their opinion, their own speciality is treated scantily, superficially, and with distortion in emphasis and selection. Indeed, it has been said that it is now no longer proper or practicable for an introduction to general linguistics to be attempted by one author, as his own competence in the different branches now recognized must be very unequal.

If this were true, it would be a great pity. The various approaches to language accepted as falling within linguistics are so accepted by virtue of some unifying theme or contribution to an integrated body of knowledge. Students are surely entitled to read, and teachers should be able to write, textbooks which take into account recent developments in the subject, as far as they may be made available to beginners, and attempt to show these in relation to its continuing course and progress as part of a set of studies sharing in common more than a mere title.

My intention in writing this book has been to produce an introduction to linguistics as an academic subject, that will be comprehensible and useful to the student entering on the study of linguistics at a university in work for a first degree or a post-graduate degree or diploma, and at the same time will serve to present the subject in outline to the intelligent general reader as one that is both important and interesting in its own right.

Where controversy still surrounds aspects of the subject encountered in the early stages of a student's acquaintance with it, I have not tried to hide this or to suggest that there is one road to salvation alone worthy of serious attention. Nothing is more pathetic than the dogmatic rejection of all approaches but one to language (or anything else) by a person who has not troubled himself even to consider the arguments in favour of others.

The writer of an introductory textbook has a further consideration to bear in mind. No branch of a living and developing subject stands still. In linguistics, outlooks, theories, and procedures are constantly being revised, and new methods appearing. Such changes, in so far as they represent or promise progress, are to be welcomed, but they inevitably alter in some degree the state of the subject during the unavoidable lapse of time between the writing of the book and its publication; and further changes must be expected in the future. Some experienced readers and teachers may well feel, as a result, that certain matters are given greater emphasis than they now merit at the expense of newer and more significant topics and viewpoints. An attempt to cover very briefly the most important developments over the last two years, and to notice fresh bibliographical material, is made on pages xviii–xx, to which the attention of students should be drawn.

In a book such as this, there is little or nothing original, except perhaps the choice of topics and their arrangement; nor should there be. I shall be well satisfied if, after reading it, people are both enabled and encouraged to go further into the subject, undertake further reading, and perhaps to specialize in one branch of linguistics or another, after achieving an adequate understanding and picture of the subject as a whole.

In writing an introductory account of linguistics, one is made very conscious of the debt owed to one's predecessors and contemporaries. Anyone engaged in linguistics in Great Britain lies greatly in debt to the late Professor J. R. Firth and to Professor D. Jones, who between them did more than any others to establish the subject in this country and to determine the course of its development. To Professor Firth, my own teacher during the eight years between my joining him at the School of Oriental and African Studies in the University of London and his retirement from the Chair of General Linguistics in that university, I owe the main directions of my work in the study of language, both in teaching and research. Equally no one engaged in general linguistics anywhere in the world can forget or treat lightly the enormous debt owed to American scholarship in this field. Without such international figures as Sapir and Bloomfield it is doubtful if linguistics would have made anything like the progress it has made, or achieved the academic recognition it enjoys the world over. Any serious student of the subject must become quickly aware of the great part American scholars in linguistics have played and are now playing in all its branches. On the continent of Europe, de Saussure, Trubetzkoy, Meillet, and Hjelmslev, to mention only four names, have been responsible for contributions to linguistic theory and method that are now indispensable components of present-day linguistic scholarship. I hope that in the form this book has taken I have discharged in some measure my debt to my predecessors and contemporaries. If I have failed, the fault is mine, not theirs.

More specifically, I am indeed grateful to successive classes of students whom I have taught in the past fifteen years. Much of what I have written here has arisen in the preparation, delivery, and revision of lecture notes and tutorial material. Some points were first brought clearly to my attention by the work of students themselves. To Professor C. E. Bazell, Professor of General Linguistics in the University of London, and to my other colleagues in the university, past and present, I owe the stimulus of constant discussion, argument, and collaboration. Professor N. C. Scott, Professor F. R. Palmer, and Dr., now Professor, J. Lyons were kind enough to read through a draft of this book. Each made many helpful and important suggestions, not least in trying to save me from a number of inclarities, inaccuracies, and downright absurdities. I hope I have made proper use of their comments; where I have not, and for all errors and imperfections remaining, I am, of course, wholly responsible. To all those who, wittingly or unwittingly, have helped and encouraged me in the production of this book, I offer my sincere thanks.

University of London   R. H. ROBINS
1964

System of reference

BIBLIOGRAPHIES

The chapters are followed by bibliographical lists of books and articles relevant to the topics discussed in them. These are numbered serially, and referred to in the chapter notes by author's surname and number; numbers following the serial number refer to pages in the work concerned. Thus '34, 11' means 'page 11 of number 34'.

The bibliographies to each chapter are independent of each other, relevant works being listed in more than one, where necessary. To avoid excessive overlapping the bibliographies of Chapters 5, 6, and 7 are combined into one, appearing at the end of Chapter 5. After Chapter 1 a general bibliography of elementary and introductory works on linguistics is given, with some brief comments.

None of the bibliographies is intended to be anything like exhaustive; they are designed simply to serve as a guide for further reading on the various aspects of general linguistics.

NOTES

In the notes to each chapter reference is made to books and articles which carry further the discussion of points made in the preceding chapter, set out alternative views, provide additional information justifying statements already made (particularly on languages not widely studied), or appear in some other way to be relevant.

Page numbers at the head of each note refer to pages in the body of the chapter to which the notes are relevant. The intention is that the beginner and general reader should be able to get a picture of the subject as a whole without the need to look at the notes at all. They are directed more towards the student who knows something of the subject already and wants to follow up in more detail questions arising from what he has read.

RECENT DEVELOPMENTS

No academic subject stands still, and a branch of scholarship that remained unaltered for any length of time would thereby betray its inherent lack of interest or the intellectual inactivity of its practitioners. Linguistics is no exception to this general statement; and, indeed, it has been making advances in our knowledge of languages and in linguistic theory and method at a remarkable rate in recent years. This inevitably fixes any textbook or introductory account of the subject at the point it had reached when the first printing was actually being prepared.

To cover what appear to be significant developments and shifts of emphasis in linguistic theory and practice during the period between the writing of this book and its publication, that should be of concern and interest to the student, a brief review has been added below. For the same reason, supplements to the bibliographies have been added at the end of each, to include important new writings published in the last two or three years, that would have been included in the main body, had they been in print at the time of writing.

While these supplementary observations and references go some way to bringing the book up to date with contemporary linguistic developments, the reader must expect further comparable movements to take place in the future, and bear in mind that new books and articles are likely to supplement and perhaps supersede some of those now recommended for study.

One of the most striking developments in linguistics in the last few years has been the increasing recognition of the transformational model of linguistic statement (6.4). Most attention has been paid to it in the United States, but work on transformational grammar is going on in Great Britain and on the continent of Europe. E. Bach's *Introduction to transformational grammars* (Chapter 5 bibliography, number 82) provides a much needed general introduction to this branch of linguistic science. Some transformationalists, as the adherents of transformational-generative grammar are called, make the claim that this approach to languages now supersedes in power all previous methods of description and analysis. Needless to say, these claims are disputed by adherents of other theories.

One aspect of transformational grammar constitutes an interesting link with Firthian theory. In contrast to the independent status of the phonological level of analysis and of the phoneme as its basic element, asserted by American linguists (and some others) in the 1940s and 1950s (pp. 144-5, 151-3, 186), transformational grammar and one interpretation of Firthian polysystemic phonological theory (4·4·3) make phonology subordinate to syntax and morphology as the link relating grammatical statements to the actual material of utterance. In this situation a phonemic analysis and transcription completely independent of any 'grammatical prerequisites' (p. 145) may be a definite hindrance to the total statement of the rules of sentence formation in a language (cp. Bach, op. cit., 126-34).

Several of the principles taught by Firth (pp. 41-3) are continued in the work of those who are coming to be known as 'neo-Firthians'. M. A. K. Halliday's 'Categories of a theory of grammar' (Chapter 1 bibliography, number 15) has been accepted as a brief outline of their theoretical position; this has been further developed in R. M. W. Dixon's *Linguistic science and logic* (The Hague, 1963). Both treat phonology as an 'interlevel' serving to relate statements made at the level of grammar with those made at the level of phonetics (Dixon, op. cit., 41-2).

One further trend should be noticed. A theory of linguistic analysis now known as tagmemics was originally suggested, in somewhat different terms, by Pike in 1954 (*Language in relation to a unified theory of the structure of human behavior*, part 1, Summer Institute of Linguistics). Its application to grammatical analysis is now made readily available to students in B. Elson and V. Pickett's *Introduction to morphology and syntax* (Chapter 5 bibliography, number 83). Its procedures are not unlike those set out in immediate constituent analysis (6·3), and involve the same concepts of basic sentence and expansion, but with the important differences that the basic sentence structures (basic 'strings') are more complex structures than those of most immediate constituent analysis (and the noun (phrase) + verb (phrase) taken as basic in much transformational grammar), and that the predominantly binary divisions of immediate constituent analysis are rejected in favour of multiple arrangements of 'tagmemes' (single morphemes and morpheme sequences filling specific functional places in string structure). See further Longacre, 'String constituent analysis' (Chapter 5 bibliography, number 49) and Z. S. Harris, *String analysis of sentence structure* (The Hague, 1962), which latter gives a brief comparison of immediate constituent analysis, string analysis, and transformational analysis.

For a further comparison of tagmemic and transformational linguistics, see W. A. Cook, *On tagmemes and transforms*, Washington, 1964.

P. Postal, 'Constituent structure: a study of contemporary models of syntactic description' (*IJAL* 30·1 (1964), part 3), sets out a vigorous criticism of both immediate constituent and tagmemic analysis from the standpoint of transformational grammar.

J. J. Katz and P. Postal, *An integrated theory of linguistic descriptions*, Cambridge Mass., 1964, incorporates a theory of linguistic semantics within transformational-generative grammar, attempting, in their own opening words, 'to reveal the nature of a fluent speaker's mastery of his language.'

While it is highly desirable that students should make themselves aware of these and similar developments in linguistics, it must be remembered that they presuppose and make use of many of the basic principles common to all linguistic analysis and description, and also assume the general setting and comprehension of the subject, which should, therefore, be studied first. These newer trends can best be appreciated against the general background of theory from which they themselves grew up.

Transcriptions and abbreviations

Linguistic material cited in this book in the examples is generally represented as follows :

English words and sentences are written in the normal orthography, followed by a reading transcription where necessary.

Words and sentences from most other languages that have a roman orthography are cited in this, followed, from Chapter 3 (Phonetics) onwards, by a reading transcription.

Languages without a recognized orthography and a few that have one but are little known, together with languages written in orthographies other than roman, are cited in reading transcriptions alone. The only exception to this is that Ancient (Classical) Greek words and sentences are given in the Greek script followed by the reading transcription.

Reading transcriptions are enclosed in slant lines / . . . /.

The reading transcription for English is the same as the one used by D. Jones in his *Outline of English Phonetics* and his *English Pronouncing Dictionary* (London, 1948). In other living languages the transcriptions are broad transcriptions, on phonemic lines. They are not necessarily strictly phonemic transcriptions; in some of the languages cited, an agreed phonemic analysis covering all the relevant features has still to be achieved, particularly in such features as stress. Sometimes deviations in the direction of narrower transcription are made if it is felt that a reader without a knowledge of the language will be helped to realize something of the sound of the words more readily thereby (thus in the German examples the glottal stop [ʔ] occurring initially in words like *arm* /ʔarm/ poor, and medially in some compound words, though not usually reckoned a separate phoneme, is transcribed). The terms *broad transcription* and *narrow transcription* are explained in 4·2.

The transcription of Ancient Greek is a transliteration, since in dealing with a dead language the phonetic information required as the basis of an adequate transcription is not ordinarily available; this transliteration follows the method set out by A. Martinet, 'A project of transliteration of Classical Greek', *Word* 9 (1953), 152–61. The transcription of Latin is the same as the traditional spelling except that all long vowels are marked as long, and this is done with the length sign :, not the macron ⁻.

It is hoped that these conventions will assist the reader unfamiliar with any of the languages from which examples are taken, without inconveniencing or annoying those already enjoying some acquaintance with them.

Transcriptions narrower than the reading transcriptions are printed, where necessary, between square brackets [. . . .].

ABBREVIATIONS

BSOAS	*Bulletin of the School of Oriental and African Studies*
BSOS	*Bulletin of the School of Oriental Studies*
IJAL	*International Journal of American Linguistics*
JAOS	*Journal of the American Oriental Society*
Lang.	*Language*
Sociol. rev.	*Sociological Review*
TCLC	*Travaux du cercle linguistique de Copenhague*
TCLP	*Travaux du cercle linguistique de Prague*
TPS	*Transactions of the Philological Society*

1

General Linguistics : The Scope of the Subject

1·1 GENERAL LINGUISTICS AS THE STUDY OF LANGUAGE

1·1·1 *Language and languages*

General linguistics may be defined as the science of language. As with other branches of knowledge and scientific study, such a definition involves the subject in certain relations with other disciplines and sciences outside itself, and in subdivision into different branches of the subject comprised within it. At the outset something must be said under both these headings, but it should be made clear that in these, as in several other important topics which must be examined even in an introductory account, the opinions of scholars differ in quite considerable respects.

It must also be realized that a subject like general linguistics, in common with most other subjects of systematic study, is not static. Viewpoints, including some of quite fundamental importance, may change or receive different degrees of emphasis in the course of years. No book can honestly pretend to deal with the subject in a way that will both be accepted in all respects by every recognized scholar in the field and remain unaltered for all time. In this book, some account is taken of major unresolved controversies, and the reader must be prepared for others to arise.[1]

In the first place it is desirable to consider the difference between

1. The section *Recent developments* in *System of reference*, p. xviii–xx, should be read and kept in mind.

general linguistics as the science or scientific study of language and the study of individual languages. This latter study is, indeed, more familiar to the majority of people, and has played a major part in all stages of education in many parts of the world for some time; the study of linguistics, on the other hand, is, at least in its present form, a relative newcomer in the field of scholarship, though in the present century and particularly in the past decade it has shown marked growth in the numbers of its students and teachers in the universities of Great Britain, Europe, the United States, the U.S.S.R., and several of the newly developing countries of the rest of the world.

General linguistics is concerned with human language as a universal and recognizable part of human behaviour and of the human faculties, perhaps one of the most essential to human life as we know it, and one of the most far-reaching of human capabilities in relation to the whole span of mankind's achievements. Needless to say, there is no 'general language' as the specific subject-matter of linguistics other than and apart from the numerous and so far uncounted different languages (estimated at around 3,000) spoken in the world; but the general linguist, in the sense of the specialist or the student concerned with general linguistics, is not as such involved with any one or more of them to a greater extent than with any others. As an impractical ideal he would know something about every language; this is, of course, impossible, and in practice most linguists concentrate on a limited number of languages including their own native languages, the number of languages studied, and the depth of knowledge acquired of each, varying by personal factors from one linguist to another. Thus it has been pointed out that the linguist as here defined and as understood in the context of general linguistics must be distinguished from the sense of the word *linguist* as often used by the public, to refer to someone who necessarily has a practical knowledge and command of a number of foreign languages. It is, of course, desirable that the linguist should know quite a lot about some languages, and the more languages (especially those representing types different from his own and from each other) with which he has some acquaintance, the better he is equipped for his subject.

Language in all its forms and manifestations, that is all the languages of the world and all the different uses to which in the various circumstances of mankind they are put, constitutes the field of the linguist. He seeks a scientific understanding of the place of language in human life, and of the ways in which it is organized to fulfil the needs it serves and the functions it performs. Several of the subjects he has within his purview and several of the questions to which he seeks answers correspond to long-established divisions of the study of foreign languages and of the institutionalized study of one's own language. Pronunciation (phonetics) and grammar are familiar enough, and some study of meaning and of the way in which meanings are discoverable and statable is presupposed in the compilation and use of any dictionary or vocabulary book. It is, in fact, partly as a result both of the search for improvements in the techniques of such indispensable aids to the study of foreign languages, and of questions arising on the theoretical basis of their production, that people have been led to the investigation of the properties and characteristics of language as such. Part of the justification of general linguistics lies in its undertaking the examination of the theory lying behind the practice of the language teacher and the language learner. The practical teaching of languages will, for obvious reasons, be largely confined to languages possessing a world-renowned literature or serving considerable numbers of speakers either as a first (native) language or as an acquired second language for the purposes of trade, education, etc. (such as English in large areas of the British Commonwealth and elsewhere, Spanish and Portuguese in Central and South America, and Russian over much of the Asiatic area of the Soviet Union). But it is an article of faith for the linguist that any language, no matter what the level of civilization reached by its speakers, how many speakers make use of it, or what area of the world they occupy, is a valuable and worthy object of study, able to teach him something more about language in general and the theoretical and practical considerations involved in the study of language.

It is well to reflect on the great diversity of the languages of the world. Some of the ways in which different languages may be compared are discussed in Chapter 8; here one may notice that language, and linguistics, the science of language, embrace equally living languages, that is languages still used today as means of communication, and dead languages, that is languages like Ancient Greek or Old English (Anglo-Saxon) now no more spoken but known from written records (manuscripts, printed texts, or inscriptions). Among the living languages the linguist finds his material both in the languages of world-wide use and with long literary traditions as the vehicles of civilization, and in languages devoid of writing, unknown outside their own community, except to the linguist, and (as is the position of many North and South American tongues) spoken perhaps by less than a hundred speakers and so in peril of extinction before the spread of some more extensively used language.

1·1·2 *Descriptive, historical, and comparative linguistics*

General linguistics includes a number of related subjects involved in the study of language as understood in the preceding paragraphs, and each may be considered both from the point of view of theory and from that of its actual operations or procedures. The most important and immediate subdivisions of the subject are **descriptive linguistics**, **historical linguistics**, and **comparative linguistics**.

Descriptive linguistics, as its title suggests, is concerned with the description and analysis of the ways in which a language operates and is used by a given set of speakers at a given time. This time may be the present, and in the case of languages as yet unwritten or only recently given written form it will inevitably be the present, as there is no other way of knowing any earlier stages of them, though there are methods by which certain facts about such earlier stages may be inferred (8·1). The time may equally well be the past, where adequate written records are available, as in the case of the so-called dead languages like Ancient Greek and (except in a few special circumstances) Latin, and in the case of earlier stages of languages still spoken (e.g. Old French and Old English). The line between these two categories of language is not easily drawn, and in part depends on the point of view from which they are looked at; the literary prestige attached to Ancient Greek and Latin and the distance that separates our knowledge of them and of the early stages of the languages that are, in fact, divergent continuations of them, Modern Greek, and French, Italian, Spanish, etc. (8·1), probably justifies the distinction. What is more important is that the descriptive study of a language, and of any part of a language, present or past, is concerned exclusively with that language at the period involved and not, as a descriptive study, with what may have preceded it or may follow it. Nor is the descriptive study of a particular language concerned with the description of other languages at the same time. Such statements verge on the obvious and would hardly justify their making but for the fact that the prestige of certain classical languages, especially Latin, and the familiarity of widely spoken languages, lie heavily on the study of all others, both in Europe and elsewhere, with the result that languages have been described and analysed, or rather misdescribed and misanalysed, not in terms best suited to them but in terms traditionally employed for Latin, Sanskrit, English, or some other well-known language; and likewise the grammatical descriptions of English and Spanish, for example, have been forced into moulds found suitable and hallowed by time for the teaching of Latin. Naturally all languages have a great deal in common, or there would hardly be a unitary subject of general linguistics, but to attempt in advance to describe one language in terms of another just because that other is well known or enjoys literary prestige, or because the language to be described may be shown to have descended from it, is as sensible as trying to fit a man into a suit of clothes designed in the first instance for someone else, either because the latter person is eminent or because he is the man's older relative.

Descriptive linguistics is often regarded as the major part of general linguistics. Be that as it may, it is certainly the fundamental aspect of the study of language, as it underlies and is presupposed (or ought to be presupposed) by the other two subdivisions, historical linguistics and comparative linguistics.

Historical linguistics is the study of the developments in languages in the course of time, of the ways in which languages change from period to period, and of the causes and results of such changes, both outside the languages and within them. This sort of study, whether undertaken in general terms or concentrated on a particular language area (e.g. English from Old English to the present day), must properly be based on at least partial descriptions of two or more stages of the continuous language series being treated.

The terms *synchronic* and *diachronic* are in general use to distinguish respectively linguistic statements describing a stage of a language as a self-contained means of communication, at a given time, during which it is arbitrarily assumed that no changes are

5

taking place, and statements relating to the changes that take place in languages during the passage of years.

Historical linguistics might from one point of view be regarded as a special case of comparative linguistics, the third subdivision of general linguistics. In **comparative linguistics** one is concerned with comparing from one or more points of view (and the possibilities of this are very wide) two or more different languages, and, more generally, with the theory and techniques applicable to such comparisons. In historical linguistics the comparison is limited to languages which may be regarded as successive stages of the speech of a continuing speech community differing from one period to another as the result of the cumulative effects of gradual changes, for the most part imperceptible within a single generation.

As will be seen in more detail in Chapter 8, comparative linguistics is principally divided into comparison based on or made with a view to inferring historical relationships among particular languages, and comparison based on resemblances of features between different languages without any historical considerations being involved.

In Europe and America historical linguistics and historically orientated comparative linguistics played a dominant role in linguistic studies during the nineteenth century, for reasons of academic history (8·1), rather antedating general linguistics in definite recognition and in the development of rigorous methods and scientific theory. These studies are familiar under the title of 'comparative philology' in English, and in some universities today what are in fact general linguistic studies are carried on and administered under this name.

1·1·3 *The term* philology

In connection with the study of language the term *philology* is in frequent use. In some ways this is unfortunate, as the word and its equivalents in some European languages (French *philologie*, German *Philologie*) are understood and used in rather different senses.

In British usage philology is generally equivalent to comparative philology, an older and still quite common term for what linguists technically refer to as comparative and historical linguistics (8·1). In German, however, *Philologie* refers more to the scholarly study of literary texts, especially those of the ancient Greco-Roman world, and more generally to the study of culture and civilization through

6

literary documents, comparative philology in the British sense being designated *Vergleichende Sprachwissenschaft*. This meaning of *Philologie* is matched by similar uses of comparable words in other European languages, and with the use of *philology* in American learned circles. It may be held that in this usage the word is a convenient term to employ with reference to the links between linguistics considered as a science and the aesthetic and humanistic study of literature, and to the field wherein the historian of different aspects of a culture draws on the findings of the linguist in the decipherment of texts and inscriptions and in the establishment of reliable versions of manuscripts and other documents as materials that provide him with part of his evidence. The relations of linguistics with philology in this last sense are very close and allow of considerable overlapping. Linguistics in its narrowest interpretation (1·3·4) concentrates on the formal analysis and description of languages as its central domain; in so far as linguists widen the scope of their subject in dealing with meanings they may be said to approach the realm of philological studies.

1·2   LINGUISTICS AS A SCIENCE

1·2·1 *Implications of the term* science

The term *science* has been used in the definition of general linguistics. It may be understood in two ways. In the widest terms it refers to the fact that the study of language in general and of languages in particular, as described in outline above, is considered worthy of scholarly attention and that a systematic body of facts and theory is built up around it. In more specific and particular terms it indicates the attitude taken by the linguist today towards his subject, and in this perhaps it marks a definite characteristic of twentieth-century linguistics.

In saying that linguistics is a science in the stricter sense, one is saying that it deals with a specific body of material, namely spoken and written language, and that it proceeds by operations that can be publicly communicated and described, and justified by reference to statable principles and to a theory capable of formulation. Its purpose in this proceeding is the analysis of the material and the making of general statements that summarize, and as far as possible relate to rules and regularities, the infinite variety of phenomena (utterances in speech or writing) that fall within its scope. In its operations and statements it is guided by three canons of science:

1. Exhaustiveness, the adequate treatment of all the relevant material;

2. Consistency, the absence of contradiction between different parts of the total statement, and within the limits imposed by the two preceding principles;

3. Economy, whereby, other things being equal, a shorter statement or analysis employing fewer terms is to be preferred to one that is longer or more involved.

One can make the position of linguistics within the sciences more precise. It is an empirical science, in that its subject matter is observable with the senses, speech as heard, the movements of the vocal organs as seen directly or with the aid of instruments (3·1, 3·2), the sensations of speaking as perceived by speakers, and writing as seen and read. Within the empirical sciences linguistics is one of the social sciences, in that the phenomena forming its subject-matter are part of the behaviour of men and women in society, in interaction with their fellows. This last statement is not invalidated by the existence of purely secondary uses of language by persons alone and out of earshot of others, in monologue ('talking to oneself'), ejaculations of joy, terror, or annoyance, addressing animals, and the like; the essence of language, and the vast majority of its uses, involve two or more persons in social intercourse.

A brief reference to what is often referred to by the title of 'intuition' is not out of place here. Manifestly people differ in their ability to understand languages, analyse meanings, and pick out the significant features within a mass of material, and to hit on satisfactory ways of explaining how sentences are constructed or words pronounced in particular languages. It is often said that a good deal of what goes on under the name of language learning makes use of intuition or a feeling for the language (*sentiment linguistique, Sprachgefühl*) acquired by long familiarity with it rather than explicitly learned; and in linguistic descriptions appeal has been made to a native speaker's intuitive reactions in approving or rejecting a particular mode of analysis. Much of the controversy centred on such uses of intuition is the result of a confusion. Progress in any branch of knowledge and the breaking of new ground, whether in bringing more phenomena within the scope of one's science or improving on the existing treatment of phenomena already dealt with, must in the first instance depend on the intuition or insight of some individual. The objection to intuition in a scientific discipline is not to its use (or all science would at once cease to progress), but to its use as the final justification of a particular statement or manner of analysis. Intuition is part of the equipment of the scientist, not a criterion of appeal or a means of justification. Insights, 'hunches', and guesses of the linguist, and the reactions of native speakers to particular analyses, must in the end be brought down to and justified by statements about the forms of what is spoken and heard, written and read; and they become thereafter no more the private intuitions or feelings of a privileged individual, but the public property of anyone able and willing to follow through the procedures and refer to the material by which they are validated. This point has been well summarized: 'Intuition is personal; science requires that its methods be public, and that its results be subject to multipersonal check.'

There is one inference that might be made from the assertion that linguistics is a science, and it must be disclaimed at once. This is that because linguistics is a science, it is necessarily not one of the humanities or a humane discipline, and that in consequence linguistics is in some way hostile to the study of literature and the linguistic study of language inhibits its literary enjoyment and the pleasures that come of literary appreciation. The relations of linguistic studies and literary studies will be examined more closely in a subsequent chapter (9·5); but it should be made clear at once that nothing in linguistic science is such as to interfere with the analysis and appreciation of literary values in what is read or written. Indeed the reverse may be true, and if a linguist finds himself insensitive to the music of poetry, the appeal of oratory, or the flow of an unfolding story, he has only himself, and not his subject, to blame.

In the present educational situation disquiet has been expressed about the gulf that has widened between what are loosely called the arts and the sciences, with the implied suggestion that scholars, and indeed the educated public in general, must either be 'literate', somewhat despising the sciences as pedestrian and illiberal, or, as it has been termed, 'numerate', considering the humanities and what

9

are traditionally regarded as the mainstays of a liberal education to be largely subjective, irrelevant, and marred by imprecision. In any much needed rapprochement between scientific studies and what are called humane studies, linguistics, along with some of the other disciplines devoted to the ways of mankind, may have an important part to play. Indeed among all branches of knowledge linguistics is in a special position. Science, like all other publicly shared knowledge, demands the use of language to talk about its particular subject, and is a refinement and elaboration of our general habit of talking about the world in which we live. Linguistics differs from other studies in that it both uses language and has language as its subject-matter. Linguistics has, for this reason, been described as language turned back on itself, or as language about language; and since every branch of knowledge makes use of language, linguistics may, in some respects, be said to lie at the centre of them all, as being the study of the tool that they all must use. The Danish linguist, Hjelmslev, has eloquently expressed the uniquely central situation of linguistics: 'Linguistic theory is led by an inner necessity to recognize not merely the linguistic system, . . . but also man and human society behind language, and all man's sphere of knowledge through language. At that point linguistic theory has reached its prescribed goal: *humanitas et universitas*.'

1·2·2 *Practical applications*

From what has been said about linguistics as a science, it should be clear that it is self-justifying as an academic subject. Language and the means whereby the forms of language and the working of language may be analysed and described are themselves regarded as proper subjects of academic study, without any further consequences being involved. Nevertheless, certain consequential and important by-products do result from linguistic work. One may consider a few examples. The greater one's understanding of language in general, the better one may expect to be able to set about the task of teaching foreign languages, both in their general aspects and with an eye to the many specialized needs for the knowledge of second languages in limited ranges of activities that the modern world seems increasingly to require. This covers both the actual techniques of teaching and the production of textbooks; textbooks differ from pure descriptions of languages in that their aim is to impart particular skills in speaking and understanding and in reading and writing (or in both), in a given language on the part of speakers of some other language. Such books are normative rather than simply descriptive; they set a standard, by some means or other, of what is correct and serve to impart a knowledge of it and foster familiarity with it.

Linguistic studies are already being applied to the practical problems of automatic or machine translation and the exploitation of statistical techniques connected with the use of language. The communications engineer is helped by some knowledge of the basic composition of the language signals whose transmission and reception are his responsibility. An understanding of the power language can exert among men and of the different ways in which this power may be exploited and directed has proved to be a potent weapon in the hands of those who with the aid of what have come to be called 'mass media' are engaged in moulding opinions, disseminating views, and exercising influence on their fellows, whether politically, commercially, or socially; the fact that such activities may often be regarded as undesirable and even disastrous is, of course, to be recognized; by-products are not necessarily always beneficial. In another sphere of activity linguistic knowledge is a powerful aid in the remedial treatments known as speech therapy, for patients whose speech mechanisms, through injury or defect, are damaged or imperfect. The applications of linguistics to other activities serving particular purposes in the world are collectively known as applied linguistics.

It is important to recognize the by-products that may come from linguistic studies; but linguists themselves need not engage in applied linguistics. Their subject is of sufficient interest and significance in the world to maintain itself in its own right, just as is botany without reference to horticulture, and as is entomology without reference to the control of insect-borne diseases or crop pests.

1·3   THE RANGE OF GENERAL LINGUISTICS

1·3·1 *Levels of analysis*

Language is immensely complicated. How complicated one discovers in the process of learning a foreign language; and the ability of all normal persons to acquire structural mastery and the basic vocabulary of their own language in childhood is one of the many wonders of human kind. The obvious complexity of language makes it unworkable for the linguist to try and describe it all at once. Language itself, speaking and writing, is a unitary activity; people speak and write, and understand what is spoken and written in their own language, without necessarily being aware of such things as grammar and pronunciation, but merely reacting unfavourably to the mistakes of a foreigner without being able to specify in what respects he has transgressed one or more recognized standards.

The linguist, in order the better to make scientific statements about language and languages, concentrates at any one time on different though interrelated aspects of his subject-matter, by attending to different types of features and by applying different types of criteria (asking himself different sorts of questions). These different and partial approaches have been called **levels of analysis** and the statements made about them **levels of linguistic statement**. Such relatively familiar terms as *phonetics* and *grammar* refer to two such levels. By extension the term **level of language** is used to designate those aspects of a language on which at any time the linguist is focusing his attention. The nature of language, as it exists, gives rise to the distinction of different levels; it must, however, be emphasized that it is not language itself which is divided like this, but the operations of the linguist and his resultant analytic statement.

Just as the limits and comprehension of an academic subject may vary between one scholar or group of scholars and another, so do the different levels that it is considered profitable to recognize. Even those who agree on the overall range of topics proper to the linguist's purview may disagree on the number of levels with which to operate and the criteria to be applied to them. In an introduction such as this, no more than a general survey can be given.

The faculty of language consists in man's ability to make noises with the vocal organs and marks on paper or some other material, by means of which groups of people 'speaking the same language' are able to interact and co-operate as a group. The noises made and the marks written down are the material of the forms of language, and the uses made of these forms in social intercourse constitute their meaning. One must recognize at the outset and as the basis of any division of linguistic analysis (or of language) into levels the two aspects of all utterance, form and meaning. Utterance is purposeful, and form and meaning are related at least in part as means and end. An understanding of language in human life requires both an understanding of the formal composition of utterances and of their relations with the rest of the world outside language.

1·3·2 *Language and symbol systems*

Language makes contact with the world on two sides. Speaking makes use of certain organs of the human body, the physical properties of the air, and the physiological properties of the ear; writing makes use of visible marks on a surface and the physiology of the eye. On this side the connection is with a very limited part of the total realm of human experience and human capabilities. On the other side, language uses the audible movements of the vocal organs and the visible marks of writing in relation to the vastly greater and potentially infinite totality of human experience, past, present, and to come. In this use of a restricted range language falls within the wider scope of symbol systems; and symbols are a special class of signs. The science of sign and symbol systems, sometimes called semiotics, lies outside the range of an outline introduction to general linguistics, but a brief clarification of the terms is desirable. Signs in general are events or things that in some way direct attention to, or are indicative of, other events or things. They may be related naturally or causally, as when shivering is taken as a sign of fever, or as when earthquakes are, or were, said to be signs of the subterranean writhing of the imprisoned god Loki; or they may be related conventionally and so used, and they are then called symbols, as, for example, the 'conventional signs' for churches, railways, etc. on maps, road signs, and the colours of traffic lights. Languages clearly include members of this class of conventional signs or symbols, and as a great many different symbols are involved, languages are regarded as incorporating symbol systems (this latter term will require further elaboration, 2·1·2).

Among symbol systems language occupies a special place, for at least two reasons. Firstly, it is almost wholly based on pure or arbitrary convention; whereas signs on maps and the like tend to represent in a stylized way the things to which they refer, the words of a language relate to items of experience or to bits of the world in this way only in the proportionately very small part of vocabulary called onomatopoeic. The connection between the sounds of words like *cuckoo, hoopoe,* and such imitative words as *dingdong, bowwow, rattattat,* etc. and the creatures making such noises or the noises themselves is obvious; and in a wider set of forms in languages a more general association of sound and type of thing or event is discoverable, as in many English words ending in *-ump,* such as *thump, clump, stump, dump,* which tend to have associations of heaviness, thickness, and dullness. It has been found experimentally that made-up words, like *maluma* and *oomboolu,* and *takete* and *kikeriki,* are almost always treated alike by persons who hear them for the first time and are asked to assign them to one or the other of a pair of diagrams, one round in shape and the other spiky; the first pair are felt appropriate to the former shape, and the second pair to the latter. The onomatopoeic and 'sound-symbolic' part of language is of great significance, but its extent in any vocabulary is quite small, and despite attempts by some to see the origin of language in such imitative cries, it must be realized that the vastly greater part of the vocabulary of all languages is purely arbitrary in its associations. Were this not so, languages would be much more similar the world over than they are, just as the conventional picture signs of several historically   unrelated   pictographic   systems   show   obvious resemblances.

The second special feature of language is far more important, and puts language in a unique position. Language alone is able to relate its symbols to every part and every sort of human experience and to all the furniture of earth and heaven; and for this reason all other symbol systems are explained by reference to it. Languages are infinitely extendable and modifiable according to the changing needs and conditions of the speakers; this is clearly seen in the immediate adaptation of the vocabulary of English and other languages to the scientific discoveries and concomitant changes that took place in the eighteenth, nineteenth, and twentieth centuries. This alone sets language quite apart from such symbolizing as gesture, and from the communication systems of certain creatures such as bees, fascinating and revealing as these are. The immense power and range of human language has been perceived by all societies, and the realization of it is no doubt partly responsible for the magical associations felt among some peoples in certain words relating to things or events vital to their lives or fearful in their effects. Traces of such a magical outlook on language are to be seen today in some familiar attitudes to certain words and expressions in most communities (2·2·1).

1·3·3 *'The origin of language'*

One topic connected with the study of language that has always exercised a strong fascination over the general public is the question of the origin of language. There has been a good deal of speculation on this, usually taking the form of trying to infer out of what sort of communicative noise-making fully fledged languages in all their complexities gradually developed. Imitative exclamations in response to animal noises, onomatopoeia and more general sound mimicry of phenomena, exclamations of strong emotion, and calls for help have all been adduced. Linguists, however, tend to leave this sort of theorizing alone, not because of any lack of intrinsic interest, but because it lies far beyond the reaches of legitimate scientific inference. Language as a human faculty is immeasurably older than the earliest attested languages (some 4,000 years old), and writing, by which alone extinct languages are known to us, is, as compared with speech, a very recent introduction, the product of settled and developed civilization. In relation to the origin of language, every known language is very recent.

Two frequently used analogies for attempted inference on the origin of language are the acquisition of speech by children and the structures and characteristics of so-called 'primitive' languages. Both are invalid for this purpose. Children acquire their native language in an environment in which language is already established and in constant and obvious use all around them for the satisfaction of needs, some manifestly shared by themselves. Even if they are not actually 'taught' to speak, as most are, their situation is entirely different from that of mankind as a whole in the circumstances assumed to obtain while language itself was taking shape.

The second argument, based on the alleged nature of 'primitive' languages, rests on a common, though deplorable, misconception of

15

these languages. Linguistically, there are no primitive languages. There are languages of peoples whose cultures as described by anthropologists may be called primitive, i.e. involving a low level of competence in the exploitation of natural resources and the like. *Primitive*, however, is not a proper qualification of *language*. Investigations of the languages of the world do not bear out the assumption that structurally the languages of people at different levels of cultural development are inherently different. Their vocabularies, of course, at any time reflect fairly closely the state of the material and more abstract culture of the speakers; but languages are capable of infinite adjustment to the circumstances of cultural development, and their phonetic and grammatical organization may remain constant during such changes. It is a palpable fact of informed observation in the linguistic study of the languages of culturally primitive peoples that phonetically and grammatically their languages are no less (and no more) systematic and orderly than the languages of western Europe and of the major world civilizations. Nor are the processes of change, that affect all parts of languages, any less active or any slower in operation in these languages than in others; indeed, the converse may be the case, as it has been held that the establishment of writing systems and standards of correctness tend, if anything, to retard linguistic changes in certain situations. Every language has aeons of changes, irretrievably lost to knowledge, lying behind it. To argue from the language of primitive peoples to the nature of a primitive stage in the evolution of language is valueless.

What can profitably be done is to compare human language and its place in human life with the most language-like communication systems observed in the animal kingdom. Several such systems, more complex and significant than mere cries, have been studied in their relations to human speech, notably bee dancing and the different calls of the gibbon apes in response to different situations (danger, friendship, etc.). Physiologically, gibbon calls are more akin to human speech in being the product of corresponding parts of the body, and received and responded to through the ears of the hearer. In the dance system of bees, some bees that have located a source of nectar can indicate its distance, direction, and richness by a set of movements made by them in the hive on their return. The 'substance' or medium of this form of communication is quite other than that of

16

human speech, but in certain respects, for example, reference to things outside the range of immediate perception, it comes closer to it.

For all the interest to the linguist that behaviour systems of this sort have, the gulf that separates them from language is an extremely wide one, and there is at present little to bridge it except scientifically untestable theorizing. In particular one must notice the vast complexity of human speech, its great flexibility, and its limitless ability to cope with the entire range of human experience.

Human speech is transmitted from generation to generation by a process of learning on the part of children, often accompanied by conscious teaching by their parents or others. It is not instinctive or inherited, though, of course, the physiological and neurological capacity for speech is. This transmission through successive generations gives the occasion for the phenomena of linguistic change, the material of historical linguistics. There is no reason to suppose that within a continuing species animal cries or bee dances change to anything like the same extent, or vary between members of the same species in geographical isolation from one another, as is the case with human languages.

Human progress is vastly speeded by the use of language in cultural transmission (one of its functions); the knowledge and experience acquired by one person can be passed on to another in language, so that in part he starts where the other leaves off. In this connection the importance of the invention of printing can hardly be exaggerated. At the present time the achievements of anyone in any part of the world can be made available (by translation if necessary) to anyone else able to read and capable of understanding what is involved. From these uses of language, spoken and written, the most developed animal communication system, though given the courtesy title of language, is worlds away.

1·3·4 *Phonetics, phonology, grammar, semantics*

That part of linguistics that deals with the material of speech itself is called **phonetics**. Chapter 3 is devoted to this, and here it need only be said that it is immediately concerned with the organs of speech and the movement of articulation, and, more widely, with the

17

physics of sound transmission and the physiology of hearing, and ultimately with the neurological processes involved both in speaking and hearing. The subsidiary and less extensive study of written language in its different forms is sometimes called **graphics** or **graphonomy**, or on the model of *phonetics*, **graphetics**; but as this material is less complex, and writing is a secondary manifestation of language compared with speaking (3·1·1), this has not been accorded such an important place in linguistic studies.

Within the scope of meaning are involved the relations between utterances, written and spoken, and the world at large. Meaning is an attribute not only of language but of all sign and symbol systems, and the study of meaning is called **semantics**, which, therefore, embraces a wider range than language alone. However, since language incorporates by far the most extensive symbol system in man's use as well as the central one, much of semantics and of semantic theory is concerned with language and languages.

In order to fulfil their symbolizing and communicative functions, languages must organize the available noises that can be produced by the vocal organs into recurrent bits and pieces arranged in recurrent patterns. This formal patterning and arrangement in languages is studied at the levels of phonology and grammar. These two levels of linguistics are the subjects of separate chapters (4 and 5, 6, 7); here it need only be said that **phonology** is concerned with the patterns and organization of languages in terms of the phonetic features and categories involved, and **grammar** is concerned with the patterns and arrangements of units established and organized on criteria other than those referable to phonetic features alone. It is for this reason that in the case of languages studied only in their written forms, such as Ancient Greek or Latin, a full grammatical statement and analysis of the written language, based on orthographic texts, is possible, but any phonological analysis of such languages must necessarily be uncertain and incomplete, since it can only be made from such phonetic descriptions of the languages as can be deduced from the orthography itself or gathered from the contemporary accounts of ancient scholars and commentators. Further discussion of the relation between these two levels may be deferred until Chapter 5.

The two levels of phonology and grammar (which latter is divided by many into morphology and syntax) are often regarded as the central province of linguistics. Indeed, there are some linguists who feel that semantics is less strictly within the field of the linguist than phonology and grammar; and some consider phonetics also as peripheral to linguistics itself. It must be emphasized in an introduction to the subject that an understanding of the phonic basis or 'substance' of language, and some consideration of the relations between language and the world, under the heading of meaning, are necessary to a proper approach to the subject of linguistics. In particular it seems unfortunate to relegate the study of meaning wholly to disciplines other than linguistics, since being meaningful or having meaning is one of the main criteria that distinguish speaking from babbling and identify shapes inscribed on a surface as writing and not mere scribbling or decoration.

For these reasons both phonetics and semantics will be included in the levels of analysis properly comprised by linguistics and within the competence of the linguist. But one sees the reasons why phonetics on the one hand and semantics on the other are sometimes felt to be on the fringe of the subject as compared with phonology and grammar. In both of the former, appeal may be made to the findings of other empirical sciences to a large extent. In the case of phonetics the other sciences that are relevant are restricted in number; physiology is immediately involved as far as concerns the structure and movements of the vocal organs, and in any specialized study of phonetics the physics of sound wave transmission, the physiology of the hearing process, and the neurology of the processes of both hearing and speaking are brought into relevance. In semantics, however, since the meanings of utterances may relate to the whole world of the actual and potential experience of the speakers, the appeal to sciences and disciplines outside linguistics, as well as to the whole range of unscientific acceptance called common sense, is, in theory, unlimited. But in view of the essentially social nature of language, the sciences principally concerned with men in society, such as social anthropology, are especially involved. The limited number and the exact nature of the sciences brought into relevance by phonetics, as compared with the potentially unlimited number and the inherently lesser precision of the sciences to which appeal may be made in semantics are among the reasons why some linguists regard phonetics as more properly within their field than semantics.

But in both cases it must be pointed out that the statements made, the categories established, and the terms employed are still primarily linguistic in relevance, even though they must necessarily rely on the findings of other sciences. They are linguistic in that they are made specifically with linguistic ends in view, that is the study and analysis of language and languages, and they are not necessarily the sort of statements, categories, or terms, that the specialists in these other sciences would want to make. For example, an important distinction is made in phonetics between the front and the back of the tongue (3·2·2); physiologically and with reference to other activities, such as gustation and swallowing, this distinction may not be of fundamental importance.

1·4 SEMANTICS

1·4·1 *Philosophical and linguistic interest in meaning*

As has already been said, the study of meaning, **semantics**, brings in symbol using and symbol systems outside language; but the central place of language in human symbol systems makes language very much its primary concern. The problems arising from the study and analysis of meaning have been recognized and have received attention during the whole of man's intellectual history. Much of the work involved has been undertaken by philosophers, especially logicians (to whom linguistics in the West owed much of its original impulse, 9·6). The study of logic is closely connected with the study of language, however the relations between the two may be interpreted by successive generations of philosophers, since language is the vehicle of philosophical discourse and even the specially devised systems of modern symbolic logic are derived from and refer to particular types of sentence in natural languages. The logician is, however, primarily concerned with the inferential uses of language, the formal means by which statements or propositions may be reached or inferred as valid conclusions from preceding statements or propositions acting as premises. Much of Aristotelian logic is devoted to the different types of syllogisms, as sets of premises followed by conclusions are called, that may be used in valid chains of reasoning.

The concern of the linguist for the uses of language is much wider. Formalized logical inference and philosophical discourse in general

are an important part of men's use of language in several civilizations; but they are by no means the only, or indeed anything like the
most frequent uses. The linguist's concern is with language in all its
uses and manifestations as part of the processes of daily living and
social interaction by members of groups, as well as in the specialized
applications that form the provinces of philosophers and literary
critics, and the approach to meaning on the part of the linguist must
be based on this much wider range of language use and types of
utterance.

1·4·2 *Word meaning*

For much of the history of semantic studies, and still to a considerable extent today, the investigation of meaning has been based on the
relationships of reference and denotation. Certainly meaning includes the relations between utterances and parts of utterances (e.g.
words) and the world outside; and reference and denotation are
among such relations. But for the purposes of linguistics it is
desirable to deal with meaning by a more comprehensive treatment.

At the outset it must be realized that the meaningful activity of
speaking consists immediately not of words as such, but of utterances
or stretches of speech consisting of sentences and delimited by pauses,
silence, or the speech of other people. Words are part of the material
into which utterances may be analysed, and the stock from which
speakers may be said to put their utterances together; but they are
not themselves actual discrete stretches of utterance, except in the
case of the limited number of utterances consisting of one word only;
and, of course, they are not all separated in speech by pauses in the
way that in texts printed in roman alphabets words are separated
by spaces.

Utterances have meaning, are meaningful; and a child learns the
meaning of many words by hearing them in other people's utterances
and practising such utterances himself subject to the correction of
others and the test of being understood by those to whom he is
talking. This process goes on all our lives, and we learn new words
and extend and increase our knowledge of the words we already know,
as we hear and see them in fresh utterances and used slightly differently from the ways which we are accustomed to. The meaning of
a word, therefore, may be considered as the way it is used as a part

21

of different sentences; what the dictionary does is to try and summarize for each word the way or ways it is used in the sort of sentences in which it is found in the language.

The potential sentences of any language that may be uttered and understood by a speaker of it are infinite in number, but they are formed from the total stock of words known to the speaker at any time. A speaker's word stock is always variable, but it may be regarded as fixed at any given point in time. Words, therefore, are, in general, convenient units about which to state meanings, and no harm is done provided it is borne in mind that words have meanings by virtue of their employment in sentences, most of which contain more than one word, and that the meaning of a sentence is not to be thought of as a sort of summation of the meanings of its component words taken individually. This is important for three reasons: 1. As has been seen, the sentence or the utterance comprising several sentences is the primary linguistic phenomenon; 2. The grammatical structure and certain phonological features such as intonation may themselves give an indication of part of its meaning (3·5·4, 4·3·7, 7·3); 3. With many words particular meanings or uses are only found when they are used in conjunction with other words, and these are often scarcely deducible from their other uses apart from such combinations (one need only think of such phrases as *cold war*, *featherweight* (boxing), *wildcat strike* (unofficial strike, particularly in American English), *white noise* (acoustic engineering); this topic is further discussed under 'Collocation', 2·4·2).

Reference and denotation are clearly a part of the meaning of many words in all languages. The many problems arising about the nature of these relations have been the subject of much philosophical discussion and cannot and need not be treated at length here. It suffices to point out that by the use in sentences of certain words one is able to pick out from the environment of speaker and hearer particular items, features, processes, and qualities, draw attention to them, give or elicit further information about them, make them the objects of action or speculation, and, most importantly, recall them from past experience and anticipate them in the future provided only that the words used have had such associations in the previous experience of speaker and hearer. These are the words whose meanings may, in part, be learned and taught by pointing, or deixis. But the relationship between the word and that to which it may be said to refer is not a simple one. Proper names (*John*, *Mary*, etc.) refer to individuals as single individuals, however many there may be so referred to; *boy*, *girl*, etc. refer to an indefinitely large class of individuals by virtue of their being grouped together in some respect; in the same way, *climb*, *fly*, *swim*, and *walk* refer to four different types of bodily movement in space. In the strict terminology of logic *denotation* is sometimes used in a specific and technical sense, but in general usage the term is more loosely made equivalent to *reference*.

It is often said that the meaning of a word is the idea it conveys or arouses in the mind of speaker or hearer. This is associated with a general definition of language as 'the communication of ideas by speech' or the like. Such accounts of the meaning of words and the working of languages are objectionable for two reasons: 1. They try to explain and define public phenomena (speech, writing) primarily by reference to necessarily private phenomena; 2. It is not easy to say what an idea is, or how it helps, except, circularly, that it is the meaning of a word. The first objection follows from the status of linguistics as an empirical science dealing with publicly observable phenomena. The second merits further examination. *Idea* is often taken as equivalent to *mental picture*, for which drawings are sometimes made in books dealing with linguistic meaning. Mental pictures are no doubt perfectly genuine parts of our private experience, but as such they seem of little relevance to linguistics. Firstly, it would appear that they are not aroused by anything like all the words in a language, even of those for which a referential meaning is fairly easily statable in isolation; secondly, even in the most favourable cases, the idea as a mental picture does not help explain one's ability to use a word correctly and understand it. Any picture is necessarily particular; as Berkeley pointed out, *triangle* refers to all of the mutually exclusive sorts of triangles (isosceles, scalene, right-angled, etc.), but any picture, mental or otherwise, of a triangle must be of one triangle only. Even if we did recognize what a word referred to by having a mental picture in our mind, we should have to be able to justify the classing together of what is actually observed and the mental picture by some further piece of knowledge. It is best to regard knowledge of the meaning or meanings of a word as a performative knowledge (like knowing how to ride a bicycle), an ability

23

to use the word in ways other people will understand and to understand it when uttered by other people; this knowledge includes knowing the range of items, processes, and the like to which words that do have referents of one sort or another may be said to refer.

The use of words in utterances to focus attention on particular bits and features of the world involves a segmentation and an organization of our experienced environment. Verbalization is not a mere passive labelling of discrete items and objects; the process of classification implicit in the use of what are often called common nouns (*boy*, *girl*, *tree*, *house*, etc.) has already been noticed. Moreover, the very permanence of names and designations presupposes that we recognize continuing identities in the stream of successively observed phenomena. Recognizing John today as the John of yesterday and this table today as the same as this table yesterday is more than just perceiving what is before one's eyes; it is imposing some order on such perceptions. Other words with more abstract meanings involve a much more far-reaching organization of the world of immediate experience; words like *cause* and *effect* do not refer to things in the way words like *table* and *chair* do (still less do they call up definite pictures in the mind), but they have distinctive and important meanings, and their use is a mark of the high degree of order and systematization imposed by us on the world we live in. In the same way the use of words like *right* and *wrong*, *duty*, *crime* (and many others subsumed under them: *property*, *theft*, *punishment*, *reform*, etc.), and of comparable words in other types of society, presupposes a social nexus of expected ways of behaviour enforced by precedent and the sanctions of disapproval and legal penalties.

Some of these orderings of experience appear to be universally recognized in the use of words in all languages, and must therefore be regarded as the general property of mankind (for example, the recognition of objects occupying space and persisting through time). In other matters languages differ in the way they most readily tend to organize parts of the speakers' experience. Relatively trivial instances of such differences are the obvious non-correspondences of the colour words in different languages (2·4·3); more significant are the difficulties involved in trying to translate words relating to moral, religious, legal, and political matters between the languages of communities having different social systems in these respects. Such difficulties arise from the differences in peoples' ways of life, and are made prominent by the work of anthropologists in examining societies far removed historically from the Greco-Roman and Hebraic inheritance characterizing western Europe and those countries most influenced by it. We do not all inhabit exactly the same world, and differences in the significant items of vocabulary in languages bring this out clearly.

Not only does reference cover a very wide divergence of relationship between words and the bits and pieces of the world, but many words in all languages can scarcely be said to refer to anything by themselves, for which, consequently, pointing is useless as a means of explaining their use. This does not mean that such words are meaningless, which is nonsensical as they have quite definite uses in languages; words like English *if*, *when*, *of*, *all*, *none*, *the* are frequent and essential components of sentences. But as it has been seen that it is the utterance and the sentences in it that are the primary meaningful stretches, the meanings of the component words must be taken as the contribution they make to the meaning of the sentences in which they appear. The fact that the contribution of some words is partly that of reference does not make reference the same as the whole of meaning; and it is not to be assumed that the meaning of a word when it constitutes a one word sentence is the same as its meaning when it forms part of a larger sentence.

The ease with which a statable meaning can be assigned to a word in isolation varies very considerably, and in part it depends on the degree to which the word is likely to occur in normal discourse as a single (one word) sentence; and even in the case of such favoured words one has no right in advance of the analysis to assume that there will be found a common 'core' of meaning underlying all the various uses the word has in the sentences in which it may occur. With words scarcely ever occurring in isolation, like those cited in the preceding paragraph, it is almost impossible to describe their meaning adequately in any other way than by saying how they are typically used as part of longer sentences and how those sentences are used. The question whether a word may be semantically described in isolation is more a matter of degree than of a simple answer yes or no.

Preoccupation with reference and denotation has troubled semantic theory, by putting an excessive importance on that part of word meaning which can be stated easily in isolation and treated either as a two-term relation between the word and the referent or thing meant (*signifiant* and *signifié*), or as a three-term relation between word, speaker or hearer, and referent. The meanings of sentences and their parts are better treated in linguistics in terms of how they function than exclusively in terms of what they refer to. The different types of reference indicated above are then included as part of the function performed, the job done, by certain words in the sentences in which they are used, and the dictionary entry of a word simply summarizes the function or functions, referential or other, of the word in the sort of sentences in which it typically occurs.

In addition to reference, excessive emphasis on historical considerations largely colours popular discussion on language, especially on word meanings, as when it is urged that the 'real' meaning of a word is to be found in its etymology or earlier form and use in the language. Thus it is claimed that the 'true' meaning of *holiday* is 'holy-day' or day set apart for religious reasons, and that *awful* and *awfully* are wrongly used like *considerable, very* (*there was an awful crowd there, awfully nice of you to come*), since its 'real' meaning is 'awe-inspiring'.

If it is accepted that statements of word meanings in descriptive linguistics are simply summaries of the ways words are used in sentences by speakers at a particular time, it is clear that historically antecedent meanings are outside the scope of such statements. Without specialized study speakers are ignorant of the history of their language; yet they use it to communicate with each other and they understand each other. Certainly the meaning of any word is causally the product of continuous changes in its antecedent meanings or uses, and in many cases it is the collective product of generations of cultural history. Dictionaries often deal with this sort of information if it is available, but in so doing they are passing beyond the bounds of synchronic statement to the separate linguistic realm of historical explanation.

1·4·3 *Context of situation*

The synchronic approach to meaning is intended to deal with the description and analysis of the many important factors observable in the use of different words in sentences in addition to any specific reference to isolated bits of the environment. In Great Britain meaning in linguistic analysis and linguistic theory has in the main been dealt with in terms of **context of situation**, a concept developed by Malinowski and Firth as a means of explaining the working of language in society. By setting up contexts of situation, the observer or analyst undertakes to state the relationships of utterances to the situations or environments in which they are said or could be said. In a context of situation the utterance or the successive sentences in it are brought into multiple relations with the relevant components of the environment. Meaning is, in the first place, the functioning of the sentence or the utterance, though for reasons already given it is convenient to refer a good deal, but by no means all, of the description of sentence meaning to the separate meanings of its component words.

Language serves a great variety of purposes, and utterances perform a very wide range of functions. Within any one language notable differences of use, in part employing differences of vocabulary and composition but mainly drawing on a common grammatical and lexical stock, must be recognized. To mention only a few uses of language, one can distinguish poetry of all kinds, rhetoric, narrative and historical records, ritual and ceremonial utterances, the forms of legal, political, commercial, and administrative operations, the professional intercourse of technical, learned, and academic persons, as well as all the general functions of talking and writing in the maintenance of the daily life of every individual in cooperation with his family and other members of the community, including the sort of idle chatter and modes of greeting and leave-taking engaged in where silence would be taken for discourtesy.

Language, which is the concern of the linguist in all its aspects and functions, thus embraces very much more than the formal discourse of philosophy and the works of written literature, just as mastery of a foreign language in anything like completeness involves the command of its uses in all manner of different environments and different circumstances. Native speakers, as the result of experience gained from early childhood in the process of acculturation, know how to behave in speaking in the various roles they come to fulfil in their lives. To describe this the linguist tries to pick out the essential

27

features of the situations that are characteristic of these different roles and to state them in sets of related categories as contexts of situation. In doing this he is trying to formalize and systematize, to set down, succinctly and explicitly, the vital information about the working and the use of languages that native speakers, for the most part unconsciously, discursively, and gradually, acquire throughout their lives in a community.

The schematic framework by which the information relevant to the functioning, the meaning, of utterances can be stated is the context of situation. A typical outline context has been given by Firth as an example, bringing the utterance and its parts into relationship with the following categories:

The relevant features of participants (persons, personalities):

 (i) The verbal action of the participants.
(ii) The non-verbal action of the participants.
     The relevant objects.
     The effect of the verbal action.

Treated in terms of contexts of situation, the meaning of utterances includes both those aspects that can be described as the reference or denotation of individual words, and those that must be stated as belonging to the sentences, or even the total utterance as a whole. Differences of personal status, family and social relations, degrees of intimacy, relative ages, and other such factors, irrelevant to the consideration of sentences as the expression of logical propositions are all handled under the appropriate headings of a context of situation.

Meaning in language is therefore not a single relation or a single sort of relation, but involves a set of multiple and various relations holding between the utterance and its parts and the relevant features and components of the environment, both cultural and physical, and forming part of the more extensive system of interpersonal relations involved in the existence of human societies.

1·4·4·*Translation*

Questions of translation are very closely connected with semantic analysis and the contextual theory of meaning. The details of this part of language study cannot be covered in an elementary introduction, but the existence of bilingual speakers and the possibility of learning foreign languages and of forming utterances in one language serving nearly if not exactly the same purposes as corresponding utterances in another (i.e. of translating) are universally obvious facts that must be taken into consideration. Indeed, Malinowski was led to the framing of his theory of context of situation in working on the translation into English of key words and sentences found in the accounts given him of their way of life by some of the Trobriand islanders, a people inhabiting a small group of islands to the east of New Guinea, a people whose whole culture, to which he devoted a great deal of study, was entirely removed from that of the western European culture of his readers.

The term *culture* is widely used in a number of different ways, and it will be useful to make explicit its use in this book, a use fairly general in present-day linguistic writing. The term is taken from the technical vocabulary of anthropology, wherein it embraces the entire way of life of members of a community in so far as it is conditioned by that membership. It is manifest that on such a conception of culture language is a part thereof, and indeed one of the most important parts, uniquely related to the whole by its symbolic status.

The need for contextual explanations of meaning was made clear in working on languages whose speakers were culturally remote from Europe; but context of situation is just as pertinent to the explanation of linguistic meaning in any language, though obviously the relevant factors and components of such contexts will differ according to the cultural differences between peoples. The need is less noticeable in dealing with familiar languages, just because the common inherited culture surrounding the use of one's own language and, though to a lesser extent, the use of other languages within the same cultural area, is taken for granted and so not made explicit. Translation, in Malinowski's words, implies 'the unification of cultural context'. This is apparent when one considers the sort of words in other languages that are relatively easy to translate into English and the sort that are not. Word translation, or the finding of lexical equivalents, is easiest with the words of languages within the unified culture area of West Europe or of parts of the world that have come under European influence, or with words in other languages which are such as to have a referential meaning more or less uniform in all cultures, for example the names of many physical objects and natural parts of the world's surface, widely distributed botanical and zoological species, and the like, although any of these words may for one reason or another have special uses and therefore special meanings peculiar to the culture of a particular linguistic community.

Wherever a cultural unity is lacking, the translation of words having reference to particular features or having particular uses in a limited field is more difficult to achieve by means of single lexical equivalents, and requires at best circumlocutions and often more lengthy explanations themselves in part recreating the relevant contexts of situation. One may instance the words peculiar to the ceremonies of particular religious communities, and in recent years the misunderstandings of such words, however translated, as *freedom*, *democracy*, *equality*, across the cultural frontier between communist and capitalist Europe; on either side such words are used in contexts different in certain important respects from each other. Translation and mutual understanding across such frontiers are not impossible; but much hard work in making explicit the essential components of the contexts of situation in which these sorts of key words are used, and taken for granted as so used on each side, is a prerequisite, and the existence in several languages of words formally resembling English *democracy* and ultimately derived from Ancient Greek δημοκρατία /de:mokratía/ is in itself of little assistance.

Further difficulties of translation arise when all the complex functions of words in extralinguistic reference and in sentence composition, as well as the sentences themselves in their contexts of situation, must be considered and sometimes weighed against one another in the choice of the means of translation. In its most familiar form, the choice may have to be between the literal and the literary, in cases where the nearest translation equivalents of individual words taken in isolation are stylistically unattractive or misrepresent some other aspect of the original when they are put together in sentences. This sort of difficulty arises especially in the translation of works of literature, of some kinds more than of others, in which features at other linguistic levels (1·3·4), such as the grammatical form of sentences and the phonetic form of words, are stylistically exploited as parts of the literary form of the whole piece. At one extreme, in the case of certain types of poetry the production of a translation that fulfils anything like all the functions of the original may approach the impossible. The ability to achieve as excellent a translation as may be, balancing all the components at all levels against one another in constructing a version as near in all respects to the original as is possible, requires a delicate and sensitive appreciation of all aspects of language; though its principles can be referred to linguistic science, its achievement is more in the nature of an art, in which individual and personal feeling for the artistic possibilities of the two languages is of the highest importance.

Because language is able to deal with any and every part and feature of human life and experience, the setting up of contexts of situation may have to call on equally large areas as part of the relevant environment, and to seek the aid of other sciences, particularly other sciences devoted to mankind. Of the sciences of man, linguistics, from the nature of its subject-matter, may be one of the most systematizable and exact, and for these reasons the analysis of meanings may not be able to achieve the same degree of precision as analysis at other levels where appeals to phenomena outside language are not needed, or as in phonetics wherein the range of such phenomena is strictly limited.

The complexities and practical difficulties of semantic analysis in language study must not be disguised; but it is very desirable that linguists should seek to develop a theoretical understanding of the place of language in the world of human life and experience, and a framework whereby the functioning of utterances and their components may be reduced to ordered and systematic statement.

A considerable number of books have been written in the present century to give an introduction to general linguistics and the coverage of the subject as the authors see it. It must constantly be borne in mind in reading more widely in this field that no two books on linguistics agree in all respects with each other. Scholars have differed sharply not only on what range of studies should properly be comprised within linguistics, but also on points of linguistic theory and methods of analysis and description, some being ones of quite basic importance. No attempt is made here to provide a complete bibliography of the subject. A number of the general books mentioned below contain bibliographies of varying extents; at the times of publication those in Bloomfield's *Language* and Vendryes's *Le Langage* were very comprehensive. Since 1949 an annual bibliography of linguistic publications, covering the years from 1939 onward, has been published: *Bibliographie linguistique*, Utrecht and Brussels.

The following general books may be recommended.

EUROPEAN

F. de Saussure, *Cours de Linguistique générale*, fourth edition, Paris 1949. This is the posthumous compilation of de Saussure's teaching course on linguistics, based on his notes and those of his pupils. De Saussure in many ways marks the beginning of linguistics as an independent academic subject in its present form, and many of the distinctions and topics now almost universally recognized as essential to it were first made explicit by him. The book is not hard to read, though the circumstances of its publication involve occasional lack of clarity on certain points. There is an English translation by W. Baskin, New York, 1959, but those who read French should use the original text.

J. Vendryes, *Le langage*, Paris, 1921, also translated, P. Radin, London, 1925.

O. Jespersen, *Language*, London, 1922. Though rather old-fashioned in some respects by now, this book is well worth reading. Jespersen was a Danish scholar, but this, like a number of his other books, was written in English and published in England.

A. Martinet, *Eléments de linguistique générale*, Paris, 1960.

AMERICAN

E. Sapir, *Language*, New York, 1921.

L. Bloomfield, *Language*, London, 1935.

These two books of the same title by American scholars are probably the most important books in the development of American linguistics, and their influence has been felt over the whole world of linguistic scholarship. Of the two, Bloomfield's book is the larger and perhaps the more important, though the style of Sapir makes his *Language* one of the most brilliant and readable books on the subject ever to be published. Bloomfield's *Language*, first published in America in 1933, defined and circumscribed the subject and at once established itself as a textbook that has not yet been superseded. Probably most United States linguists would consider themselves as in some sense Bloomfield's disciples, whether they actually studied under him or not, and a great deal of American work has taken the form of working out questions raised and methods suggested in Bloomfield's *Language*. The two writers are very different in outlook and complement one another. Sapir's interests were wide-ranging, and though his linguistic scholarship was unchallenged he was always probing the boundaries of linguistic studies and the contribution they could give to and receive from other fields, such as anthropology, psychology, philosophy, and literary criticism, subjects in which he himself was qualified. Bloomfield deliberately concentrated on the theory and techniques of linguistics as a circumscribed and defined science. Many of the generally used technical terms in linguistics today were introduced into the subject by Bloomfield in his book *Language*.

Sapir and Bloomfield have been contrasted more than once, as centrifugal and centripetal by S. Newman (*IJAL* 17 (1951), 180–6), and as genius and classic by M. Joos (*Readings in linguistics*, Washington, 1957, 31). American linguistic scholarship is indeed fortunate to have had two such men during its formative years.

Sapir's work can be seen in greater detail in his *Selected writings* (ed. D. G. Mandelbaum, Berkeley, 1949). Bloomfield's attitude to language studies is further illustrated in 'A set of postulates for the science of language', *Lang.* 2 (1926), 153–64 and 'Linguistic aspects of science', *International encyclopædia of unified science*, 1 (Chicago, 1939), part 4.

Further general introductions by American authors are:

B. Bloch and G. L. Trager, *Outline of linguistic analysis*, Baltimore, 1942; E. H. Sturtevant, *An introduction to linguistic science*, Yale, 1947; C. F. Hockett, *A course in modern linguistics*, New York, 1958; R. A. Hall, *Linguistics and your language*, New York, 1960; and H. A. Gleason, *An introduction to descriptive linguistics*, second edition, New York, 1961. A. A. Hill's *Introduction to linguistic structures*, New York, 1958, is, in fact, largely a linguistic analysis, on Hill's lines, of English, concentrating on phonology and grammar; it also contains brief appendices on Latin and Eskimo. A rather different type of book is seen in Z. S. Harris's *Methods in structural linguistics*, Chicago, 1951, which concentrates on phonology and grammar, working out procedures and methods in great detail and with great rigour of theory, exemplified from a number of languages. It is scarcely an elementary book, and it presupposes a knowledge of Bloomfieldian linguistics, developing certain aspects of it to their logical conclusion.

The course of development of American linguistics from the twenties of this century is partly set out in a collection of important articles and monographs arranged in chronological order, *Readings in linguistics*, ed. Joos.

BRITISH

J. R. Firth, *Speech*, London, 1930, brief and provocative.

Firth, *The tongues of men*, London, 1937, a popular book, with relatively little detail.

L. R. Palmer, *An introduction to modern linguistics*, London, 1936, an excellent short survey.

Firth's contribution to British linguistics, and to the subject generally, was very considerable, but it was not in the main made by his books. His most influential writing took the form of articles, the most significant of these being collected together in his *Papers in linguistics 1934–1951*, Oxford, 1957. He provided a summary of his theoretical opinions, with numerous quotations from earlier works, in his 'Synopsis of linguistic theory', appearing in *Studies in linguistic analysis*, special publication of the Philological Society, Oxford, 1957.

C. E. Bazell, *Linguistic form*, Istanbul, 1953, is a condensed and critical survey of current linguistic methods and assumptions. It ought to be more widely known, but it is certainly not elementary.

S. Potter has published two books, both popular and discursive rather than technical, enjoyable and easy to read, and likely to arouse an interest in the subject: *Modern linguistics*, London, 1957, and *Language in the modern world*, Penguin Books, 1960.

Dictionaries of technical terms in linguistics:

J. Marouzeau, *Lexique de la terminologie linguistique*, Paris, 1943, concentrates on European work and is rather old-fashioned.

M. A. Pei and F. Gaynor, *Dictionary of linguistics*, London, 1958.

E. P. Hamp, *A glossary of American technical linguistic usage 1925–1950*, Utrecht, 1958, confines itself, as the title indicates, to recent American terminology (second, expanded edition, 1963).

Many of the developments in linguistics take the form of articles rather than of books, and there are periodicals in several countries devoted to the publication of linguistic papers. One may notice particularly:

EUROPEAN: *Le bulletin de la société de linguistique de Paris*, France.

Lingua, Holland (published in English, French, and German).

Acta linguistica, Denmark (also published in English, French, and German).

AMERICAN: *Language*, the journal of the Linguistic Society of America.

International journal of American linguistics, principally devoted to studies in the American-Indian languages, but containing a number of articles and separately published monographs of general theoretical interest.

Word, the journal of the Linguistic Circle of New York, an internationally edited periodical.

BRITISH: *Transactions of the Philological Society.*
Archivum linguisticum.

ADDENDA

Attention may be drawn to the following recently published books that serve the purpose of general introductions to the subject:

B. Malmberg, *Structural linguistics and human communication*, Berlin, Göttingen, and Heidelberg, 1963. Malmberg covers the general range of topics indicated in the title, though with predominant attention to phonetics and phonology.

A. Martinet, *Elements of general linguistics*, London, 1964. This is an English translation of Martinet's *Eléments de linguistique générale*, noticed on page 32, above.

Both these books follow through the developments initiated by de Saussure in his *Cours de linguistique générale*. Martinet introduces some terminology and points of theory of his own, also seen in his less elementary *A functional view of language*, Oxford, 1962, and the chapter on the evolution of languages (historical linguistics) presents in simplified form the approach set out in his *Economie des changements phonétiques* (44 in chapter 8, bibliography).

An additional British linguistic periodical, the *Journal of linguistics*, published for the Linguistics Association of Great Britain, appeared in 1965.

A clear and concise presentation of the subject in Italian may be found in G. C. Lepschy, *La linguistica strutturale*, Turin, 1966.

GENERAL BIBLIOGRAPHY—ADDENDA

CHAPTER 1, BIBLIOGRAPHY

1. B. BLOCH and G. L. TRAGER, *Outline of linguistic analysis*, Baltimore, 1942.

2. L. BLOOMFIELD, *Language*, London, 1935.

3. G. M. BOLLING, 'Linguistics and philology', *Lang.* 5 (1929), 27–32.

4. R. CARNAP, *Introduction to semantics*, Cambridge, Mass., 1948.

5. C. R. CARPENTER, *A field study in Siam of the behaviour and social relations of the gibbon*, Comparative psychology monographs 16 (1940), part 5.

6. J. B. CARROLL, *The study of language*, Cambridge, Mass., 1953.

7. J. R. FIRTH, *Speech*, London, 1930.

8. ——, 'The technique of semantics', *TPS* 1935, 36–72.

9. ——, 'Personality and language in society', *Sociol. rev.* 42 (1950), 37–52.

10. ——, 'Synopsis of linguistic theory 1930–55', *Studies in linguistic analysis*, special publication of the Philological Society, Oxford, 1957, 1–32.

11. ——, 'Ethnographic analysis and language with reference to Malinowski's views', *Man and culture*, edited by R. W. Firth, London, 1957, 93–118.

12. K. VON FRISCH, *Bees, their vision, chemical senses, and language*, Ithaca, 1950.

13. A. L. GARDINER, *Theory of speech and language*, Oxford, 1932.

14. W. HAAS, 'On defining linguistic units', *TPS* 1954, 54–84.

15. M. A. K. HALLIDAY, *The language of the Chinese 'Secret history of the Mongols'*, publication of the Philological Society 17, Oxford, 1959.

16. ——, 'Categories of the theory of grammar', *Word* 17 (1961), 241–92

17. S. I. HAYAKAWA, *Language in thought and action*, London, 1952.

18. L. HJELMSLEV, *Prolegomena to a theory of language*, translated by F. J. Whitfield, Baltimore, 1953 (originally published in Danish, 1943).

19. ——, 'Structural linguistics', *Studia linguistica* 1 (1947), 69–78.

20. C. F. HOCKETT, 'A system of descriptive phonology', *Lang.* 18 (1942), 3–21.

21. ——, *A manual of phonology*, Indiana University publications in anthropology and linguistics 11, 1955.

22. ——, *A course in modern linguistics*, New York, 1958.

23. O. JESPERSEN, *Language*, London, 1922.

24. E. KIECKERS, *Die Sprachstämme der Erde*, Heidelberg, 1931.

25. W. KÖHLER, *Gestalt psychology*, New York, 1947.

26. A. L. KROEBER, 'Sign and symbol in bee communications', *Proc. National Academy of Sciences* 38 (1952), 753–7.

27. B. MALINOWSKI, *Coral gardens and their magic*, London, 1935.

28. A. MEILLET and M. COHEN, *Les langues du monde*, Paris, 1952.

29. T. F. MITCHELL, 'The language of buying and selling in Cyrenaica', *Hespéris* 1957, 31–71.

30. C. MORRIS, *Signs, language, and behaviour*, New York, 1946.

31. C. K. OGDEN and I. A. RICHARDS, *The meaning of meaning*, eighth edition, London, 1946.

32. F. R. PALMER, 'Linguistic hierarchy', *Lingua* 7 (1958), 225–41.

33. J. P. POSTGATE, *Translation and translations*, London, 1922.

34. E. PULGRAM, 'Phoneme and grapheme: a parallel', *Word* 7 (1951), 15–20.

35. G. REVESZ, *Der Ursprung und Vorgeschichte der Sprache*, Berne, 1946 (translated by J. Butler, London, 1956).

36. R. H. ROBINS, 'A problem in the statement of meanings', *Lingua* 3 (1952), 121–37.

37. ——, 'John Rupert Firth', *Lang.* 37 (1961), 191–200.

38. E. SAPIR, 'The status of linguistics as a science', *Lang.* 5 (1929), 207–14.

39. F. DE SAUSSURE, *Cours de linguistique générale*, fourth edition, Paris, 1949.

40. T. H. SAVORY, *The art of translation*, London, 1957.

41. W. SCHMIDT, *Die Sprachfamilien und Sprachenkreise der Erde*, Heidelberg, 1926.

42. N. C. SCOTT, 'Obituary, John Rupert Firth', *BSOAS* 24 (1961), 413–18.

43. H. SPANG-HANSSEN, 'Glossematics', *Trends in European and American linguistics 1930–1960*, Utrecht, 1961, 128–64.

44. G. L. TRAGER, 'The field of linguistics', *Studies in linguistics*, occasional paper 1 (1950).

45. S. ULLMANN, *The principles of semantics*, second edition, Glasgow and Oxford, 1957.

46. ——, *Semantics*, Oxford, 1962.

47. L. WITTGENSTEIN, *Philosophical investigations*, translated by G. E. M. Anscombe, Oxford, 1953.

ADDENDA

48. J. LYONS, *Structural semantics, an analysis of part of the vocabulary Plato*, publication of the Philological Society 20, 1963.

49. C. E. Bazell, J. C. Catford, M. A. K. Halliday and R. H. Robins (editors), *In Memory of J. R. Firth*, London, 1966.

50. J. C. CATFORD, *A linguistic theory of translation*, London, 1965.

p. 2. On the languages of the world, Meillet and Cohen, 28, give brief accounts of all languages so far as information is available. See also Schmidt, 41, and Kieckers, 24.

On the linguist as opposed to the polyglot, Bloch and Trager, 1, 8.

p. 5. *Synchronic* and *diachronic*, like a number of other basic terminological distinctions in linguistics, are Saussurean in origin (39, 114–43). De Saussure gave us the term *état de langue* to refer to a stage of a language at a particular period; thus Chaucerian, Johnsonian, and contemporary English are each different *états de la langue anglaise*.

p. 6. On the different uses of the word *philology*, Carroll, 6, 3, 65–6; Bolling, 3.

p. 9. N. McQuown, *Lang.* 28 (1952), 495.

p. 10. The quotation comes at the end of Hjelmslev, 18; so also does the use in linguistics of *metalanguage* to designate language about language or language turned back on itself, a use borrowed from the logician's distinction of metalanguage (language about language) and object language (language about things); see Carnap, 4, chapter 1. Hjelmslev's *Prolegomena* was first published in Danish in 1943, and represents a statement of the glossematic theory of language and linguistics, as developed by Hjelmslev and those associated with him (loosely called 'the Danish school'). Glossematic theory is characterized by a high degree of abstraction and systematization, and is an important part of contemporary linguistic theory; but it can hardly be said to be easily grasped, nor is the *Prolegomena* a beginner's book. A briefer and simpler outline of the theory appears in Hjelmslev's 'Structural linguistics' (19), see also H. Spang-Hanssen, 43.

p. 12. On levels of analysis, Firth, 8; Hockett, 20; F. R. Palmer, 32.

It is desirable to maintain clearly the distinction between different levels of analysis, employing different kinds of criteria, and different ranks within the analysis at any level, when the same kinds of criteria are used to establish elements or structures of greater or lesser extent. Thus:

LEVEL	RANK	
	lesser	*greater*
phonological	syllable	syllable group
grammatical	morpheme	construction

cp. Halliday, 16.

pp. 12-13. cp. the definition of language in Bloch and Trager, 1, 5. On sign and symbol, cp. Morris, 30, 23–7.

p. 14. On sound symbolism and onomatopoeia, Jespersen, 23, chapter 20; Firth, 7, chapter 6; Köhler, 25, 224–5.

It is sometimes said that certain mystical experiences, perfectly real to the percipient, are 'ineffable', quite literally inexpressible in human language. It is not for the linguist to deny such aspects of some people's experiences, and if they are truly inexpressible then this forms an exception in the case of certain persons to the power of language. Such personal phenomena can hardly be discussed further here.

p. 15. On the question of the origin of language, Révész, 35 and Hockett, 22, chapter 64, and in *The scientific American*, September 1960. On bee dancing, von Frisch, 12; Kroeber, 26. On gibbons, Carpenter, 5.

Parrots' 'speech', though superficially nearest to human speech, is functionally an artificial development of parrots in human company, and quite unimportant.

p. 18. On graphonomy, Hockett, 22, chapter 62. On the analogy of *phonemics* (4·3) a branch of linguistics called graphemics has been suggested (Pulgram, 34).

p. 20. On linguistically orientated statements involving the subject-matter of other sciences, Palmer, 32, 234.

On the narrower interpretation of *linguistics*, Trager, 44, cp. Hjelmslev, 18, 50; Hockett, 21, 14.

p. 23. George Berkeley, *A treatise concerning the principles of human knowledge*, 1710, introduction, §13.

pp. 24-5. On different cultural worlds, Sapir, 38.

p. 26. On 'thing meant', Gardiner, 13; *signifiant* and *signifié*, de Saussure, 39, 99; triadic relationship of meaning, Ogden and Richards, 31, chapter 1.

On meaning as function, Bazell, *Word* 10 (1954), 132; cp. Wittgenstein, 47, 126 etc.

Bloomfield develops a rigorous theory of meaning in behaviourist or mechanist terms (2, chapters 2 and 9). These topics are discussed from a number of points of view by Ullmann, 45; cp. 46.

p. 27. *Phatic communion* was used by Malinowski (in Ogden and Richards, 31, 315) as a technical term to denote the type of socially necessary 'idle chatter'; cp. Hayakawa, 17, 72: 'The prevention of silence is itself an important function of speech.'

p. 28. By a somewhat more specialized use of *semantics*, Morris, 30, distinguishes *semantics*, the study of the sorts of meaning relation covered by *reference*, and *pragmatics*, the wider range of associations between what is said and other aspects or features of human behaviour.

On context of situation, Malinowski, Supplement 1 in Ogden and Richards, 31, and 27, volume 2, chapter 1; Firth, 9 and 10, 7–11.

Malinowski and Firth do not use *context of situation* in quite the same way. In part this is due to the fact that Malinowski was an anthropologist led to an interest in language through his ethnographic studies, while Firth was a linguist concerned with the rest of human culture in so far as it was involved in the framing of a theory of language. Malinowski's context consisted of the actual relevant features, cultural and physical, of the environment in which the utterance took place. This conception led to his being criticized, perhaps excessively, for 'particularism' (Carroll, 6, 39–40), in that every utterance must be treated separately and general statements of meaning are precluded. Firth's context of situation is an abstract set of related categories at the level of semantic analysis, of the type exemplified on p. 28, but which may be as varied in its composition as the semantic explanation of the material requires. Its categories are applied to the actual environment and provide the means whereby in each individual case the features relevant to the functioning (meaning) of the utterance and its parts may be singled out for attention.

See further: Robins, 36; Mitchell, 29; Firth, 11; Halliday, 15, chapter 3.

The contextual theory of meaning was developed by Firth to form a general theory of language and of linguistic analysis, that has been of considerable influence in Great Britain. Starting from the axiomatic conception of language as meaningful activity, Firth extended the treatment of meaning as function in a context to the other levels of linguistic analysis, namely those of linguistic form, in particular grammar and phonology. This involved him in such expressions as *grammatical meaning* and *phonological meaning*, which in a way are unfortunate as his *grammatical meaning* is often misunderstood as the semantic correlations of grammatical classes, constructions, and categories (Chapter 7), and *phonological meaning* is at first sight startling. His attitude is wholly compatible with the rigorous distinction of the different levels into which linguistic analysis and description is divided by the application of different criteria. But the theory underlying it has the definite advantage of giving a certain unity to the study of language, and binds together the investigation of the two different aspects of it, form and meaning ($1\cdot3\cdot1$). Essentially, in this theory, meaning is defined as the function of some linguistic form or element in a context. The meaning treated contextually by Malinowski, and covering the usual sense of the word as used non-technically, is regarded as the function of the utterance and its parts in a context of situation and distinguished as semantic meaning or meaning at the situational level. In grammar and phonology, the elements and categories abstracted or set up to describe the forms and patterns of utterances in a language function (i.e. have their meaning) by their relations with other elements belonging to (abstracted at) the same level. Grammatical meaning is the function of grammatical elements in relation to the context of other grammatical elements; and phonological meaning is the function of phonological elements in the context of other phonological elements. In terms of this theory and system of analysis, the description of linguistic form in phonology and grammar, as well as the description of semantic function in relation to the external world by means of the categories of a context of a situation, all help to make up the statement of meaning. The working or functioning of language, considered as meaningful activity, is split up for analysis and description into a series of separate functions of elements and forms abstracted by the appropriate criteria at each level.

This general theory of language and linguistic analysis is set out in Firth, 8 and 10. A complete bibliography of Firth's publications is to be found at the end of his obituaries, by Scott, 42, and by Robins, 37.

Haas, 14, discusses Firth's theoretical position.

p. 29. On culture as a technical term, Bloch and Trager, 1, 5. While the use of the term in the present book is typical, it must not be assumed that all anthropologists use it in the same way.

On translation, Malinowski, 27, volume 2, 14; Postgate, 33; Savory, 40; *IJAL* 20 (1954), part 4, translation issue; Catford, 50.

ADDENDA

p. 20. On semantics in linguistics, see Lyons 48, chapters 1–4.

p. 28. A number of linguistic studies in one way or another relating to Firth's teaching and interests may be found in Bazell and others, 49.

2

Theoretical and methodological considerations

2·1 ABSTRACTIONS

2·1·1 *The status of linguistic abstractions*

Linguistic analysis proceeds in the manner of other empirical sciences by making abstractions, at different levels (1·3·1), of elements having the status of constants and of categories expressing the relations between the elements, to which the continuous flux of the phenomena comprising its subject-matter can be referred, and by means of which the phenomena may be explained and accounted for. At any level the abstractions can be of different degrees of generality. Thus at the grammatical level, in relation to English, the word *foot* (abstracted from utterances containing certain sound sequences), *noun*, and *word* are progressively higher degrees of abstraction, that is, they subsume successively more material under themselves. Phonetically, *the consonant* /b/, *plosive consonant*, and *consonant* show a similar gradation in degree (for the phonetic terms here used as examples, see 3·3).

The status of the abstractions employed in the description and analysis of linguistic form has been the subject of considerable debate. It has been variously maintained:

1. That the constants abstracted in an analysis, if the analysis is correct, are in some way inherent in the actual material of the language under analysis;

2. That the linguist's abstractions are also abstracted, albeit unconsciously, by native speakers of the language as the result of their

having learned the language in childhood, and are part of the content of the speakers' minds or brains;

3. That the linguist's abstractions have no other status than as part of his scientific terminology, and are justified by their utility in stating regularities and making predictions about the forms of utterances, but have no express relevance to the speakers' mental or cerebral states or equipment, though certain correspondences between the two are not ruled out and are *prima facie* quite probable.

These three viewpoints follow somewhat along the classical philosophical lines of realism, conceptualism, and nominalism respectively. In so far as their differences fall within the field of philosophy or of general scientific theory, they need not be the direct concern of the linguist. But there are certain implications for linguistics in each view, which should therefore be mentioned.

The first view implies as a consequence that languages have an organization independent of any analyst, and that the analysis consists in discovering the inherent patterns of that organization, so that one's statements are correct or incorrect according as they correspond or do not correspond with the pre-existing organization of the language, even though it may never be actually possible to declare for certain that any particular analysis or analytic statement is the correct one.

The implication of the second view is that the linguist's analysis of a language as he observes it corresponds in some way to the linguistic working of the speaker's mind or brain, and that the language should be described in the same terms as could be used to describe the production of speech by a speaker and its comprehension by a hearer.

The third view is in many ways the easiest to adopt. It makes no demands outside the realm of linguistic description and analysis. The descriptions of languages may in part correspond with descriptions of the production and comprehension of speech, but that is not their province. As regards 'the language itself' apart from the work of any analyst, it is not, of course, maintained that chaos reigns until a linguist appears and imposes an order from outside; languages clearly differ from one another, in as much as different analyses are required for them. But it is simply held that the questions whether an organization and its constant elements exist in the phenomena, what they are like, and how they are related to one another independently of the analyst are not sensibly or profitably asked. The description and its elements are justified by their explanatory power and validated by their application to further material, i.e. by their ability to predict by extrapolation from a necessarily limited body of material the forms and functions of a much larger and in living languages necessarily unlimited body of similar material. Nothing more is claimed or required of them.

Of course, language, in so far as it is deemed a proper subject of an empirical science, is held to be such that a systematic description is feasible and that the statements made therein have a predictive value. This merely puts language within the class of phenomena accessible to science; it does not endow the elements employed in a description and analysis with any existential status outside and apart from the statements in which they appear. This does not imply any scientific irresponsibility towards the data, language in general and languages in particular. The fact that the analyst does not see himself as uncovering a pre-existing 'true' state of affairs, or mapping an actual configuration present in the speaker's mind or brain, but only as framing descriptive and predictive general statements, does not justify him in lowering his standards in any way. Different analyses of the same data and different procedures of analysis are to be evaluated and judged in merit against one another by their fulfilling the standards of scientific work, exhaustiveness, consistency, and economy (1·2·1), and are in all cases justified by their successful application to further data. But it must be allowed that two or more different descriptions or descriptive procedures may be equally justifiable, or that each of several is to be preferred for highlighting different parts or different facets of the phenomena in question.

In this introduction to the subject of linguistics, the third approach will be assumed in dealing with the treatment of linguistic phenomena, but it should not be difficult to make use of linguistic literature written from one of the other points of view. In the approach followed here, the elements or constants are established at each level of analysis by abstraction from the relevant phenomena (utterances). Those features and parts of utterances that are held to give rise to and justify each abstraction may be said to represent it or serve as its exponents. Thus from the English utterance 'Take care', the phonetic consonant and vowel segments, the phonological consonantal and vocalic elements, the grammatical elements verb and noun related as imperative verb and object noun, and the lexical items *take* and *care* are all abstracted at their appropriate level, and are severally represented by exponents in the actual or assumed utterance. The validation of an analysis by applying it to fresh material of the same sort and finding adequate exponents for the abstractions made therein may be called the renewal of connection.

In the illustration given above the exponency of all the levels of analysis was sought in the actual utterance; but it is usually convenient to employ the elements of one level to serve as exponents of the analysis at another. This is done, for example, when lexical items and grammatical elements are indicated and identified by means of a phonological transcription (4·2), and when phonological elements have their exponents stated as phonetic segments and features, themselves abstractions at the phonetic level from the actual utterance. When levels are treated as related in this way, a hierarchy is established between those levels that make use of or presuppose at least part of the results of analysis at other levels and those other levels themselves, in the total analysis or theory of analysis.

Strictly speaking, in such a scheme of analysis one should not talk of such and such elements or items (literally) 'occurring' in a text or in a language, or of phonological elements as 'found in' or as 'constituting' grammatical or lexical elements. Such forms of statement are, rigidly within the terms of the theory, more accurately made by saying that the abstractions concerned are statable at the different levels and that the abstractions at two or more levels may show specific congruences of exponency. However, provided the simpler and more 'realistic' language of 'occurrence' and the like is recognized as a convenient metaphor and no more, its use is well justified by the resultant convenience and brevity. It will, in fact, be frequently adopted, with the proviso just mentioned, in this book.

2·1·2 *Structural linguistics: syntagmatic and paradigmatic relations*

It is a commonplace today to say that linguistics is **structural**, and that languages, as analysed by linguists, are treated **structurally**. This is a statement about the elements (constants) set up by abstraction in t he description and analysis of languages. These are considered and treated as being all related to one another by their very nature and so forming interrelated systems rather than mere aggregates of individuals. A metaphor may clarify this distinction. The members of an orchestra are all related to each other by their specific rôles as orchestral players therein, both within smaller groups and in the whole orchestra (e.g. member of the woodwind section, first fiddle among the strings, and so on). Each performs his function by virtue of his place in relation to the others, and players cannot be added to or taken away from an orchestra without altering its essential musical quality and potentialities. On the other hand the audience at a concert is more like a simple aggregate; ten more members or five fewer, be they men or women and wherever they may choose to sit, make no difference to the whole audience in its capacity as an audience.

At each level the formal constituents of the analysis, the elements abstracted, are established and defined as parts thereof by their relations with other constituents at the same level. Some linguists go so far as to say that the actual 'content' or exponential features assigned to an abstracted element are of little account, or of none, in determining and defining it. This is not necessary; the actual material of utterance in a language is the ultimate basis of any analysis or description, and reference to phonetic features in phonological analysis and to phonological (or phonetic) shapes in grammar is perfectly compatible with the prime consideration being given to the interrelations within the level in determining the status of analytic elements.

Essentially the relations between linguistic elements are of two kinds or dimensions, usually designated syntagmatic and paradigmatic. **Syntagmatic** relations are those holding between elements forming serial structures at a given level, referable to, though of course not identical with, the temporal flow of utterance or linear stretches of writing. To take again the previous example: the word sequence *take* and *care*, the transcription /ˈteik ˈkɛə/, the more abstract phonological representation CVVC CVV (C = consonantal element, V = vocalic element), and the grammatical arrangement verb + noun are all, at different levels, structures of syntagmatically related components. By reason of their referability to the actual material of the spoken (or written) utterance, syntagmatic relations may be considered the primary dimension. **Paradigmatic** relations are those holding between comparable elements at particular places in structures, e.g.

initial consonant *take* /teik/

           m   /m/

           b   /b/

post-verbal noun *take care*

               pains

               thought

               counsel

and more generally between the comparable elements of structures in classes (e.g. consonants, verbs), or in the language as a whole (e.g. phonemes (phonological elements), word classes ('parts of speech')).

Structure and *system*, and their derivatives, are often used almost interchangeably, but it is useful to employ *structure*, as in the preceding paragraph, specifically with reference to groupings of syntagmatically related elements, and *system* with reference to classes of paradigmatically related elements.

Relations may be manifold between linguistic elements, and so structures may be divided into substructures, and systems may comprise various subsystems. In particular, the paradigmatic dimension, at both the phonological and the grammatical levels, covers many different types of contrast, according to the different criteria employed.

The use of relational criteria in the analysis of the forms of languages is apparent in practically all modern descriptions. The status of a particular case as a grammatical category applicable to certain word endings in a language like Latin is stated syntagmatically in terms of the different syntactic structures (constructions) in which it may be used in relation to other grammatical constituents (verbs, prepositions, etc.), and paradigmatically in terms of the number of different cases formally marked in the language; it is not stated in terms of a common semantic meaning ascribable to all words exhibiting the particular case (often leading to a fruitless search). The status of a phonological element (e.g. a particular consonant) is not established solely by reference to its exponents (phonetic segments or fractions of utterance), but syntagmatically in terms of its possible places in relation to other phonological elements in phonological structures, and paradigmatically in terms of the different elements with which it contrasts in the different places of its occurrence.

The illustrative statements of the preceding paragraphs are necessarily anticipatory; the terms employed and the processes of analysis involved at the different levels will be dealt with in subsequent chapters. Here it may be said that in this explicitly structural approach to the description and analysis of languages modern linguistics most sharply contrasts with earlier traditional linguistic attitudes.

2·2   DIALECT, IDIOLECT, STYLE

2·2·1   *Dialects as subdivisions of languages*

Among the abstractions that are made in linguistics, one of the most important has so far been assumed without receiving any examination. This is the term *language*, in the sense of *the English language*, *the French language*, etc. It is an empirically obvious fact that no two individuals have identical speech. One is seldom unable to recognize the voice of one acquaintance as distinct from that of another and from that of a stranger. Nevertheless in everyday affairs one readily speaks of *the English language*, etc. without confusion of misunderstanding, and the linguist in making statements about a given language at any level of analysis does the same. In each case one is deliberately ignoring certain differences between the speech habits of separate individuals. The linguist, who must recognize explicitly what he is doing, bases his abstractions, generalizations, and descriptive statements on features and characteristics that can be ascribed to all speakers recognized for his purposes as speakers of the language concerned. Science must proceed in this way, seeking to compass the manifold diversity of phenomena by statements applying to what can be said to be common to them. In the case of languages one can proceed in two ways, either making one's statements general enough, admitting permissive variation of structures and systems in one's description and a wide range of actual exponents, so that the inherent diversity of different speakers is allowed for, or, more usually, selecting certain speakers only and restricting one's statements to them alone as fictitiously representing the language as a whole.

In practice, except with languages spoken by a few people in a compact area, the second procedure is normal. Traditionally and customarily, the speech of educated persons in the capital city of a country is selected as representing 'the language'. Grammars of English and French and books on English or French pronunciation, unless it is expressly stated otherwise, describe educated English as spoken in London and the south-east of the country and educated Parisian French. These are the types of English and French taught as foreign languages in schools, though as types of speech they may represent the speech habits of only a minority in each country.

Whatever the practical merits of this procedure, linguistic science and linguistic theory must be able to deal with the actual diversity of linguistic phenomena more precisely. Within the domain generally recognized of 'one language', many clearly observable differences of pronunciation, grammar, and vocabulary are not haphazardly mixed, but occupy different regions within the territory, shading continuously into one another in all directions. This sort of situation is apparent to anyone journeying by stages, for example, west from London to Cornwall or north from London to Edinburgh.

To cope with this state of affairs, the linguist distinguishes within all but the smallest language areas different dialects. **Dialect** is an abstraction of the same sort as language; but as it covers fewer people, it enables one to keep one's statements closer to the actual speech of the speakers; each abstracted element in the description of a dialect covers a less wide range of actually different phenomena. The number of dialects to be recognized within a language is clearly not fixed in advance; it depends on the fineness of the scale on which the linguist is working; the smaller each dialect is taken to be and therefore the greater the number of dialects distinguished, the more precise each description can be, as each generalization will cover a smaller range of divergence. In such circumstances dialects will fall into successively larger groups of dialects, the largest group being the language itself as a unity. The lower limit of dialect division comes down to the individual speaker, and for this limiting case of dialect the term *idiolect* (the speech habits of a single person) has been coined.

Even here, however, one has not reached the end of the possible subdivisions of linguistic phenomena. Each individual's speech habits vary according to the different situations he is in and the different roles he is playing at any time in society. One readily distinguishes the different types of speech used by the same person in intimate family circles, among strangers and with persons of different social positions, in official, professional, and learned discourse, and so on, though with indeterminate borderlines between each; and in writing, the composition of a family letter is very different from that of a technical article. As an obvious example, in educated London English the word sequence *the author to whom I was referring* is considered natural and appropriate in a formal lecture, and the sequence *the author who I was referring to* is likewise felt appropriate to conversation. The latter might be found in a lecture, especially in an extempore one without a full script, but the former would appear strangely stilted in general conversation.

These differences within the linguistic range of a single person are often called **styles**. At the present state of linguistics, the style chosen in first investigating the speech of an individual as representing a particular dialect or language is conventionally that designated 'slow colloquial', the style appropriate to fairly formal discourse with strangers, other styles being described usually by reference to the description of this.

The peculiar slangs and jargons of closely knit groups within a community, such as some schools and colleges, certain skilled trades, semi-secret societies, and the like, fall under the general heading of style; their use on appropriate occasions by the individuals concerned helps to give the 'insiders' an enhanced sense of group unity and to distinguish them from the 'outsiders', to whom such modes of discourse are unfamiliar and in part unknown.

A special case of style variation is seen in the working of linguistic taboo, the avoidance by speakers either of whole topics or of certain words in particular situations (e.g. the presence of strangers, members of the opposite sex, children, older persons, etc.). As far as is known, this phenomenon is found in all communities, though the sorts of topics and the types of vocabulary thus interdicted and the situations in which the taboos operate vary considerably. In England such topics as excretion and sexual reproduction ('obscenity', 'dirt'), details of one's own professional activities ('talking shop'), personal successes ('swank'), and the making and investing of money have all been found objectionable to varying degrees in certain types of situation and company. If certain types of bodily processes and some much feared or unpleasant diseases have to be mentioned, a different vocabulary is substituted in most circumstances, usually having reference to other less distressing activities or experiences (euphemism), and the vocabulary whose principal reference is to taboo topics is reserved for intimate and other special situations. A similar taboo often lies on the sort of vocabulary that may be used in ejaculations of anger, enthusiasm, and the like, in the hearing of strangers. Names of the deity and words with religious associations (doubtless relics of earlier magical attitudes towards language), as well as those labelled obscene, sometimes seem to relieve tense feelings merely by being uttered; but in most situations their use is disapproved of as 'swearing', and other expressions are substituted. For this reason it has been said not without truth that to be able to swear convincingly in a foreign language is one of the marks of its thorough mastery.

2·2·2 *Dialect mapping: isoglosses*

The differences of personal styles and of dialects are the summations of large numbers of individual differences of speaking (and writing), discernible at all levels, in pronunciation, in grammar, and in the meanings of particular words. Examples from English are the trilled 'r' of parts of Scotland, the separate second person singular pronoun forms of parts of the north of England, the use of local words not current in other regions, such as *nesh*, 'liable to damage or distress from cold' (parts of North and West England), and the use of words in senses not generally current, e.g. *to starve*, 'to perish of cold' as well as 'of hunger' (parts of North England and the Midlands), *homely*, 'comfortably disposed' (British English), 'ugly, plain' (parts of the United States).

Considerable attention has always been paid to dialectical differences within languages. Though their accurate and systematic description and differentiation are matters for the linguist, the division of most languages into dialects has always been a matter of general knowledge and acceptance. Among amateur scholars dialect observation has always been a favourite linguistic topic, and the several dialect societies in existence bear witness of this. Antiquarianism (where modern conditions are tending to displace an earlier distinct dialect) and local pride are two main motivating causes. Some linguists specialize in dialect studies within one or more language areas, and *dialectology* is available as the title for this specialization.

Dialects are constituted at any degree of abstraction by their features at each level of analysis, both those they share with others

Diagram 1

Representation of the definite article, 'the', in spoken dialects of Yorkshire, England (based on the map in W. E. Jones, 'The definite article in living Yorkshire dialect', *Leeds studies in English and kindred languages* 7–8 (1952), 81–91).

The lines (isoglosses) within the unshaded area of the map divide the county of Yorkshire into three areas, according to their spoken representation of 'the':

1. A t-sound and/or a glottal stop (ʔ)* before consonants and vowels;
2. A t-sound and/or a glottal stop before consonants, a th-sound (θ) or tth-sound (tθ) before vowels;
3. No spoken representation.

* For the phonetic symbols, see chart on pp. 92–3

54

Diagram 2

Map of the *maken/machen* line (isogloss), based on Map 1, in T. Frings, *Grundlegung einer Geschichte der deutschen Sprache*, Max Niemeyer Verlag, Halle, 1950, 67.

and those peculiar to a particular dialect. So dialects have been defined as the sum of their characteristics, a statement equally applicable, of course, to whole languages. In so far as these characteristics are locally distributed, they can be plotted on a map of the area concerned. This is done in 'dialect geography' by drawing lines as closely as the nature of the material allows demarcating areas exhibiting a particular feature and so dividing them off from areas exhibiting other features. These lines are called **isoglosses**, a term modelled on geographical terms like *isotherm* (a line joining areas of equal temperature) and *isobar* (a line joining areas of equal atmospheric pressure). In several countries (e.g. Britain, France, Germany, and the United States) semi-official dialect surveys have been, or are being, made, covering features at all levels.

As was said above, the dialect features plotted by isoglosses are

55

not randomly scattered over an area, but tend roughly to coincide in distribution, so that a dialect map shows several isoglosses more or less following the same track, especially those relating to features of grammar and pronunciation, though it must be remembered that every time a speaker of one dialect moves or settles in another dialect area without changing his own speech, he infinitesimally blurs several isoglosses.

Examples of isoglosses on dialect maps are given in diagrams 1 and 2. Lines followed by several bundles of isoglosses are taken as dialect boundaries, the number required being partly dependent on the degree of fineness of scale in dialect division employed by the linguist; but sometimes a single isogloss, especially if it joins together several bundles in different localities or if it lies along the mean of several roughly convergent isoglosses is partly arbitrarily taken as a dialect boundary marker. The so-called 'Benrath line' is an example of this, running roughly east-north-east across Holland and Germany, just north of Benrath on the Rhine (to the south of Düsseldorf) and keeping north of Berlin, to the limits of German-speaking territory, and often regarded as the dividing line between the group of Low German dialects to the north and the group of High German dialects to the south. The particular features distinguished by this line are the pronunciations of the word spelled *machen* in German, with a 'k' sound as second consonant to the north and a 'ch' sound (as in Scots *loch*) to the south.

2·2·3 *Class dialects and 'standard languages'*

So far geographically marked dialect differences have been considered, but in many language areas there are, beside these, manifest 'vertical' or social dialect divisions. The special status often accorded to educated speech of capital cities has already been mentioned, and in many areas differences in speech can be correlated with social or class differences. There is, however, usually a connection between the two dimensions of dialect division; educated speech tends to be less markedly different as between one region and another than the speech of less educated people, presumably because of the greater mobility of educated people, aided in Britain by the upper-class addiction to boarding school education often away from the child's home area. The spread of universal education is one among the factors tending at the present time toward the lessening of dialect divisions.

A dialect, or some closely similar group of dialects enjoying prestige as the speech of educated people of the capital city or of some other socially respected group, is often designated '**the standard language**', 'standard English', 'standard French', and so forth; and the pronunciation characteristic of this type of English has been called 'received pronunciation' or 'R.P.'. The use and consequent spread of 'standard languages' outwards and downwards in the social scale, as it were, is often encouraged in modern states by their employment in official broadcasts, as the approved types of speech for school instruction, and in other similar ways. The term *capital city* may be more in the nature of a cultural focus or centre than just the political capital of a country; Parisian French sets the standard of educated speech in the French-speaking areas of Belgium and Switzerland as well as of France.

The term *standard language* must not mislead. Such forms of speech are descriptively dialects, just like any other dialect, to be described and delimited on just the same criteria as the less socially and officially favoured 'regional' dialects. It is a popular assumption on the part of those speaking standard dialects that other dialects, especially those spoken by groups lacking any social prestige or recognition, are both 'incorrect' and more or less formless, lacking a true grammar or precise means of discourse. Epithets such as 'ugly', 'slovenly', and the like are freely employed with reference to the pronunciation of such dialects (countered to some extent by accusations of 'affectedness' and 'putting on airs' made by some non-standard speakers of those speaking a standard dialect). Needless to say, the linguist faithful to the principles of objective scientific statement must abjure all such modes of expression and value judgments, aesthetic and quasi-moralistic, as outside his field. The statement that certain utterances are 'incorrect' (e.g. *we ain't done nothing*) is to the linguist equivalent to the statement that in a corresponding situation the speaker of the standard dialect would say something else (*we haven't done anything*). Reactions to other people's speech is valuable evidence of part of the social function of language within a community; but the linguist, whatever his private feelings on these and kindred matters, can, as a linguist, have no part in them. His task is to describe and analyse the phenomena of languages (and of the dialects within them) as he finds them, and his techniques and procedures are devised for this purpose. He has no concern with preferring one dialect over another, nor with prescribing how people should use their language. Description, not prescription, is his work, and it is work enough.

It may be worth insisting that any claims for some dialects being better organized than others do not bear examination. Of course the social situations in which they are predominantly used determine the sort of sentences produced and the vocabulary most frequently employed; but the phonetics, phonology, and grammar of non-standard dialects are as amenable to exact description as are those of standard dialects (one may compare the similarly prejudiced misapprehension about the so-called 'primitive' languages, 1·3·3).

2·2·4 *Criteria for determining dialect status*

At this point the question is properly raised as to the reasons for describing some differences of speech habits as being dialects within a language and others as being different languages. In one usage, springing from the misguided attitude referred to in the preceding section, forms of speech without a writing system, or those held to be characteristic of uneducated persons, are regarded as 'dialects' and contrasted with the 'true language' of the literate and educated. By this usage, certain types of colloquial Arabic are contrasted, as 'the dialects', without further discrimination or qualification. Apart from this, several different and often conflicting criteria are commonly and tacitly admitted. *Dialect* is used for:

1. Forms of speech that are different but mutually intelligible without special training;
2. The forms of speech current within a politically unified area; and
3. Forms of speech of speakers sharing a common writing system and set of written classics.

By 1, the various types of English spoken in the British Isles are regarded as dialects of English, whereas Welsh, Irish, and Scots

Gaelic are different languages. By 2, the various types of Low German spoken on either side of the Dutch–German frontier are sometimes described as dialects of Dutch and German respectively, without regard to their mutual similarities and intelligibility. In the same way Swedish, Norwegian, and Danish are usually termed different languages, despite their relative intercomprehensibility, and in particular that between standard Norwegian and Danish. By 3, the different tongues spoken in China and among the Chinese outside China (Malaya, Formosa, etc.) are traditionally called dialects, although spoken North Chinese (Mandarin) and spoken Cantonese (a South Chinese tongue) are mutually incomprehensible. These usages are somewhat reinforced by such factors as the existence and official use of standard Dutch and standard German over the whole of Holland and Germany, respectively, and by the quasi-official status of Mandarin Chinese.

Linguists tend to concentrate on the first criterion, mutual intelligibility, as relating to specifically linguistic facts, though from a sort of courtesy *dialect* is used in certain areas, such as Chinese, of what would strictly be regarded elsewhere as separate languages, themselves each subdivided into many dialects. Mutual intelligibility, however, is not an all-or-none matter, and admits of degrees from almost complete and unhindered comprehension to nearly total incomprehension without special training. In such situations the standard of intelligibility (which need not be the same each way; speakers of dialect A may understand speakers of dialect B more readily than the other way round) that is required to admit of dialect status must be decided by the linguist, unless reliance is placed on traditional or extra-linguistic factors. Ways of quantifying fairly accurately relative intelligibility have been devised, by the use of texts in each of the types of speech under investigation divided into short stretches, each of which speakers of the other types of speech are asked to translate into their own tongue. In this way they can be awarded a graded or numerical mark against each stretch and their total summed up and compared. To some extent the degree of mutual intelligibility correlates with the number of major structural and lexical isoglosses dividing dialect from dialect, but this correlation need not be anything like uniform.

A special situation obtains in some areas, in that there are successions of different dialects lying next to one another so that each is mutually intelligible with its near neighbours but those at either end are mutually unintelligible (e.g. a succession ABCDEFGH, in which ABCD, DEFG, and FGH are sufficiently intercomprehensible to rank as dialects, but not A and F, B and H, etc.). Here the linguist must either recognize some mutually unintelligible tongues as comprised within one language, or, better, divide the area into several languages with the admission that some dialects of one may be also intelligible with some dialects of another that lie adjacent to them. Or he may fall back on extralinguistic, political, or geographical divisions. In a more complex form, such a situation is said to hold between the French of North France and the Italian of South Italy, with a chain of mutually intelligible dialects linking the more distant and mutually unintelligible types of speech (e.g. Parisian French and Roman Italian). Here, at least among educated people, speakers of dialects on the French side of the frontier are likely also to be able to use standard French, or something like it, as a common dialect, and those on the Italian side are similarly likely to be able to use standard Italian. This can be said to help justify linguistically the politically based division of the speech chain into French and Italian respectively.

Such a situation does not exist across all frontiers. Between France and Germany there is an area of bilingualism, in which many speakers, with varying degrees of proficiency in each, use both French and German (each in many ways influenced by features of the other), as occasion requires; but a chain of mutually intelligible dialects as such is not found. This same state of affairs is found in Britain, as between English and Welsh in several parts of Wales, though unilingual speakers of Welsh are now becoming increasingly rare and it may be expected that they will soon cease to exist. This does not, of course, mean that the Welsh language itself need face extinction.

2·2·5 *Linguistic tendencies affecting dialectal divisions*

Dialect divisions must be seen as the product of the universal tendency of speech habits to vary, at every level, in the course of transmission from one generation to another. This will be discussed further in Chapter 8; here one may notice two factors in constant conflict, that govern the genesis and spread, and also the obliteration of dialect differences. One's speech habits are normally acquired in early childhood and are more or less fixed, in the absence of special circumstances or efforts, thereafter. It is during those years that one's circle of acquaintance is most limited, and consequently differences peculiar to one's parents are easily acquired along with the rest of one's mother tongue. But membership of an expanding circle, with the objective need to be able to communicate readily with all its members and the subjective need to integrate oneself therewith, tends towards the acquisition by all members of similar modes of speech and the lessening of purely personal differences. Among small isolated groups of persons, rarely moving beyond their own localities and having little external intercourse, regional differences of speech habits readily develop and become affectionately regarded as part of the personality of the members of the group. Conversely, in conditions favouring large-scale travel, regional mobility, urbanization, and the like, local speech differences, especially where they are such as to hinder intercourse or where they have come to be associated with lack of education, low social prestige, or other unfavourable circumstances, are liable to be replaced with conscious effort on the part of speakers by a more widely recognized and socially advantageous type of speech. The ultimate product of this tendency is the spread of 'standard languages' over whole regions; but a frequent result, especially where a regional dialect has a fairly wide extent and where local feeling remains strong, is the acquisition by many speakers of two separate dialects, local and standard (or an approximation thereto), used according to the type of situation prevailing at the time, the local dialect being reserved for more intimate family occasions (as in many parts of North England). In these circumstances, speech in the local dialect acquires a special meaning or function in the situations in which it is used.

It is noticeable that bundles of isoglosses tend to coincide with or to follow boundaries that either now hinder mutual intercourse or did so in earlier times, such as physical barriers, wide rivers, mountain ranges, etc., or political frontiers. It may be surmised that the fairly extensive dialect differences in Germany and Italy are in part the result of the relatively late political unification of those territories.

61

The two constantly counteracting tendencies in dialect development were called *l'esprit de clocher* (parochialism) and *la force d'intercourse* (pressure of communication) by de Saussure. Clearly modern civilization greatly favours the latter, with the forces of urbanization and centralization everywhere rampant. One must assume that dialect differences were more numerous in earlier days, despite the smaller populations; it has been estimated that in medieval Europe a peasant could live and die without having enlarged his circle of acquaintance beyond 300. Today local dialects are generated and persist more easily in scattered rural communities than in urban ones, and in regions where from geographical or other causes movement is restricted. In most modern countries the dialect differences of town dwellers are less noticeable than those of rural people in corresponding parts of the country. Those engaged on dialect surveys in France noticed the spread of features from one urban centre to another along the main railway lines and roads, missing out more isolated intervening rural areas.

The recognition of dialect divisions in language areas, and a cognizance of the principles and methods of dialect study are an important part of general linguistics for a number of reasons. The linguist is enabled to make a more precise statement of the phenomena of the language or languages he is concerned with at any time. The reactions of speakers to each other's dialects often throw much light on the social working of language in communities and on its functions both as a unifier and as a diversifier of social groups. Moreover in the more minute and detailed scale possible in dealing with the relatively small areas of some dialects, one has, as it were, a small-scale picture of the linguistic situation of the world as a whole. The frontiers between totally distinct and mutually unintelligible languages are, in fact, very closely packed bundles of coinciding isoglosses. In the processes of dialect splitting and dialect merging, dialect contact and interaction, in the spreading of some features and the disappearance of others, the rise of prestige dialects and national 'standard languages', and so on, one is able to study closely and on a small scale the same types of occurrence which give rise on a much larger scale and over long eras of time to the distribution of languages over the globe and the material of linguistic history (8·1).

62

2·3 GENERAL AND PARTICULAR

The nature of linguistic abstractions has already been discussed, and it was pointed out that at any level of analysis they may be of different degrees of generality, and that all abstractions are necessarily referable to an infinite number of exponents in the utterances of a living language (2·1·1). But of the abstractions that form the language system set up by the linguist for the description and analysis of any language, or dialect, some are by their nature and purpose abstracted as general categories, and others are abstracted as particular items. The categories of **phonetics, phonology**, and **grammar** are general; the components of the **lexicon** of a language are particular. Abstractions like *plosive, bilabial, consonant, noun, genitive case*, etc. apply repeatedly to parts of utterances that must be referred lexically to different words in a complete description. Traditionally the dictionary or lexicon of a language has been regarded as that part which requires particular and different statements for each item, and grammar, phonology, and phonetics as dealing with what can be brought under general rules, classes, and categories, embracing many individually different words. The same material is under examination all the time, but in the one case what is peculiar to particular items is the focus of attention, and in the other what can be abstracted as common to many such items or parts thereof. Hence in general usage the 'grammar' of a language often includes, in addition to grammatical categories and rules, details of its pronunciation, transcription, and orthography, topics often treated separately as different levels of analysis in the technical language of the linguist.

Bloomfield described the lexicon as an appendix of grammar and the list of basic irregularities. This is because, as has been said, it deals with that part of the functioning of words that has not already been and cannot be treated under the general classes and categories of grammar (and phonology and phonetics). This does not imply that it is exclusively concerned with meaning or with reference (1·4). A good deal of the particular function of some words must be stated in terms of their relations with other words in the sentences of which they typically form a part. None the less, the reference and semantic (situational) function that can be stated of a word must be dealt with in the dictionary entry; it is probable that there are no

63

two words that are exactly equivalent semantically in all the sentences in which they can occur. Each word's semantic function or meaning must be described separately.

Dictionary-making presupposes grammar and phonology in a way that they do not presuppose it. The grammar and phonology of a language can be stated with the use of no more of its words than are required to exemplify the classes, categories, and structural rules involved; nor, provided they are sensible, does it matter much what sentences are used as examples and illustrations of grammatical constructions. But the dictionary entry dealing with each word must assign it to its grammatical class and any subclass (6·6), and must transcribe it, unambiguously represent its pronunciation, which is not necessarily done by its orthographic spelling (4·1), though in a dictionary of an unwritten language the transcription alone will necessarily constitute the word as entered in the dictionary. In particular, the grammatical class of a word cannot be inferred just by looking at it; its assignment to a class as a member thereof (or 'part of speech') is therefore part of the individual information to be given for each word. In most cases such a class assignment is all that the dictionary needs to do as far as the grammatical level is concerned; the rest of the grammatical information about it may be found in the appropriate parts of the grammatical description. But what are called 'irregular' forms, just because they are irregular (i.e. exceptional, individual), cannot be inferred from the class assignment and must be stated in the dictionary entries of the words concerned. An obvious example in English is the verb *go* with past tense form *went*, as against *walk*, *walked*, *tramp*, *tramped*, and countless others. Often, in fact, this same information is given twice in the description of languages, in the grammar as breaches of general rules, and in the dictionary as the peculiarities of individual words. This topic is treated in more detail in Chapter 6·6.

For the semantic information to be given in dictionary entries summaries are obviously required; no entry could possibly list every potential use in a sentence, and even in a dead language with a consequently restricted body of material it is not feasible to refer to every use except in a few rare words. The extent of the summary is necessarily governed by the size of the dictionary as a whole. The easiest and generally least helpful means is to give one or more synonyms, or near translation equivalents in a dictionary of a foreign language, and no more. As words have their meanings by virtue of their potential use in sentences (1·4·2), the citation of typical sentences containing the word in question with a succinct description of the distinctively relevant features of the contexts of situation in which such sentences are used (1·4·3) is very much more useful, and is the practice of larger dictionaries (see, for example, the lay-out of entries in the full edition of the *Oxford English Dictionary*). In this way the individual meanings of words that are not fully statable in terms of direct reference to the external world may be more adequately described.

The techniques of successful dictionary-making lie rather outside the scope of an elementary introduction to linguistics, but one question that arises is relevant to general linguistic theory: how many separate meanings are to be recognized amid the often continuous ranges of potential uses of words? The question is partly one of convenience and ready accessibility of the information to be conveyed by the dictionary entry. Subdivisions are more easily presented and understood than overlong unsystematized accounts purporting to fall under a single head. But in part criteria can be given in the degree of relatedness of the different contexts of situation in which the word in question is used. In many words, their meaning ranges are related in recognized and similar ways; physical and abstract (metaphor: *summit of a mountain, summit meeting; depth of water, depth of despair*), or personal and non-personal (*Prince Edward; Cox's Orange is a prince among apples*). Further elaboration is easy to the native speakers of any language, and would be tedious here. The different semantic usages of these kinds of words share contextual links and also share somewhat similar lexical company in sentences (*reach the summit, plumb the depths,* etc.), which speakers intuitively understand and which can be explicitly stated. Different, though there may be borderline cases, are apparently unrelated meanings of single word forms, perhaps due to historical accidents or to associations now forgotten (e.g. *case* (container), *case* (circumstance); *premises* (building), *premises* (of a syllogism); *mail* (post), *mail* (armour); *port* (wine), *port* (harbour); *post* (stick), *post* (mail), *post* (appointment), etc.). Historical connections can in some cases be shown between meanings now very disparate; some dictionaries, like the *Oxford English Dictionary*, include historical facts such as the earlier forms of the words and their presence in earlier stages of the language or their entry from a foreign language as 'loans' (8·1·7); but synchronically, such facts are strictly irrelevant to the listing of the lexical components of a language at a given time and the description and classifying of their meanings or uses by speakers at the time, just as they are unavailable in dealing with the dictionaries of hitherto unwritten languages.

The related question of word forms that occur in more than one grammatical class (e.g. English *work* as noun and as verb) is more easily dealt with, as the criteria for the assignment of words to word classes (6·2) are in general clear-cut and lead to determinate classifications. Multiple entry often is the simplest solution. Here also one meets quite unconnected homophones (words pronounced alike): *bear* (the animal), *bear* (endure); pairs with some semantic connection: *stomach* (part of the body), *stomach* (put up with); and pairs very close in semantic function: *paint* (the material), *paint* (cover with paint, or depict with paint).

2·4   THE STRUCTURAL TREATMENT OF LINGUISTIC MEANING

2·4·1 *The distributional analysis of meaning*

In much of the statement of meanings in dictionary entries, the linguist necessarily looks beyond the realm of language, as he is dealing with the use of words in sentences in relation to the whole of human experience, and he may have to rely on sciences other than linguistics and on unsystematized 'common sense' (1·4). For this reason some linguists have tried to redefine or reconsider meaning in so far as it is relevant to linguistics as equivalent to distribution. That is to say, the meaning of a word, as far as it concerns the linguist within the strict confines of his subject, is to be understood as the range of its occurrences in sentences consisting of other words. Just as there are probably no words exactly alike in meaning in all contexts, so there will probably be no two words in any language sharing exactly the same lexical environment (distribution). The temptations of this treatment of meaning are strong. Reliance on sciences and experience outside linguistic competence is eliminated; and, especially with the use and development of statistical methods and computer techniques (the mechanical collection and sorting of data), considerable precision and exhaustiveness, not available in semantics otherwise, seems within reach.

The objection, however, to this method of treating meaning is that it fails to 'save the phenomena'. Meaning is everywhere understood as involving the relation of language to the rest of the world, and such meaningfulness is an essential part of any definition of language. Distributional studies enable one to state a great deal about the total functioning and use of words in a language, but just not what is ordinarily understood to be their meanings and what is rightly expected from the entries in a dictionary, for which information such traditional terms as reference and denotation, and more modern systems of analysis such as context of situation, however imprecise they may be in many cases, have been devised.

The distributional approach to meaning, while inadequate as a complete treatment of it, or at least as the way one would ordinarily expect it to be treated, brings to notice the significant fact that part of the total meaning of many words in all languages is to be determined by their individual relations with other words, in both the basic dimensions of linguistic analysis, syntagmatic and paradigmatic. Words, as individual lexical items, are structurally related to each other in languages and the uses of languages, as they are as members of grammatical classes and as are grammatical and phonological elements generally, though in different ways. The syntagmatic relations between words as lexical items have been studied under the title of *collocation*, and the paradigmatic relations are considered in the theories of the *linguistic field*.

2·4·2 *Collocation*

By **collocation** is meant the habitual association of a word in a language with other particular words in sentences. Collocation is distinct from syntax in that one is concerned in collocation with each word as an individual lexical item in the company of other words as individual lexical items, and not, as in syntax, part of the grammatical level of analysis, with words as members of classes in relation to other words also as members of classes. Speakers become accustomed to the collocations of words and the mutual expectancies that hold between them in utterances irrespective of their grammatical relations as members of word classes or as 'parts of speech' (6·1, 6·2, 6·3). A rather obvious example is given by Firth, who made use of the term as part of the technical terminology of linguistics: *dark* collocates with *night*, and vice versa. 'One of the meanings of *night* is its collocability with *dark*, and of *dark*, of course, collocation with *night*.' This statement does not, of course, exclude word groups like *bright night*, *dark day*, but just because of the less usual concomitance of such pairs, they stand out as more prominent in an utterance in which they occur than do *dark night* and *bright day*. Collocations such as these are manifestly related to the referential and situational meaning of the words concerned, but collocation and situational meaning are different parts of the total statement of the use of words. In some other cases collocations are habitual but less closely connected with extralinguistic reference. *White coffee*, *black coffee*, *white wine*, *white race* all have a range of situational reference, but apart from the collocation of the particular second words in each pair the word *white* would not, in most utterances, be used with reference to the colours of the referents. Similar collocations in English involving colour words, but further removed from reference to actual colour surfaces, are *green with jealousy*, *red revolution*, *purple passage*. Some words in languages have, at least in certain styles, very limited uses, almost wholly circumscribable in their collocations. The word *maiden*, for example, in modern spoken English, is scarcely ever used as a synonym for *girl*, but principally occurs in collocation with a limited set of other words such as *voyage*, *speech*, *over* (in cricket), *aunt*, *lady* (English speakers can readily supply the others).

Conversely, words like *the*, *a*, *if*, *when*, and so on, are hardly subject to any collocational restrictions, and are found in almost any lexical company in the language that the grammar permits. For such words collocation is not a relevant part of the statement of their use; but with others (the majority) it is possible to set up collocational ranges of words with which given words will be found associated in their various grammatical constructions. The conjunction of two or more words quite outside the range of collocation and unprepared by any explanation, is likely to be incomprehensible or downright nonsensical, although its grammatical composition may be unexceptionable. A now famous example of such a grammatical but non-sensical sentence is: 'Colourless green ideas sleep furiously.'

Collocational ranges are unlike grammatical classes in that they are peculiar to each word, and almost certainly no two words in a language share exactly the same range and frequency of occurrence within a range, whereas grammatical classes may each contain many different words as members. Moreover collocations are far more personally variable among speakers of a single dialect within a language than are grammatical classes; borderline cases there are in grammar, where speakers may differ, or be uncertain, as to whether a particular word form or word sequence is grammatically acceptable; but these are very few compared to the personal differences in collocational use and acceptance.

Sometimes different styles, types of utterance appropriate to specific types of situation (2·2·1) are characterized by different collocations (consider the differences between *He's a proper rascal* and *that is a very proper observation*, and between *we've had a nice time today* and *we have here a nice point to decide*).

In some uses of language precision for particular purposes is obtained by deliberately excluding certain collocations. Some philosophers (John Locke, for example) would hold that in the context of philosophical discourse *free* does not collocate with *will* ('it is as insignificant to ask whether man's will be free, as to ask whether his sleep be swift, or his virtue square').

It obviously does in everyday speech (*he did it of his own free will*, etc.); but it is said that if this collocation is used and understood in the same way as *free* in other collocations, such as *free agent, free man*, and so on, one will be misled in argumentation. So, too, it has been suggested that in the language of philosophy the verb *to exist* is not collocable with nouns in the same way that other verbs and verbal phrases (*eat, stand, move, be visible, be perceptible*, etc.) are, and that its use in such collocations has given rise philosophically to a 'systematically misleading' sort of statement.

The justification of these philosophical views and their further implications lie outside the sphere of the linguist's jurisdiction; but they are examples of the deliberate restriction of collocation in a particular context of situation.

Special cases of collocations are what are called idioms and clichés. *Idiom* is used to refer to habitual collocations of more than one word, that tend to be used together, with a semantic function not readily deducible from the other uses of its component words apart from each other (e.g. English *she went for him hammer and tongs, they ran off hell for leather*). Knowledge of such individual features of a language, acquired by long experience, but unnecessary for ordinary intercourse, usually comes at the end of one's learning of a foreign language; hence a complete or near-complete mastery of one is often said to be 'idiomatic'. Some idioms preserve in use words that have otherwise become obsolete (e.g. English *to and fro, waifs and strays, kith and kin*).

When a collocation has become almost universal in a particular style, the contribution of some of its words comes to be nugatory, and often appears irritating and inelegant to listeners or readers who do not relish (as some seem to) that mode of discourse (for example the house agent's *desirable residence* (residence), the politician's *this modern age in which we are living* (this age), the journalist's *inside information* (information); the reader will be painfully able to multiply the examples from his own experience). Clichés of this sort form a notable part of the public speaking style of many politicians all over the world, presumably because of intellectual laziness or in the hope of appealing to the emotions of people in political meetings, broadcasts, and the like, by the repeated use of words, such as *freedom, peace,* etc., to which favourable responses are normally accorded; cliché-ridden talk is a good deal easier to produce than a serious examination of current political problems.

2·4·3 *Semantic field theory*

The theory (or theories, as the basic conception has been developed in different ways) of the **linguistic field**, or the field theory of meaning, is concerned to show that the lexical content of a language, its total vocabulary, or such of it as is available to a speaker at any time, is not a mere conglomeration or aggregation of independent items, and that word meanings cannot be understood or adequately described as if it were. Word meaning is best understood as the contribution a word can make to the meaning or function of the sentences in which it may appear (1·4·2); and this depends, not just on its reference, or any other aspect of its meaning considered simply as the property of the word in isolation from all other words in the language. In part the meaning and use of most words are governed by the presence in the language or availability to a speaker of other words whose semantic functions are related in one or more ways to the same area of situational environment or culture.

It was observed above (1·4·2) that the use of many words presupposes the imposition of order and stability on the sequences of sensory experience, and that the employment of certain words rests on a high degree of such abstract ordering. It appears that certain features of this sort of ordering are universal, or at least very general, and this is the basis of the translatability of the utterances of one language into those of another; but other features are peculiar to particular cultural traditions of particular areas, with the consequence that the translation of words and sentences relating to such features requires more explanation and circumlocution. In no case is the lexical content of a language equivalent to a nomenclature, the labelling with separate words of independently existing entities. Nomenclature is possible when linguistic labels are secondarily put to entities already distinguished as a class by the lexicon of a language, as in the cases of the naming of individual houses in a street, of streets in a town, or of rooms in a mansion. 'The world as we know it' is in part the product both of our culture and of the lexical system of our own language.

In a language each word with a reference to the external world bears the meaning it does, functions as it does in sentences, in that it relates to a part of the world in some way differently from all other words. Every such word is, therefore, determined in its meaning by the presence of other words in the vocabulary of the language related to the same or to associated ranges of phenomena, and its meaning is liable to be further determined or altered both by the appearance of other words in a speaker's available vocabulary or by changes in the meanings of associated words.

By the nature of things as they are perceived by all men, and by the nature of certain specific aspects of different cultures, some words are more tightly bound in systems than others, and the semantic fields involved are more readily separated. Colour terms, which notoriously do not correspond from one language to another, are an obvious example of naturally delimited fields. Every language has a range of words that divide up the potentially all but unlimited range of colour differences in visible phenomena. It is probable that children learn the principal colour words fairly closely together in time (e.g. in English, *red, green, blue, yellow, white, black*; the fact that green is not a primary colour and that white and black are not colours in the sense that the others is is not relevant here). Certainly one only knows the meaning of *red* as a colour word (knows how to use it in sentences) when one knows also the colour words bordering on it in various directions (*pink, purple, orange, brown*, etc.) and the principal words for colours comprised within the class designated by *red* (e.g. *vermilion, scarlet, rose*).

Colour constitutes a naturally separable field of reference, or semantic field, for which every language may be expected to provide sets of lexical terms in which the meaning of each is determined by the co-presence of the others in a speaker's vocabulary. It is well known that languages do not correspond in their most used colour vocabulary. Welsh *gwyrdd, glas*, and *llwyd* roughly cover the same colour range as English *green, blue, grey*, and *brown*, but do not have the same approximate boundaries. The same surfaces designated *green, blue*, and *grey* in English might all be called *glas* in Welsh. Likewise in Japanese the adjective *aói* refers to much of the range of colour distinguished in English by *blue* and *green*.

Military ranks and ranks in any strictly hierarchical organization of people in relationships of seniority, command, and subordination are examples of a culturally produced field that is closely delimited and ordered. Part of the meaning of any military rank word (*major, captain, corporal*, etc.) is the product of the whole system of such terms in the relevant part of the language and of the exact place of each in relation to the others. These factors may be decisive in the translation of words referring to ranks in armed services and the like from one language to another.

In a very practical context of situation, the selection and grading of hotels, the word *good* has a very different meaning when used non-technically (in the field of *bad, indifferent*, etc.) from when it is used, as it is by some travel agents, in a strictly limited system of comparative gradings as the lowest in the field of *first class, luxurious, superior, good*.

Part of the power and flexibility of language lies in the ability of speakers to multiply their vocabulary in any given field in the interests of greater precision and clarity. It follows that the more words there are closely associated in meaning the more specific each one's meaning may be in the particular field (irrespective of its uses in other fields). As an organization becomes more complex and its members more numerous, new ranks and grades appropriately named may be devised, restricting the holders to an exact place in the hierarchy. Occupations whose operations involve much colour discrimination (paint manufacture, textile manufacture, etc.) develop an extensive technical vocabulary, partly from existing colour words, partly by adding new and specialized meanings to words having reference to coloured things (e.g. *magnolia*, *cream*), partly by adapting other words and phrases to give them a definite place in the technical field of colour terms (*summer blue*, *mistletoe green*, etc.). Such technical vocabularies may sometimes employ numbers of words unknown to non-technical speakers of the language and devise meanings for others quite different from those they bear outside these specialized contexts.

The supreme example of this infinite flexibility is in the use of numerical terms with reference to measurable features of the world. Between any two adjacent number terms another may be added for greater precision; between *eleven* and *twelve* may be put *eleven and a half*, and between *eleven* and *eleven and a half* may be put *eleven and a quarter*, and so on indefinitely. Those who speak of the infinite divisibility of matter may be doing no more than drawing attention to this potentiality of the mathematical language of the physical sciences.

It is apparent from the investigation of collocations and semantic field associations in their relations with the full description and analysis of the meanings of words, that syntagmatic and paradigmatic relations are nearly as important in dealing with the lexicon of a language as they are at the levels of grammar and phonology. Internal relations of elements within complex wholes are of the essence of language. 'Un système ou tout se tient', one all-embracing system, was the characterization of language by the French linguist Meillet. This emphasizes one of the most fundamental features of language and of the treatment of language in modern

73

linguistics. But it might be more appropriate to think not so much of one overall system, as of many interlocking and interdependent structures and systems at all levels, the functions of every linguistic element and abstraction being dependent on its relative places therein.

CHAPTER 2, BIBLIOGRAPHY

1. C. E. BAZELL, *Linguistic form*, Istanbul, 1953.

2. L. BLOOMFIELD, *Language*, London, 1935.

3. C. D. BUCK, *Introduction to the study of the Greek dialects*, Boston, 1928.

4. N. CHOMSKY, *Syntactic structures*, The Hague, 1957.

5. ——, 'Some methodological remarks on generative grammar', *Word* 17 (1961), 219–39.

6. E. DAUZAT, *La géographie linguistique*, Paris, 1922.

7. J. R. FIRTH, *Speech*, London, 1930.

8. ——, 'Personality and language in society', *Sociol. rev.* 42 (1950), 37–52.

9. ——, 'Modes of meaning', *Essays and studies*, 1951, 118–49.

10. ——, 'Synopsis of linguistic theory 1930–55', *Studies in linguistic analysis*, special publication of the Philological Society, Oxford, 1957, 1–32.

11. Z. S. HARRIS, *Methods in structural linguistics*, Chicago, 1951.

12. ——, 'Distributional structure', *Word* 10 (1954), 146–62.

13. S. I. HAYAKAWA, *Language in thought and action*, London, 1952.

14. H. HICKERSON and others, 'Testing procedures', *IJAL* 18 (1952), 1–8.

15. L. HJELMSLEV, *Prolegomena to a theory of language*, translated by F. J. Whitfield, Baltimore, 1953.

16. C. F. HOCKETT, *A course in modern linguistics*, New York, 1958.

17. H. M. HOENIGSWALD, *Language change and linguistic reconstruction*, Chicago, 1960.

18. F. W. HOUSEHOLDER and S. SAPORTA (editors), 'Problems in lexicography', *IJAL* 28 (1962), no. 2, part 4.

19. I. IORDAN, *Introduction to Romance linguistics*, translated by J. Orr, London, 1937.

2 THEORETICAL CONSIDERATIONS

20. K. JABERG, *Sprachgeographie*, Aarau, 1908.

21. M. JOOS (editor), *Readings in linguistics*, Washington, 1957.

22. R. E. KELLER, *The German dialects*, Manchester, 1961.

23. E. H. LENNEBERG and J. M. ROBERTS, *The language of experience*, supplement to *IJAL* 22 (1956), part 2.

24. R. I. MCDAVID, 'The dialects of American English', chapter 9 of W. N. Francis, *The structure of American English*, New York, 1958.

25. A. MCINTOSH, *An introduction to a survey of the Scottish dialects*, Edinburgh, 1952.

26. ——, 'Patterns and ranges', *Lang.* 37 (1961), 325–37.

27. A. MEILLET, *Aperçu d'une histoire de la langue grecque*, third edition, Paris, 1930.

28. ——, *La méthode comparative en linguistique historique*, Oslo, 1925.

29. ——, *Linguistique historique et linguistique générale*, Paris, 1948.

30. E. A. NIDA, 'The analysis of meaning and dictionary-making', *IJAL* 24 (1958), 279–92.

31. S. ÖHMAN, 'Theories of the "linguistic field"', *Word* 9 (1953), 123–34.

32. L. R. PALMER, *Introduction to modern linguistics*, London, 1936.

33. P. PASSY, *Petite phonétique comparée*, third edition, Paris, 1922.

34. M. PLATNAUER, 'Greek colour-perception', *Classical quarterly* 15 (1921), 153–62.

35. S. POP, *La dialectologie*, Louvain, 1950.

36. E. SAPIR, 'The status of linguistics as a science', *Lang.* 5 (1929), 207–14.

37. F. DE SAUSSURE, *Cours de linguistique générale*, fourth edition, Paris, 1949.

38. E. SIVERTSEN, *Cockney phonology*, Oslo, 1960.

39. N. C. W. SPENCE, 'Linguistic fields, conceptual systems, and the Weltbild', *TPS* 1961, 87–106.

40. R. H. STETSON, *The bases of phonology*, Oberlin, 1945.

41. H. SWEET, *Collected papers*, Oxford, 1913.

42. W. F. TWADDELL, *On defining the phoneme*, Language Monograph 16, 1935.

43. S. ULLMANN, *The principles of semantics*, second edition, Glasgow and Oxford, 1957. ·

44. C. F. VOEGELIN and Z. S. HARRIS, 'Methods of determining intelligibility among dialects of natural languages', *Proc. of the American Philosophical Society* 95 (1951), 322–9.

45. I. C. WARD, *The phonetics of English*, Cambridge, 1948.

46. J. WRIGHT, *A grammar of the dialect of Windhill in the West Riding of Yorkshire*, English dialect society, London, 1892.

47. ——, *The English dialect grammar*, Oxford, 1905.

ADDENDUM

48. G. L. BROOK, *English dialects*, London, 1963.

p. 44. For a general discussion on the status of linguistic abstractions see Twaddell, 42 (also in 21, 55–80, where see comments by Joos).

The realist and nominalist points of view were nicknamed 'God's truth' and 'hocus-pocus' respectively by F. Householder (*IJAL* 18 (1952), 260–8), and have since then been discussed under these titles. Firth took up a strongly non-realist 'hocus-pocus' line (8, 42).

On exponency and renewal of connection, Firth, 10, 15–17.

p. 48. The unimportance of the actual phonetic exponents of phonological elements was maintained by de Saussure, among others (37, 166); cp. Hjelmslev, 15, 50.

The terms syntagmatic and paradigmatic go back to de Saussure (37, part 2, chapter 5), though he actually used the term *associative* (*associatif*) instead of paradigmatic. The latter term, whose use in this Saussurean distinction is now general, was first suggested by Hjelmslev (*Acts of the fourth international congress of linguists*, 1936, 140–51).

p. 49. On the distinction of *structure* and *system*, Firth, 10, 17.

p. 52. On 'slow colloquial' as the accepted basis of the linguistic analysis of spoken language, Passy, 32, 4; Stetson, 40, chapter 5.

p. 53. In connection with linguistic taboos, it is amusing to notice that among some *soi-disant* 'progressive' circles of people who pride themselves on their freedom from the 'irrational' taboos of obscenity and blasphemy, by which others in their community feel bound, the serious discussion of moral issues in specifically moral terms arouses very similar reactions of discomfort, embarrassment, and contempt. Taboo restrictions, though doubtless an irrational feature of linguistic behaviour, are more pervasive than some like to think.

p. 55. On dialects as the sum of their characteristics, Palmer, 32, 132.

p. 56. On the 'Benrath line', see further Bloomfield, 2, 343–4.

On the relative delocalization of standard dialects, Firth, 7, chapter 8.

p. 58. Many detailed descriptions of non-standard English dialects have been made, e.g. Wright, 47 and 46, and recently Sivertsen, 38.

On the relations between standard and non-standard dialects, see further I. C. Ward, 45, chapter 1.

A possible exception to the statement that every dialect is equally capable of precise description may be found in the special standards of 'correctness' laid down in some countries with reference to the speech approved for educated persons by such bodies as the French Academy, which attempts to prescribe the semantic and grammatical use of some words within strict limits; but these prescriptive rules are by no means always followed by speakers generally recognized as speakers of the standard dialect of the language.

p. 59. On quantifying mutual intelligibility, Voegelin and Harris, 44; Hickerson and others, 14.

On the French-Italian dialect chain, Hockett, 16, 324.

p. 62. The course of dialect history is well illustrated in the Greek language. By the time at which written records are available, Ancient Greek was split into a number of major dialect divisions, North-west Greek, Doric, Attic-Ionic, Aeolic, and Arcadocyprian, themselves sub-divided into smaller dialects. This dialect fragmentation was due to the different periods of the settlement of the classical Greek world by Greek speakers, and to the mountainous terrain and the numerous islands of the area. Classical Greek, other than the Homeric poems, is mostly written in Attic, the dialect of Athens, which spread during the Hellenistic and Roman periods over much of the rest of Greece and Asia Minor as the language of administration and general intercourse. In the course of this spread it suffered considerable changes; New Testament Greek is an example of this resultant κοινή, /koiné:/, as it came to be called (κοινή διάλεκτος /koinè: diálektos/ common dialect). Modern Greek dialects are for the most part the result of the Byzantine and post-Byzantine fragmentation of this κοινή, not survivors of other ancient dialects, which largely disappeared during these years. But Tsaconian, spoken today in part of the Morea (Peloponnese), is said to preserve features of the old Laconian dialect of Sparta. See further Meillet, 26; Buck, 3.

On the terms *esprit de clocher* and *force d'intercourse*, de Saussure, 37, part 4, chapter 4; limited world of the medieval peasant, J. A. Williamson, *The evolution of England*, Oxford, 1931, 86; spread of urban features, Palmer, 32, chapter 7.

On the relevance of dialect study to comparative and historical linguistics, Meillet, 28, chapters 5 and 6. On dialect study in general linguistics, Bloomfield, 2, chapter 19; Hockett, 16, chapters 38 and 39; Palmer 32, chapter 7.

A considerable amount of specialist literature has been devoted to the study of dialects. The following books may be noticed: Jaberg, 20; Dauzat, 6; Pop, 35; McIntosh, 25; McDavid, 24; Keller, 22.

A special aspect of dialect study is known as *Wörter und Sachen* (words and things). This involves the detailed study in different dialects of the forms of words relating to material objects and processes of all kinds found in the dialect localities, and of the forms of the objects and processes themselves (plants, agricultural implements, etc.), together with general ethnographical investigations of the areas. This study was instituted formally by R. Meringer and H. Schuchardt around the turn of the present century, largely centring on Romance dialectology.

In 1909 a journal *Wörter und Sachen* was started; it has now ceased publication, and the specific *Wörter und Sachen* studies, though still undertaken, have somewhat receded in attention with the development of modern structural linguistics, although these two aspects of linguistic study, as far as dialectology is concerned, would not appear to be antagonistic. See further Iordan, 19, 62–74; Y. Malkiel, *Lang*. 33 (1957), 54–76.

p. 63. On the individual nature of dictionary information, as against the general information given in grammar and phonology, Bloomfield, 2, 274; cp. Sweet, 41, 31.

On the methods and purposes of the dictionary writer, cp. Hayakawa, 13, 56: 'The way in which the dictionary writer arrives at his definitions is merely the systematization of the way in which we all learn the meanings of words beginning at infancy and continuing for the rest of our lives.'

p. 65. On metaphor, Bloomfield, 2, 149.

p. 66. On the theory and practice of lexicography (dictionary-making), Nida, 30; Householder, 18.

The reader should consider just what information he would wish to find in a comprehensive dictionary entry for a particular word in a language in which he is interested, and how that information could best be set out. He should then turn to a recognized dictionary (e.g. the large *Oxford English Dictionary*), and see how far he is satisfied with what is there given.

p. 67. On meaning as distribution, Harris, 11, 7, note 4; 12; Hoenigswald, 17, 16. Criticism in R. B. Lees, *Lang*. 33 (1957), 394–5.

On collocation, Firth, 9; 10, 11–13. For a somewhat similar notion of 'attachment', Bazell, 1, 36–7.

p. 69. On collocational ranges, McIntosh, 26.

Colourless green ideas sleep furiously appears in Chomsky, 4.

Attempts have been made to include what have here been treated as collocational incompatibilities all under the heading of grammar, as being of the same nature as the material of grammatical rules (Chomsky, 5). The advantages of this seem very doubtful, but their discussion lies outside the scope of this book.

John Locke, *Essay concerning human understanding*, ed. A. S. Pringle-Pattison, Oxford, 1934, 140.

On 'systematically misleading expressions', (editor) A. Flew, *Logic and language*, Oxford, 1951, 11–36.

p. 70. On idiom, Hockett, 16, 171–3.

p. 71. Language not a nomenclature, de Saussure, 37, 34, 97; cp. Sapir, 36. This is part of what has come to be known as the 'Whorf hypothesis' (note to page 291, below).

p. 72. Colour words in Welsh and English, Hjelmslev, 15, 33; cp. Platnauer, 34; Lenneberg and Roberts, 23.

The germ of the field theory of meaning is to be found in de Saussure's 'associative relations' (37, 173–5). For a brief account and further references, see Ullmann, 43, 152–70; Öhman, 31; Spence, 39.

The field theories of meaning have largely been developed in terms of a conceptualist approach to meaning, and with prime reference to historical studies. This in no way reduces their relevance to synchronic descriptive linguistics, and they are equally compatible with the contextual theory of meaning set out here.

Meillet, 29, 16.

ADDENDUM

p. 58. On English dialects, Brook, 48.

3

Phonetics

3·1 ARTICULATORY PHONETICS

3·1·1 *The spoken foundation of language*

It has been observed that language makes contact with the world outside language at two ends, in the physical medium employed in communication from person to person, and in its interaction with the world at large or in its meaning (1·3·2).

The only universal medium of linguistic communication among all normal human beings (i.e. excluding the deaf and dumb, some congenital idiots, etc.) is speech, and the scientific study of speech is known as **phonetics**.

It is sometimes maintained (cp. 1·3·4) that the study of phonetics, of speech sounds, their production and perception, is not an essential part of the study of linguistics as such, and for reasons similar to those adduced for the comparable relegation of semantics, the study of meaning, to a peripheral status, namely that in both· phonetics and semantics one may have to rely to some extent on sciences concerned with fields outside that of language itself. It is, of course, open to any practitioner to define the limits of his study as he thinks fit and as suits his purposes; but there would seem to be several reasons for which those seriously interested in language and linguistics should include in their purview the study of speech sounds in phonetics, and for which a general book on the subject should include a chapter devoted to this aspect of language study.

As was said above, speech is the only universal mode of human communication in language. We must assume a period of many thousands of years when it was the exclusive manifestation of language, before the development of writing systems at the dawn of recorded history. In many communities today languages are spoken for which no system of writing has been devised, and whose speakers are illiterate (or, as it is optimistically put in the context of educational developments the world over, preliterate, with the consequential use of the term *preliterate language* to refer to the languages of such peoples). It may be observed (cp. 1·3·3) that, contrary to a widespread assumption, the languages of such totally illiterate communities do not differ in any significant way as regards their speech sounds from the languages of peoples long literate and well known as the foci of world civilizations.

Moreover, a moment's reflection shows that in literate communities speaking antedates writing in the acquisition of language by normal children and the output of spoken language, speech, far exceeds the output of written language, books, newspapers, letters, notices, private notes, and the like, on the part of every member of the community. The same applies still more to the other media of communication in language such as Morse code signals, deaf and dumb symbols, and telegraphic codes, which are all derivatives of written language.

While, therefore, some may think it feasible to exclude the nature of the noises themselves used in language from the essence of language as the subject-matter of linguistics, it seems obvious that the physiological conditions of speaking and hearing have always permitted and governed the existence and development of language in general and of every particular language, and are, therefore, very relevant to the proper study of this part of human behaviour. Certainly a full understanding of language as a form of man's activity requires an understanding of the basis and nature of human speech.

3·1·2 *Primacy of articulatory phonetics*

The essence of speech is that one human being, by movements beginning at his diaphragm and involving various parts of his chest, throat, mouth, and nasal passages, creates disturbances in the air around him, which within a limited distance from him have a perceptible effect on the eardrums and through them on the brains of other people, and that the hearers can, if they belong to the same language community, respond to these disturbances, or noises, and find them meaningful.

Speech can therefore be studied in phonetics from three points of view.

1. It can be studied primarily as the activity of the speaker in terms of the articulatory organs and processes involved; this is called **articulatory phonetics.**

2. It can also be studied with the main attention focused on the sound waves generated by speaking and their transmission through the air.

3. The perception of these sound waves by the hearer's ears can be given primary emphasis, both in terms of the physiology of the ear and associated organs of hearing, and in terms of the psychology of perception.

These two latter aspects (2 and 3, above) are referred to as **acoustic phonetics** and **auditory phonetics**, respectively.

From the point of view of the study of language and as a part of general linguistics (which it is here considered to be), there are good reasons for prime attention being paid to articulatory phonetics. The principal parts of the body responsible for the production and differentiation of speech sounds, the vocal organs or organs of speech, are fairly easily accessible to visual observation, either directly or by means of various devices such as laryngoscopes and X-ray photography. Several of them, such as the lips, teeth, and tongue are familiar to everyone, and almost all of them can be described as far as concerns the part they play in speaking by the use of terms not difficult of comprehension to the non-specialist. The processes of speech are in the speaker's control to the extent that he can choose to speak or not to speak, and what to say in his language. Moreover, everyone has some kinaesthesis of the processes of speaking, that is to say, an awareness of some of the organs involved and of what they are doing (the widespread use of words like *tongue* in many languages both in the physiological and in the linguistic sense is an obvious illustration of this); and this kinaesthesis can be developed by attention, training, and practice to a considerable extent in most people and to a very marked extent in some.

With this development of the awareness of the processes involved in articulation come the increasing ability to recognize and discriminate different speech sounds not forming part of one's own language ('ear training'), and a practical control over the speech organs not merely as regards speaking one's own or a foreign language, but in the conscious control of particular organs as such in making particular movements productive of speech sounds of definite sorts. These latter skills are part of the equipment and qualification of the phonetician, or linguist who has developed this branch of the subject to a high degree of specialization.

None of the foi :going statements applies to anything like the same extent to the physical and auditory aspects of speech. One is not normally aware of sound waves as one is aware of the movements of the tongue, teeth, and lips; nor are their diffusion and impingement on the ear readily observable visually, without the use and specialized interpretation of appropriate machines. One has virtually no kin-aesthesis of hearing (an awareness of the hearing process apart from the hearing of the noise itself); nor has one control of hearing in being able to start and stop as one can start and stop speaking; and the physiology and working of the ear-drum and the bones and membranes of the inner ear associated with it are inaccessible to the naked eye. and much less amenable to observation through the sort of apparatus whose operation and understanding are likely to be available to the general linguist.

Linguists can and should acquaint themselves with the work and findings of specialists in acoustic phonetics, in the physics of sound-wave transmission, and in the physiology and psychology of hearing; and it is proper that some linguists should specialize in the aspects of these branches of knowledge of concern to the study of language; but for the non-specialist general linguist and for the student entering on the study of the subject, attention should be concentrated on articulatory phonetics, wherein speech can most readily and profitably be studied. In fact, linguists all along have concentrated on the articulatory aspect of phonetics, and it is from this that the bulk of technical phonetic terminology and phonetic categories has arisen.

In the general study of phonetics it is very desirable that a student, at the same time as he reads about the mechanisms and processes of speech, should make a practical study of the phonetics of his own language and of at least one other language. A great deal of work has been done on the phonetics of English, and for this and obvious practical reasons the phonetics of English, whether as one's native language or as a foreign language, is one of the most useful practical accompaniments of theoretical phonetics. What is written in this chapter is in no sense a substitute for such practical study.

3·1·3 *The physiological basis of speaking*

Speech is in one sense a wonderful by-product of the physiologically necessary process of breathing. The great majority of speech sounds are originally generated by the force of expiration, breath expelled through the mouth or nose from the lungs. Those initiatory processes other than pulmonic or lung pressure, which play a restricted part in the languages in which they are used at all, will be referred to later. Just as the main material of speech, expiratory breath, is itself part of the biologically necessary process of breathing, so it may be said that the organs of speech are themselves not organs or parts of the body specifically devoted to speech production, but organs that are used for this purpose among others. Of all the main organs controlling articulation it would be hard to assert that this is the exclusive function of any one of them, as is obvious from a consideration of the other uses of the tongue, teeth, lips, and throat. It has, however, been asserted that man's acquisition of upright posture, and his adoption and subsequent abandonment of an arboreal habitat liberated part of the throat mechanism from prime attention to other processes and enabled it to develop as the means of voice production.

Expiration is ordinarily silent. But air passing under pressure, if checked or obstructed, generates noise. The operation of wind instruments in music, and the sighing of the wind in trees or round rocks or on a hillside are familiar examples of this. In speaking one is checking and obstructing the outward passage of expiratory air at various places in the vocal tract and in various ways. Perceived differences in speech sounds are the result and correlate of differences in the place and manner of this interference, and the terms and categories of phonetic description are in the main drawn from this source.

A brief account of the principal articulatory processes will be given here. For a complete general description recourse should be had to

86

THE ORGANS OF SPEECH

1. Lips	5. Soft palate	8. Front of tongue	12. Position of
2. Teeth	(Velum)	9. Back of tongue	vocal-cords
3. Teeth-ridge	6. Uvula	10. Pharynx	13. Tip of tongue
4. Hard palate	7. Blade of tongue	11. Epiglottis	

a textbook on phonetics, and for a detailed description of the articulation of the sounds of a particular language a book on the phonetics of that language should be consulted.

3·2 THE ORGANS OF SPEECH

3·2·1 *The glottis*

Air passing up and out through the windpipe passes through the glottis, a part of the larynx, itself part of the throat. Across the glottis lie two membranes known as the vocal cords, though they are more in the form of curtains. These can be pulled together wholly to cut off the outward (or inward) stream of air, as in 'holding one's breath'. They can be relaxed and folded back at each side, as in normal breathing, when they permit the air to flow through freely and silently. Momentary obstruction by the vocal cords followed by the release of expiratory air produces a sound called the glottal stop, used in a number of languages, for example Arabic, and frequently in the Cockney dialect of English (as in the Cockney pronunciation of *what a lot*). The vocal cords may also be held together tautly so that the air stream vibrates them regularly at different speeds in its forced passage through them. This vibration is known technically as voice or voicing, and is a component of many of the speech sounds of all languages. It is also the source of voice pitch, the material of intonation, and of the pitch phenomena of 'tone languages' (3·5·4). It may be felt externally by lightly touching the front of the larynx or 'Adam's apple' with the finger-tip while humming or saying 'Ah'. Its absence is called voicelessness, and several pairs of similarly articulated sounds are distinguished in many languages as voiced and voiceless (e.g. the initial sounds in *van* and *fan*, and the *d*'s of *did* as against the *t*'s of *tit*).

Apart from voicing, the vocal cords may be held fairly close together, so as to interfere with the egressive air by making it push through a restricted aperture. This process is not fully understood at present, but it plays some part in the type of speech called whispering (in which the glottal vibrations of voicing are not made). The audible passage of air through the glottis is responsible for the production of h-like sounds (as in English *hand, behind*).

3·2·2 *The supraglottal organs of speech*

Above the glottis and the vocal cords, obstruction can be caused principally between a part of the tongue and the upper teeth or part of the roof of the mouth, between the upper front teeth and the lower lip, or between the two lips. The main places involved are the back, front, and blade of the tongue (the extreme front of which is the tip), the uvula, soft palate (velum), hard palate, teeth ridge (alveolus), teeth, and lips.

These places illustrate part of the theory of phonetic categorization. Terms like *teeth*, *lips*, *hard palate*, *soft palate*, and *uvula* designate physiologically distinct parts of the mouth, recognized as such quite apart from any articulatory function they may have, and are terms used in any physiological description of the human body. The tongue, however, as a physiological organ, is a unity; as a structure the blade, front and back are not sharply distinguished (whereas the boundary between the hard (bony) palate and the soft (fleshy) palate may be easily felt with a finger or the tip of the tongue). These divisions in the tongue are imposed by phoneticians to facilitate the description and analysis of different articulations; the relative position of the part of the surface of the tongue in contact or proximity with the other part of the mouth involved in a particular articulatory obstruction is a necessary part of the accurate description of many speech sounds.

The tongue is an extremely mobile organ and is responsible for more varieties of articulation than any other. Broadly speaking five places on the roof or upper surface of the mouth are involved in articulation with some part of the surface of the tongue. Behind and below the soft palate the uvula, a small tab of flesh, hangs down; and in some languages, for example Arabic, but not English, sounds are articulated with closure between this and the extreme back of the tongue. The other positions of obstruction or closure involving the surface of the tongue are the soft palate or velar area (closure here with the back of the tongue produces the initial sounds of English *come* (voicelessness) and *go* (voiced)), the hard palate (narrowing of the space between here and the front of the tongue produces the initial sound of English *yet* and *yeast*), the teeth ridge (alveolar ridge), just behind the upper front teeth and in front of the hard palate (closure here with the tip of the tongue produces the initial sounds of English *tooth* and *den*), and the upper front teeth (partial obstruction between these and the tip of the tongue produces the initial sounds of English *thin* and *then*, and closure produces the French *t* and *d* sounds, which differ in articulation and acoustic effect, among other factors, by this slight difference of the place of closure with the tongue tip).

Apart from the tongue and the area of the roof of the mouth, obstruction or closure can be made between the upper teeth and the lower lip (where the English *f* and *v* sounds are produced, as in *five*), and between the two lips (the articulatory place of English *p* and *b* sounds, as in *pip*, *bib*).

3·2·3 *Nasalization*

Any articulation at any place in the mouth may be accompanied by **nasalization**. The soft palate can take up two positions in articulation; when raised it seals off the nasal cavity from the mouth; when lowered the two cavities are united at the back (this is the position in normal breathing). The articulations just described were illustrated with sounds produced with the soft palate raised. When it is lowered, part or all of the air passes out through the nose. This is called nasalization, nasality, or nasal articulation; and with nasalization all articulations produce a different sound from that of their non-nasalized counterparts (i.e. articulated with the soft palate raised and the nasal cavity sealed off). Nasalization is what distinguishes English *m* from *b* (*mad*, *bad*), *n* from *d* (*not*, *dot*), and the sound represented by *ng* at the end of a word from that represented by *g* (*bung*, *bug*).

3·3 SEGMENTATION: VOWEL AND CONSONANT

3·3·1 *Segmentation*

Speech sounds are, very broadly, classified in two dimensions, according to the place of articulation (lips, tongue tip, and teeth ridge, etc.) and according to the manner of articulation (complete closure, partial closure, and other factors to be described later). It must be realized that speech is a continuous process, broken by pauses, and that in speaking the various movable organs involved are more or less continuously in motion. Speech sounds are not separate and discrete events or actions serially put together to form utterances in the way that the letters of the roman alphabet are serially put together to form printed words. One is, in a literate community, so used to thinking of speech as represented by spelling, which in a sense it is, that care must be taken to avoid considering speech as a kind of audible analogue to using a typewriter. Particularly tiresome is the habit of some older books on languages which refer to the constituents of spoken forms as 'letters'.

It is, however, possible, with the reservations just mentioned, to analyse the continuous process of speaking by reference to various events taking place in time but merging into one another. Many recognized speech sounds, indeed, cannot in the nature of things be articulated all by themselves, but only as part of an utterance including at least one other sound. Letters are discrete entities that can be put together to produce words; speech is a continuum which, for the purpose of description, may be segmented into speech sounds in order to analyse and symbolize the articulatory movements involved in its production. The speech sounds or segments that result from this analysis are abstractions of the nature referred to above (2·1·1).

3·3·2 *Vowels and consonants: transcription*

Traditionally and familiarly speech sounds are classified as **consonants** and **vowels**, though this division is not always as easy as it looks, and a clear-cut definition of *vowel* and *consonant* valid for all languages is very hard to arrive at. Less appropriately letters of the alphabet are distinguished as consonants and vowels according to the type of speech sound most usually represented by them. The vowel–consonant distinction is a convenient point at which to begin in the description and classification of speech sounds, but it must be emphasized that there are several important types of sound and sound features in language that must be described in other terms (3·5).

Two definitions of *vowel* as a general phonetic category may be quoted, with *consonant* in each case being defined as a segmental speech sound other than a vowel: 'Vowels are modifications of the

91

CONSONANTS	Bi-labial	Labio-dental	Dental and Alveolar	Retroflex	Palato-alveolar
Plosive . . .	p b		t d	ʈ ɖ	
Nasal . . .	m	ɱ	n	ɳ	
Lateral Fricative . .			ɬ ɮ		
Lateral Non-fricative .			l	ɭ	
Rolled . . .			r		
Flapped . . .			ɾ	ɽ	
Fricative . . .	ɸ β	f v	θ ð | s z | ɹ	ʂ ʐ	ʃ ʒ
Frictionless Continuants and Semi-vowels	w ɥ	ʋ	ɹ		

VOWELS					
Close	(y ʉ u)				
Half-close . . .	(ø o)				
Half-open . . .	(œ ɔ)				
Open	(ɒ)				

(Secondary articulations are

OTHER SOUNDS.—Palatalized consonants : ṭ, ḍ, etc. ;
palatalized ʃ, ʒ : ɕ, ʑ. Velarized or pharyngalized consonants : ɫ, đ,
z, etc. Ejective consonants (with simultaneous glottal stop) : p',
t', etc. Implosive voiced consonants : ɓ, ɗ, etc. ɼ fricative trill.
σ, ᵹ (labialized θ, ð, or s, z). ꞎ, ʑ (labialized ʃ, ʒ). ʇ, ʗ, ʖ (clicks,
Zulu c, q, x). ɹ (a sound between r and l). ŋ Japanese syllabic
nasal. ʅ (combination of x and ʃ). ʍ (voiceless w). ɩ, ʏ, ɷ
(lowered varieties of i, y, u). з (a variety of ə). ɵ (a vowel
between ø and o). Affricates are normally represented by groups of
two consonants (ts, tʃ, dʒ, etc.), but, when necessary, ligatures are
used ‿(ʦ, ʧ, ʤ, etc.), or the marks ⌒ or ‿ (t͡s or t‿s, etc.). ⌒ ‿ also
denote synchronic articulation (m͡ŋ = simultaneous m and ŋ). c, ɟ
may occasionally be used in place of tʃ, dʒ, and ʦ, ʣ for ts, dz.
Aspirated plosives : ph, th, etc. r-coloured vowels : eɹ, aɹ, ɔɹ, etc.,
or eʳ, aʳ, ɔʳ, etc., or ęᶦ, ąᶦ, ǫᶦ, etc. ; r-coloured ə : əɹ or əʳ or ɹ or ə̣

Alveolo-palatal	Palatal	Velar	Uvular	Pharyngal	Glottal
	c ɟ	k ɡ	q ɢ		ʔ
	ɲ	ŋ	N		
	ʎ				
			R		
			R		
ɕ ʑ	ç j	x ɣ	χ ʁ	ħ ʕ	h ɦ
	j (ɥ)	(w)	ʁ		

	Front	Central	Back		
	i y	ɨ ʉ	ɯ u		
	e ø		ɤ o		
		ə			
	ɛ œ		ʌ ɔ		
	æ	ɐ			
	a		ɑ ɒ		

shown by symbols in brackets.)

or ɝ,

LENGTH, STRESS, PITCH.— : (full length). ˙ (half length). (stress, placed at beginning of the stressed syllable). ˌ (secondary stress). ‾ (high level pitch) ; _ (low level) ; ′ (high rising) ; ╷ (low rising) ; ˋ (high falling) ; ˎ (low falling) ; ^ (rise-fall) ; ˇ (fall-rise).

MODIFIERS.— ~ nasality.   ₒ breath (l̥ = breathed l). ᵥ voice (s̬ = z) ' slight aspiration following p, t, etc. ᵕ labialization (n̫ = labialized n). ᵥ dental articulation (t̪ = dental t). ˙ palatalization (ż = ʑ). ˎ specially close vowel (e̝ = a very close e). ˌ specially open vowel (e̞ = a rather open e). ⊥ tongue raised (e⊥ or e̝ = e). т tongue lowered (eт or e̞ = e). + tongue advanced (u+ or u̟ = an advanced u, t̟ = t). - or ᴴ tongue retracted (i- or i̠ = ɨ+, t̠ = alveolar t). ᵓ lips more rounded. ᶜ lips more spread. Central vowels: ï(= ɨ), ü(= ʉ), ë (= ə˔),   ö (= ɵ), ̈ë, ̈ö. ˌ (e.g. n̩) syllabic consonant. ˘ consonantal vowel. ʃˢ variety of ʃ resembling s, etc.

voice-sound that involve no closure, friction, or contact of the tongue or lips' (Bloomfield); 'A vowel is defined as a voiced sound in forming which the air issues in a continuous stream through the pharynx and mouth, there being no obstruction and no narrowing such as would cause audible friction' (Jones; the presence of voicing in the articulation of vowels is not, in fact, essential, as Jones admits with regard to whispered speech, qualifying his definition by reference to 'normal speech'; though not found as essential components of European languages, voiceless vowels do occur in the normal speech of some few languages (e.g. Comanche), but they are admittedly rare).

Essentially a distinction is being drawn between short stretches or segments (with the reservations made above) wherein the sound is formed by the shape of the supraglottal cavity as a whole (in addition, in most cases, to voicing from the vibration of the vocal cords) and those wherein in addition to this there is audible obstruction at a particular point or points within the cavity. Inevitably there will be marginal sound types hard to assign definitely to either category, and an element of arbitrary decision may be necessary in particular cases, but the main principle of the division seems clear enough.

Segmentation and orthographic representation go closely together, and in fact the invention of an alphabet depended on some sort of early analysis of the utterances of particular languages into series of identifiable speech sounds. Different writing systems vary in the degree to which they faithfully represent the actual sound sequences of the words for which they stand. This is discussed elsewhere (4·1). Among languages written in a roman alphabet, English spelling comes quite a long way down in the scale of phonetic clarity (for example, -*ough* represents a different sound sequence in each of the following words: *cough, rough, dough*, and the following three words, all spelled differently, are exact rhymes: *whey, neigh, gay*).

For the purpose of accuracy in phonetic detail, phoneticians have developed systems of **transcription**, using symbols whose only purpose is to indicate on paper precisely the sounds or sound features into which an utterance has been analysed. Such transcriptions whose sole aim is accuracy of phonetic detail are called **narrow** transcriptions, to be distinguished from **broad**, sometimes called reading transcriptions, which make use of fewer different symbols but rely on some further linguistic analysis; the differences between the two are further discussed in 4·2. While the complete representation of every discriminable sound difference is an unattainable ideal, transcriptions can be more or less narrow according to the amount of detail required. The International Phonetic Association has been responsible for a set of symbols for narrow transcriptions that are widely used in Great Britain, and a table wherein these symbols and modification marks expressing finer shades of phonetic detail have been brought together is known as the International Phonetic Alphabet (I.P.A.); it is revised periodically in the light of progress in phonetic research, the latest edition (1951) being reproduced on pages 92–3.

It was said above that, with few exceptions, speech sounds are produced by the audible interference with expiratory breath from the lungs; and in practice the resultant acoustic differences can be accounted for by reference to a limited number of articulatory factors or components. Other than the glottal stop itself (3·2·1), expiratory sounds are all either voiced or voiceless, with intermediate degrees of partial voicing according to whether and to what extent the vocal cords are vibrating during the articulation. This applies equally to h-sounds or aspirates; the glottal friction involved in their production does not preclude some vocal cord vibration characteristic of voicing. Voiced and voiceless h-sounds are symbolized [ɦ] and [h], respectively, in the I.P.A. Except in whispering, voiceless vowel sounds are rare, but their production presents no difficulties.

3·3·3 *Vowels*

Vowel sounds are differentiated principally by two factors, the position of the tongue in the mouth and the shape of the lips. The tongue may be kept low in the mouth, or raised in varying degrees in the front towards the hard palate or in the back towards the soft palate. These positions give what are called open, front close, and back close vowels, respectively, with as many intervening grades (front half open, etc.) as may be required. Open vowels may also be distinguished as front or back according to the part of the tongue that is highest, but the latitude of variation when the tongue is low in the mouth is more restricted. The tongue may also be raised centrally in the mouth, producing central or neutral vowels (i.e. neither distinctively back nor front). Concomitantly with these different tongue positions, the lips may be rounded or spread, both in varying degrees, or neutral (neither rounded nor spread, rather as when the mouth is relaxed). These lip features, which distinguish vowel qualities, may vary independently of the position and height of the tongue, though obviously the more open vowel positions give less scope for lip spreading and for strong lip rounding, because the jaw and mouth are wide open.

To provide a referential frame of general validity, independent of the vowel sounds of any particular language, eight vowel sounds, articulated at fixed positions of the tongue and lips, four front and four back, have been recorded as Cardinal Vowels, transcribed [i], [e], [ɛ], [a], [ɑ], [ɔ], [o], [u], by reference to which the vowel sounds of languages can be roughly placed and identified.

Vowel positions may be maintained for relatively longer periods in one word than in another (symbolized in transcription by :), giving a distinction between **long** and **short** vowels, of which use is made in some languages, usually with other qualitative differences as well (long close vowels are often closer than their short counterparts).

The different categories of vowel may be illustrated from standard English, in which the following vowel types are found. (It must be made clear that in these sections a full account of the phonetics of English is not being given. English is being used as a convenient and familiar source for examples of many phonetic categories. For the phonetics of English in detail, books such as Jones's *Outline of English phonetics* or Ward's *Phonetics of English* should be studied):

/i/   short front close, with spread lips (*bit* /bit/; *fin* /fin/)
/i:/ long front close, with spread lips (*beat* /bi:t/; *feel* /fi:l/)
/u/   short back close, with rounded lips (*put* /put/; *pull* /pul/)
/u:/ long back close, with rounded lips (*boot* /bu:t/; *fool* /fu:l/)

(In addition to greater duration, /i:/ and /u:/ in English are closer and respectively more front and more back in articulation than /i/ and /u/; indeed, the qualitative difference is often as noticeable as the length difference.)

/e/   short front half close, with spread lips (*met* /met/; *tell* /tel/)
/æ/   short front half open, with lips neutral[1] (*man* /mæn/; *hat* /hæt/)
/ɑ:/ long back open, with lips neutral (*calm* /kɑ:m/; *hard* /hɑ:d/)
/ə/   short back open, with rounded lips (*cot* /kət/; *on* /ən/)
/ɔ:/ long back open, with rounded lips (*cord* /kɔ:d/; *caught* /kɔ:t/)

(In the last pair of English vowels, /ɔ:/ is less open than /ə/.)

/ʌ/   short central half open, with lips neutral (*cut* /kʌt/; *hum* /hʌm/)
/ə/   short central half close, with lips neutral (*sofa* /'soufə/; *upon* /ə'pən/) [2]
/ə:/ long central half close, with lips neutral (*herd* /hə:d/; *earn* /ə:n/)

It will have been noticed that the English front vowels are mostly accompanied by lip-spreading, and the back vowels by lip-rounding. These are certainly the most common combinations, but others are perfectly normal and quite frequently found. French and German have front vowels with lip-rounding, symbolized [y], [ø], and [œ], corresponding to [i], [e], and [ɛ] (e.g. French *tu* /ty/ you (singular); *deux* /dø/ two; *boeuf* /bœf/ ox); and a number of Far Eastern languages have back vowels with spread lips, symbolized [ɯ], and [ɣ] corresponding to [u] and [o].

Long vowels involve the maintaining of an articulatory position relatively constant, but temporally equivalent articulations may be made by moving from one vowel position to another through the intervening positions. These are called **diphthongs**, and English furnishes several examples of them:

/ei/ front half close to close with spread lips (*may* /mei/; *made* /meid/)
/ou/ back half close to close with rounded lips (*hole* /houl/; *go* /gou/)
/ai/ central open with lips neutral to close front with spread lips
                                        (*lie* /lai/; *might* /mait/)
/au/ central open with lips neutral to close back with rounded lips
                                        (*cow* /kau/; *owl* /aul/)
/ɔi/ back open with rounded lips to front close with spread lips
                                        (*boy* /bɔi/; *coil* /kɔil/)
/iə/ front close with spread lips to central half close with lips neutral
                                        (*pier* /piə/; *fierce* /fiəs/)

1. Customarily but illogically *half close* and *half open* are used distinctively in a system of four terms in English phonetic terminology, *half close* being closer than *half open*. More detailed and therefore more precise descriptions of the English vowels may be seen in the appropriate sections of Jones's *Outline*.

2. The special phonological status of short /ə/ in English, which necessitates its illustration in words containing more than one vowel, is referred to in 4·3·4.

/ɛə/ front half open with spread lips to central half close with lips neutral
(*air* /ɛə/; *pared* /pɛəd/)
/uə/ back close with rounded lips to central half close with lips neutral
(*poor* /puə/; *gourd* /guəd/)

These last three diphthongs are often called centring diphthongs, from the direction of their movement.

The passage from one vowel position to another may not be by the most direct route; where a detour, as it were, is made, a sequence sometimes called a triphthong results. Examples of these in English are:

/aiə/ central open with lips neutral via front close with spread lips to central half close with lips neutral (*tyre* /'taiə/; *hired* /'haiəd/)
/auə/ central open with lips neutral via back close with rounded lips to central half close with lips neutral (*tower* /'tauə/; *hours* /'auəz/)
/ɔiə/ back open with rounded lips via front close with spread lips to central half close with lips neutral (*coir* /'kɔiə/; *loyal* /'lɔiəl/)

In the articulation of these triphthongal sequences the movement towards the midway position is normally not as marked as in the corresponding diphthongs.

All vowel sounds may be characterized by **retroflexion**, the slight upward turning of the tongue tip toward the centre of the hard palate. Retroflex vowels such as [ɑɹ] and [əɹ] are common in American English and in most south-western dialects of British English in the pronunciation of words spelled with an 'r' after a vowel letter (*hard, word*, etc.). This retroflexion is one of the characteristics of what is loosely called in Britain 'an American accent'.

All types of vowel sounds may be uttered with **nasalization**, that is with the soft palate lowered and with the air passing partly through the nasal cavity and nostril as well as through the mouth. Nasalized vowels, as such vowels are called, are not distinctive (4·3·1) in English as they are in some languages, for example, French, but they are often heard from certain speakers. People who use such vowels very noticeably or frequently are said to 'talk through their nose', which is a true though rather careless way of putting it. In French nasalized and non-nasalized vowels are found distinguished by this feature alone, though here, as apparently in all such languages, the number of distinctively nasalized vowels is smaller than that of the non-nasalized vowels (e.g. *son* /sɔ̃/, sound; *un* /œ̃/ one). In whispered speech voiceless vowels can be nasalized in the same way as voiced vowels.

3·3·4 *Consonants*

As the vowel sounds in speech can be classified and described by reference to a limited number of articulatory factors, so the **consonant sounds** can be similarly treated, and broadly speaking these are the terms in which the I.P.A. chart is set out. In consonants the two most important components are the place of articulation and the manner of articulation. The glottal stop (symbolized [ʔ]) and the voiced and voiceless aspirates ([ɦ] and [h]), which are in a rather special class as being glottally articulated, have already been described. At the main supraglottal points of articulation already mentioned (3·2·2), obstruction may be total, producing what is called a **stop** and, when the obstruction is released and the air passes out again, a **plosive**; or it may be partial, when the air is made to pass through a narrow passage with resultant noise, for which the general term *continuant* may be used. Each may be voiced or voiceless. Continuants wherein the air is forced through a very narrow passage in the mouth are called **fricatives**.

Some of these articulations may be illustrated from standard English:

/g/   voiced velar plosive (*get* /get/; *gag* /gæg/)
/k/   voiceless velar plosive (*kick* /kik/; *neck* /nek/)
/d/   voiced alveolar plosive (*did* /did/; *hand* /hænd/)
/t/   voiceless alveolar plosive (*tot* /tɔt/; *hate* /heit/)
/b/   voiced bilabial plosive (*bet* /bet/; *bib* /bib/)
/p/   voiceless bilabial plosive (*peck* /pek/; *cup* /kʌp/)
/ð/   voiced dental fricative (*then* /ðen/; *wreathe* /riːð/)
/θ/   voiceless dental fricative (*thin* /θin/; *wreath* /riːθ/)
/v/   voiced labiodental fricative (*vote* /vout/; *thieve* /θiːv/)
/f/   voiceless labiodental fricative (*fife* /faif/; *fifth* /fifθ/)

Velar fricatives are not found in English, but the voiceless velar fricative [x] is the final consonant of the Scots *loch*. The voiced counterpart is symbolized [ɣ]. Both these sounds occur in Dutch.

Uvular plosives, voiced and voiceless, are found in some languages; the voiceless plosive is commoner, occurring, for example in Arabic. Voiced and voiceless palatal plosives, in which the front of the tongue makes closure with the hard palate, [(ɟ) and [c]), are found in Hungarian and in some other languages.

The distinction between voiced and voiceless consonants is a basic and important one in many languages, but the terms are sometimes used more in the way of labels than as complete designations. Other differentiating factors often accompany voicing and voicelessness, reinforcing their distinctiveness. In particular, voiced consonants are frequently articulated more laxly, i.e. with less breath force and muscular tension than the corresponding voiceless consonants, since, with the same force of expiration, the vibration of the vocal cords in voicing reduces the pressure of air above the glottis and so the force of the supraglottal articulation.

Various processes accompanying obstruction and release produce different types of sound at the articulatory places mentioned above. Closure may be released slowly, with partial obstruction, as in fricatives, audibly intervening before the free passage of air, producing **affricates** (plosive plus fricative). The initial and final consonant sounds of English *church* /tʃəːtʃ/, and *judge* /dʒʌdʒ/, are examples of palato-alveolar affricates.

Release of closure (with or without affrication) may be followed by a small puff of air (**aspiration**). This is the case with the standard English voiceless plosives in initial position (narrowly symbolized [pʰ], [tʰ], [kʰ]), and distinguishes them from the French voiceless plosives and from those in some northern English dialects, which do not have this aspiration; these latter are called unaspirated voiceless plosives. Voiced plosives can be aspirated, with voiced aspiration intervening, though these are less common. Some languages of India have all four types ([t], [tʰ], [d], [dʱ], etc.). In English whispered speech the aspiration of the voiceless plosives is one of the features maintaining the distinction between normally voiced and voiceless consonants (compare the whispered words *pack* and *bag*).

The lateral surface of the tongue instead of being more or less flat may be made slightly convex and cause stoppage in the centre of the roof of the mouth while allowing air to pass at the sides. Consonants so articulated are called **laterals**. Voiced laterals are found in English and French, at the alveolar and dental points of contact respectively, [l] and [l̪]. Voiceless fricative laterals are found in Welsh and some other languages, and a few languages use laterals with velar contact distinctively, but these are rare. Voiced laterals are seldom produced with enough friction to be classed as fricatives, though there are languages employing voiced lateral fricatives.

When the lateral surface of the tongue is made slightly concave, as opposed to convex, release of air is down the centre of the tongue with closure between the sides and the roof of the mouth. English /s/ and /z/, as in *size* /saiz/, are produced in this way (voiceless and voiced), respectively; and so is one pronunciation of English /r/, [ɹ], with the tongue tip a little further back in the mouth and the main part of the tongue kept low. There are a number of r-sounds in English, and the letter 'r' stands for a variety of different pronunciations. In standard English /r/ as a consonant only occurs before a vowel, where it is usually an alveolar fricative as described just above in this paragraph; but a flapped or tapped /r/, [ɾ], when the tongue tip lightly and momentarily touches the alveolar ridge, is common between two vowels (as in *merry* /meri/; *very* /veri/). In parts of Northumberland a voiced uvular fricative (the 'Durham burr') is heard as a pronunciation of /r/. In standard English 'r' finally or before a consonant letter represents not a consonant at all but usually a long vowel or a centring diphthong (*farm* /fɑːm/; *near* /niə/). In Scotland /r/ is often pronounced as an alveolar trill, an articulation wherein the tongue tip vibrates against the teeth ridge; in Scots English, /r/ occurs both prevocalically and postvocalically (*cart*, standard /kɑːt/, Scots /kart/). In Parisian French, /r/ is often pronounced as a uvular trill, with the uvula vibrating against the back of the tongue in a stream of air [R]. r-sounds are generally voiced, but voiceless ones are found sporadically in many languages and distinctively in some.

In the speech of most speakers of standard English, words whose orthographic form ends in an -r have two pronunciations: with a final /r/ when followed without any break or pause by a word beginning with a vowel sound, the /r/ being thus intervocalic, and without the final /r/ in all other positions. Thus in isolation *fear* is /fiə/ and *war* is /wɔː/, but the phrase *the fear of war* would be /ðə ˈfiər əv ˈwɔː/.

When articulations similar to /s/ and /z/ are made with the tongue slightly further back in the mouth, the consonants /ʃ/ and /ʒ/ are produced, palato-alveolar fricatives as against alveolar fricatives. These are exemplified in English *shine* /ʃain/ (compare *sign* /sain/)

101

and *measure* /ˈmeʒə/. Voiceless and voiced affricates are articulated in this position in English (/tʃ/ and /dʒ/, as in *church* /tʃəːtʃ/ and *judge* /dʒʌdʒ/).

In addition to making contact at various places in the mouth with its upper surface, the tongue may have its tip curved upward in the mouth in varying degrees, as in retroflex vowel articulation. This retroflexion is found in a number of languages. Some Indian languages have a series of markedly retroflex consonants, which are distinct from their dentally articulated [ṭ], [ṭʰ], [ḍ], [ḍʰ], [ḷ].

The different types of supraglottal consonant articulations can **have a nasal** counterpart, when the air is released through the nasal **cavity** and the nostrils with the soft palate lowered. In the case of **total** mouth obstruction (the nasal counterparts of the stop consonants) the air passes exclusively through the nose; with other, partial, obstructions, it passes out through both mouth and nose, as with the nasalized vowels. Nasal consonants with complete mouth closure are common in almost all languages, and may be exemplified by English /m/, /n/, and /ŋ/, the counterparts of /b/, /d/, and /g/ (*mob* /mɔb/; *bomb* /bɔm/; *nod* /nɔd/; *don* /dɔn/; *gang* /gæŋ/). /ŋ/ is not found initially in English words. All nasal consonants are continuants as the egress of air is never completely cut off; they are commonly voiced, though voiceless nasal consonants, as in English whispered speech, do occur; and nasalized fricatives and laterals are found in some languages, but rather rarely.

A rather marginal category of articulation, usually classed with the consonants of a language, is designated '**semivowels**'. In English this category is exemplified in /j/ and /w/, both normally voiced, as in *yet* /jet/ and *wet* /wet/. They are formed in the same manner as the vowels /i/ and /u/, sometimes with a narrower passage between the tongue and the hard palate or between the lips, to cause some slight noise from the local obstruction. In assigning articulatory segments to the category of vowel or semivowel in a particular language, recourse is often made rather to phonological considerations of patterning in relation to other segments than to purely phonetic criteria in the strict sense (4·3·4).

Just as vowels can be long (i.e. longer than other vowels in the same position in an utterance and at the same speed of speaking), so

102

consonants can be long, or geminate, when the closure or obstruction is held momentarily before release. This is found in English words such as *night-time* /ˈnaittaim/ and *solely* /ˈsoulli/; consonant gemination distinguishes the two Italian words *fato* /ˈfato/ fate, and *fatto* /ˈfatto/ fact.

Pulmonic or expiratory lung air was mentioned as the principal source of speech in all languages; but certain other initiatory processes are found and need brief treatment. Although a weird but intelligible sort of speech can be made while breathing in instead of breathing out (and may be used by some people when talking very quickly) no language is known to make regular use of this method. But three non-pulmonic types of consonant articulations are used in some languages: ejectives, implosives, and clicks, in this order of commonness of occurrence in languages.

In **ejective** consonants, which are found at all the previously mentioned places of articulation and with all types of obstruction and release, air pressure is created, not by expulsion from the lungs, but by contraction of the space between the closed vocal cords and closure or restriction at some supraglottal point in the mouth, and consequent compression of the air prior to release. Ejective consonants, which are sometimes also called glottalized consonants, are most commonly found with plosive or affricate release, and a series of this type at several places of articulation matching a series of pulmonic consonants is found in Georgian and in a number of languages of the Caucasus as well as elsewhere. The acoustic impression of these sounds on someone in whose language they do not occur is one of sharpness when the glottalic pressure is released. They are usually symbolized with an apostrophe after the letter sign ([p'], [t'], [k'], [tʃ'], etc.).

Implosion is something of the reverse process, and is found in Swahili and several other African languages, and sporadically elsewhere. Closure is made at one of the supraglottal places already referred to, and a partial vacuum is created by closing the glottis completely or bringing the vocal cords together to vibrate as in voiced articulation and then drawing the glottis downward. When the supraglottal closure is released air flows momentarily inward, giving a different sound from that produced by closure released outwards. Implosive consonants can be voiced or voiceless, but the voiced implosives are much the commoner. In Swahili, implosive and plosive (egressive) voiced consonants are found.

Clicks are probably confined as regular components of utterances to certain languages of southern Africa, though sounds of the click type are found elsewhere, and in English the exclamation of distaste (usually spelt *tut-tut*) is in many speakers a sort of click, as is the 'clucking' sound used to urge horses on. Essentially, clicks consist of the creation of a suction between the tongue surface and the roof of the mouth by making closure at two places (bilabial, alveolar, palatal, etc., and velar) at the same time, drawing the centre of the tongue downward and then releasing the partial vacuum. The English click is generally alveolar, but some African languages have a series of such sounds as an integral part, with velar closure combined with closure at one of a number of other places distinctively.

3·4   ACOUSTIC PHONETICS

For reasons given earlier it was said that articulatory phonetics was the proper object of the initial study of the speaking process in general linguistics. But as the term *sound wave* has been used, a brief account of the physical acoustics of speech may be useful.

Noise of whatever source or origin consists physically of displacements in the air involving rapid increases and decreases of pressure moving outwards from the source and gradually decreasing to vanishing point. Comparison with the waves caused by a stone dropped into a smooth surface of water is often made, though differences in pressure are not involved in liquids in such cases.

The properties that characterize sound waves are:

1. The amplitude, or the distance from the highest and lowest pressures to the mean; this is the main physical counterpart of the perceived loudness of a sound, the greater the amplitude the louder the sound, other things being equal.

2. The frequency, or the number of oscillations between the high and the low points in pressure in a given time, say a second; this is the physical counterpart of pitch, the higher the frequency, the higher in scale the pitch.

3. Simplicity or complexity; a simple sound wave consists of oscillations like this:

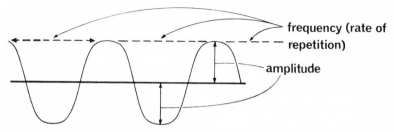

and is generated by a regular source of vibration such as a tuning fork; complex sound waves involve waves of different frequencies superimposed on one another to produce wave forms like:

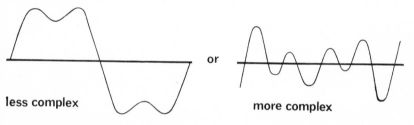

In speech, the vocal cords (when vibrating in voicing), the various places and processes of articulation, and the different shapes of the whole supraglottal cavity in the production of consonant and vowel sounds generate sound waves at specific frequencies, which added together constitute the sound waves of speech. These are far more complex than those just illustrated. The supraglottally generated frequencies are often called inherent, in contrast to the glottal frequency which is variable according to the speed of the vibration of the vocal cords and produces the different pitches of voiced speech sounds irrespective of their own specific supraglottal frequencies. This glottal pitch is, of course, only a feature of voiced speech sounds. Glottal pitch differences may be illustrated by singing a scale on any sound sequence (*la la la*, etc.), or on the conventional *do re mi* syllables. Differences of inherent pitch may be noticed by alternating between hissing and 'hushing' (saying *sh sh*), when the lower inherent note of 'hushing' is heard.

105

In the acoustic analysis of speech sounds it has been found that in addition to the glottal pitch of voiced sounds (and it has been calculated that about eighty per cent of the speech sounds of connected utterance in English are voiced), perceptible phonetic differences are the result of sound waves generated at different areas or 'bands' of frequency. In vowels and certain continuants the features distinguishing one from another are caused by a combination of a small number of separate bands of frequencies, called formants, of which two are the most important, ranging from about 200 cycles per second to about 750 cycles per second and from about 700 cycles per second to about 3,000 cycles per second respectively.

In the artificial production of speech sounds by mechanical devices, or speech synthesis, as it is called, recognizable vowels and consonants can be produced by generating and combining sound waves at a limited number of different frequencies that have been found essential for each sound. Many other components are involved in the sound waves of actual speech, some of which are not fully understood yet, but the basic and essential nature of the sound waves in the air by which speech is transmitted is now clearly known.

3·5   PLURISEGMENTAL FEATURES

3·5·1 *The continuum of articulation*

It was stressed earlier that speech is essentially a continuum of movements by the vocal organs and that the segmentation of it into successive consonants and vowels is an artificial process, though a practical and necessary one in the study and analysis of language. Inevitably the assignment of features to a particular place in the stream of utterance represented by a discrete symbol in the transcription is a distortion of the actual state of affairs, and it is often found in careful analysis and experimentation that the transitions from consonant articulation to the following vowel, and from vowel to the following consonant, are the most important clues to the hearer as to what speech sounds are being uttered. The continuous temporal interpenetration and overlapping of articulation processes must be constantly kept in mind, and certain features of speech that are of great significance in all languages must be referred to

106

sequences of at least one consonant and one vowel segment and often to longer stretches, sometimes from pause to pause, or even to a whole utterance.

The most important features that must be treated as pluriseg-mental, extending over stretches of various lengths, are stress, pitch, and general voice quality. But certain articulatory processes them-selves, though assignable to individual consonant or vowel segments, are often best regarded in this light.

3·5·2 *Supraglottal features*

Lip-rounding has already been referred to as a feature of the articula-tion of some vowels. It is also a feature of certain consonants such as [w] and in some languages of a set of velar plosives with con-comitant lip-rounding called labiovelars (symbolized [kʷ], [gʷ], etc.). It is often appropriate to regard this lip-rounding as a phonetic feature of a sequence of such a consonant and the following vowel, as it may persist to some degree in the articulation of both segments and characterize them both acoustically, even if, as in English *queen* /kwi:n/, the lips move from a rounded to spread position as the vowel articulation takes place.

Glottalization is a feature that may characterize short stretches. Its production involves a series of irregular total or partial glottal closures like a succession of glottal stops, giving an effect of 'creaki-ness' to the sounds, as well as single glottal closures briefly inter-rupting a vowel articulation or nearly concomitant with a consonantal obstruction. Ejective consonants are a special case of glottalization, where in addition to closure pressure on the air above the closed glottis replaces pulmonic pressure in the consonantal articulation. Such consonants are often followed by vowels in which glottal con-striction persists. Non-ejective glottalized plosives, with concomitant glottal and supraglottal closure, are a feature of Cockney English, distinct from the Cockney use of simple glottal stops in the place of the /p/, /t/, and /k/ in the middle of some words as pronounced in standard English.

The spread of a feature over vowel and consonant segments is found with **retroflexion**, well exemplified in several languages of India, in which the acoustic effect of the upturn of the tip of the tongue is heard in the vowels adjacent to a retroflex consonant. Likewise in **palatalization,** the raising of the front of the tongue towards the hard palate, the position of the articulation of the palatal consonants themselves, may characterize the articulation of other consonants, as an additional feature, together with their adjacent vowels. The effect of this is that front vowels are more front in articulation than the corresponding vowels adjacent to non-palatalized consonants, and other vowels are somewhat fronted. What may be regarded as the opposite process to palatalization is known as **velarization,** in which the back of the tongue is raised, as during the articulation of the velar consonants themselves. A velarized or back /l/ is heard in English in final position (e.g. *ill* /il/). In Arabic four velarized consonants contrast with the four non-velarized [s], [z], [t], and [d]; vowels adjacent to such velarized consonants are generally more back in articulatory position than the corresponding vowels in other positions. The alternation of palatalized and non-palatalized (sometimes velarized) consonants, often called 'soft' and 'hard' respectively, together with concomitant differences in the quality of adjacent vowels, plays an important part in a number of languages, for example Russian and Irish.

The acoustic analysis of the sound waves of speech is now a well-developed part of the work of phonetics laboratories, and the tracings or other translations into visual representation of the different components of the waves resulting from different articulatory processes show very clearly how the features mentioned above, and many others, extend over the boundaries (in so far as these are themselves sharply definable) of the successive consonants and vowels to which they are attributed. Indeed, there have just been given only some examples of a principle always to be kept prominently in mind in phonetic analysis.

3·5·3 *Stress*

Stress and pitch differ from the sort of features mentioned in the preceding section, in that they are not related to any particular process of supraglottal articulation. **Stress** is a generic term for the relatively greater force exerted in the articulation of part of an utterance. It is, therefore, an articulatory term, and it is to be distinguished from prominence, a more subjective term relating to the more noticeable acoustic impression conveyed by certain parts of a stretch of speech as against the rest. Stress is often associated with greater loudness, and it may be a component part of prominence, but other factors involved include the inherently greater prominence, or sonority, of certain speech sounds as compared with others (vowels are more prominent than consonants, voiced sounds more prominent than voiceless ones, etc.), and the prominence of a pitch level higher or lower than neighbouring pitches (4·3·7).

Two fairly distinct types of stress, as defined above, may be seen in language. As a general and perhaps universal process, the whole or any part of an utterance may be stressed, that is to say uttered more loudly and with more forceful articulation for the purpose of emphasis, so as virtually to compel the hearer to take more notice of it than to the rest. This exploitation of the greater noticeability of strongly stressed utterance is one of the less arbitrary features of speaking as a symbolic activity (1·3·2), comparable to the use of capital letters, boldface type, and the like for similar purposes in printing. Moreover, it admits of an infinite number of gradations in loudness correlatable with different degrees of emphasis in both the intention of the speaker and the effect on the hearer. Separable from this is the use of differences of stress in normal speech as an inherent part of the articulation processes of particular languages, but not of all languages.

Stress in this latter sense is often accompanied by differences in vowel qualities as between stressed and unstressed segmental sequences. Unlike stress for emphasis, its extent and function in languages differs considerably from one to another, and this aspect is a matter for phonological analysis (4·3·3). One may distinguish fairly readily languages in which stress placement occurs at fixed points between pauses, as in French wherein the final prepausal segments are somewhat stressed, those in which its place is determined in the main by word boundaries (cp. 5·3·2), such as Hungarian (putting stress at the beginning of words) and Polish, Swahili, and several others (stressing in the main one place before the end of words), and languages like English, in which its position may vary from word to word. Stress falls on a different place in each of the following four words: *solitary* /ˈsɔlitəri/; *dependency* /diˈpendənsi/; *apperception*

109

/æpəˈsepʃən/; *carabineer* /kærəbiˈniə/. Some pairs of otherwise identical spoken words are distinguished in English by different stress placements (e.g. *export* (noun) /ˈekspɔ:t/, *export* (verb) /eksˈpɔ:t/, *billow* /ˈbilou/, *below* /biˈlou/.

In longer English words there may be, and usually are, more than two different degrees of stress, or force of articulation, on different parts; in *apperception* there is more force on /æ/ than on /pə/ or /ʃən/. It is placement of the major or full stress that is discussed and marked here.

The statement of stress occurrence in isolated words, wherein one part must be regarded as bearing full stress, and the stress is therefore left unmarked in words having only one available position, must be distinguished from the statement of stress occurrence in the words of connected discourse. Here, according to the speed of utterance and some other factors, many words are uttered unstressed or with a lesser degree of stress. Thus the phrase quoted above in 3·3·4 would most naturally be stressed in connected speech:

/ðə ˈfiər əv ˈwɔ:/, and *after that they went away* would be /ɑ:ftə ˈðæt ðei went əˈwei/.

3·5·4 *Pitch*

Pitch is the acoustic result of the speed of the vibration of the vocal cords in the voiced parts of utterances. It follows that the term does not properly apply to voiceless sounds, nor to whispered speech. But the latter is a fairly infrequent variation from normal utterance, and in all languages voiced sounds outweigh voiceless ones in frequency and in numbers. The ratio in English speech has been calculated as eighty to twenty.

Irrespective of the supraglottal components of individual consonants and vowels and features like those mentioned above (3·5·2), variations in the speed, or frequency as it is called, of the vocal cord vibrations produce sounds acoustically higher or lower. The faster the cords vibrate the greater the number of regular changes in pressure in the sound waves and the higher the pitch as heard.

Speech is nowhere said on a monotone, except for special purposes such as the intoning of parts of some church services. One is not normally very conscious of the rises and falls in one's own speech and that of persons of one's own immediate dialect, but unfamiliar sequences of pitch levels, in persons from other dialect areas for example, are immediately noticeable.

Pitch variation is found in all languages, but its function is very different from one type of language to another. Broadly, there are two ways in which languages make use of pitch variations in speech. In languages such as English, French, and German, and many others, regular sequences of different pitches characterize stretches of speech between pauses and are known collectively as **intonation**. Individual and personal variations are numerous, but there are general patterns of intonation characteristic of the utterances in each language and usually in different dialects within a language. These differences of intonation may correlate with different types of utterance. As an example from English one may compare the normal intonation of *Thursday at ten o'clock then*, as a statement of a fixed time for an appointment with that of the same sequence of words *Thursday at ten o'clock then?* as a request for confirmation of the time of the appointment.

In some languages, widely scattered over the world, but perhaps most notably in China and parts of Africa and South-east Asia, pitch differences help to distinguish one word from another and may be the only differentiating feature between two or more words whose composition in terms of consonants and vowels is the same. Pitch differences used in this way are called **tones**, and these languages are called **tone languages**. The different Chinese languages are the most widely spoken group of tone languages. Tones may be mainly on a single level of pitch (level tones), the relative height being what differentiates one such tone from another, or they may rise or fall, or rise and fall, or fall and rise (rising, falling, rising-falling, falling-rising tones, respectively), and be distinguished by the actual direction in which the pitch moves.

In certain tone languages, particular tones or distinctive pitches are regularly accompanied by other features of articulation, such as 'creakiness' (caused by glottal constriction) and breathiness.

The difference between the two uses of pitch features may be seen in the fact that in English, a non-tonal language, wherein pitch sequences (intonation) are the property of sentences and parts of sentences, the lexical content of a sentence does not affect the pitch sequences, except that the substitution of longer or shorter words may spread the intonation over more or fewer sounds, and differently stressed words may alter the position of the high and low pitches; thus if one takes the simple question *are you feeling hungry?*, usually said on a sequence of pitches falling to a low pitch on *hun-* and then rising, this pitch sequence is not altered by the replacement of *hungry* by *thirsty, sleepy, happy*, and so on. But in a tone language, in which the pitch levels or the rising and falling pitches are properties of the words as lexical items, the substitution of a different word in a sentence may change the pitch sequence, if the two words concerned are different in tonal composition. In northern (Mandarin) Chinese, the sequence /ta/, for example, may represent four different words according to the tone on which it is said: level tone, to raise; rising tone, to penetrate; falling-rising tone, to hit; falling tone, great.

These two types of language are not sharply exclusive of each other. Many tone languages have a well defined set of intonations superimposed on the tones of the words in sentences, so that the tones of each word may be somewhat different in actual pitch, while remaining distinct from other tones, according to the intonation on which the whole sentence is uttered. And some European languages (e.g. Norwegian, Swedish, and Serbo-croat) are partially tonal, in that certain words have a pitch pattern inherently different from the patterns of other words. Occasionally these patterns may be the only differentiator of otherwise identical word forms (e.g. Norwegian *bønner* /ˈbønnər/ with the 'double', falling-rising tone, beans; *bønder* /ˈbønnər/, with the 'single', rising tone, farmers). These languages have their own intonation patterns, and the tonal distinctions just mentioned are generally maintained in the different intonation tunes as are the tonal distinctions in fully tonal languages.

The different ways in which pitch differences are exploited intonationally and tonally in languages of all types will be dealt with further in 4·3·5 and 4·3·7. They fall within the purview of phonology, rather than of phonetics, which is concerned primarily with the physiological basis of pitch differentiation and the actual types of pitches that occur.

112

3·5·5 *Voice quality*

Voice quality is one of the most elusive aspects of utterance to analyse adequately. The words, and phrases like them, are in frequent use non-technically, and it is terms like these, rather than technical terms specifically invented for linguistics (even though linguists often differ in the exact way in which they define them), that are likely to cause trouble. In general parlance, the 'quality of a person's voice', like the 'tone of someone's speech', may cover almost any part of his utterance, such as the actual sense of what is said, the general impression made on the hearer, the choice of vocabulary, or dialectal features differentiating it from what the hearer is accustomed to or was expecting. All of these features are handled separately elsewhere in linguistic description, but there remains in utterance a residue of pronunciation features, not accounted for in the description of the segmental articulations and the plurisegmental features such as have been illustrated hitherto, but which are perceptible and may be significant, and are consequently part of the subject-matter of the phonetic level of linguistic analysis.

Voice quality in this sense refers to differences in what is heard, caused, like everything else heard in speech, by differences in some part or parts of the whole process of articulation reflected in differences somewhere in the resultant sound waves. It covers a multitude of rather different components, some of which are at present not fully understood as regards their articulatory basis. Some are nearly, if not quite, universal, as for instance, the greater loudness and force of articulation of an entire discourse, as against the greater relative loudness of a single utterance or part of an utterance referred to as emphatic stress; this correlates with, and communicates to the hearer, excitement, anger, or some other emotional involvement in what is being said.

At the opposite pole to this is quiet speech, which is not the same as whispering, though this by its very absence of voicing throughout is necessarily quiet and is employed for similar purposes and in similar situations. Quietly spoken, but normally articulated speech, carries connotations in both speaker and hearer of secrecy, confidentiality, intimacy, tenderness, and the like. It may be observed that both quietness and loudness of speech are, rather like onomatopoeia, directly suggestive, as features, of their functions, part of the total meaning of the utterances. As with stress for emphasis, both these features are infinitely variable in degree on a scale; there are as many degrees of forceful utterance as speaker and hearer can distinguish, whereas significant distinctions of consonant and vowel segments and of most other features, including stress as an inherent part of normal speech in some languages (3·5·3), are organized into contrasts of a fixed number of categories by each language according to its phonological system.

Apart from the use of pitch differences in intonation tunes, or as lexically distinctive tones in tone languages (accompanied in some languages by other articulatory features), persons vary both in the ranges of high and low pitch within which they speak, and in the relative height of their overall range. The speech of children is generally, for physiological reasons, higher than that of adults, and in many communities the speech of women is higher than that of men. Within these general limits each individual has his own normal pitch range. The deliberate use of a pitch range wider than one's usual one, or higher or lower than that normally used, correlates in various speech communities with various situations and intentions on the speaker's part (excitement, mockery, wheedling, and so on) and is understood in these lights by others of the same community.

Other aspects of voice quality are purely personal. It is highly unlikely that any two people are exactly alike in their speech (the articulations and the sound waves produced thereby), even if we had ways of determining what 'exactly alike' actually is. Everyone is aware that differences in voice quality are part of each person's total individuality, and different speakers can be distinguished behind closed doors, and the voices of acquaintances recognized even over such imperfect lines of transmission as telephones.

The totality of such features includes several different items. Some are probably physiological; different types of facial structures are likely to condition one's general speech production. These physiological differences do not affect the ability of any physically normal person to articulate all the speech sounds and maintain all the contrastive differences of any language. A baby born into a speech community will in the absence of interference acquire a perfect (i.e. native speaker's) mastery of the language, or dialect, of that community, whatever his physiological type. The belief that the actual physiology or race of certain peoples prevents them pronouncing certain sounds or enables them to pronounce others is nothing but a myth of ignorant ethnocentricity, on a par with travellers' tales of languages with no more than 600 words and no proper grammar. It is, incidentally, part of the task of general linguistics to dispel such harmful prejudices about other people's languages. None the less the different configurations of the jaw, lips, nose, and other organs of speech in different physiological types do probably contribute something to the differences in the overall quality of people's voices that are universally recognized, though without effect on their use of language.

Some features may be cultural, acquired by speakers as part of the general behaviour patterns of their community, and so characterizing a dialect or even a whole language. Types of speech popularly categorized as 'harsh', 'precise', 'careful', and 'slurred', and referring to specific though as yet ill defined aspects of the sound waves and their production, belong to this group. Thus it is said that French consonants are articulated more sharply, giving something of a staccato effect, than are English consonants.

It has already been said that little is known yet about the exact articulatory basis of all these subtle though highly significant differences between the speech habits of groups and of individuals falling under the general heading of voice quality. Clearly this side of phonetics cannot be pursued further in an elementary treatment of linguistics such as this; but it is important that these aspects of speech should be recognized as a proper (and perhaps urgent) object of phonetic study and research.

3·6 PHONETICS IN LINGUISTICS

The account of speech sounds, their production, description, and analysis, given in this chapter has been intended as no more than a brief introduction to this part of the study of language in general linguistics. It can and should be supplemented by the further reading of books specifically devoted to phonetics, both general and that of particular languages, together with, if at all possible, some practical acquaintance with and control over the recognition and production of different speech sounds by oneself (practical phonetics).

Speech is certainly the oldest form of language, and everywhere the most widespread form. The physiological conditions of its production and reception, and the physical means of its transmission, must have helped to determine the ways in which languages have developed and are organized as systems of human communication. These are sufficient reasons why an understanding of the principles of phonetics is a necessary basis for the study of other branches of linguistics, and for a reasonable comprehension of the working and significance of language the world over.

CHAPTER 3, BIBLIOGRAPHY

1. L. E. ARMSTRONG, *The phonetics of French*, London, 1932.
2. —— and I. C. WARD, *A handbook of English intonation*, Cambridge, 1926.
3. E. O. ASHTON, *Swahili grammar*, London, 1944.
4. J. BITHELL, *German pronunciation and phonology*, London, 1952.
5. L. BLOOMFIELD, *Language*, London, 1935.
6. S. C. BOYANUS, *Russian pronunciation*, London, 1965.
7. J. R. FIRTH, *A short outline of Tamil pronunciation*, in A. H. Arden, *A progressive grammar of common Tamil*, Madras, 1934.
8. W. H. T. GAIRDNER, *The phonetics of Arabic*, London, 1925.
9. M. GRAMMONT, *Traité de phonétique*, Paris, 1950.
10. R. S. HARRELL, *The phonology of colloquial Egyptian Arabic*, New York, 1957.
11. R. S. HEFFNER, *General phonetics*, Madison, 1952.
12. C. F. HOCKETT, *A manual of phonology*, Indiana University publications in anthropology and linguistics, 11, 1955.
13. D. JONES, *Outline of English phonetics*, sixth edition, Cambridge, 1947.
14. ——, *The phoneme*, Cambridge, 1950.
15. M. JOOS, *Acoustic phonetics*, Baltimore, 1948.
16. J. S. KENYON, *American pronunciation*, Ann Arbor, 1935.
17. P. LADEFOGED, *Elements of acoustic phonetics*, London, 1962.
18. T. F. MITCHELL, *Introduction to colloquial Egyptian Arabic*, London, 1956.
19. V. E. NEGUS, *The mechanism of the larynx*, London, 1929.
20. B. Ó CUÍV, *The Irish of West Muskerry*, Dublin, 1944.

3 PHONETICS

21. K. L. PIKE, *Phonetics*, Ann Arbor, 1943.

22. ——, *The intonation of American English*, Ann Arbor, 1946.

23. ——, *Tone languages*, Ann Arbor, 1948.

24. E. SAPIR, *Language*, New York, 1921.

25. A. SOMMERFELT and I. MARM, *Teach yourself Norwegian*, London, 1943.

26. R. H. STETSON, *The bases of phonology*, Oberlin, 1945.

27. ——, *Motor phonetics*, Amsterdam, 1951.

28. I. C. WARD, *The phonetics of English*, Cambridge, 1948.

ADDENDA

29. A. C. GIMSON, *An introduction to the pronunciation of English*, London, 1962.

30. H. MOL, *Fundamentals of phonetics 1: The organ of hearing*, The Hague, 1963.

31. J. D. O'CONNOR and G. F. ARNOLD, *Intonation of colloquial English*, London, 1961.

32. R. G. POPPERWELL, *The pronunciation of Norwegian*, Cambridge, 1963.

33. D. CRYSTAL and R. QUIRK, *Systems of prosodic and paralinguistic features in English*, The Hague, 1964.

34. J. L. FLANAGAN, *Speech analysis, synthesis and perception*, Berlin, 1965.

35. R. KINGDON, *The groundwork of English intonation*, London, 1958.

36. M. SCHUBIGER, *English intonation: its form and function*, Tübingen, 1958.

p. 86. On the phonetics of English (British standard English), Jones, 13; Ward, 28. The transcription in Jones's *English pronouncing dictionary* follows that of his *Outline*.

No organs of speech as such, Sapir, 24, 7.

On the development of the larynx as an organ of voice production, Negus, 19, appendix 1.

p. 88. On general phonetics, Pike, 21; Heffner, 11; Grammont, 9. With special reference to instrumental techniques, Stetson, 26 and 27.

On American English, Kenyon, 16.

On French phonetics, Armstrong, 1.

On German phonetics, Bithell, 4.

p. 91. On segmentation, and some of the problems involved, Pike, 21, chapters 3 and 7.

p. 94. Jones, 13, 23; cp. Pike, 21, 78. Vocoid: 'a sound during which air leaves the mouth over the centre of the tongue and without friction in the mouth'. Contoid: 'any nonvocoid'. The use by Pike of *vocoid* and *contoid* as newly invented terms in general phonetics is in order to keep *vowel* and *consonant* for use exclusively as phonological terms with reference to particular languages (cp. *Phonemics*, Ann Arbor, 1947, 253).

On the voiceless vowels of Comanche, E. D. Canonge in *IJAL* 23 (1957), 63–7.

p. 96. Cardinal vowels, Jones, 13, 28, 34.

p. 104. Swahili, Ashton, 3.

pp. 104, 106. For detailed treatment of this aspect of phonetics, Joos, 15; Hockett, 12; Ladefoged, 17.

p. 107. Glottalization in Georgian, Robins and N. Waterson, *BSOAS* 14 (1952), 55–72.

On retroflexion, Firth, 7.

p. 108. On Arabic phonetics, Gairdner, 8; Mitchell, 18; Harrell, 10.

On Russian and Irish, Boyanus, 6; B. Ó Cuív, 20. In Russian four different words involving the sequence bilabial nasal, open unrounded vowel, and voiceless dental stop are distinguished according to whether palatalization affects neither consonant, both consonants, or one of the consonants, with concomitant differences of vowel quality (Jones, 14, 26).

pp. 108–10. On stress, Jones, 13, chapter 29.

On prominence and sonority, Jones, 13, §§101–2; Bloomfield, 5, 120–1.

p. 110. Ratio of voiced to voiceless sounds in English, Jones, 13, 255.

p. 111. On British English intonation, Jones, 13, chapter 31; Armstrong and Ward, 2. On American English intonation, Pike, 22.

On tone languages, Pike, 23.

p. 112. On intonation in tone languages, Pike, 23, 16–17, 85–6.

On tone distinctions in Norwegian, Sommerfelt and Marm, 25, 33–41; Bloomfield, 5, 116.

p. 115. It may be that further understanding of all the features involved will enable us ultimately to demonstrate and describe the individuality of each person's speech sounds.

ADDENDA

p. 84. On auditory phonetics, Mol, 30.

p. 86. On English phonetics, Gimson, 29.

p. 111. On English intonation, O'Connor and Arnold, 31; Kingdon, 35; Schubiger, 36.

p. 112. On Norwegian phonetics, Popperwell, 32.

p. 115. On what have been called paralinguistic features of speech, Crystal and Quirk, 33.

p. 106. Further on acoustic phonetics, Flanagan, 34.

4

Phonology

4·1 SPEECH AND WRITING

The two media or substances used by natural languages as vehicles for communication are air disturbed by the movements of articulation and marks made on a flat surface by chisel, writing brush, pen, pencil, etc. These two modes of linguistic communication, speech and writing, virtually exhaust the field, as one may, particularly in an elementary account, leave aside such specialized and restricted systems as the gestural communications of the deaf and dumb, and such other secondary systems as semaphore, heliograph, and the like.

The familiar languages of Europe, but not all their dialects, and the languages of the major areas of civilization in the world are both written and spoken; that is to say a system of writing and a system of speaking are recognizable and recognized as 'the same language'. Many languages are spoken languages only, and the spread of literacy does not necessarily bring them all within its compass; spoken languages of relatively small communities, living within a larger political or cultural group, are often bypassed as the speakers are taught to be literate in a more widely used language of the area as a 'second' language or one acquired in the course of education and not in infancy (as is also the case with many speakers of non-standard dialects of written languages). This situation is found among the American Indians of North America (literate in English), the American Indians of Central and South America (becoming literate in Spanish or Portuguese), many of the inhabitants of parts of Africa (literate in English, Swahili, or some widely used language), and the people of several other parts of the world.

Some languages are known at the present time only in their written forms, the so-called dead languages, though one can make estimates with varying degrees of confidence and exactitude as to their once spoken forms. Ancient Greek and Hittite are well-known examples of such languages. Latin is virtually a dead language, though in a specialized development it is used as a spoken medium, always a second language, in services in the Roman Catholic Church and more widely in certain religious communities.

As in spoken languages, one recognizes various different styles, usually merging into one another through intermediate styles. Some written styles are virtually unintelligible if read aloud or if used as a spoken medium, for example the formal language of legal contracts and legislative enactments. But ordinarily the written words and sentences of a language represent in one way or another its spoken forms, and a spoken sentence in a literate language can be written down, and a written sentence can be read aloud. The relationship between these two forms of language is not uniform, and several different systems of representing speech by writing (which one can always regard as temporally subsequent to spoken language) are found, with varying degrees of phonetic accuracy, that is the direct indication, without the reader necessarily knowing the word represented, of the sounds of the corresponding spoken form.

Chinese is the best-known example of a language wherein the written symbols are graphic representations of individual lexical and grammatical items as wholes. There are in consequence several thousand such individually different written symbols, or **characters**, as they are often called, often thought of as directly representing ideas and hence also called ideograms, but more sensibly treated as the representations of spoken forms, in many cases words, but more strictly morphemes (5·4). Though the representation is directly of the word or of its grammatical components (morphemes) bypassing its phonetic composition, an indication is given in many Chinese characters of something of the sounds by a part of the character, called for this reason 'the phonetic'. The invariable nature of Chinese words, whether containing one or more than one morpheme, makes such a writing system more usable than in a language with considerable word form variation (5·3·1, pp. 196–7).

Most writing systems use written shapes to represent in some way the phonetic composition of spoken forms directly, thus avoiding the need for as many different written symbols as there are lexically different items in the language. These systems recognize the phonetic segments referred to in the preceding chapter as consonants and vowels, and represent them by written signs as they appear in the spoken forms, usually isolated spoken forms, forms spoken alone and not as parts of larger sentences (4·2, p. 126).

Some orthographic or writing systems use a single written sign to indicate a consonant, and sometimes two consonants, followed by a vowel, with other special signs to mark consonants not followed by a vowel. Such systems are called **syllabaries**, and there is reason to regard them historically as intermediate between the character type of writing still used in Chinese and attested in parts of the Middle East and elsewhere, and the alphabetic systems widely used all over the world today. The main writing systems of several of the languages of India are syllabaries, as is the orthography of Javanese. The recently deciphered Mycenaean script (the earliest written records of Greek) is largely syllabic, with some character-like symbols as well. The ancient Semitic writing system used by the Phoenicians and the Hebrews was of the syllabary type; modern Hebrew writing is a development of this, and so is the Arabic script as used in the Middle East today. But in these languages it is the consonant articulations of the spoken forms that are in the main indicated by the syllabary symbols, the different vowels being indicated by dots or other marks separate from the symbol itself and not always put in where the consonantal outline in its context is considered clear enough without them.

This sort of development of syllabary writing seems half way to the **alphabet** or letter systems of Europe and elsewhere, in which consonant and vowels articulations are separately marked by individual letters. Indeed, our alphabet (the Roman alphabet) and other alphabets, such as the Cyrillic, used for Russian and some other East European languages, are derived historically via the Greek alphabet (still used in Greece). This was an adaptation, subsequent to and separate from the Mycenaean syllabary, of the symbols of the Phoenician syllabary, to represent individually by separate symbols the consonants and vowels of the Greek language. Alphabetic writing, which has now spread all over the world, and is being developed

123

either at the expense of syllabary writing, as in Java, or alongside it as a second system of writing, is just one of the many debts that civilization owes to the peculiar genius of Ancient Greece.

Not all orthographic systems are anything like pure examples of the above mentioned types. Mixed writing systems are found. To a very limited extent written English makes use of characters not unlike those of Chinese in principle in employing the numeral signs *1, 2, 3*, etc. and the ampersand (&). More typical of such a mixture is written Japanese. The Japanese learned writing along with a good deal else from long cultural contact with the Chinese, and took over the Chinese system of characters; but, unlike Chinese, Japanese is a language with a high proportion of variable words, or groups of word forms sharing a common part or root, rather like English word series such as *walk, walks, walking, walked*. In dealing with this situation, Japanese writing today employs a set of characters substantially the same as those in use in Chinese (from which they were acquired) together with a syllabary script formed by the use of fragmentary parts of certain characters; broadly speaking invariable words and the root parts of variable words are represented by the character and the affixes are indicated by the signs of the syllabary (called *kana*, borrowed names).

Alphabetic systems may vary considerably as regards the closeness they bear to the phonetic composition of the forms they represent, or, put another way, in the degree to which they mark the actual pronunciations. English is well known as a language wherein spelling and pronunciation may be far apart; the same sound sequences may be spelled in several different ways and the same series of letters may represent several different sound sequences (3·3·2). In so far as alphabetic spellings are ambiguous phonetically, and the pronunciation of the words must be known by knowledge of the spelt form of the word as a whole, the groups of letters function in part rather like a Chinese or other character. Other languages, for example Italian, have a far closer correspondence of spelling and pronunciation; French and some other languages stand in a peculiar position, in that the pronunciation is usually (not always) inferable from the spelling, but the spelling system employs a remarkably high proportion of 'silent letters' or differently spelt variants of the same sound sequence (*donne, donnes, donnent* /dɔn/; *à, a* /a/; *cas* /ka/, *chat* /ʃa/;

thé, nez, aller, quai, et, all end in /-e/, etc.). Languages like English, wherein spelling and pronunciation frequently disagree, receive the constant attention of spelling reformers. The anomalies of English spelling, however, are not wholly a nuisance; orthographic *-s* as the sign of the plural in *dogs, cats,* and *horses,* though it indicates three different pronunciations /-z/, /-s/, and /-iz/ which a more 'accurate' spelling might represent differently with separate letters, does give a single sign for a single grammatical element, and this may be a definite advantage.

However, in the course of centuries, orthographies are bound to become out of line with pronunciations in some words, as spoken forms change (8·1) while spellings tend to be conservative especially since the invention of printing, though in Norway and Holland, for example, official spelling reforms have been made. English *fine, line,* and *mine* (for minerals), and some other words were once pronounced with a final sound sequence more like that of *machine,* having been taken from French (in which the /i:/ vowel has persisted, *fine* /fi:n/, *ligne* /li:ɲ/, *mine* /mi:n/); but in English at a later date the /-i:n/ changed to /-ain/, so that *-ine* now represented this pronunciation; but the change had come to an end by the time the French word *machine* was introduced. In the normal course of the development of a language the creation of such disharmonies between orthography and pronunciation is inevitable unless the spellings of words are constantly adjusted to pronunciation changes.

4·2 NARROW AND BROAD TRANSCRIPTION: PHONETICS AND PHONOLOGY

During the nineteenth century and after, when phonetics was rapidly advancing as the scientific study and accurate analysis of the speech sounds used in languages, the representational inadequacies of orthographies became more and more apparent and more and more a nuisance, not to be overcome by any tinkerings in the way of spelling reforms. In two respects all orthographies are deficient in representing the spoken sounds of utterances, though they are satisfactory for their purpose of recording spoken utterances and forms as wholes for ordinary purposes. Firstly, they are usually inadequate in marking the different forms words take in continuous discourse as compared

125

with isolated utterance. To some extent English spellings like *'ll*, *'d*, *'s* (*I'll do it, he'd be there, he's all right*) help to fill the gap, but the normal pronunciation of *the*, /ðə/ or /ði/ as against the isolate pronunciation /ði:/, and the common variants of *for*, /fə/ as against isolate /fɔ:/, and *to*, /tə/ and /tu/ as against isolate /tu:/, etc., are hardly indicated at all, and, far worse, when they are written *fer* and *ter*, etc., this is done as a supposed mark of uneducated speech, whereas it is in fact a normal and indeed essential part of any dialect or style of English. Secondly, sound features such as stress and pitch, noticed in the preceding chapter, which are equally a part of uttered sentences and essential to correct pronunciation, are often entirely unrepresented.

The International Phonetic Alphabet was devised and is progressively modified to provide a precise and universal means (i.e. valid for all languages) of writing down the spoken forms of utterances as they are spoken without reference to their orthographic representation, grammatical status, or meaning. This is an essential part of phonetic analysis and of the phonetic study of the sounds of languages; but the increasingly accurate '**narrow**' transcriptions that are produced in this way led to the realization of their inherent inadequacy as a means of systematically and unambiguously representing the pronunciation of the spoken forms of a particular language for the purpose of reading. It is at once apparent that anything like a phonetically accurate narrow transcription (an unattainable though approachable ideal, since one cannot assume that any two utterances of 'the same sound', i.e. intended repetitions, are in fact precisely and demonstrably the same, and as between any two speakers they are often demonstrably not the same) is far too unwieldy to serve just as an unambiguous representation of what is pronounced; what it is is a detailed symbolization of each successive sound segment and sound feature.

It was discovered that transcriptional systems of far fewer symbols and diacritical signs (signs of the type appearing at the bottom of the I.P.A. chart) could be devised for each language separately, to serve the purpose of unambiguous representation of the pronounced forms. These are known as **broad** transcriptions, and there is clearly a minimal number of distinct symbols required for the unambiguous indication of the pronunciations, as opposed to the potentially infinite number needed to symbolize separately each difference of actual sound. Two facts stand out as a result of distinguishing these two types of transcription. Firstly, many of the differences between sounds in a language may be shown to be conditioned by the phonetic environment of each sound, i.e. the other sounds or strictly speaking the articulations, near it in the uttered form, and therefore do not need separate symbolization in a transcription devised for the language in question. Secondly, this conditioning differs from language to language; and consequently, whereas a narrow transcription can be indifferently used of the material of any language, or indeed of a series of speech sounds made up for the purpose and belonging to no language, such as are used in phonetic training in pronunciation and recognition (ear training), a broad transcription must be separately worked out for each language, and often each dialect, under analysis.

The study of the phonetic composition of utterances in the light of these considerations led to a realization that different languages both make use of different selections from the articulatory possibilities of the human vocal tract, and may be shown to organize these selections differently in systems of contrasting sounds and combinatory possibilities in utterance. As a result, two separate ways of studying speech sounds are recognized in linguistics: phonetics, the study and analysis of the sounds of languages, in respect of their articulation, transmission, and perception without reference to any particular language or to their function therein, and phonology, the study and analysis of the exploitation of different ranges of speech sounds by different languages and of the systems of contrasting sound features (phonological systems) maintained by languages.

Phonetics and phonology are both concerned with the same subject-matter or aspect of language, speech sounds as the audible result of articulation, but they are concerned with them from different points of view. Phonetics is general (that is, concerned with speech sounds as such without reference to their function in a particular language), descriptive, and classificatory; phonology is particular (having a particular language or languages in view) and functional (concerned with the working or functioning of speech sounds in a language or languages). Phonology has in fact been called functional phonetics. General accounts of phonology and phonological theory, such as are to be given in outline in this chapter and are set out in detail in books devoted specifically to this part of linguistics, are general only in the sense that they deal with the functioning of speech sounds in the phonological systems of various languages, with the analysis of such systems, and with the phonological possibilities of languages; phonology always has in view a language as a communication system in its theory and procedures of analysis.

It will be seen from this summary statement of the province of phonology that it goes considerably beyond the question of workable broad transcriptions; but such a transcription, as opposed to a narrow, purely phonetic, transcription, presupposes some phonological analysis, as does an adequate alphabet, even though it is implicit and unrealized; and it is a fact that while the phonological analysis of a language and the working out of a broad transcription for it are different, though related, matters, the development of phonological theory and of the procedures of phonological analysis has been largely conditioned by transcriptional requirements. This must be borne in mind in the understanding and evaluation of the approaches by different linguists to this part of their subject.

4·3   THE PHONEME THEORY

4·3·1   *The phonemic principle*

The theory of phonology that evolved over the years as the result of the search for adequate and efficient broad transcriptions centred round the phoneme concept, and today the great majority of linguists base their phonological analysis and derive their principles of phonology from the theory of the phoneme. The theory has in the course of its evolution taken a number of rather different forms, and has been carried to greater extremes by some scholars than by others. A great deal of ink has been spilled on controversies within and about the phoneme theory which it is neither necessary nor profitable to follow through in an elementary treatment of the subject. The essentials of the theory and the analytic methods that are based on it can be presented relatively simply in outline.

In terms of the phoneme theory and by means of phonemic analysis languages can be shown to organize the selection they make of the available sound differences in human speech into a limited number of recurrent distinctive units. These are called **phonemes**, and it is found that their number in any language is relatively small, as compared with the great and potentially unlimited number of actually different sounds uttered by speakers. The numbers of phonemes in any language differ both from one language to another and according to the way in which the linguist analyses his material, but upper and lower limits of around fifty and fifteen have been calculated, the most frequent count being around thirty. Moreover the same phonemic system is found to be valid for large numbers of speakers of the same language or dialect, despite their obvious differences of individual speech. Phonemic analysis and the theory behind it were first worked out in regard to the segmental consonant and vowel elements of languages, and the basic principles can well be illustrated in these terms.

4·3·2 *Segmental phonemes*

The linguistically essential property of a sound segment or feature in an utterance or in any fraction of an utterance is that it should be distinct or differentiatable. De Saussure, indeed, went so far as to say that the differences were all that mattered in languages, the means by which the differences were maintained being irrelevant. To differ distinctively, two sounds must be able to occur in the same position and in the same environment as far as other distinctive sound units are concerned. Where two phonetically different sounds are restricted to different positions in relation to other sounds, their differences are accounted for and cancelled out by their environment or distribution, and in these terms serve no distinctive purpose (this is not the same as saying that their differences are phonologically irrelevant). They need not, therefore, be represented by more than one symbol in a broad transcription, as the different sound involved will be clearly indicated in each case by the copresence of the other symbols, to anyone knowing the phonological system of the language on which the broad transcription is based.

The two notions of phonemic distinctiveness and phonetic difference may be illustrated from English. English /p/, /t/, and /k/, when pronounced in initial position are aspirated ([pʰ], [tʰ], [kʰ]), as in *ten* /ten/ ([tʰen]). But immediately following initial /s/ in a consonant cluster they are without aspiration, as in *steam* /stiːm/, [stiːm]. Such

129

a difference is not necessarily noticed by a native speaker of standard English, but a little attention and phonetic training make these differences readily apparent. As aspirated [tʰ] and unaspirated [t] cannot replace one another in the same environment in English, they cannot contrast or distinguish one utterance from another. One therefore groups these two sounds, phonetically different as they are, into one phonologically distinctive unit, or phoneme, symbolized by /t/, whose phonetic implications are determined by its phonological environment in an utterance, as represented in terms of other phonemes established in the same way. The phoneme /t/, therefore, consists of several phonetically different sounds, or 'members', and may be regarded logically as a class. Likewise the phonemes /p/ and /k/ consist of different sounds similarly distributed in their environments, compare the [pʰ] and [p] of *pan* and *span*, and the [kʰ] and [k] of *can* and *scan*). Sounds are grouped into a single class or phoneme if they can be shown to be phonetically similar (containing some sort of articulatory feature in common) and in complementary distribution (not occurring in the same environment and so not distinctive). The condition of phonetic similarity keeps [t] and [tʰ], [p] and [pʰ] in the same phonemes respectively, as against the equally non-contrastive [t] and [pʰ], [p] and [tʰ].

The condition of complementary distribution is supplemented by that of free variation; where two phonetically different sounds may occur in the same environment but are always interchangeable therein in all utterances, they are equally non-distinctive, and are grouped into the same class or phoneme. As the pronunciation of either variant is indifferent a broad transcription need only represent the phoneme by one symbol. English utterance final /p/, /t/, and /k/ illustrate this; they may be exploded (audibly released) or released without sound (i.e. outward air pressure has ceased during the maintenance of the closure). In utterance final position, either sort of stop consonant can occur without any distinction being made thereby. In some languages this is not the case; in Thai (Siamese) and Vietnamese, voiceless final stop consonants are never audibly released and there is no free variation of the English type in this position.

All the segmental sounds used in each language can be classed into a limited number of phonemes, and conversely the consonant and vowel phonemes exhaustively cover all the consonant and vowel sounds so occurring. All consonant and vowel contrasts between distinct forms in a language can be referred to one or other of its component phonemes. Thus English *man* /mæn/, containing three phonemes, may contrast at three points or places wherein a distinctively different sound unit may be substituted: *man, pan* (/pæn/); *man, men* (/men/); *man, mad* (/mæd/). In establishing the phonemes of a language 'minimal pairs', or pairs of words differing by one phoneme only like the above examples, are a convenience, if they can be found; but they are not essential to the analysis or to its justification. The essence of phonemic distinctiveness lies in phonetic differences between two or more sounds that are neither in free variation nor wholly determined by their environments. The phoneme has been defined as 'a class of phonetically similar sounds, contrasting and mutually exclusive with all similar classes in the language'.

Phonemic analysis consists in allotting all the indefinite number of sounds occurring in the utterances of a language to a definite and limited set of phonemes contrastive in at least some environments; and a phonemic transcription or broad transcription at its simplest consists in the use of one letter or symbol and one only for each phoneme. Manifestly, while there is a minimal number of symbols required for a broad transcription, transcriptions of different degrees of narrowness can be made employing more or fewer separate signs for actual phonetic differences among variant members of phonemes.

Members of phonemes are often called **phones** or **allophones**, and it is common practice to write phone symbols between square brackets and phoneme symbols or the symbols of a broad transcription between oblique brackets. Thus in English, [t] and [tʰ] are allophones of the /t/ phoneme. The use of oblique brackets in this book is explained on page xxi, Transcriptions.

Apart from the criterion of phonetic similarity, which is usually maintained in the phonemic analysis of languages, the ways in which sounds are distributed and contrast with one another may vary very considerably from one language to another. The degree of phonetic difference required to maintain a distinction is a matter for the language system and not merely the phonetic nature of the sounds themselves, provided there is some perceptible difference. [t] and [tʰ], non-contrastive in English, are contrastive, and so belong to different phonemes, in several varieties of Chinese and in a number of Indian languages (in North Chinese /tan/ and /tʰan/ are both found as distinct parts of utterances, alike in all other respects including the range of possible tones (3·5·4, 4·3·5), and in Hindi /t/ and /tʰ/ are in contrast in the distinctive pair /sat/ seven and /satʰ/ with).

Other examples of allophonic differences and phonemic groupings in English are:

1. 'Clear' and 'dark' /l/ (respectively with the front of the tongue raised toward the hard palate and the back of the tongue raised toward the soft palate) in prevocalic and postvocalic position, as in *Lil* /lil/, or in *lip* /lip/ as contrasted with *pill* /pil/. This distinction is phonemic in some dialects of Polish, in which 'clear' and 'dark' /l/ can occur in the same phonological environment and so be contrastive.

2. Fricative and flapped /r/ are in free variation intervocalically in words like *very* /veri/, *merry* /ˈmeri/, and *marry* /ˈmæri/, in many varieties of standard English: an alveolar fricative [ɹ] or an alveolar flapped [ɾ] may be uttered indifferently; the two sounds are treated as members of the same /r/ phoneme, freely variant in this environment.

3. Three slightly different qualities of the vowel /ə/ are heard in many speakers, a lower central vowel in utterance final position as in *china* /ˈtʃainə/, and *colour* /ˈkʌlə/, a higher and rather back vowel when the /ə/ in non-final position adjoins a /k/ or a /g/, in *again* /əˈgein/, and a vowel somewhat between the two in other environments, as in *along* /əˈlɔŋ/, *salad* /ˈsæləd/.

In general, all English vowels are pronounced with slightly shorter duration before final voiceless consonants than before final voiced consonants, without obscuring the relatively greater length of the distinctively long vowels (e.g. *hit* /hit/, *hid* /hid/, and *heat* /hi:t/, *heed* /hi:d/).

Many of the allophonic differences in the members of phonemes in languages may be accounted for by the fact that speech is a continuous process and that the segments that form the basis of the consonant and vowel phonemes are more or less artificially abstracted from the stream of speech. Necessarily the position of the organs in one segment will affect the articulation of the following segment, as will the movement towards the position of a subsequent segment; indeed, the conditioned variants juxtaposed to a segment frequently assist the recognition of its distinctive qualities, and while in phonemic analysis environmentally conditioned features are as such non-distinctive, they cannot be dismissed as phonologically irrelevant or neglected in language learning.

This conditioning of allophonic differences is clearly illustrated in English by the different varieties of the /k/ and /g/ phonemes found according to the nature of the following, or in final position the preceding, vowel. A slightly different position of contact between the back of the tongue and the soft palate may be observed for each different adjacent vowel phoneme, but three varieties illustrate this variation best: with /iː/ a very front contact point is used, as in *keep* /kiːp/ and *peak* /piːk/; with /ʌ/, as in *cup* /kʌp/, and *muck* /mʌk/, a middle contact point is used; with /uː/ a back contact point is used, as in *coop* /kuːp/, and *flook* /fluːk/. These differences can be made clear by preparing to say *keep* and from that point of closure uttering *coop*, or vice versa, when a noticeably unnatural pronunciation results.

It will have been noticed that so far the terms *contrast* and *distinctive* have been used in the description of the phoneme and of phonemic analysis, and in the preceding chapter, without further comment. Many linguists are prepared to accept these terms as primitives, i.e. as requiring no further definition within linguistics; but others have sought to define the terms. Generally the distinctiveness or contrast between phonemes has been taken as their ability to differentiate one form from another; thus /p/ and /b/ are distinctive in English because words like *pan* /pæn/, and *ban* /bæn/, are different words with different meanings. The phrase *ability to differentiate* is important in this context, as some pairs of phonemes, generally distinguishing forms with different meanings, are in a few words used interchangeably; thus *difficult* may be pronounced with /i/ or /ə/ (/ˈdifikəlt/ or /ˈdifəkəlt/), and *economic* may be pronounced indifferently /iːkəˈnɔmik/ or /ekəˈnɔmik/; but /i/ and /ə/, and /iː/ and /ə/ are minimally distinctive elsewhere (e.g. *city* /ˈsiti/, *sitter* /ˈsitə/; *eel* /iːl/, *ell* /el/). An alternative explanation of *distinctive* or *contrasting* has been made in terms of the 'pairs test', in which it is asserted that a native speaker can consistently tell apart members of pairs of utterances differing by one phoneme, but not when they differ solely by one of two allophones in free variation in a certain position. Both of these accounts of the terms, it will be seen, involve an appeal to a native speaker's necessary, though unconscious, awareness of how his language works, and what units are functionally distinctive in providing for a sufficient lexical stock. Considerable discussion on the theoretical basis and necessary presuppositions of phonemic analysis has taken place, but what has been said above may be sufficient in an introduction to the subject.

4·3·3 *Phonemic analysis of length and stress*

The difference between long and short vowels has been mentioned in the preceding chapter (3·3·3). Not all languages make use of this sort of difference (often referred to as quantity) as phonemically distinctive. It is, of course, always possible to vary the length of any articulatory segment, but in some languages this is a matter of style or even of random variation, and not part of the distinctive apparatus of the phonological system. The phonemic analysis of the distinctively long vowels of English has been subjected to different analyses, and it is instructive to compare some of these as an illustration of how different and equally valid analyses of the same material may produce different phonemic systems and different numbers of phonemes. This is simply an illustration of the general situation obtaining in the descriptive analysis of languages and of the view adopted in this book on the status of the abstractions involved (2·1·1), namely that at any level the same body of data may be liable to a number of different analyses, depending on the criteria employed and on the relative weight given to them. Each analysis is justifiable in the terms in which it is worked out; though sometimes one will be preferable to the others, or preferable for certain purposes (e.g. highlighting particular features of a language), often there is little to choose between them, each having some advantages and some disadvantages as a means of explaining the phenomena involved.

One analysis of the British English long vowels simply treats and transcribes them as separate vowel phonemes, with the differences of relative length just one of the features distinguishing them from other vowels; this treatment may be reinforced by the use of special symbols and no length mark (e.g. /i/ = /i:/, /ɪ/ = /i/, /u/ = /u:/, /ɷ/ = /u/, /ɔ/ = /ɔ:/, /ɒ/ = /ɔ/, /ɜ/ = /ɜ:/, /ə/ = /ə/, /a/ = /ɑ:/). Another treats the long vowels as sequences of two corresponding short vowels, with the differences of quality accounted for as allophonically conditioned by the environments of the two vowels concerned (the first vowel of each pair being part of the environment of the second, and vice versa (/i:/ = /ii/, etc.). A third treatment, substantially that followed by Jones,[1] is to treat length as having phonemic status itself as a length phoneme (or chroneme, in his usage), symbolized by /:/, so that /i:/ and /i/ both represent the /i/ phoneme, with and without length, respectively. Any of these analyses is legitimate, and they may be weighed against one another according to the results achieved. The first makes use of more phonemes and therefore of more transcriptional symbols than the second or third, and obscures a definite phonetic relationship between several pairs of vowels in English; but it does serve to emphasize that differences of quality, and not simply of relative duration, help to distinguish the long and short vowels of English; the second employs fewer phonemes, but perhaps obscures the qualitative differences between the members of long and short vowel pairs; the third is nearly as economical in phonemic inventory, marks the length correlation without suggesting that a long vowel is the equivalent to two short vowels, which phonetically it is not, and is, generally speaking, the system most used as a phonemic analysis of the British English vowels and as the basis for a broad (phonemic) transcription of the language.

In English, as in some other languages, vowel and consonant articulations and vowel length are not the only phonetic differences employed to produce lexically distinct forms. Stress in the second sense referred to above (3·5·3), or relatively greater force of articulation on one part of a word form, is an essential part of the correct pronunciation of English words of more than two vowels or consonant-vowel sequences, and its position cannot be predicted or explained by reference to other phonetic factors. Distinctions of stress must therefore be included in the inventory of the English phonological system, and in a few word pairs, as was seen above, difference of stress placement alone may differentiate lexically distinct forms. Linguists have differed as to the number of distinctive degrees of stress required for the analysis of the potentially infinite

1. Jones's transcription, employing the two symbols /æ/ and /ɑ:/ is, phonemically, redundant at this point.

number of actually different degrees of phonetic stressing. Jones operates with one degree of stress (rarely with two) contrasting with the absence of stress (there can, of course, be no absence of all force in an audible sound; phonologically unstressed segments are uttered with varying amounts of phonetic stressing always contrastively less than those of stressed segments).

Most linguists regard the function of stress in languages like English as justifying phoneme status for the distinctive degrees recognized, and stress phonemes are usually set up for English phonology. Jones, however, does not make use of the term *phoneme* with regard to stress distinctions. Several American linguists have set up three degrees of stress as well as absence of stress as four phonemically distinctive elements, symbolized by /´/, /ˆ/, /`/, and /˘/ or by the absence of a mark, and illustrated in the compound word *elevator-operator* /élĭvèitŏrŏpŏrèitŏ/. The phonetic phenomena of stress are very similar between British and American English, and the difference in the number of distinctive degrees of stress recognized by Jones and by American linguists is partly accounted for by their different attitude towards the phonological relevance of word boundaries and the boundaries between the elements of compound words (4·3·6).

In addition to the phonemic degrees of stress already mentioned some linguists recognize a phoneme of extra-loud contrastive or emphatic stress, symbolized /″/, on a particular word or part of a word, as in *that's mine (not yours)* /ðæts″ main/. This phoneme, which relates to the first use of stress described in 3·5·3, is of a rather special nature in that it includes not only a contrast with normal unemphatic pronunciation, but also the possibility of an infinitely gradable scale of extra-loudness (within the limits of articulatory possibilities) correlated with a similarly gradable scale of emphasis or the like, meant and understood. For this reason some linguists do not recognize this as a phoneme in its own right. Much the same sort of effect can, of course, be achieved in languages making use of stress contrasts in normal diction, by putting full stress on a different word or different part of a word from that whereon it would otherwise fall (e.g. *uncommon* (ʌnˈkɔmən/, but *uncommon (not common)* /ˈʌnkɔmən/).

Phonemes of stress and length, when abstracted as phonemes in their own right, are often classed among what are called the supra-

segmental phonemes, to distinguish them from the segmental consonant and vowel phonemes, as the suprasegmental phonemes do
not relate to phonetic segments so much as to phonetic features
concomitant with and characterizing a whole segment or succession
of adjacent segments.

4·3·4 *The syllable*

Word is a term primarily of grammatical significance, though in
many languages it may be phonologically delimited as well (5·3·2).
The principal purely phonological term for a group of consonants
and vowels with the status of a unit is *syllable*. This term, familiar
enough in general usage, has not been employed as a technical term
so far in the main text of this book. It is, in fact, used technically in
at least two ways, as a phonetic unit and as a phonological unit.
Phonetically the term *syllable* has frequently been used to refer to a
sequence of speech sounds having a maximum or peak of inherent
sonority (that is apart from factors such as stress and voice pitch)
between two minima of sonority. Generally speaking, vowels are
more sonorous than consonants, and continuant consonants than
stop consonants; to a large extent, though not wholly, sonority varies
with the degree of openness of the vocal tract, and this has led some
to delimit phonetic syllables by such features as the degrees of 'stricture' or obstruction of the air passage in articulation. In each case
the results are similar.

However, the term is more widely used in general linguistics as
part of the phonological level of analysis, and the **syllable** is defined
as a unit for each language separately. In this usage *syllable* refers to
a number of different sequences of consonants and vowels, together
with other features such as length and stress, or to single consonants
or vowels, which in the language concerned are suitably considered
as a unitary group for further analysis. The linguist decides by
criteria that may include purely phonetic factors what sequences
comprise the syllables of the language he is describing in the course
of devising a full phonological analysis thereof; and it is normally
found that there is a considerable correspondence between syllables
established on purely phonetic criteria of stricture or sonority and
those established for the purpose of further phonological description.

137

It is frequently the case that the syllable may be defined phonologically as the unit that can bear a single degree of stress, as in English, or a single tone, as in many tone languages (3·5·4, 4·3·5). Words may be classified as monosyllabic, disyllabic, trisyllabic, etc., according to the number of syllables they contain. Phonetically it is often hard to decide to which syllable an intervocalic consonant belongs, as the minimum of sonority and the maximum of stricture may occur in the middle of its articulation, and such consonants may have to be described phonetically as ambisyllabic, belonging to both. But when a decision is taken phonologically to allot the consonant to a particular syllable, in general single intervocalic consonants within a word are assigned to the following vowel (V-CV, not VC-V). This is done principally on the distributional grounds that CV is in all languages a commoner sequence than VC, and indeed in some languages VC sequences are very much restricted and found only with certain consonants; moreover in a word stressed on a non-initial syllable, in stress-marked languages, the stressed articulation usually begins on the consonant in such sequences. In the case of intervocalic sequences of consonants the phonetic criteria of sonority and stricture may be referred to for a decision, but sometimes stress is observed to begin on an inherently less sonorous consonant and the syllable division is, accordingly, made before that consonant. Thus in English words like *astray* and *mistake*, the stress often begins on the /s/, and despite the sequence /st/ being fricative followed by stop, the syllable division is made /ə-ˈstrei/ and /mi-ˈsteik/. Sometimes phonetic features characteristic of a final consonant may assign an intervocalic consonant to the preceding syllable, especially in fairly loosely compounded words like *book-end* /ˈbuk-end/, and this is a common practice in English across word boundaries, as in the contrasting sequences such as *an aim* and *a name*, /ən-ˈeim/ and /ə-ˈneim/. In this respect English is in marked contrast to French, wherein word final consonants are generally syllabified with the initial vowels of words following without pause, irrespective of the boundaries. Some English words classed phonologically as monosyllables could by strictly phonetic criteria be regarded as disyllabic, as, for example, *strain* /strein/, but the stress always begins on the /s/.

In English and in the majority of languages phonological syllables (the term *syllable* will henceforth be used in this sense unless it is stated otherwise) consist of one or more consonants and a vowel. But a single vowel can constitute a syllable, as in *ah* /aː/, and a syllable division can be established between two vowels as in *seeing* /ˈsiːiŋ/, where one observes a fall in sonority in the transition between the two vowels. Conversely a syllable may contain no vowel, as is the case in English with syllables ending in /n/, /m/, and /l/, in words like *cotton* /ˈkɔ-tn/, and *apple* /ˈæ-pl/. In quick speech a syllable consisting of a single consonant may be found in utterances like *'s terrible*, *'s true*, /s-ˈterribl/, /s-ˈtruː/, in which the longer duration of the [s] sound, the onset of stress, and the aspirated [tʰ] establish /t/ as initial consonant of the second syllable. In Japanese /ŋ/ occurring after a vowel, or in initial position, constitutes a separate syllable, as in /saŋ/, *three*; this is established on the grounds of its having its own pitch possibilities as well as on its greater relative duration than non-syllabic consonants.

A phonological analysis, based on the identification of the phonemes to be set up in a language, must take into account not merely the paradigmatic dimension of contrast but also the syntagmatic dimension of the permitted phoneme sequences in the lexical forms of a language (cp. 2·1·2). Phonologically the syllable is of prime importance as a unit within which the relative distributions or possibilities of sequential occurrence of phonemes and phonological features can be stated. Languages differ very much in the types of syllable structures they exhibit and the places they occupy in words. While CV is a universal structure, beyond that each language has its own rules. Some languages, like Arabic, do not allow any syllable not beginning with a consonant; others, like Fijian, do not permit any syllable ending with a consonant. Italian allows no word-final syllables ending in CC sequences, and not many ending in a single consonant compared to some other languages. English and German allow a good deal of consonantal clustering both initially and finally, exemplified in such words as *strengths* /streŋθs/ and *sprichst* /ʃpriçst/ you (singular) speak, both very difficult to pronounce for speakers of languages not permitting such clustering. It seems to be a general observation that types of consonant clustering in syllable initial and syllable final position are often comparable, though several sequences may be found in one position that are not permitted in the other.

Languages thus differ both in the selection they make from the available articulations of the vocal apparatus and in the positional arrangements or syllabic groupings that they impose on them; and the principal difficulty in learning to pronounce foreign languages lies in overcoming these two sorts of limitation ingrained into one in learning one's native language as a child. It has been said that the greatest obstacle to learning a language is speaking one already. The mastery of foreign sounds is one obvious difficulty, but learning to pronounce sounds found in one's own language in positions from which that language excludes them presents almost equal difficulty. English /ŋ/ is confined to intervocalic and postvocalic positions (*singer* /ˈsiŋə/, *sing* /siŋ/). For an English speaker to pronounce and to recognize correctly words like Swahili /ŋgoma/ ([ŋgoma]) drum, and Sundanese /ŋaran/ name, requires training, attention, and effort, as does the pronunciation and recognition of syllable final [h], as in Malay /təŋah/ middle, a sound confined to initial and intervocalic position in English (*hand* /hænd/, *behind* /biˈhaind/).

Considerations of syllable structure often help in deciding on the best analysis of sounds and sound groups that are phonetically ambiguous. There has been some discussion on whether English /ʧ/, as in *church* /ʧə:ʧ/, is one consonant phoneme, like /t/, or two, as /tr/ and /ts/ are regarded. In favour of treating /ʧ/ as a sequence of /t/ and /ʃ/ are the economy in phoneme inventory, as /t/ and /ʃ/ are both required anyway as English phonemes, and the phonetic similarity of /ʧ/ and /ts/; but in favour of treating it as a single affricate phoneme, the usual practice, is its occurrence in syllable final position, unlike /tr/, and in syllable initial position, unlike /ts/, except in a few words of obvious foreign origin such as *tsetse* (*fly*) /ˈtsetsi/ (also often pronounced /ˈtetsi/).

So, too, considerations of syllable structure, in which the /w/ and /j/ of words like *wet* and *yet* (/wet/ and /jet/) occupy consonantal rather than vocalic places, are often decisive in classing them, as semivowels, among the consonants of language (cp. p. 102).

English diphthongs have been variously analysed, as have the diphthongs of other languages. Some, like Jones, have chosen to regard them as separate unitary phonemes, phonetically complex but otherwise like other vowel phonemes; others analyse them as sequences of two phonemes functioning in the syllable like a long vowel, and identify the starting and ending points of each diphthong with one of the phonemes already set up elsewhere in the English phoneme system. Thus the first phonemes of English /ei/, /ou/, and /ɔi/ may be regarded as /e/ and /ɔ/, with a closer allophone of /ɔ/ being used before /u/ than before /i/ or before consonants; the initial phonemes of /ai/ and /au/ are identified with /ɑ/, as allophones of the vowel phoneme otherwise found with length as /ɑ:/. It must be remembered that the transcription in which these diphthongs are represented in this book follows the system of Jones (Transcriptions, p. xxi) not the phonemic analysis just mentioned. The second phonemes of these diphthongs have been variously identified with the semivowel consonants /j/ and /w/ and with the vowels /i/ and /u/. There seems little to choose between the two, but the phonetic nature of the sounds themselves and the parallelism with the centring diphthongs /iə/, /ɛə/, and /uə/, where the matching of the second part with /ə/ in standard English seems obvious, may be held to argue in favour of analysing the second elements of all the English diphthongs as a vowel phoneme. English triphthongs are probably best analysed as disyllabic sequences of a diphthong followed by /ə/ (hence the stress marking in the examples on p. 98, above).

In many languages making use of stress as a distinctive feature in their phonological systems, the segmental composition of stressed and unstressed syllables differs in its range of possibilities. This can be illustrated from English, though some other languages carry the differences further. All English vowels and diphthongs, except short /ə/, can occur in stressed or unstressed syllables; but /ə/ and the consonant syllables with /l/, /m/, and /n/, can only occur in unstressed positions. The working of this distributional rule can be seen in some pairs of words similar to pairs like *export* /ˈekspɔ:t/ and /eksˈpɔ:t/, mentioned above (3·5·3): *convict* (noun) /ˈkɔnvikt/, (verb) /kənˈvikt/; *permit* (noun) /ˈpə:mit/, (verb) /pəˈmit/.

4·3·5 *Tone phonemes*

The phonetic feature of pitch variation was mentioned in the preceding chapter, where the traditional distinction between tonal and non-tonal languages was referred to (3·5·4). In phonology the tonal phenomena of tone languages were the first to be brought within the scope of the phoneme theory. This became necessary as soon as phonemic analysis was applied to such languages. In tone languages differences in pitch, or tone, as it is called, exhibit a limited set of contrastive distinctions, on one or more syllables of words, and these serve to differentiate one word from another just as segmental contrasts do, and may frequently constitute the only differentiation in 'minimal pairs' (e.g. North Chinese /tanpau/ with level and falling-rising tones, to guarantee, with falling and rising tones, diluted; Mixteco (a language of Mexico) /ʒuku/ with two mid level tones, mountain, with mid level and low tone, brush).

Tones as phonetic features present their own problems of apperception and description; as phonemes, however, the principle of their establishment is not different from that of segmental phonemes or phonemes of stress. As they may characterize more than a single segment, they are, like length and stress, often called suprasegmental phonemes. Sometimes the term *toneme* is used to refer to tone phonemes, but this is perhaps undesirable as it suggests that as phonemes they are in a class apart, which they are not, if phonemes are regarded as the units of distinctiveness of whatever sort into which linguistic forms may be analysed and by which they are distinguished by one another.

The potentially infinite variations in the actual heights of pitches and in the types of pitches (level, falling, rising, falling-rising, rising-falling, etc.) are analysed into a limited number of pitch or tone phonemes, each of which contrasts in at least some environments with at least one other such phoneme. The number varies from language to language, as do the types. In some tone languages, for example Yoruba, a language of West Africa, only level tone phonemes are found (phonetic falls and rises of pitch are analysed as successions of two different level tones each influenced allophonically by the other; thus [/]=/_ ⁻/, and [\]=/⁻ _/). Other languages require rises and falls and combinations of the two to be recognized among their distinctive tone phonemes; thus North Chinese has four tone phonemes: (high) level, rising, falling-rising, and falling. Usually the domain of one tone, or the sequence of segments with which it is associated, is a single syllable, though in a few tone languages two distinct tones are found on the same syllable in sequence; for example in Mazateco, another language of Mexico, /ti/ with low followed by high tone, bowl, but with a single high tone, it burns. In speaking of the domain of a tone as a syllable it must be borne in mind that while this includes all its consonants and vowels, the actual manifestation of tones by vibrations of the vocal cords at different speeds is only possible in the voiced segments thereof.

Distinctive differences of pitch in tone phonemes are wholly a matter of relative height. There are within the limits of the pitch possibilities of the human vocal cords no fixed points. In a system of two level tone phonemes, high and low, the high must be higher than the low in all positions where they can contrast, and a similar situation obtains with a three-term system of high, mid and low. In the speech of a single speaker at one time the tones must preserve their relative positions on the scale, but different people's voices vary in overall height, and clearly a child's low tone may be absolutely higher in pitch than the high tone of an adult speaking the same language.

In tone languages syllable structure must be stated jointly in terms of segmental and tonal phonemes, and sometimes length and stress are also involved as additional phonemic distinctions. The tones and segments are seldom, if ever, wholly independent of one another, and one finds that some tone phonemes are restricted to syllables of a certain segmental composition. Thus in Thai, syllables containing a long vowel and ending in a stop consonant are only found with two of the five tone phonemes set up for the language as a whole. In North Chinese certain unstressed syllables may be 'toneless' phonologically; that is to say the pitch on which they are said in connected discourse is wholly determined by the nature of the tone on the preceding syllable.

Phonetic features other than relative pitch height and pitch movement and belonging phonetically more to the sphere of voice quality are sometimes involved in maintaining tonal distinctions. In Vietnamese two of the six phonemically distinct tones are additionally characterized by 'creakiness' or glottalization (intermittent momentary closures and constriction of the glottis in addition to the vibrations of voicing).

The general category of tone languages conceals a number of different types. Such languages may be classified according to the number of distinct tones (e.g. North Chinese four, Thai five, Vietnamese six, Cantonese six, and in some dialects more), and according to the nature of the tones (e.g. all level, or with falls and rises, or with additional features such as glottalization). But perhaps more significant linguistically are the different functions that tone distinctions play in tone languages. They are grouped together as a class of languages by the fact that, in them all, distinctive tones are a phonological property of individual words as such. Lexical contrasts between words are the most well known function of tones, but in addition tonal differences may in some languages mark grammatical categories, grammatical relationships, and syntactic groupings (6·5·6), just like the segmental or other suprasegmental phonemes of a language, from which considered simply as part of the distinctive signalling equipment of a language they are not essentially different.

4·3·6 *Juncture phonemes*

The apparatus of phonemic analysis as described so far served the requirements of many British, European, and American linguists until fairly recently. The need for a further range of phoneme types arose from the methods of American linguists, and was partly the result of their refusal to work within a frame that had hitherto satisfied linguists in phonological analysis, and still does satisfy many.

The question was raised to what extent, if at all, should considerations at levels other than those of phonetics and phonology be admitted in carrying out phonological analysis; or, put another way, should phonemes be established and defined for a language without the aid of any criteria other than what can be derived from phonetic observation only? In several well known works on phonology in Britain and elsewhere, mostly concerned with languages having a long established writing system, terms such as *word, compound word, word group*, and the like have been used as part of the environment for assigning speech sounds to phonemes and determining distinctions of stress; that is to say, word final position and word initial position are used as part of the relevant data in phonemic analysis. In transcriptions based on such procedures, the spaces between words and the hyphens in some compound words as found in the orthography are themselves used as symbols and their significance is taken as part of the environment of the phonemes represented in the transcription, without their own status being questioned. In many languages, as in English, the boundaries of words and the junctions within compound words are often relevant to the assignment of sounds to phonemes; or, conversely, phonemes are often represented by different members or allophones in word initial and in word final positions. The distribution of English 'clear' and 'dark' /l/ is a case in point (4·3·2, p. 132). But word boundaries as such and the boundaries between the components of compound words are not heard; they are not themselves part of the articulatory or the acoustic stream of speech, in the way that consonants and vowels, and features like stress and pitch are; nor, of course, are words in speech all separated by pauses, as words in print are in many writing systems separated by spaces. Word initial and word final are not, therefore, as such, phonetically observable positions like utterance initial and utterance final are (since silence is observable), though in isolated words they coincide.

Many linguists accept the practice of assuming non-phonetic data from other levels of analysis (principally the grammatical level, 5·1·1) in arriving at and stating phonemic systems and the phonemic structure of linguistic forms, the use of non-phonetically based signs like word spaces and hyphens in phonological transcriptions, and the mixture of levels involved in such procedures. But many American linguists and some others have objected to any facts other than those derivable from what is actually heard or able to be heard in the stream of speech being used as the basis of phonemic analysis or for providing symbols, including spaces, in phonemic transcriptions. Such views have been strongly held by those who have been dealing with unwritten languages wherein no preexisting orthographic word boundaries thrust themselves on the analyst, but this theory and method of phonemic analysis has been developed and applied in working on the analysis of very well known languages, and notably of English.

Students of linguistics are likely to come across theoretical writings and actual descriptions of languages based on both procedural attitudes, and so some familiarity with the different approaches is desirable.

Linguists who admit in varying degrees what are sometimes called grammatical prerequisites in phonological analysis need not elaborate phonemic analysis further as regards grammatical inter- and intra-word divisions. But, theoretical objections apart, one of the chief difficulties is that in languages phonological and grammatical divisions usually neither consistently correspond nor consistently fail to correspond. In a case of consistent non-correspondence, perhaps approached in French, word spaces could simply be ignored in transcriptions as merely serving the purposes of ready comprehension and of no more phonological significance than the division of the text into successive lines. Pauses are, of course, phonologically relevant, but as periods of momentary or indefinite silence they are audible as breaks in speech, and the marks by which they are symbolized in transcriptions are clearly significant and based on actual phonetic observation.

Conversely, in a language, if there is one, in which a phonetic feature such as fixed place stress invariably marked every word boundary, a type to some extent represented in several languages (e.g. Hungarian word initial stress, Polish and Swahili stress on the penultimate syllable of words), the grammatical word could be shown to correspond exactly with a phonologically definable unit (the phonological or phonemic word), and the spaces marking word divisions would be no more than a symbolization of phonetically marked and phonologically relevant divisions in the audible material (though in the case of penultimate word stress the spaces would not occur at the same places as the features themselves).

Many languages exhibit partial correspondences between grammatical words and phonetically marked divisions. In English the phonetic marking of word divisions is often potential rather than actual; that is, the phonetic features that serve to mark them are such as may occur rather than such as invariably do occur. As an example most English words do not contain more than one full stress, but in connected speech many words are uttered without any syllable bearing a full stress, and a number of words (such as *the* and *a*) are very seldom stressed. Some orthographic and grammatical word divisions in English are not marked by phonetic division; words ending in *-r*, when pronounced with an /r/, link this syllabically with the initial vowel of the following word (3·3·4, p. 101), and some phrases like *not at all*, and with certain speakers *it is* and *at home* are regularly syllabified /nɔ-tə-ˈtɔ:l/, /i-ˈtiz/, and /ə-ˈtoum/, thus reversing the more usual correlation of word and syllable division in the language. Phonemic purists insist on two things in this connection:

1. Word boundaries phonetically unmarked must not be incorporated into the transcription nor used in phonemic analysis; and

2. Word boundaries that can be shown to be phonetically indicated in some way shall be replaced in the transcription and the analysis by phonemes derived directly from the phonetic features themselves.

Such phonetic features are called **junctures**, and the phonemes based on them **juncture phonemes**. While the theory of juncture analysis is by no means settled as yet, its main principles can easily be illustrated. English pairs such as *an aim* and *a name*, *an ocean* and *a notion*, *at ease* and *a tease* (cp. 4·3·4) are in many utterances audibly different, and exemplify differences that are found in many other environments across word boundaries where no minimal distinctions are involved. The phonetic differences are not hard to state; they involve different phonetic syllable division, with onset of stress and syllable initiality at the consonant in the second member of each pair, with forcible release and aspiration of the /t/ in *tease*, as against onset of stress and syllable initiality on the vowel in the first member, with weaker articulation of the syllable final consonant, somewhat prolonged and 'drawled' in the case of /n/, and inaudibly or only weakly released with little or no aspiration in the case of /t/. The second members of each pair do not ordinarily differ audibly from single words of the same segmental and stress composition (cp. *attack*, *a tack* /ə-ˈtæk/, and *at Ac(ton)* /ət-ˈæk(tən)/), and so no phoneme of juncture or phonemic symbol is posited. In the first members a phoneme of inter-word juncture, assumed as part of the phoneme inventory of the language, is said to occur in the place between the segments corresponding to the orthographic space, in order to provide for the phonetic differences. It is often symbolized /+/ or /#/, but spaces could be used equally well in the transcription if consistently and solely so used. In this method of analysis a juncture phoneme /+/ would be set up to account for the syllable division in examples such as those quoted above (4·3·4): *'s terrible* /s+ˈterribl/, *book-end* /ˈbuk+end/. In the first example /+/ would provide the environment for the greater duration of /s/ and the initiality of /t/ (hence [tʰ]), as against its non-initiality in such words as *steam* /sti:m/ (cp. pp. 129–30, above).

Two things must be noticed in connection with juncture phonemes in this type of analysis: the features on the basis of which the juncture phoneme is set up may in some cases not occur in the part of the utterance corresponding to the place at which the phoneme is located (this is so, for example, when penultimate word stress is taken as the mark or exponent of inter-word juncture); and these junctures are solely set up on the basis of phonetic differences; they are not, as such, grammatical symbols marking grammatical divisions, though in many languages, such as English, their occurrences in a great many cases parallel the inter-word spaces resulting from the separate process of analysis at the grammatical level. Word sequences in which a final /r/ is syllabified with the initial vowel of a following word (3·3·4, p. 101), and sequences like *a loan* /ə ˈloun/ and *a tack* /ə ˈtæk/, show word divisions not marked by juncture, and the pronunciation by some speakers of the name *Plato* /ˈpleitou/, with the first diphthong somewhat lengthened as if the word were '*play-toe*' has been adduced as an example of juncture occurring in the middle of a grammatically indivisible unit.

4·3·7 *Intonation*

The phonological function of pitch differences in what are called tone languages has already been dealt with (4·3·5). Students of European languages are more familiar with the function of pitch sequences as intonations, that is the property of sentences or parts of sentences as such, and not of individual lexically different words. Isolated words are, of course, said with a regular pitch pattern, but this is, in other than tone languages, an intonation applied to a one-word sentence, and any differences between one word and another will be due either to a different sentence intonation or to differences consequential on the syllable structure and in some languages on the stress patterning of the word.

Intonations or intonation **tunes**, as they are often called, are regular sequences of pitch differences coextensive with a whole sentence or with successive parts thereof, and constituting an essential feature of normal spoken utterances. As with distinctive tones in tone languages, it is the sequence of pitches of different relative heights that matters; the actual height of the pitches is determined in part by the age and sex of the speaker as well as any personal habit of speaking with a high- or a low-pitched voice.

The intonation tunes of a language may usually be associated in general, though not entirely, with particular contextual functions of speech and with various general semantic categories, such as emphasis, excitement, surprise, and the like. The two English tunes (Tune I and Tune II in Jones's terminology) associated respectively with statements and with questions expecting an answer *Yes* or *No* have already been noticed (3·5·4); questions introduced by a specific interrogative word, like, *Who have you come to see?*, are normally uttered with Tune I). These two are not the only intonations recognizable in English, but they cover a good deal of ordinary speech. Similar differences of intonation with approximate semantic correlations can be discovered in other languages, including tone languages; but in the analysis of intonation, as in the analysis of all other formal features of speech, the different elements (intonation tunes) must be established by their actual composition (rises and falls and different levels of pitch), and not by their apparent meaning correlations. These latter are never exact in their correspondences, and in the nature of things they can only be made explicit within rough limits.

Single intonation tunes in sentences differ mainly as the result of differences in the length of the stretches of speech with which they occur, and, in languages with phonologically different stress patterns, according to the occurrence of the stressed syllables. The statement tune, Tune I, in English is in outline a rise to a relatively high falling pitch followed, unless it is final in the tune, by a sequence of lower pitches. In a longer sentence other high level pitches may precede the final fall; conversely in very short sentences the intonation may start at its highest point, and in monosyllabic utterances a single falling pitch will represent the entire intonation tune. If in one sentence a sequence of more than one such intonation tune occurs (as in very long sentences, or sentences slowly enunciated), the non-final tunes generally fall less at the end than does the final tune.

In English, as in several other stress languages, stressed syllables carry more intonational weight than unstressed syllables; and, indeed, much of the prominence accorded to stressed syllables results from the fact that these syllables stand out in intonation tunes. Generally speaking, in a falling or level sequence the stressed syllables are slightly higher in pitch than the unstressed or intermediately stressed, and the final falling pitch of Tune I occurs on the last stressed syllable, any following unstressed syllables being uttered on a series of more or less low level pitches with a slight final fall. Where a 'change of direction' is involved, as when the highest point of Tune I is reached, or the lowest point in Tune II (a sequence of descending levels followed by a rise), the extreme point is always a fully stressed syllable. This may be easily noticed if the intonations are compared in the sentences *it was yesterday* and *it was today* said on Tune I, and in *was it yesterday?* and *was it today?* said on Tune II:

/it wəz ˈjestədi/   /it wəz təˈdei/

/ˈwɒz it ˈjestədi/   /ˈwɒz it təˈdei/

Intonation tunes may be modified and varied, often with the effect of emphasizing a particular word, by using an extra-high pitch standing above the rest of the sequence, or by a fall from high to low in the middle, as in such a sentence as *it's quite impossible to go any higher*:

/its kwait imˈpɒsibl tə ˈgou eni ˈhaiə/

Such a fall can only occur on a stressed syllable, which is often uttered with the additional force of emphatic stress.

So far, intonation, as opposed to tone, has not been here discussed in terms of the phoneme theory. Its treatment in relation to this differs considerably among linguists who may otherwise agree tolerably well together in their methods of phonological analysis.

Many European linguists have been content to use the phoneme concept for the phonological analysis of phonetic phenomena within accepted or established word boundaries (including the tones of tone languages), and to leave intonation, together with inter-word juncture features, outside its scope. Such, substantially, is the treatment of intonation by Jones; the sequences or tunes are classified, and sub-classified where this is appropriate, with such semantic correlations as are readily statable, and systematic modifications within the tunes (for example, contrastive intonation) are analysed both in regard to their phonetic form and their possibilities of occurrence in the tunes. This part of phonological analysis is not regarded by him as falling within the bounds of the phoneme theory.

The extension of phonemic analysis to cover phonetic features associated with inter-word boundaries has already been mentioned. The motive behind this extension of the scope of the phoneme has been the theoretical principle that all phonetic differences anywhere and of any sort in utterance that can be shown to be contrastive, or distinctive in the same phonological environment, must be assigned to an appropriate phoneme or phonemes, whose linguistic status is essentially the same as that of the first recognized segmental con-sonant and vowel phonemes, although the phonetic phenomena in-volved are of different kinds. This is the counterpart of the view already referred to, that only phonetic phenomena can be admitted as the basis for phonemic analysis.

Within these requirements two general types of procedure have been adopted in dealing with intonation. The significantly different intonation tunes themselves have been analysed as single phonemes and symbolized /,/, /!/, /?/, /./, etc. at the end of the stretches referred to. The fact that these symbols are also orthographic punctuation marks has no bearing on their function as elements in a phonemic transcription, but, of course, in written texts punctuation marks serve similar purposes, along with others, though not very efficiently. This method was used by Bloomfield, and it has been applied to tone languages wherein intonations are separately recognizable and certain differences in tones within tone phonemes are regarded as being conditioned by their intonational environment. In such lan-guages intonational tunes are found overlying, as it were, the lexically distinctive tones, and are separately abstractable by the way they determine certain variations in them, such as the height of level tones and the distance between the end points of rises and falls, sometimes

151

together with additional rises and falls at the end of final lexical tones.

More recently, however, the phonemic analysis of intonation has fallen more into line with the analysis of other suprasegmental features, and the tunes of non-tonal languages are being treated as sequences of separate pitch phonemes. The individual pitches on syllables are grouped into phonemes according to the number of distinctively different pitch levels discovered in the languages. Successive syllables not contrasting in height may be said to have a single phoneme common to them all, and rises and falls may be interpreted as sequences of two different pitch phonemes on the same syllable, or, in some cases, as allophonic variations conditioned by adjacent pitch phonemes. In English four phonemes of relative pitch height have been established in analyses. These phonemes are numbered from /1/, the lowest, to /4/, the highest, and symbolized in transcription by superscript numbers written above the syllable or the first of a group of syllables bearing the same pitch phoneme.

In this type of phonemic analysis, the juncture phonemes have been extended in number and scope to cover the regularly occurring pauses and accompanying prepausal modifications of intonation pitches, their number again depending on the number of such contrasting sets in a language. Three such terminal junctures, as they have been called, have been recognized in English, according as the last pitch phoneme before a pause maintains its level /||/, rises slightly /|||/, or falls slightly /#/. Sometimes the pause itself is scarcely noticeable, and the juncture is marked just by the maintenance or change in direction of the pitch.

The first two British English examples on p. 150, above, could be transcribed in these terms:

$$\overset{2}{/\text{it}} \text{wəz} \overset{3}{\text{'jest}}\overset{1}{\text{ə}}\text{dei} \#/ \qquad \overset{2}{/\text{it}} \text{wəz tə}\overset{31}{\text{'dei}} \#/.$$

As the result of the extension of the phoneme concept to cover all the relevant phenomena of pause, phonetically marked word division, stress on words in connected discourse, and intonation, the complete phonological analysis of a language and of utterances in it is, it is claimed, achieved in terms of phonemes and without recourse to other levels of analysis or to orthographic tradition; moreover it is asserted that the results of such an analysis can be wholly incorporated in a transcription with the use of the additional phonemic symbols just mentioned. Recent treatments of English on these lines make use, therefore, in addition to the segmental consonant and vowel phonemes, of four stress phonemes (least stress being usually unmarked in transcription), four junctures (one medial, the other three terminal or pausal), and four intonational pitch levels.

Intonation is an essential part of spoken utterance, and its recognition and analysis are an essential part of the study of language. It is regrettable that this part of phonetic and linguistic description has often lagged behind the rest. In this chapter only a brief outline of intonation has been presented; the reader should supplement this by studying a more detailed treatment of the intonation of English or of any language known to him of which a satisfactory account is available.

4·3·8 *Distinctive features: neutralization*

So far the account that has been given of phonemic analysis has been mainly concerned with the progressive extension of the concept, from the field of the consonant and vowel segments that needed separate symbols in a broad transcription, to cover all the distinctive phonetic differences in utterances, and with the corresponding development of additional transcriptional signs.

Besides this extension of the phoneme concept (which, it must be remembered has not been universally accepted), the segmental phoneme itself has been subjected to further analysis. Considered simply as the basis and justification of a separate transcriptional sign in a broad transcription, the segmental phoneme is no more than one of the contrasting phonological units of a language, into which its spoken utterances may be analysed, and its linguistic essence lies in its being, at least in some phonological environments, contrastive, or distinct from every other phoneme in the language; the way in which this distinctiveness is maintained is of secondary importance.

However, phonology has always been concerned with wider linguistic considerations than the needs of an adequate transcription, although its development in terms of the phoneme theory has throughout been in large part determined by those needs. If the

153

consonants and vowel phonemes are envisaged as the minimal distinctive units into which the sentence and word forms of a language may be analysed, their further analysis is revealing. This further analysis of the phoneme as a scientific concept rather than simply as a transcriptionally devised unit was first undertaken systematically by Trubetzkoy, the Russian linguist and leader of the Prague school of phonology between the two world wars, and is especially associated with his colleagues and those who have been most influenced by him.

It is obvious on the most cursory examination that some phonemes are phonetically more closely related than others; thus English /p/ and /b/ are much more akin than are /p/ and /ŋ/. If the phonemes of a language are compared and their members phonetically analysed, it is found that they are distinct from one another by differing in certain features of articulation, and that these same features serve in many cases to distinguish a number of other pairs of phonemes. This has appeared already in the grouping together of /i/ and /e/, /u/ and /ɔ/ as front spread and back rounded vowels respectively. In the English phonemes /p/, /b/, and /m/, /t/, /d/, and /n/, and /k/, /g/, and /ŋ/, /p/ and /b/, /t/ and /d/, and /k/ and /g/ differ from each other in the same respects, as voiceless and voiced plosives at the same point of articulation (with the other features subsumed under these labels, 3·3·4); and both phonemes in each pair differ from the corresponding nasal in being oral stop consonants as against nasal continuant consonants. Looked at the other way, the triads /p/, /b/, and /m/, /t/, /d/, and /n/, /k/, /g/, and /ŋ/ all share the same three points of articulation, bilabial, alveolar, and velar, and the corresponding phonemes in each share the same three types of articulation, voiceless stop, voiced stop, and nasal continuant. The **oppositions**, as they are called, between the nine phonemes concerned in this may be represented in the diagrams

/p/		/t/		/k/	
/b/	/m/	/d/	/n/	/g/	/ŋ/

Features that distinguish phonemes in a language in this way are called **distinctive** or **pertinent features**, and their number is always less than that of the phonemes in the language. The contrast between the presence and absence of a feature, or between two distinctive features is called an **opposition**. It will be seen that some pairs of phonemes differ by only one such opposition, others by two, and others by more than two (thus in English, /p/ and /b/ are distinguished by one, /p/ and /d/ by two, and /p/ and /z/ by three).

The nine separate phonemes of the three English triads are maintained as distinctive units by six features: plosion, voice, nasality, bilabiality, alveolarity, and velarity (orality and voicelessness being regarded as the absence of a feature, nasality and voice, respectively).

Vowel phonemes may be similarly analysed. A seven-vowel

$$/i/ \ /y/ \qquad /u/$$

$$/e/ \ /ø/ \ /o/$$

$$/a/$$

system can be analysed into the two binary oppositions front and back, and rounded and spread, together with the three distinctive degrees of openness; this latter is a feature wherein the contrast is not between two features or between a feature and its absence, but between different degrees of a feature; in the vowel system just given, closeness could equally well have been taken as the positive feature.

Two facts emerge from this sort of analysis:

1. What appears to be phonetically the same sound in two different languages may as a member of a phoneme enter into different sets of oppositions. Thus in English /b/ as a voiced bilabial plosive is opposed to /p/ and /m/ within the triad of its closest phonological neighbours; in some languages of India, for example Hindi, /b/ as a voiced unaspirated bilabial plosive enters into a contrast system with four other terms, /p/ voiceless unaspirated, /pʰ/ voiceless aspirated, /bʰ/ voiced aspirated, and /m/ nasal; and other plosive consonants enter into corresponding systems. Part of this system can be shown diagrammatically

$$/p/ \qquad /p^h/$$

$$/b/ \qquad /b^h/$$

$$/m/$$

2. Not all the oppositions of pertinent features between one phoneme and another operate in a language in all phonological environments. It has already been seen that the essence of the phoneme is
contrast or distinctiveness, in at least some environments. The
phoneme system and the phoneme inventory of a language (and so its
broad transcription requirements) are established by reference to the
environments of maximal contrast; analysis of the phoneme itself
makes clear the different contrasts obtaining in different environments. In English, in initial position /p/ and /b/, /t/ and /d/, /k/ and
/g/ all contrast; but after initial /s/ only three plosive contrasts are
possible, not six, at the three points of articulation; there is no
possibility of distinction within the syllable between voice and voicelessness in the sound segment occurring in such an environment (e.g.
spill /spil/; *still* /stil/; *skill* /skil/). The sounds are spelled with *p, t,*
and *k,* and are usually assigned to the phonemes /p/, /t/, and /k/ (as
here); but their ranges of contrast in this environment are more
restricted than in absolute initial position, where there is the additional contrast between the voiced and voiceless plosive at each
articulatory position. After initial /s/ only plosivity (*spell* /spel/;
smell /smel/) and place of articulation (*spill* /spil/; *skill* /skil/) are
functional distinctions within the syllable. This restriction of the
oppositions occurring elsewhere in a language is called **neutralization,**
and various examples of it are found in different languages. Neutralization of the distinction between two phonemes has just been
noticed; in a language like Spanish with a five-vowel phoneme
system

$$/i/ \qquad /u/$$

$$/e/ \qquad /o/$$

$$/a/$$

the distinction between the concomitant features front spread and
back rounded is neutralized in the position of maximal openness
with the single phoneme /a/. In German and Russian the contrast
between voiced and voiceless plosives is neutralized in final position,
only voiceless plosives occurring irrespective of the rest of the phonological environment. Thus while English has the contrast of *found*

and *fount* (/faund/ and /faunt/), German has only /t/ in such a position; *Bund*, bundle, and *bunt*, mottled, are both pronounced /bunt/, though they are differentiated in other case forms, *Bundes* /ˈbundes/ and *buntes* /ˈbuntes/.

The examination of facts of this kind in phonology, though it may may be irrelevant to mere transcriptional needs, leads to a fuller understanding of the different ways languages make use of their selected phonetic repertoire.

Distinctive feature analysis has developed since Trubetzkoy's time on somewhat different lines in alliance with the findings of acoustic phonetics (3·4), particularly in America. The features abstracted as distinctive components of phonemes tend to be drawn not directly from articulatory processes (though articulation is the basis of all speech sounds and their component features), but from characteristic contrasting acoustic features in the sound waves resulting from these processes. Some of the distinctions are the same as Trubetzkoy's, such as oral and nasal, consonant and vowel; but some, such as grave and acute, compact and diffuse, though referable to the different articulatory positions of the vocal organs, are primarily acoustic features, defined in acoustic terms, distinguished by the different sets of frequencies and differences in shape and structure displayed by the sound waves. It has been concluded that the consonantal and vocalic distinctions maintained in every language in the world can be reduced to combinations of members of the following twelve pairs of opposed acoustic features: vocalic, non-vocalic; consonantal, non-consonantal; interrupted, continuant; checked, unchecked; strident, mellow; voiced, unvoiced; compact, diffuse; grave, acute; sharp, plain; flat, plain; tense, lax; nasal, oral.

4·4 PROSODIC PHONOLOGY

4·4·1 *Theory of prosodic analysis*

So far this chapter has been concerned with phonological analysis based wholly or partly on the phoneme. Phonemic phonology, as has been seen, grew out of the need and search for adequate broad transcriptions; and while there has developed from it a complete theory and method of analysing and classifying phonological systems and the phonological structures of languages, the requirements of a

157

linear, readable, transcription to represent all the phonologically distinctive elements established in the analysis have always been kept to the fore. Phonological analysis and transcription have advanced together and mutually determined each other's progress.

In recent years a type of phonological theory and phonological analysis not based on the phoneme concept nor on transcriptional needs has been developed in Great Britain, and a number of phonological descriptions of parts of languages have been made in its terms. A definitive formulation of this phonological theory, which is called **prosodic** phonology, has yet to be made, but a good deal of phonological description and discussion of phonological methods has been set in prosodic terms in Britain (and to a lesser extent elsewhere), and some knowledge of its main features is desirable for students of linguistics.

Phonemic analysis concentrates on the paradigmatic relation of contrast in a given environment and on the serial treatment of the phonetic data; as far as possible all relevant phonetic features are assigned to phonemes occupying definite places in a linear succession of phonemes. This has been seen in the treatment of juncture phonemes and in the analysis of intonation into sequences of pitch phonemes; pitch and stress phonemes are distinguished from consonant and vowel phonemes as being suprasegmental, but relative to each other they are block-like units with definite segmental domains, usually syllables. Certain exceptions to this procedure are seen, for example the analysis of intonation as single phonemes extending over the whole or a part of the utterance; and work has been done on the abstraction of phonemic 'long components' from successions of consonant and vowel phonemes all sharing a common feature, such as voicing or retroflexion. But in all such cases the analysis rests on a prior segmental phonemic one, and the groundwork and the bulk of phonemic analysis consist in assigning the relevant phonetic phenomena to a linear sequential series of phonemes, and setting up an inventory of such phonemes as the phonemic or phonological system of the language, wherein are contained all the phonetic distinctions employed by the language in communication. In this sense phonemic analysis is monosystemic.

As was seen, however, in the account given of the processes of articulation in the preceding chapter, speech is a continuous activity and any descriptive segmentation into successions of consonants and vowels involves some misrepresentation of the actual material being described. Manifestly some segmentation is necessary for any analysis, and total segmentation, or something near it, is a requisite for a broad transcription; but the study of the physiology of articulation, the neurological processes controlling it, and the behaviour of the sound waves thereby produced has emphasized still more strongly the interlocking and overlapping nature of the articulations and resultant phonetic features that are the object of phonological analysis.

Prosodic analysis seeks to allow in some measure for this overlapping and partly simultaneous nature of speech, by abandoning a transcriptionally orientated and essentially unidimensional treatment of utterances and taking into account both the syntagmatic and paradigmatic dimensions in which features may be assigned to distinctive phonological elements relative to each other in ways not exclusively serial.

Broad transcription is essential to the study of a language, and phonemic analysis is a necessary procedure in the development of a broad transcription for it to be accurate, unambiguous, and usable; but phonological analysis and transcription are two different things, and there is no *a-priori* reason to assume that the most useful theory of phonological analysis will be one embodying the same concepts and employing the same procedures as are needed for transcription.

Prosodic analysis is not as such concerned with transcription, but with providing a framework of categories for the analysis of the ways in which different sound features function in the utterances of languages. In fact *prosodic analysis*, as it is usually called, is a brief title for a method of phonological analysis that employs as fundamental concepts two types of element, not reducible to a common type, **prosodies** and **phonematic units**. Phonological structures, in the terms of this theory, comprise phonematic units and prosodies. Phonematic unit in this sense must be distinguished from phonemes or phonemic units; despite the unfortunate superficial similarity of the words they are of quite separate status; particular care is needed in reading the work of some writers who use *phonematic* as the adjective of *phoneme*, a use that must be kept quite distinct from its use in the type of phonology being outlined here.

159

As is the case with phonemic analysis, different linguists employ somewhat different treatments within the broad limits of the theory they embrace, and interpret the theory in different ways; but a general account can be given in outline of prosodic analysis and the theory behind it, on lines that summarize the points of agreement between linguists working within it.

Prosodic analysis provides a theoretical framework for the analysis of all the relevant phonetic phenomena in a language; in this respect it is comparable to the fully developed phonemic theory of American linguists rather than with the phonemic phonology of many European linguists.

In the prosodic analysis of a language, phonological structures consist of phonematic units and prosodies, and the phonological system of the language comprises both sorts of element, subdivided into different types according to the structures to which they relate. The phonetic data found relevant are assigned to phonematic units and to prosodies irrespective of any graphic considerations that may arise in literate languages. The relationship of data to element is one of exponent to abstraction $(2 \cdot 1 \cdot 1)$. Broadly speaking, those features that are most conveniently regarded as primarily involving linear or temporal succession are assigned to successive **phonematic units**. Phonematic units are divided into consonant and vowels, and occupy sequential positions within structures and their relative order is significant, corresponding to some extent to the temporal sequence of articulations and the production of audible sound features in the stream of speech; but it must be emphasized that in no case does speech consist of a succession of separate sound units produced by jerks of the vocal organs, and this must be kept in mind in interpreting any analysis or graphic representation of it.

Features that for various reasons are found to be best assigned not to units but to stretches of speech actually or potentially larger than a single consonant or vowel unit are allotted to one or more **prosodies**, which by definition are elements capable of extension over or relevance to sequences of phonematic units of any length.

The consonant and vowel phonematic units bear some resemblance to the segmental phonemes of phonemic analysis, but they are not to be equated with them, and the basis of their establishment is different. Certain phonetic features that would constitute part of some seg-

160

mental phonemes in the phonemic analysis of a language are likely to be allotted to one or more prosodies in prosodic analysis, leaving the phonematic unit as an abstraction representing fewer phonetic features than its nearest correspondent in phonemic analysis.

Prosodies are abstracted from the utterance or sentence (sentence prosodies) and from parts thereof, but always with reference to a given structure; and the relevant phonetic data may be assigned to such different categories of prosody as sentence prosodies, sentence part prosodies, word prosodies, syllable prosodies, and syllable part prosodies. Where more than one phonematic unit or prosody is referable to a single structural position, these constitute a system. Systems are thus set up to state the structural possibilities of a language at the phonological level.

The order of working is generally 'downward', from the larger structure through the successively smaller structures to the units.

4·4·2 *Applications and illustrations*

An illustration of prosodic analysis may be drawn from Thai (Siamese), a tone language in which intonations are also relevant.

The phonetic data have been analysed in terms of:

sentence prosodies: intonations
sentence part and syllable group prosodies: the relations of length, stress, and tone between successions of syllables
syllable prosodies: length, stress, and tone
syllable part prosodies (including syllable initial and syllable final prosodies): plosion, affrication, labialization, unreleased closure, etc.
phonematic units: *k, t, p, n, m*, etc.

Intonation sequences or tunes, as referred to earlier, are clearly abstractable as sentence prosodies, phonological features characterizing or belonging to sentences as wholes; this does not exclude the possibility of long sentences being characterized by two or more successive intonations, each capable of constituting a sentence prosody, but, in the instance, being sentence part prosodies. The modifications to the lexical tones in Siamese and other tone languages under intonation tunes belongs to the sentence prosody, and in such languages the actual pitch phenomena may be allotted to three separate types of prosody:

1. Sentence prosodies of intonation;
2. Sentence part or syllable group prosodies, including word

161

prosodies, of the modifications imposed on tones by their presence in closely linked tone groups; and

3. Syllable prosodies of the lexically distinctive tones available on any given syllabic sequence of consonants and vowels.

In Siamese, sentence part and syllable group prosodies, in which prosodies of word units must be included, involve the relations of length, stress, and tone between the component syllables (that is to say, the ways in which the features of these kinds ascribable to the syllables in isolation actually appear in the different groups of syllables within sentences). This same category of prosody involves other features in other languages, such as the non-release or weak release of stop consonants otherwise exploded (this feature is a syllable part prosody in Siamese), and covers much of the material treated under juncture phonemes in American phonemic analysis; but the juncture phonemes concentrate emphasis on the breaks between stretches, where they are serially located in transcriptions, whereas the sentence part prosodies and word prosodies concentrate emphasis on the unity of the groups or stretches as prosodically marked whole structures.

The treatment of intonation as sentence prosodies, and of tone, stress, and length as syllable prosodies is not very unlike some phonemic treatments of such phenomena, and some features involved in syllable group prosodies and word prosodies are often similar to those assigned one way or another to juncture phonemes.

The prosodic analysis of the syllable, however, differs quite sharply from the phonemic analysis of the same sort of structure. The structure in question is the phonological, not the phonetic syllable, and it is a phonological structure defined in terms of phonematic units and prosodies. Certain syllable prosodies, such as length, stress, and tone, in languages where any or all of these are relevant categories, are comparable to the corresponding suprasegmental phonemes of a phonemic analysis; but phonemically length is usually assigned to the vowel phoneme and transcribed after it (as in one phonemicization of English, $4 \cdot 3 \cdot 3$), whereas prosodic analysis treats it as a feature of the syllable as a single structure, not linearly related to any of the consonant and vowel units. Its exponents are vowel length and any other qualitative features present with it in the rest of the syllable, all features being taken as its exponents and not divided into distinctive (phonemic) features on one segment (the vowel) and non-distinctive (allophonic) features on other segments (consonants). This difference in treatment may be most marked in languages in which length phonemically ascribed to the vowel of a syllable is accompanied by other phonetic differences elsewhere.

In diagrammatic representations prosodies are usually marked with different typefaces or are set over the linear sequence of phonematic unit symbols, in order to make their separate status clear. Thus a long syllable phonemically representable /CV:C/ could be prosodically represented $\frac{\text{L(ength)}}{\text{CVC}}$

Suprasegmental phonemes have been in practice restricted by linguists to the phenomena of length, stress, and pitch. But features of any phonetic nature can be treated prosodically if their function in the structure to which they are assigned warrants it. As has been seen, all features overlap and interlock, but certain features involving a syllable or the sequence of phonematic units in a syllable are more obviously syllable features as such, or yield a more satisfactory structural analysis of the syllable if so treated. Features such as retroflexion and palatalization involving phonetic differences in the articulation of adjacent consonants and vowels within syllables (to which reference has already been made (3·5·2)) have been analysed as syllable prosodies in a number of languages. Phonemic analysis takes account of such concomitant variations, but is obliged in its own terms to allot the exponents to phonemic or distinctive status on one segment and allophonic or non-distinctive status on the other segments. In an account of Russian phonetics it has been said that in some positions the accompanying differences of vowel quality are more readily perceived than the differences in the consonantal articulation of the soft (palatalized) and hard (non-palatalized) consonants themselves; yet it is these that are treated as phonemically distinguished and the differences in vowel quality are given allophonic status.[1] In such cases a prosodic analysis that assigned palatalization

1. It may be noted that the Cyrillic orthography (p. 123) takes the opposite course, and in general marks the difference between palatalized and non-palatalized consonantal pronunciations, not by different consonant letters, but by the use of different vowel letters.

as a syllable prosody to the syllable as a whole, with its exponents variously located in each segment, might be phonologically more suitable, if phonology were freed from the linear restraints of transcriptional requirements. The greater the weight borne in maintaining lexical and grammatical distinctions by plurisegmental features of this sort, the greater the gain may be in structural analysis by assigning them to appropriate prosodic abstractions.

Some other features in languages suggest similar prosodic analysis in relation to syllable structures. In some, but not all, languages nasal consonants are always followed by nasalized vowels within the same syllable, and nasalized vowels only appear after nasal consonants. This is substantially the position in Sundanese, a language of Java. In Georgian and Armenian it has been found that the glottalized or ejective consonants are followed by glottalization or glottal constriction in the following vowels in the same syllable, a feature not found in vowels elsewhere in these languages. Such features may be treated as prosodies of the syllables concerned, abstracted from and manifested in the sequences of consonant and vowel (phonematic units), and not assigned phonologically to any one place as distinctive or significant as against any other place.

Prosodies of the type that have been discussed above may be abstracted from sequences of more than one syllable, usually within word boundaries. In Turkish and Hungarian, for example, the vowels may be classified into the categories of front and back, according to the part of the tongue that is highest in their articulation and the part of the roof of the mouth towards which it is raised, and into rounded and unrounded, according to the position of the lips. Words in these languages (other than those of foreign origin, 8·1·7) are largely characterized by what is called vowel harmony, whereby the vowels in polysyllabic words in Turkish, and similar words in Hungarian resulting from grammatical suffixation (5·4·3), are either all back or all front in type, and in certain word structures all rounded or all unrounded (thus Turkish:

ev /ev/ house, *evler* /evler/ houses, with front vowels
ayak /ajak/ foot, *ayaklar* /ajaklar/ feet, with back vowels
ev /ev/ house, *evim* /evim/ my house, with front unrounded vowels
göz /gœz/ eye, *gözüm* /gœzym/ my eye, with front rounded vowels
yol /jol/ way, *yolum* /jolum/ my way, with back rounded vowels
kız /kɯz/ daughter, *kızım* /kɯzɯm/ my daughter, with back unrounded vowels

164

Hungarian:

tanulok /tənulok/ I learn, with back vowels
verek /vɛrɛk/ I hit, with front unrounded vowels
török /tørøk/ I break, with front rounded vowels).

In prosodic analysis these features that affect more than one syllable in word structures are abstracted from the whole word or from stated syllables of the word, as a word or word part prosody, separate from the sequence of phonematic units constituting the consonants and vowels of the structure. In such an analysis, the exponents of the prosodies are not only the vowel features concerned, but also any variations in the articulations of the consonants adjacent to them. Thus the Turkish word *yollarımız* /jollarɯmuuz/ our ways, is prosodically represented

```
o--
w---------
```
$C\alpha CC\alpha C\iota C\iota C$, or with the consonants distinguished,

```
o-
w------
```
yɑllɑrɯmɯz

In this representation o and w mark the prosodies of lip-rounding and back articulation respectively, and the broken lines mark their structural extension. The phonematic vowel units, α and ι, indicate only the distinction between open and close, all other features ascribable to vowels as phonetic segments, or as phonemes in a phonemic analysis, being allotted to the relevant prosodies.

Just as languages differ and may be classified according to the types of syllable structures they exhibit as expressed in phonemic terms (4·3·4), so different languages lay themselves open to different prosodic statements of syllable structure. When analyses of this sort are further advanced and more numerous, lines of important language type classification may be expected to emerge.

Prosodies of syllable parts fall into a rather different general category of prosody. Prosodies are abstracted from stretches and referred to structures for two main reasons. Firstly, as in the illustrations so far given, the relevant phonetic features serving as the exponents of the prosodies may themselves be articulated or realized

165

over the whole stretch of speech corresponding to the structure to which the prosody is ascribed or at various points therein. Secondly, a feature may phonetically be confined to a particular part of a structure (or, strictly, to a particular part of the corresponding stretch of speech), and even to a single segment therein, but because in the language its occurrence is restricted to a certain position in relation to the rest, it serves thereby as a signal of structural delimitation and so as a mark of structural unity. Prosodies fulfilling this type of function may be regarded as syntagmatically relevant to the structures they thus help to identify.

In Siamese, aspiration, affrication, plosion, and a number of other features are confined to syllable initial position, and unexploded closure is confined to syllable final position (that is to say, syllable final stop consonants are not released audibly). In Siamese, or in any other language where this sort of statement is possible, the occurrence of one of them necessarily indicates a syllable initial or final boundary, and is thus syntagmatically significant beyond its immediate place as a phonetic segment, in addition to any contrastive function it may have in its particular environment.

Syntagmatic relevance of this kind is the basis for regarding certain features as belonging to syllable part prosodies, while others not so positionally restricted within the syllable are assigned to the sequence of phonematic units.

As will have been seen from the examples already given, prosodic analysis is represented in diagrams or phonological formulae rather than in transcriptions.

Syllables are not the only structures that may be prosodically demarcated in this way. In languages with phonologically marked word divisions, the phonological features in question, juncturally analysed in American phonemics, are regarded in prosodic analysis as demarcative word prosodies. Languages in which such word demarcative prosodies are usefully abstractable differ in the degree to which the units grammatically defined as words are marked by phonological features; but features, such as fixed place stress, or the English phonetic qualities associated in phonemic analysis with inter-word juncture (4·3·6), are syntagmatically significant, and justify prosodic treatment for just that reason.

Fixed place stress in words, whether on the initial, penultimate, or any other syllable, may be analysed as falling into two prosodic categories, with respect to different structures:

1. By phonetic extension of the feature of forceful articulation it serves as the exponent of a syllable prosody, part of the phonological structure of a particular syllable; and

2. By virtue of its demarcative function in the word, it acts as an exponent of the prosody of word delimitation or of the syntagmatic unity of a succession of syllables having a particular grammatical status.

4·4·3 *Polysystemic phonology*

Prosodic analysis has been characterized as polysystemic in contrast to monosystemic phonemic analysis. It contrasts with phonemic analysis not only in the recognition of two basic phonological entities, prosody and phonematic unit, rather than one, but in other respects. Phonemic analysis is general throughout a language, and a sound segment assigned to a phoneme in one environment is generally held to belong to the same phoneme everywhere else. Phonemic systems are established without reliance on grammatical distinctions (e.g. between nouns and verbs or roots and affixes). They are, moreover, based on the structural places of maximal differentiation; the non-applicability of some contrasts in some environments is the basis of the theory of neutralization, already mentioned (4·3·8). Prosodic analysis admits the possibility, and often the desirability, of different grammatical elements being subjected to different phonological analyses, where a more satisfactory description can be shown to result thereby; and phonological analyses of the nominal words or the verbal words in particular languages have been separately undertaken. As was seen above, grammatical elements such as words, as well as purely phonological elements such as syllables, are open to treatment as structures from which prosodies may be abstracted.

Moreover, prosodic phonology envisages the setting up of separate systems of contrastive phonematic units and prosodies at different places in phonological structures without necessarily identifying the units in one system with those in another (though in symbolization the same letters may sometimes be used). In a language that admits

167

three nasal consonants in initial position in syllables and only two in syllable final position, as in some types of Chinese, there would be no need to identify any of the members of the initial system with any of those of the final system; and in the English case of plosive consonants after /s/ in initial position in the syllable, referred to above (4·3·8), prosodic phonology would not feel any requirement to identify the three consonantal phonematic units in this position with either the distinctively voiced three or the distinctively voiceless three that are found in absolute syllable initial position. The concept of neutralization need not, therefore, be invoked to deal with the non-comparability of some different systems that operate in different structural places.

The theory and procedures of prosodic analysis in phonology have not yet been formulated and set out at length, and there is need of further application to widely different types of language and language material before the full value of this mode of phonological analysis can be justly assessed. In particular, it may be hoped that some of the elusive phonetic features that characterize utterance at speeds faster than the 'slow colloquial' (2·2·1), that has constituted the basis of most phonological statements about languages so far, will yield to analysis in prosodic terms.

In the present chapter no more is done than to try to make explicit the main principles of this type of phonological theory and method of analysis, and to point out the ways in which it chiefly differs from most types of phonemic analysis. Further references to theoretical accounts and to applications of the method to different languages are given in the notes to this section. Linguistic theory is never static, and the subject would lose much of its interest if it were, and, as will be seen elsewhere, an elementary introduction must outline recent developments that are likely to grow in importance, while their full significance and utility have not yet been evaluated. An understanding of the theory and practice of phonemic analysis and some acquaintance with those of prosodic analysis are both desirable for anyone seeking a comprehensive picture of phonological studies in linguistics today and the ability to read further thereon with profit.

1. A. S. ABRAMSON, 'The vowels and tones of standard Thai', *IJAL* 28 (1962), part 2, section 3.

2. W. S. ALLEN, 'Notes on the phonetics of an Eastern Armenian speaker', *TPS* 1950, 180–206.

3. ——, 'Some prosodic aspects of retroflexion and aspiration in Sanskrit', *BSOAS* 13 (1951), 939–46.

4. L. E. ARMSTRONG and I. C. WARD, *A handbook of English intonation*, Cambridge, 1926.

5. T. G. BAILEY, *Teach yourself Hindustani* (edited by J. R. Firth and A. H. Harley), London, 1950.

6. J. T. BENDOR-SAMUEL, 'Some problems of segmentation in the phonological analysis of Tereno', *Word* 16 (1960), 348–55.

7. ——, 'The verbal piece in Jebero', *Word* 17 (1961), supplement.

8. B. BLOCH, 'A set of postulates for phonemic analysis', *Lang.* 24 (1948), 3–46.

9. ——, 'Studies in colloquial Japanese 4 (phonemics)', *Lang.* 26 (1950), 86–125.

10. —— and G. L. TRAGER, *Outline of linguistic analysis*, Baltimore, 1942.

11. L. BLOOMFIELD, *Language*, London, 1935.

12. ——, *Eastern Ojibwa*, Ann Arbor, 1958.

13. D. W. BOLINGER, 'Intonation: Levels versus configurations', *Word* 7 (1951), 199–210.

14. G. L. BURSILL-HALL, 'Levels analysis, J. R. Firth's theories of linguistic analysis', *Journal of the Canadian Linguistic Association* 6 (1961), 124–35, 164–91.

15. J. CARNOCHAN, 'A study in the phonology of an Igbo speaker', *BSOAS* 12 (1947–8), 417–26.

16. ——, 'Vowel harmony in Igbo', *African language studies* 1 (1960), 155–63.

17. J. CHADWICK, *The decipherment of Linear B*, Cambridge, 1958.

18. Y. R. CHAO and L. S. YANG, *A concise dictionary of spoken Chinese*, Cambridge, Mass., 1947.

19. N. CHOMSKY, *Syntactic structures*, The Hague, 1957.

20. A. COHEN, *The phonemes of English*, The Hague, 1952.

21. H. N. COUSTENOBLE and L. E. ARMSTRONG, *Studies in French intonation*, Cambridge, 1934.

22. D. DIRINGER, *The alphabet*, New York, 1948.

23. M. B. EMENEAU, *Studies in Vietnamese grammar*, Berkeley, 1951.

24. J. R. FIRTH, *Sounds and prosodies*, TPS 1948, 127–52.

25. —— and B. B. ROGERS, 'The structure of the Chinese monosyllable in a Hunanese dialect', *BSOS* 8 (1937), 1055–74.

26. E. FISCHER-JØRGENSEN, 'Remarques sur les principes de l'analyse phonémique', *TCLC* 5 (1949), 214–34.

27. H. A. GLEASON, *An introduction to descriptive linguistics*, second edition, New York, 1961.

28. M. R. HAAS, *Tunica*, New York, 1941.

29. R. A. HALL, 'Analytic grammar of the Hungarian language', *Lang.* 14 (1938), part 2, supplement.

30. Z. S. HARRIS, 'Simultaneous components in phonology', *Lang.* 20 (1944), 181–205.

31. ——, *Methods in structural linguistics*, Chicago, 1951.

32. E. J. A. HENDERSON, 'Prosodies in Siamese', *Asia Major*, new series 1 (1949), 189–215.

33. A. A. HILL, *Introduction to linguistic structures*, New York, 1958.

34. C. F. HOCKETT, 'Componential analysis of Sierra Popoluca', *IJAL* 13 (1947), 258–67.

35. ——, *A manual of phonology*, Indiana University publications in anthropology and linguistics, 11, 1955.

36. ——, *A course in modern linguistics*, New York, 1958.

37. R. JAKOBSON, C. G. FANT, and M. HALLE, *Preliminaries to speech analysis*, Cambridge, Mass., 1952.

38. —— and M. HALLE, *Fundamentals of language*, The Hague, 1956.

39. D. JONES, 'Some thoughts on the phoneme', *TPS* 1944, 119–35.

40. ——, *Outline of English phonetics*, sixth edition, 1947.

41. ——, *The phoneme*, Cambridge, 1950.

42. M. JOOS, *Acoustic phonetics*, Baltimore, 1948.

43. B. KARLGREN, *Sound and symbol in Chinese*, London, 1923.

44. J. LYONS, 'Phonemic and non-phonemic phonology', *IJAL* 28 (1962), 127–33.

45. S. E. MARTIN, 'Morphophonemics of standard colloquial Japanese', *Lang.* 28 (1952), part 3, section 2.

46. A. MARTINET, 'Un ou deux phonèmes', *Acta linguistica* 1 (1939), 94–103.

47. ——, *Phonology as functional phonetics*, publication of the Philological Society 15, Oxford, 1949.

48. G. B. MILNER, *Fijian grammar*, Suva, 1957.

49. W. G. MOULTON, 'Juncture in modern standard German', *Lang.* 23 (1947), 212–26.

50. F. R. PALMER, 'The verb in Bilin', *BSOAS* 19 (1957), 131–59.

51. K. L. PIKE, *Phonetics*, Ann Arbor, 1943.

52. ——, *The intonation of American English*, Ann Arbor, 1946.

53. ——, *Phonemics*, Ann Arbor, 1947.

54. ——, 'On the phonemic status of English diphthongs', *Lang.* 23 (1947), 151–9.

55. ——, 'Grammatical prerequisites to phonemic analysis', *Word* 3 (1947), 155–72.

56. ——, *Tone languages*, Ann Arbor, 1948.

57. ——, 'More on grammatical prerequisites', *Word* 8 (1952), 106–21.

58. R. H. ROBINS, 'Vowel nasality in Sundanese', *Studies in linguistic analysis*, special publication of the Philological Society, Oxford, 1957, 87–103.

59. ——, 'Formal divisions in Sundanese', *TPS* 1953, 109–42.

60. ——, 'Aspects of prosodic analysis', *Proc. of the University of Durham Philosophical Society*, series B (Arts) 1 (1957), 1–12.

61. R. H. ROBINS and N. WATERSON, 'Notes on the phonology of the Georgian word', *BSOAS* 14 (1952), 55–72.

62. E. B. SANSOM, *Historical grammar of Japanese*, Oxford, 1928.

63. F. DE SAUSSURE, *Cours de linguistique générale*, fourth edition, Paris, 1949.

64. N. C. SCOTT, 'A study in the phonetics of Fijian', *BSOAS* 12 (1947–8), 737–52.

65. ——, 'A phonological analysis of the Szechuanese monosyllable', *BSOAS* 18 (1956), 556–60.

66. R. H. STETSON, *Motor phonetics*, Amsterdam, 1951.

67. B. M. H. STRANG, *Modern English structure*, London, 1962.

68. *Studies in linguistic analysis*, special publication of the Philological Society, Oxford, 1957.

69. H. SWEET, *Handbook of phonetics*, Oxford, 1877.

70. G. L. TRAGER and B. BLOCH, 'The syllabic phonemes of English', *Lang.* 17 (1941), 223–46.

71. —— and H. L. SMITH, *Outline of English structure*, Studies in linguistics occasional paper 3, Norman, Oklahoma, 1951.

72. N. S. TRUBETZKOY, *Principes de phonologie* (translated by J. Cantineau), Paris, 1949.

73. W. F. TWADDELL, *On defining the phoneme*, Language monograph 16, 1935.

74. N. WATERSON, 'Some aspects of the phonology of the nominal forms of the Turkish word', *BSOAS* 18 (1956), 578–91.

75. R. S. WELLS, 'The pitch phonemes of English', *Lang.* 21 (1945), 27–39.

A number of general accounts of phonological theory and the principles of phonological analysis in linguistics are available, each treating the subject from somewhat different points of view. Attention may be drawn to the following:

> Bloomfield, 11, chapters 5 to 8,
> Bloch and Trager, 10, chapter 3,
> Gleason, 27, chapters 16 to 21,
> Hockett, 36, chapters 2 to 13.

More detailed and extensive treatment in:

Trubetzkoy, 72. This was originally published in German under the title *Grundzüge der Phonologie* (*TCLP* 8, 1939). It was translated into French by Cantineau. The translation is the more useful book, as it contains a number of articles by Trubetzkoy and Jakobson, not printed in the original German version. References are here made to the French translation.

> Jones, 41,
> Harris, 31, chapters 3 to 11,
> Twaddell, 73,
> Pike, 53,
> Hockett, 35,
> Jakobson, Fant, and Halle, 37,
> Jakobson and Halle, 38.

ADDENDA

76. K. H. ALBROW, 'The phonology of the personal forms of the verb in Russian', *Archivum linguisticum* 14 (1962), 146–56.

77. M. A. K. Halliday, 'The tones of English', *Archivum linguisticum* 15 (1963), 1–28.

78. ——, 'Intonation in English Grammar', *TPS* 1963, 143–69.

79. C. MOHRMANN, F. NORMAN, and A. SOMMERFELT, *Trends in modern linguistics*, Utrecht, 1963.

80. J. VACHEK (editor), *A Prague school reader in linguistics*, Bloomington, 1964.

p. 122. On Chinese writing, Karlgren, 43.

p. 123. On Mycenaean, Chadwick, 17.

p. 124. On the development of Japanese writing, Sansom, 62, chapter 1.

On the history of writing, Diringer, 22; more briefly, Bloomfield, 11, chapter 17; Hockett, 36, chapter 62.

p. 126. The variant forms of some commonly used words in connected speech are called 'weak forms', the isolated forms being 'strong forms' (Jones, 40, chapter 16).

Early development of the theory of broad transcription, Sweet, 69, 100–8, 182–3.

p. 127. Functional nature of phonology, Martinet, 47. Many books on the sound systems of particular languages cover both phonetic and phonological description, as does Jones's *Outline*.

p. 129. Numbers of phonemes in languages, Hockett, 35, 139.

De Saussure, 63, 166; cp. p. 48 above.

p. 131. cp. the definition of the phoneme in Bloch and Trager, 10, 40.

Notice that Bloomfield, unlike modern practice, prints his phonemes in square brackets in *Language* (i.e. his [b] = /b/, etc.).

The criterion of phonetic similarity in grouping sounds into phonemes has been challenged as being not strictly relevant in an analysis concerned solely with establishing distinctive elements and their relations with one another irrespective of the phonetic substance in which they are expressed. Most linguists do take it into account. Discussion in Fischer-Jørgensen, 26.

p. 132. On the varieties of English /ə/, Jones, 40, §§355–61.

p. 133. On the 'pairs test', Chomsky, 19, 94–7.

p. 134. Bloch, 8, makes an attempt to define the phoneme rigorously, without any semantic considerations, avoiding even any appeal to the speaker's recognition of difference or distinctiveness. This was challenged by others, and Bloch replied to their criticisms in *Lang*. 29 (1953), 59–61. It seems doubtful whether this extreme position can be fully maintained.

For further consideration on the theory of phonemic analysis, see Trubetzkoy, 72, 41–6, and Jones, 39.

p. 135. A general discussion of the treatment of English short and long vowels in phonemic analysis, and of other questions in English phonology, is to be found in Cohen, 20.

American phonemic analyses of English vowels are rather different, partly because the phonetic phenomena are themselves different in American English. cp. Bloch and Trager, 10, chapter 3; Trager and Bloch, 70; Trager and Smith, 71. This last has formed the basis of several subsequent phonological analyses of English by American linguists.

In contrast to the vowels, English geminated or 'long' consonants are normally analysed as sequences of two of the same consonant phonemes. Such occurrences within a word are always the result of grammatical composition or affixation (night-time /ˈnaittaim/, solely /ˈsoulli/).

p. 136. Jones's views on the analysis of stress in English, 41, §§462, 468–9; details in 40, chapter 29.

American treatment of stress in English, Trager and Smith, 71, 35–9; Gleason, 27, chapter 4; Hockett, 36, chapter 5.

Extra-loud stress as a phoneme, Bloomfield, 11, 91.

p. 137. On the syllable as a phonetic entity, Jones, 40, chapter 12; Pike, 51, 116–17. Stetson, 66, 33, defines the phonetic syllable in terms of a stretch of sound produced with one chest pulse. Pike, 51, 119, distinguishes checked syllables, wherein a consonantal articulation stops or reduces the outward flow of air (as in up /ʌp/), and unchecked syllables, in which the outward air flow is checked at its source in the lungs (as in too /tuː/).

p. 138. On the syllable as a phonological unit, Trubetzkoy, 72, 196–212.

On the nature of the Japanese syllabic nasal, on which there has been some discussion, Bloch, 9, 102; Martin, 45, 12; Jones, 41, 88.

p. 139. The phonemic status of German [ç] in its relation to [x] (as in Buch /buːx/), is controversial; Jones, 39, 127–32, 41, §§230–2; Moulton, 49.

On Fijian, Scott, 64; Milner, 48.

p. 140. These and similar topics are discussed in Martinet, 46; cp. Pike, 53, 130.

On the phonemic analysis of English diphthongs, Pike, 54. Jones, 41, §237, prefers to regard them as single phonetically complex phonemes, transcribed with digraphs (sequences of two symbols). American linguists generally phonemicize English diphthongs as sequences of a vowel phoneme and a consonant (semivowel) phoneme. This different treatment is partly due to the different nature of some of the sounds involved, as compared with British English (Bloch and Trager, 10, 51–2; Trager and Smith, 71, 15–20). General discussion in Cohen, 20, 89–107.

On triphthongs, Jones, 40, §§232–3.

p. 142. The term *toneme* is used by Jones, 41, chapter 25. The various problems involved in the phonological analysis of tone languages are treated exhaustively in Pike, *Tone languages*.

Mixteco and Mazateco data in Pike, 56.

Tonal distinctions cannot be maintained in their normal way in whispered speech, though some compensatory distinctive features appear to be used in certain tone languages in whispering, in ways not yet fully understood (Pike, 56, 34–6).

On North Chinese tones, Chao and Yang, 18, xiv–xix.

p. 143. On Vietnamese tones, Emeneau, 23, 8.

p. 146. Jones regards a number of English words as double-stressed (40), e.g. *archbishop* /ˈaːtʃˈbiʃəp/, thirteen /ˈθəːˈtiːn/. Many linguists insist that only one syllable in such words is fully stressed, the other stressed syllable bearing a distinctively (phonemically) lesser degree of stress. The stress patterning of such words is often variable according to the stress patterns of neighbouring words in the sentence.

p. 148. That phonetic analysis should be based on the word unit, however established, in isolation, is stated explicitly by Jones, in 39 and in 41, §34, 688–9. This attitude is strongly attacked by Smith, *Lang.* 28 (1952), 144–9. The two opposing viewpoints should be carefully studied and compared by the serious student. The phonological analysis of a language in terms of the phoneme will differ according to the position taken by the analyst on this question. Smith's views are put into practice in Trager and Smith, 71.

Support for grammatical word boundaries being taken into account in their own right in phonemic analysis is found in Pike, 55, and in replies to criticism, in 57.

Two different methods of relating the relevant phonetic material to juncture phonemes have been proposed. In one (Harris, 31, chapter 8), the juncture phoneme is itself a zero element (a unit required and justified by overt observable phenomena, but not itself comprising any variants or allophones, cp. note to p. 204. This zero phoneme provides the different phonological environment by which the phonetic features involved in the syllabification /ən ˈeim/, /ət ˈiːz/, etc. occur as allophonic variants. By the other method (Hockett, 35, 167–72), the juncture phoneme has as its members all the phonetic differences abstracted from the sequences involved which by the former method were assigned to the neighbouring segmental phonemes. The differences between these two methods of assigning phonetic material to juncture phonemes, though they are as methods totally opposed, do not seem vital from the point of view of the theory of juncture phoneme analysis as a whole.

Two phonemic degrees of juncture within and between words in English have been assumed by some to differentiate, at least sometimes, sequences such as *playful* /ˈpleiful/, *trayful* /ˈtrei-ful/, and (a) *play full (of excellent character studies)* /ˈplei≠ful/ (Harris, 31, 86–7), or similarly *minus*, *slyness*, and *my nasturtiums*. In so far as the phonetic facts are consistent and observable, these two juncture phonemes may be explained on the same lines and present no new questions of theory.

Despite the quite different status of juncture as a phonologically relevant phonetic phenomenon (or set of phenomena) and of word boundaries as grammatically established divisions, some linguists, who make use of juncture phonemes in their analyses of English, seem almost to assume a juncture phoneme at every word boundary without making clear exactly what phonetic phenomena they are relying on in each case.

Plato with internal juncture, Trager and Smith, 71, 38; Hockett, 36, 59.

p. 151. On English intonation, Jones, 40, chapter 31; see further Armstrong and Ward, 4. On French intonation, Coustenoble and Armstrong, 21.

Bloomfield's treatment of English intonation, 11, 90–2; cp. 12, 3. Haas, 28, 19–20, uses the term 'phrase final melody' in this mode of analysis.

On intonation in tone languages, Pike, 56, 16–17, 85–6; Abramson, 1, 14.

p. 152. The phonemic analysis of intonation in terms of successions of pitch phonemes was pioneered by Pike, 52, and Wells, 75. Note that Pike's numbers are in the opposite order to that now in general use in America, his 1 being highest and 4 lowest.

The pitch phenomena involved in Jones's intonation tunes are covered jointly in this method by the sequences of pitch phonemes and the terminal juncture. Phonemic descriptions of (American) English intonation on these lines may be found in Trager and Smith, 71; Hill, 33; Gleason, 27; and Hockett, 36. For a criticism of this treatment, Bolinger, 13.

A brief treatment of the intonation of British English in terms of four distinctive pitch levels may be seen in Strang, 67, 52–60. Note that, like Pike, she numbers the highest pitch 1 and the lowest 4.

p. 154. The classical exposition of distinctive feature analysis is in Trubetzkoy, 72. For a similar analysis of vowel systems, Hockett, 35, 87.

p. 155. Hindi, Bailey, 5, xi–xli. A similar system obtained in Sanskrit, the classical language of India.

p. 156. On neutralization, Trubetzkoy, 72, 80–7.

The details of this most recent mode of distinctive feature analysis, which can only be summarily presented here, are to be found in Jakobson, Fant, and Halle, 37.

An analysis of phonemes into 'componential features' on a more directly articulatory basis on Trubetzkoyan lines, though without the use of further Trubetzkoyan concepts like neutralization, has been made by some American linguists under the title *componential analysis*. See Hockett, 35, 126–37, and 34.

p. 158. Firth's programmatic article, 24, marked the beginning of prosodic analysis as an explicitly stated procedure, though the sort of method there proposed had been applied in some previous publications, such as Firth and Rogers, 25, and Carnochan, 15.

On phonemic long components, Harris, 31, chapter 10.

p. 159. The possible divergence of transcriptional requirements and the purposes of phonological analysis were stressed by Twaddell, 73.

On neurological overlapping, Joos, 42, 109–14.

The prominent place occupied by transcriptional considerations in any sort of phonemic analysis is seen in a comment by Harris on his own long component analysis, 30, 203: 'phonemics [i.e. prior to the abstraction of long components] is undoubtedly the more convenient stopping point in this development, because it fits alphabetic writing.'

In addition to the ambiguity of the term *phonematic*, one should note that some writers use *prosodic*, with reference to phonemes and features, as equivalent to *suprasegmental*. Care must always be exercised when what appears to be the same technical term is used in two quite distinct and separate senses in two different systems of analysis.

pp. 161–2. Siamese, Henderson, 32.

Another example of working downward, in a partial prosodic analysis of Sundanese, Robins, 59.

p. 163. On the phonetic limitations on suprasegmental status, Pike, 53, 63. The nearest approaches to prosodic analysis in phonemic terms have been Harris's long components and Hockett's componential analysis. Both are based on a prior segmental phonemic analysis, and are subject to the overall monosystemic principle of phonemic phonology, explicitly rejected in prosodic analysis (4·4·3).

Russian palatalization, Jones, 41, §183.

pp. 164–5. Sundanese, Robins, 58.

Georgian, Robins and Waterson, 61.

Armenian, W. S. Allen, 2.

Hungarian, Hall, 29 (phonemic phonology).

On Turkish, Waterson, 74.

Waterson's prosodic treatment of Turkish is compared with a phonemic analysis of the same phonetic phenomena by Lyons, 44. It is to be noticed that the same phonemic status must be accorded to the different vowels in each syllable in this type of word structure, though the possible vowel contrasts in suffix syllables are much fewer than in initial syllables. The allocation of the relevant features to a word prosody brings this into prominence.

A further example of the prosodic treatment of vowel harmony may be seen in Carnochan, 16.

The feature of Sanskrit grammar traditionally known as cerebralization (*cerebral* being an old-fashioned term for retroflexion) is prosodically analysed in Allen, 3.

p. 166. The theory of demarcative prosodies was partly foreshadowed by Trubetzkoy's 'boundary markers' (*Grenzsignale, signes oristiques*), 72, 290–314.

Further examples of formulaic diagrams of prosodic analysis in Scott, 65.

p. 167. Separate phonological analyses of different grammatical word classes, Palmer, 50.

In a study of part of the phonology of a language of South America, Bendor-Samuel, 6, treats the vowel segment transcribed /e/ as *o* with Y prosody in /ˈyeno/ you (singular) walked, and as *e* with zero prosody in the phonetically identical /ˈyeno/ his wife, because of the different contrast systems and phonological structures it enters into in the two grammatical contexts. In this prosodic analysis, the three grammatical categories of first, second, and third person, in both nouns and verbs, can be shown to have as exponents the prosodies of nasalization (N), palatalization (Y), and zero prosody or the contrastive absence of N and Y. Each prosody in turn has a series of phonetic exponents identified in successive segments of the words concerned. Bendor-Samuel's article, though on a remote and little known language, provides a valuable example of phonemic and prosodic analyses placed side by side with reference to the same body of data.

p. 168. Apart from Firth, 24, already mentioned, two general, though brief, accounts of prosodic phonology are available, Robins, 60, and Lyons, 44. Bibliographies of work illustrating the application of prosodic analysis to parts of the phonology or particular languages are to be found in Robins, 60, and more extensively in Bursill-Hall, 14. This latter sequence of two articles is a most valuable summary of Firth's linguistic theory, on phonological analysis and on the other aspects of the study of language. It must not be expected that all the treatments of language material in prosodic terms necessarily agree in all respects in their application of the method; in a number of cases explicit disagreements appear (as they do in any other system of analysis).

68 and 81 contain a number of examples of prosodic analysis, though it cannot be said that all of them make easy reading.

An example of the application of prosodic analysis to the phonological description of an entire language may be seen in Bendor-Samuel, 7, chapter 3.

ADDENDA

p. 151. Halliday, 78 and 79, sets out a somewhat different framework for the analysis of English intonation.

p. 163. On prosodic analysis applied to Russian, Albrow, 76.

p. 168 A short summary of prosodic phonology in the general context of British linguistics during the years 1930–1960 is to be found in Mohrmann, 79, 11–37.

p. 154. A collection of writings by members of the Prague school may be found in Vachek, 80.

5

Grammar: grammatical elements

5·1   PRELIMINARY QUESTIONS

5·1·1   *The material of grammar*

Grammar has been studied from the early days of literate civilization in several centres, both from the point of view of individual
languages and from that of general theory. It is perhaps the concentration of attention on its aims and on the best methods of achieving
them that has been the chief contribution of linguistic science in the
contemporary world to grammar.

Grammar is concerned with the structure of stretches of utterance
or stretches of writing, and with the grouping and classification of
the recurrent elements of utterances by virtue of the functional places
they occupy and the relations they contract with one another in the
structures. Grammar is thus organized on the two dimensions already referred to (2·1·2), syntagmatic and paradigmatic. It may be
approached from the point of view of the grammatical analysis of
the actual utterances of a language, or from that of the generation or
production of utterances by grammatical rules framed for that
purpose.

It is an obvious fact, and this alone makes language capable of its
infinite flexibility (1·3·2), that the unlimited possibility of different
utterances in every language reveals in each a limited number of
regular patterns composed of members of a limited number of classes
of elements in various statable relations with one another. These
elements and relations are expressible in phonological terms (as well
as in orthographic terms, though the orthographic representation of
spoken utterances does not normally indicate all their grammatically

180

relevant features), but they cannot be reduced to phonological rules, that is rules statable by reference to the phonetic categories involved; for this reason grammatical statements are not referable to the phonology of a language or to part of its phonology, but constitute a different level of analysis and description (1·3·1).

A brief illustration from English will clarify the statement just made. Sequences such as *men live* and *man lives* are acceptable English sentences, as are *the man lives* and *the men live*; but †*man live* and †*men lives* are not, nor is †*men the live* († is a convenient mark used to indicate deliberately unacceptable word forms or sentence forms with reference to a given language). But nothing in the phonetic composition of the unacceptable sequences excludes them from the language; they can be written down orthographically, as they have just been written down here, transcribed in an English broad transcription, and easily pronounced by a native speaker of English, in the way that stretches impermissible in English phonology, either employing non-English sounds or sounds in positions from which English structures exclude them (e.g. initial /ŋ/), cannot. Moreover, the possible English sentences are patterns with an infinite range of component substitutions (since vocabulary can be, and is, constantly changing). In place of *man* in *the man lives* can be put *horse, dog, cat, woman,* etc., and in place of *lives* can be put *comes, eats, dies, perspires,* etc., and likewise in *the men live, horses, dogs, cats, women,* etc., and *come, eat, die, perspire,* etc., provided always that there is adequate collocational compatability between the individual items thus linked (2·4·2). The two substitution lists just illustrated are not interchangeable and a member of each first list requires a member of each second list in the production of a three word English sentence of the type referred to. Phonetic composition and phonological structure cannot decide these permitted and excluded word sequences; the phonetic relations between *man* and *men* and between *horse* and *horses* could scarcely be more dissimilar, but they are brought together grammatically by their relations, which are typical of those between thousands of other English words, with other words in English sentences. It is this kind of relationship that provides the material of grammar.

For this reason one can deal satisfactorily with the grammar of a dead language surviving in written records, provided they comprise an adequate and representative sample, but one cannot do so for its phonology to the same extent, as the phonological analysis can only be indirectly based on the phonetic interpretation of the writing system helped out by the remarks of ancient writers on the pronunciation of the language. One can also describe the grammar of the written form of a language (e.g. the grammar of written English); this will partially correspond to the grammar of the spoken language, but in view of the different styles between the two forms of linguistic expression, the two grammars will not be the same; in particular, stress and intonation, unrepresented in ordinary English writing, are not available as marks of grammatical structures or categories in the written language, as they are in transcriptions of spoken English. For the same reasons the grammatical analysis and description of a spoken language need not be based on a prior phonological analysis and description. The exponents of the relevant grammatical elements and categories could be referred directly to the phonic material (the noises) and symbolized in narrow transcription; but in practice some phonological analysis, at least as far as is needed for a broad transcription, is desirable as a means of conveniently representing exponents and examples.

5·1·2 *Formal grammar*

Reflection on the relative simplicity of the basis of grammar (complexity, of which there is no lack, comes with its elaboration in the full grammatical analysis of languages and the theoretical apparatus required for this) should clarify the need for purely formal methods in grammatical method. This need has only been clearly and explicitly realized in fairly recent times, and it has been accompanied by the development of an adequate terminological apparatus to carry it through. **Formal grammar** is grammar that both in theory and in method is concerned solely with the observable forms, structural functions, and interrelations of the components of sentences or stretches of utterance.

Linguistics is an empirical science dealing with observed phenomena, and grammar deals with a particular part of these. Each language as a system of communication is self-contained; native speakers have no need to learn another language in order to conduct their affairs in their own and to make themselves understood and acceptable as speakers of their own language and members of their own speech community; nor need they for these purposes know anything about the history of their own language, important as this is as part of a general education. Speakers of unwritten languages are necessarily in this position, as are most speakers of written languages in fact the world over. The two besetting sins of traditional grammar that have hindered and distorted its operations and the development of theoretical consistency have been the attempts to base grammar and the categories of grammar on alleged types of meaning, or on notional, conceptual, or philosophical categories, and the description of a language in terms found suitable, or assumed to be suitable, for another language, usually one carrying cultural prestige, such as Latin or Sanskrit, or for an earlier stage of the language in question, which for the purposes of grammatical description counts as a separate language also. Frequently both tendencies are found working together, as when in a grammar of English the class of nouns is defined as those words that stand for persons, things, and notions, and when *to the man* is called a dative case, because (presumably) its Latin translation is /homini:/, dative case form of the noun /homo:/ man, but the structurally comparable *behind the man* is (rightly) called a prepositional phrase, because its Latin translation /po:ne hominem/ would be so described.

The so-called class meanings need have nothing to do with the interrelations of the components of sentences; but if there is some parallelism, as is indeed quite common, a consistent account must be achieved in terms of these interrelations and not terms of the apparent meanings. *Perspiration, death, woman, triangle,* and *virtue* are classed together grammatically in English by their similarity of formal relations and positional occurrence in sentences: each can occupy a place after *the* and before a collocationally compatible member of the class of words to which *comes, lives, seems,* etc. belong, and each can begin a sentence of which the second or third word is *is* (*death is the end of life, a triangle is a three-sided plane figure*; the distinction between those words of the class that generally require *a* or *the* before them in sentences of this sort and those which do not is a matter of subclassing within the class). These statements are made on the basis of observation of how sentences appear and are put

183

together in the language. Statements about a common type of meaning in all these and similar words, or about a common way in which their meanings are envisaged or conceived by speakers, must remain partly subjective and not amenable to public observational checking. In the process of establishing grammatical classifications one is not concerned with whether there is anything in common in the actual meanings of *cuts* in *this knife cuts the cake*, of *bisects* in *this line bisects the angle*, and of *adores* in *Jack adores Jill* (or *plum-pudding*), but with the fact that these words behave in sentences in the same way that the words like *comes*, *lives*, and *eats*, mentioned above, behave; and one groups them into the same general class accordingly.

An important part of the description of a language is the statement of the correlations that may be established, in varying degrees, between the structures, classes, and categories of its grammar, on the one hand, and those of semantics, on the other. The historical development of the grammar of a language from one period to another is, equally, a very necessary part of the linguist's study, where the evidence is available. But in the framing of a theory of descriptive grammar, and in carrying out the grammatical analysis of a language, they are always liable to be misleading and distorting. Moreover, an adequate treatment of either of these two topics requires a proper basis in formal grammatical description, if it is to be significant and free from circularity. It is profitable to investigate the types of semantic functions (in so far as these can be established) that are ascribable to different grammatical features in a language, and the degree to which such grammatical and semantic correlations can be attested; but this must come after the formal analysis of the language concerned has been consistently carried through.

It should be clear from what has been said that the quest for a universal grammar is a vain one. Attempts to devise such a system in the past have rested either on the projection of the grammatical framework of a favoured language like Latin on to the analysis of all other languages, irrespective of their actual formal patterns, or on the adoption of a single logical system as supposedly underlying the grammatical organization of every language. Formal grammar must respect the observed patterns of each language separately, though their actual description and analysis rests with the linguist; inductive experience of the formal analysis of several languages of different types may suggest certain general criteria to apply, types of unit and category to look for or set up, and types of procedure to follow. This builds up, not a universal grammar, but a **general theory of grammar** to be appropriately applied to individual languages. In part the categories employed and the results obtained will be different from those of traditional grammar; in part they are likely to resemble earlier work. Provided formal methods are consistently applied, traditional terms often prove useful, though, of course, their definitions arise from within formal analysis and do not depend on their traditional connotations; and traditional grammar, without realizing it or indeed ever really making explicit its principles and methods, has always been partially guided by formal procedures.

5·1·3 *Grammar and phonology*

In dealing with the theory of grammar and the procedures of grammatical analysis, one is at the present time faced with a number of controversial points, which even in an elementary introduction cannot well be avoided.

Three points in particular need to be discussed, and on them there is considerable diversity of opinion among scholars whose writings are likely to be met by the student at an early stage in the study of linguistics.

The first concerns the relation of **grammar** to **phonology**. In a wide and imprecise sense, *grammar* often covers what would more strictly be divided into grammar and phonology, together with some account of the writing system of a written language. For the purposes of general linguistics the two distinct levels of grammar and phonology are usually maintained; and one is intuitively aware that categories such as syllable and stress are of a different nature from categories such as nouns and verbs. It is mainly on the relations between the two levels that controversy arises.

Some maintain that the two levels are of equal status within the system of description and essentially independent, between them providing the total framework of categories necessary for the description of the recurrent patterns and regularities of utterances. Another view is that grammar constitutes the central part of the organization of a language and so of its description, phonology serving to relate grammatical structures and categories to the phonetic categories by which speech is described. This view has to commend it the fact that roughly similar grammatical statements can be made about the written and spoken forms of a single speech community, while the description of a writing system differs much more from the phonological analysis of spoken utterances. Apart from the different overall pictures that result of linguistic systems and linguistic theory, the main significance of this question turns on the degree of inter-dependence allowed in devising descriptive categories. As was seen in the preceding chapter, many phonologists have made use, tacitly or explicitly, of grammatical entities such as words (for whose status see 5·3·1) in the statement of the distribution of phonological elements and for the grouping of allophones into phonemes. Such a view is inherent in any phonological transcription that employs grammatically established inter-word spaces as phonologically significant. Prosodic phonology is prepared to go further, in applying separate phonological analyses to grammatically different classes of words, if the material seems to permit the productive use of such methods (4·4·3).

It has, however, been strongly held by many, particularly in America, that phonological analysis must be exclusively based on phonetic observation alone and that no reference to the level of grammar and no employment of grammatical categories may legitimately be made in establishing or describing phonological categories, if the total analysis is to be scientifically precise and consistent. The implications of this view in phonemic analysis have already been described (4·3·6); in it linguistics is organized into a hierarchy with unilateral dependence of grammar on phonology. But it is possible to argue that the alleged rigour and consistency of this approach is purchased at the price of excessive complexity. The two levels are clearly to be distinguished, and each has its own objects and criteria, but it may well be that some grammatical factors may profitably be taken into account in making phonological statements; vicious circularity would only arise if the same sets of items at each level were made mutually defining (if, for example, the occurrence of a particular feature were said to be confined to a particular position in the word, and then word divisions were established by sole reference to the occurrence of this feature).

Related questions on whether grammatical elements contain or consist of phonological elements in any literal sense are, strictly speaking, made irrelevant by the attitude towards the descriptive and analytic categories of linguistics put forward in this book (2·1·1). All categories are part of the descriptive apparatus or frame set up by the linguist to deal with the particular language, and the relation between them and the material of utterance (or, *mutatis mutandis*, of writing) is one of class and category to exponent or manifestation, with no other status accorded to the classes and categories than that of terms in a system of description. Inter-level dependence may be exploited in either direction: in dealing with spoken language, phonological transcription is usually the most convenient way of representing grammatical elements; and congruence of analysis at the two levels may make one phonological analysis preferable to another in dealing with the same material in the interests of facilitating grammatical statement.

5·1·4 *Grammar and meaning*

The second question, on the relation between **grammar** and **semantics**, is partly concerned with the topic just discussed. It is often maintained that the distinction between the levels of grammar and phonology lies in the alleged fact that phonology operates with meaningless elements (phonemes, syllables, etc.), while grammar sets up and operates with essentially meaningful elements (in particular the morpheme, or minimal element of grammatical structure, 5·4, has been defined by several writers as the minimal meaningful element of language).

The status and the means of establishment of morphemes in the grammatical analysis of a language will be discussed below, 5·4; here it is desirable to point out some of the difficulties that arise on this criterion of grammar and the grammatical level of analysis. What is implied is that the minimal elements of grammar are semantically meaningful elements in their own right, whereas the basic element of phonemic phonology, the phonemes, are not. As matters of fact there is something in these statements, but not as part of the definition of what constitutes grammar. Many grammatical elements or morphemes can have a semantic meaning ascribed to them with tolerable

187

ease; one may instance the plural formative written -*s* in English, as in *cats*, *dogs*, and *horses*, meaning 'more than one', and the past tense formative, written -*ed* or -*d*, as in *walked*, *cured*, and *performed*, meaning 'action or process in past time', but no-one would pretend to ascribe any specific meaning to /p/, /s/, or /u/, considered simply as phonological entities in the English language (the fact that the letter *s* and the consonant unit /s/ are in some words the exponents of the plural formative or morpheme is a contingent matter, not relevant to their status as a letter and as a phoneme).

There are, however, serious objections to the view, admittedly widespread, that it is in this that the distinction between grammar and phonology lies, and, as was seen above, there is no need of this alleged semanticity of the morpheme to maintain the distinction between the two levels. Many elements and categories that must be recognized in grammatical analysis defy the ascription of any plausible semantic function to them as individual components, which is what the use of meaningfulness as part of the definition of grammar comes to. It is scarcely possible to give an individual meaning to the word endings that mark the accusative case in Latin nouns, or to the categories of masculine and feminine gender and the parts of words that mark them in French nouns referring to abstract and inanimate entities, in most of which sex reference or any other semantic correlate of grammatical gender is totally irrelevant. But these are essential parts of the grammar of Latin and French. In English certain 'bound roots', -*ceive* and -*lieve* (5·4·3), may be formally abstracted from words like *deceive*, *receive*, *relieve*, *believe* and, of course, each of these words has a different meaning of its own; but this does not enable one to locate the meaning in either of the two grammatical constituents which are recognized as such simply on the comparison of word forms in the language. It is implausible to assign a specific meaning to English formatives like -*tion* in *imagination*, etc. or -*ize* in *economize*, etc.; one may say that the meaning of such formatives is to form nouns and verbs respectively, but this is a grammatical statement, not a semantic one, and only refers to meaning in the most general sense by which everything in language is meaningful, a sense covering all linguistic elements and functions, and not at issue here.

These are instances of the theoretical objection to the use of meaningfulness as against meaninglessness as a criterion for distinguishing grammar from phonology; but there is a more practical objection, which may carry greater weight. The whole emphasis of grammatical theory and grammatical method today is on formal analysis and formal criteria for the establishment of grammatical elements and grammatical categories, in keeping with the status of linguistics as one of the empirical sciences. Loosely applied semantic and notional considerations have in the past hindered and distorted the grammatical analysis of newly discovered languages and the efficient presentation of the grammar of well-known ones (not least of modern English). It is, therefore, highly desirable that from the start grammatical theory and grammatical practice should be independent of semantic considerations, as they can be, for any of their elements, criteria, and procedures. Of course grammatical analysis presupposes that the material used (utterances of particular languages) is meaningful, in the sense that it would mean something to a speaker of the language, but so does phonological analysis, and *meaningful* in this sense is no more than *genuine*, applying not to the individual bits and pieces of the analysis but to the sentences as wholes.

5·1·5 *The basic units of grammar*

The third general question to be faced at the outset in an account of grammatical theory and practice is that concerning the unit or units recognized as basic (in the way that in phonemic phonology the phoneme is taken as basic, and in prosodic phonology the phonematic unit and prosody are taken as basic).

Traditionally grammar has been built on the word as the basic unit. But some linguists have reacted against this, and argue that since the morpheme (5·4) must be recognized anyway as the minimal unit of grammar, in many cases smaller than the word, grammar is better built on this unit, with words occupying a relatively less important place in the system, along with such larger groupings as phrase and clause.

It has indeed been a weakness of traditional grammar that it failed to recognize sufficiently the place of the morpheme in word structures, which restricted considerably its descriptive power and clarity. But words, as formal elements of a language, can be established and

189

defined within its grammatical system; and when the sort of criteria on which their definition rests have been made clear (5·3), they can serve as a suitable basis, together with morphemes, for the description and analysis of languages at the grammatical level.

The general principles of formal grammatical analysis, which are the subject of this and the following two chapters, apply equally whichever unit is made basic, though with differences of procedure and treatment at certain points, and for elementary purposes there is much to be said for basing grammar on the word, properly established, and not assumed or taken for granted; and this course will be followed here.

The retention of the word as a basic, though not the minimal, unit of grammatical description allows the retention of the traditional division of the grammar of most languages into **morphology**, the study of the grammatical structure of words, and **syntax**, the study of the grammatical structure of sentences as built up of words, though the relations between the two were never made clear in traditional grammar and need careful consideration.

5·2 THE SENTENCE

Grammar is concerned, in the syntagmatic dimension, with the description and analysis of structures that may be abstracted from stretches of utterance. At the grammatical level, the structures are abstracted and analysed in terms of recurrent elements and patterns that are not explicable merely by reference to the phonetic categories involved. Traditionally the longest structure within which a full grammatical analysis is possible has been taken as the **sentence**, or potentially complete utterance. The interrelations of the grammatical elements and groups of elements within a sentence are completely describable in the terms of the grammar of the language to which the sentence belongs.

Certain links may be established between the sentences of a continuous narrative or conversation, relating the grammatical elements and structures of one with those of another, such as cross-reference and anaphora, whereby in English, for example, *he, she, it,* and *they* may refer to previously mentioned persons or things, and the word chosen for this purpose is partly determined by the type of word to which reference is made (*house*, *stone*, *baby*, and *principle* may be followed by *it* in a subsequent sentence; *man*, *horse*, and *minister* by *he*; *woman*, *mare*, and *ship* by *she*; there are further refinements and variations of these relations which need not be followed up here). But such links are only partial, whereas within the sentence the interrelations of all the grammatical elements can be brought within the compass of grammatical rules. Therefore the sentence is conveniently taken as the largest unit of grammatical analysis and the upper limit of structural statement at the grammatical level.

Certain consequences follow from this. A sentence is by definition grammatically complete (the alleged 'incomplete' or 'elliptical' situationally tied sentences are complete in those situations, cp. 6·3·1); it may, therefore, be preceded and followed by indefinite pause or silence, together with those phonetic features associated in each language with prepausal position; it is usually marked in writing by final punctuation, full stop, question mark, exclamation mark, or semicolon, and in speech by a characteristic intonation tune. Intonation tunes coextensive with a sentence often do, and in all cases may, close with a sentence final pattern of pitches. While in continuous discourse sentences may follow one another without pause or intervening silence, there is always potentiality of pause at sentence boundaries. Thus the sentence can be phonologically defined as a stretch of speech that may be uttered with a prepausal intonation tune. More briefly a sentence may be called a potentially complete utterance. This congruence between the grammatical and phonological levels, though it is potential rather than always actual, is an additional characteristic of the status of the sentence as a structural unit.

Since language is by definition meaningful (1·3·4), it follows that a potentially complete stretch of utterance will be, as a whole utterance, meaningful within the situation in which it is uttered. As a whole it can be functionally related to the relevant components of the situation, and its meaning explained by reference to a context of situation abstracted from the total extra-linguistic environment for this purpose (1·4·3). This may also be true of some or all of its constituent parts. But these are not, when occurring as sentence parts, themselves complete utterances (though in many cases they could be); they need not themselves have an independently statable semantic function or meaning; and the meaning of a word or group of words forming part of a larger sentence is not necessarily the same thing as the meaning of that same word or group when constituting a sentence complete in its own right.

Traditional grammar went further than this and declared that sentences expressed a complete predication, question, or command, and that each had a specific logical form. The predicative sentence was often equated with the proposition of logic. But as linguistics, and therefore grammar as part of linguistics, is distinct from logic, though both are in different ways concerned with language and its use, the same definitions will not produce satisfactory structures for both studies alike. Propositions are defined, classified, and analysed by their logical form and content, which are matters for logicians; sentences are defined, classified, and analysed by their grammatical (and secondarily by their phonological) structures, which are matters for the linguist to determine. In all languages in which logical enquiries have been systematically undertaken, there are certain general, though not universal, correlations between sentence types and proposition types; and in all languages there are similar correlations between sentence forms and types of meaning or situational function (command, enquiry, statement, and the like). Linguists try to state them in any account of a language that purports to be complete, and to allow for them in any theory of language; and the relations between linguistic or grammatical form and logical form are a very proper subject of interdisciplinary investigation. But for statements in these fields to be informative, sentence types and sentence form must first be described and analysed by strictly formal linguistic means.

Grammar thus operates between the **upper limit** of the **sentence** and the **lower limit** of the **morpheme** or minimal grammatical unit. Between these limits structures given such titles as clause, piece, phrase, and word may be abstracted and formally delimited. Of these, in all languages the word appears as a particularly stable element, and serves as a basic grammatical unit in grammar as outlined in this book. The status of the word and the morpheme as formal units of grammatical structure and grammatical analysis will be considered in the following sections.

192

5.3   THE WORD

5.3.1   *Grammatical criteria of word status*

The term *word* has been used hitherto in this book without comment on its linguistic status. To those brought up in the literate tradition of the West any such discussion may seem otiose. This is part of the legacy of western literacy, with words listed in dictionaries and distinguished unambiguously in writing by spaces, whereby their self-evident status in both spoken and written discourse comes to be taken for granted. Experience in the analysis of unwritten languages, and the need to devise theories and procedures of grammar that may be applicable to any language have shown that words cannot be assumed at the outset, but must be established as grammatical units for the language under investigation. They are essentially units of the language as a system rather than of speech, wherein they are not, save in quite exceptional circumstances, delimited by inter-word pauses as printed words are delimited in the roman alphabet by inter-word spaces. Malinowski went so far as to say that words 'are in fact only linguistic figments, the products of an advanced linguistic analysis'; and this is justifiable in so far as it stresses the need for the word, whether institutionalized by writing or not in a particular language, to be formally established, if it is to serve as a basic unit of formal grammar. But diverse experience goes to show that native speakers have an intuitive awareness of word-like entities in their own language, whether written or not, to a greater extent than they have of other grammatical elements and structures set up by the linguist. The use of orthographic spaces, or other marks as in some non-roman scripts, is evidence of this, and Sapir noticed how readily linguistically untrained speakers of unwritten languages could come to recognize stretches of utterance between which pauses could be made (as in dictation) but which were themselves in some way felt as indivisible. It is likely that this intuitive and ready awareness of such a unit is an implicit response to a variety of formal criteria in the speaker's language, which the linguist in making his abstraction of word units must set out fully and systematically, and which linguistic theory must enable one to formalize and make explicit.

When sentences of the same language are studied and compared, it is seen that certain stretches in them exhibit an internal stability peculiar to themselves. These stretches may appear at different places in sentences relative to each other (*the kitten saw the pigeons, the pigeons saw the kitten; two and five make seven, five and two make seven*), may be separated by other stretches (*the kitten I bought saw the pigeons*), and by momentary pauses (*the puppy, the kitten, and the children were all playing, when it started to rain*); but they do not permit internal rearrangement of their constituent parts, nor the insertion of comparable and virtually unlimited further stretches of utterance, and they may not in normal speech be interrupted by any pause. Moreover, most of these stable stretches may themselves stand alone to constitute a complete sentence or whole utterance.

These unitary stretches represent what are called **words** in formal grammar; in written languages they usually (but not always or necessarily) correspond to the orthographic words, but they are equally well establishable in unwritten languages, since they are based on the inspection and comparison of spoken utterances by the linguist.

Definitions of the word unit have not been lacking, but those relying on non-formal, extra-grammatical criteria such as 'possessing a single meaning' or 'conveying a single idea' are of little value. Bloomfield's classic definition of the word as the 'minimum free form' of a language is really a special application of the criterion of stability. The word as a stretch of speech that admits momentary pause on either side may also appear between indefinite pauses as a minimal utterance or minimal sentence. The sentence is a free linguistic form, and the word is its minimal version. The word, defined as a minimum free form, is an element corresponding to a stretch of speech that, with differences of intonation and in some languages of stressing, and sometimes differences of segmental composition, may both appear recurrently and recognizably in longer sentences, and stand alone to constitute a sentence, but cannot be divided without remainder into such stretches. Thus in English *man* is a word, and so is *manly*, because, though *man* can stand alone (*Who was made like the angels? Man*), *-ly* (/-li/) cannot (except as a citation of a grammatical form, and any element in a language can be cited in this way, virtually becoming a word in its own right in such a use).

Words, like many other analytic entities, are the products of several different though related criteria. Thus they comprise nuclear members of the category, to which all the criteria apply, more peripheral or marginal ones to which only some apply, and very marginal or doubtful cases in which the criteria may conflict and different conclusions may be reached by the different weighting of the conflicting criteria. Stability is the basic criterion, which splits into a number of separate features; of these minimum free form status is perhaps the most obvious. The actual probability of individual words in a language occurring in normal discourse as independent sentences accompanied by sentence final intonation and followed by indefinite pause is obviously variable, with proper names and a few exclamative words like *hello, goodbye,* and *bother!* being the commonest types so used; but most words can appear acceptably as one word sentences. A small number of very frequently occurring items are very implausibly regarded as constituting complete sentences, and some may be positively excluded from such a function. Here the criteria of positional mobility in the sentence and separability from what preceded and follows are invoked. English *a* and *the* hardly ever occur as complete sentences (and then as /ei/ and /ði:/, instead of the normal /ə/ and /ðə/ or /ði/ of connected discourse); but in other respects they behave as independent words, being parallel in sentence structures to *this* and *that* (*the man is here, in this room*; *that man is here, in the room*), which obviously do occur as complete sentences, and being separable from the words following them (*a dog; a big dog; the big black shaggy dog*). In this respect it is clear that English *the* is quite different in grammatical status from the suffixed 'definite article' of the Scandinavian languages and Rumanian, which, however intertranslatable they may be with most uses of English *the*, are always attached to a preceding word to form part of it. Thus, Norwegian *hus* /hu:s/ house, *huset* /ˈhu:sə/ the house; Rumanian *lup* /lup/ wolf, *lupul* /ˈlupul/ the wolf, *lupul mare* /ˈlupul ˈmare/ the big wolf; Scandinavian languages do also have a separate definite article similar to English *the*, used with adjective noun groups: *det store hus* /də ˈsto:rə ˈhu:s/ the big house.

More marginal as members of the class of words are the French unemphatic pronouns, *je* /ʒə/ I, *tu* /ty/ you (singular), *il* /il/ he, etc.; they are never found alone as in this position the independent or emphatic pronouns are used instead, *moi* /mwa/, *toi* /twa/, *lui* /lɥi/, etc., and in sentences they always form part of a closely knit verbal group. Some can occur in the same place as a proper name, clearly a free form (*Jean commande* /ʒɑ̃ kɔmɑ̃d/ John orders, *il commande* /il kɔmɑ̃d/ he orders), but others such as *y* /i/ cannot, but are only found in fixed positions relative to other similar forms in a verbal group, though separable from them by limited possibilities of insertion of other unemphatic pronouns and a few other elements, such as negatives (*il l'y met* /i li mɛ/ he puts it there; *il ne l'y met pas* /il nə li mɛ pɑ/ he does not put it there). These unemphatic pronouns are generally regarded as words, but of strictly limited mobility in sentence structures. The fact that historically they are descended from free words (mostly pronouns) in Latin, though of significance in the history of the French language, is quite irrelevant to the statement of their grammatical status in the language today.

Still more marginal in regard to word status is English *'s* (/s/, /z/, or /iz/), usually called the 'possessive suffix' or '-s genitive'; it is never free to occur alone, and it mostly consists of a single consonant (*-iz* occurs always and only after words ending in /s/, /z/, /ʃ/, /ʒ/, /tʃ/, and /dʒ/), and then it has no alternative longer form, as the 'weak forms' of English words do (*I'll go* /ail ˈgou/, *I will go* /ai wil ˈgou/, etc.). Moreover, it is very limited in its positional possibilities in sentences. But word groups do occur, in spoken rather than in written English, in which it belongs grammatically to a series of words rather than to the word to which phonologically it is attached (cp. 6·3·4), such as *member of Parliament's salary*, and *the boy I saw yesterday's jacket*, and these make it unlike other English suffixes in its grammatical behaviour. It has been variously analysed as a suffix of unique behaviour and as a word of unique form; the balance of evidence is probably in favour of its treatment as a peculiar suffix, not as a word, but with elements as marginal as this, where the relevant criteria that normally reinforce one another are in conflict, more than one analysis can be justified.

Most languages contain both **variable** and **invariable** words. Variable words are those in which ordered and regular series of grammatically different word forms are found, wherein part remains relatively constant and the variations in the other parts are matched by similar variations in other words; in English *walk, walks, walking, walked, follow, follows, following, followed*, etc., and *cat, cats, car, cars, house, houses*, etc. are variable words, and the ordered series of forms are called paradigms. Words appearing in only one form are invariable words, such as English *since, when, seldom*. Languages differ in the number and complexity of the paradigms of their variable words; German has more grammatical word form variation than English, and Latin and Sanskrit have more than German. Some languages, mostly in the Far East and parts of South-east Asia, of which the Chinese languages form the best known examples, contain virtually only invariable words, without grammatical paradigms.

5·3·2 *Phonological markers of the word unit*

It will have been seen that in setting out the criteria of grammatical word status no attention was paid to meanings, nor to questions of phonological features, other than the actual phonological shape representing the word in spoken utterance. As regards meaning, since words are by definition mostly free forms, i.e. potential sentences, and as sentences are as such meaningful, words are generally speaking suitable units for the assignment of a meaning of some sort; and they are so used in dictionary making. But definitions of the individual word unit in terms of its having a simple meaning are quite useless; particular words can be glossed in a dictionary with a greater or lesser degree of precision, depending on their various uses in sentences, but no observations can determine whether any meaning statable of a word is simple or complex. Pairs such as *lovelier* and *more lovely*, and *oculist* and *eye doctor* are formally one and two words respectively, though their lexical meanings are practically the same.

As regards phonological features, certain correlations can be found with grammatical word status in many languages, and in such languages this should be brought out clearly in the description. Languages differ considerably in the amount of such correlations exhibited between the phonological and grammatical levels. At one extreme French is often cited as a language wherein little information is given by phonological criteria on word divisions in connected discourse. In the feature of liaison in French, words ending phonetically (not orthographically) with a consonant and followed without pause by a word beginning with a vowel syllabify the consonant and vowel across the word boundary; English has the possibility of distinguishing between pairs such as *a name* and *an aim*, *a tease* and *at ease*, etc., by the sort of features referred to in the preceding chapter and treated as juncture phonemes or as word prosodies (4·3·6, 4·4·2). Some other languages show much more correlation; as noticed already (4·3·6), Hungarian stresses the initial syllable of most grammatical word units, while generally speaking Polish, Swahili, and Sundanese (spoken in Java), three totally unrelated languages widely separated from one another geographically, stress the penultimate syllable of words. Some languages restrict severely the consonants that can appear in word final position; Japanese only allows the syllabic nasal (4·3·4, p. 139), and Ancient Greek has only the following word final consonants: /n/, /r/, /s/, /ks/ and /ps/; /k/ and /kʰ/ occur in two words only (ἐκ /ek/ out, and οὐκ /ouk/ not, before words beginning with a vowel, οὐχ /oukʰ/ before words beginning with h/). As a consequence in such languages, other consonants give the negative information of word non-finality. Vowel harmony, or the restriction of the categories of vowels within words, whose working in such languages as Turkish and Hungarian has already been described (4·4·2), is a further example of grammatical and phonological correlations.

It must be remembered that phonological features of the types mentioned in the preceding paragraph, relevant as they are in the languages that exhibit them, are, of necessity, logically secondary considerations in the establishment of grammatical word units. They are seldom, if ever, entirely in agreement with the grammatical criteria over the whole of the vocabulary of a language, and where there is conflict between grammatical criteria of the types described in 5·3·1 and phonological features normally coinciding in delimiting the same stretch of speech, the grammatical criteria must be allowed to carry the day. Examples of this conflict are seen in some words of foreign origin in Swahili, stressed on syllables other than the penultimate, and words such as *a, az* /ɔ/, /ɔz/ the (definite article), in Hungarian, seldom stressed at all. A unit or a category must be established and defined by criteria from the same level of analysis as that at which it will subsequently be used. If the word is to be employed as a basic unit of grammatical description, both in morphology and syntax, grammatical criteria are the primary ones in its delimitation. It may be the case in some languages that usually congruent phonological features, such as fixed-place stress, are more obvious and so more immediately recognizable in analysis, but they remain secondary. A trivial illustration from another field may help: students in an examination room might be divided into two groups, those taking domestic science papers and those taking electrical engineering papers, and for the invigilators this would be the fundamental distinction. If in a particular year it so happened that all those taking domestic science were women, and all those taking electrical engineering were men, this would be the most noticeable feature by which the two groups could be differentiated for the distribution of papers and so on. There may be a likelihood that the sex difference and the subject difference will show some degree of correlation, just as there is a likelihood that the grammatical and phonological levels of the same language will show correlations, but this cannot be assumed, and the distribution of papers by an invigilator on the basis of a sex difference would be justified in that particular year only because they had previously been divided into the two groups on the basis of primary criteria (courses of study followed and the like) and the sex correlation then observed.

In cases where a language does exhibit any marked degree of phonological and grammatical correlations in its word forms, this is an added reason in a complete linguistic description of the language for treating the word as a basic unit of grammar, since one is then bringing into prominence a structure of which the grammatical and phonological description are maximally congruent and so giving a more coherent total analysis of the language. This virtue in linguistic description, where the language permits it, may be called congruence of levels, and it is in many languages a characteristic of the word as a generic unit that it is the point below the sentence at which grammatical features and phonological features are most convergent. (The syllable and the morpheme (5·4) are usually more exclusively phonologically and grammatically characterized units, respectively.) It has already been seen that prosodic phonology treats phonological features that are characteristic of word structures as such, either demarcatively or by extension of their exponents over more than one place therein, under a particular category of word prosodies (4·4·2).

5·3·3 *Variant word forms*

Languages differ not only in the phonological correlations they ex-hibit with grammatical word boundaries, but also in the degree to which words vary in form phonologically in sentences. In all lan-guages, words differ in such features as intonation pitches and rela-tive speed of articulation and stressing, according to whether they are uttered alone or as part of a larger sentence and according to their position and environment in the sentence. But other differences of word form in sentences vary from language to language. The exist-ence in English of 'weak' and 'strong' forms of some words has already been mentioned, whereby a considerable number of com-monly used words appear in one form when used in isolation or when stressed in a sentence, and in a number of other forms, usually shorter, in connected discourse with normal stress patterning (4·2). Thus the sentence *I should have thought so* may appear as /ai ˈʃud həv ˈθɔːt sou/, with *should* stressed and emphasized, or, with normal stressing, as /ai ʃəd həv ˈθɔːt sou/, and more quickly as /ai ʃədəv ˈθɔːt sou/ or /aiʃtəfˈθɔːtsou/. Such differences are to a limited extent marked in spelling, but never completely; this was one of the considerations that led to the devising of transcriptions to deal adequately with facts of speech like this.

In French several words have two different forms, with and without a final consonant, according to whether they are followed without pause and in close grammatical relation by a word beginning with a vowel (again it must be emphasized that this is a statement about the phonological form of French words as spoken, not about their spelling). Thus *est*, is, in isolation and before consonants is pro-nounced /ɛ/, but before a vowel initial word /ɛt/ (*il est brave* /il ɛ braːv/ he is brave, but *il est aimable* /il ɛt ɛmablə/ he is agreeable; so, too, *bon* /bɔ̃/ good, but *bon air* /bɔn ɛːr/ good appearance). In Sanskrit word shapes are considerably affected by the shapes of adjacent words and the final consonants of many words differ in connected discourse according to whether the word is final in its group or sentence and according to the initial consonant of an immediately following word. These differences were represented in the Sanskrit spelling and are therefore known in some detail (*tat* /tat/ that; *taj jāyate* /taɟ ɟaːjate/ that is born; *tac chinatti* /tac chinatti/ he cuts that; *mahat* /mahat/ big; *mahad dhanuḥ* /mahad dhanuh/ big bow). The term used of this sort of word form variation by the ancient Indian grammarians was *sandhi* ('putting together'), and this has been generalized as a technical term in linguistic description for all such phenomena. The differences between the tones of words in tone languages when conditioned by the tonal patterns of neighbouring words (4·3·5) have been called tone-sandhi.

A special case of word form variation is found in Celtic languages (e.g. Irish, Welsh, and Gaelic), whereby some words appear in a number of forms differing in their initial consonant or its absence and dependent on the particular preceding word or on the grammatical relation between them. Thus Welsh:

tad /ta:d/ father	*gardd* /garð/ garden
fy nhad /və/or/ə nha:d/ my father	*fy ngardd* /və ŋarð/ my garden
ei dad /i da:d/ his father	*ei ardd* /i arð/ his garden
ei thad /i θa:d/ her father	*ei gardd* /i garð/ her garden
eu tad /i ta:d/ their father	*eu gardd* /i garð/ their garden

It will be noticed that in some cases the distinction between 'his', 'her', and 'their' is shown by the differences in the initial segment of the second word form. The traditional name for these Celtic initial sandhi differences is *mutation*.

Sandhi differences are not generally regarded as paradigms like the paradigms of variable words referred to above (5·3·1), because they are often determined by the phonological shape of adjacent word forms, as in Sanskrit and French, and are not tied to specific grammatical relationships or limited to specific grammatical classes of words; they may affect words that are grammatically variable or invariable.

5·4   THE MORPHEME

5·4·1 *The morpheme as the minimal grammatical unit*

The word has been treated in this account of grammatical analysis as a fundamental and unique grammatical unit; but it is demonstrably not the minimal grammatical unit. The most casual comparison of such word forms as *cats, dogs,* and *horses,* with *cat, dog,* and *horse* reveals the divisibility of the former set into two grammatically significant elements, *cat-*, *dog-*, *horse-*, and *-s* (or, in phonological transcription, /-s/, /-z/, and /-iz/).

These elements are grammatically significant, not primarily because of a 'more than one' meaning attaching to most words with such a plural formative, but because of the formal patterning in English sentences *the cat eats*, and *the cats eat*, etc. It is further apparent that below this, at the grammatical level, no further analysis of these words into smaller units is possible; phonologically /kæt/, /dɔg/, and /hɔ:s/ are further divisible into consonant and vowel elements, but this division does not make for the abstraction of any grammatically relevant pieces.

These minimal grammatical units are called **morphemes**. It is remarkable that adequate recognition of the morpheme as a grammatical unit, and consequently a proper treatment of morphological word structure was not achieved in western scholarship until fairly recently, despite the preoccupation of grammarians throughout antiquity and the Middle Ages with the morphological aspect of grammar. Recognition of the status of the morpheme in linguistic analysis was one of the achievements of the ancient Indian linguists, of whom Pāṇini is the most famous, and this is one of the debts Western linguistic scholarship owes to Indian work, which became known in Europe during the course of the nineteenth century.

Morphemes are established and delimited in a language by comparing word forms with one another and noting the recurrent pieces that compose them, and every word is wholly analysable into one or more morphemes. Thus *-s* /-s/, is revealed by comparing *cap*, *caps*, *cat*, *cats*, *lock*, *locks*, etc., and *-ment* /mənt/, by comparing *establish*, *establishment*, *embarrass*, *embarrassment*, *atone*, *atonement*, etc. Morphemes may be represented by, or correspond to, any phonological feature or shape, and may be monosyllabic or polysyllabic. /-z/ in /dɔgz/ is a single consonant; /-li/ in *lovely* /ˈlʌvli/, shows a CV structure, /-i/ in *doggy* /ˈdɔgi/, is a single vowel; *tobacco* /təˈbækou/ contains three syllables. The syllabic (phonological) structure of a word and its morphemic (grammatical) structure do not necessarily correspond; in *loveliness*, syllabically and morphemically /ˈlʌv-li-nis/, they happen to coincide, but in *teller*, syllabically /ˈte-lə/, morphemically /ˈtel-ə/, they do not.

202

5.4.2 *Morpheme variants (allomorphs)*

It has already been seen that words may exhibit different shapes according to their position in spoken sentences; this is much more characteristic of morphemes in almost all, if not in quite all, languages. But whereas variant word shapes in most languages (i.e. other than those in which rigid sandhi rules apply) are fairly freely variable and depend for the most part on style and speed of utterance, most variant morpheme shapes are strictly dependent on their environment within the word, like the variant allophones within a phoneme in phonemic phonology (4.3.1, 4.3.2). Thus the regular formatives of English noun plurals,[1] /-s/, /-z/, and /-iz/, are distributed according to the final vowel or consonant of the word base or singular form: words ending in a voiced consonant, other than /z/, /ʒ/, or /ʤ/, or in a vowel (which are all voiced in English), have /-z/ (*dogs* /dɔgz/, *cows* /kauz/, *hens* /henz/); those ending in a voiceless consonant, other than /s/, /ʃ/, or /ʧ/ have /-s/ (*cats* /kæts/, *tacks* /tæks/); those ending in /s/, /z/, /ʃ/, /ʒ/, /ʧ/, and /ʤ/ have /iz/ (*horses* /ˈhɔːsiz/, *prizes* /ˈpraiziz/, *rushes* /ˈrʌʃiz/, *churches* /ˈʧəːʧiz/, *judges* /ˈʤʌʤiz/).

In order to make the parallelism with phoneme and allophone more clear, some linguists reserve the term *morpheme* for the whole grammatically relevant class of shapes that are in complementary distribution or in free variation in a given environment, and call the different shapes themselves morphs or **allomorphs**. This, however, is not universal practice, and provided it is remembered that the word *morpheme* may be used by different writers both for the individual form and for the whole class, confusion need not arise.

The allomorphs or variant morpheme shapes /-s/, /-z/, and /-iz/ are phonologically predictable in their distribution relative to one another, but there are plenty of examples of allomorphs of a morpheme in complementary distribution but not predictable by any phonological criteria. The English plural *-en* /-ən/, is a case in point; the pair of words *ox, oxen*, grammatically parallel to *dog, dogs*, establishes it as a member of the same morpheme (or morpheme

1. Traditionally familiar terms like *noun* and *plural* are used in this section for convenience. Their status and establishment in formal grammar are dealt with subsequently. These categories have no special bearing on the questions discussed other than providing suitable exemplification.

class) as /-s/, /-z/, and /-iz/, but inspection of the singular form does not lead one to expect the form *oxen*, as inspection of the regular noun *box* leads one to expect *boxes*. Plurals like *oxen* have to be learned individually in learning English.

English noun plurals illustrate a number of the problems that arise in the morphemic analysis of word structures in different languages (it must be emphasized at this point that this and subsequent chapters do not set out to give an account of English grammar; English is simply used more than other languages to illustrate the theory and procedures of formal grammatical analysis and description). Beside the regular forms /-s/, /-z/, and /-iz/, and the irregular /-ən/, other irregular plurals of nouns are found, such as *children, sheep, feet, men*. In the analysis of these word forms, the aim, as in all linguistic analysis and description, is to state the observed facts in as economical and consistent a manner as completeness permits. With *child, children* (/ʧaild/, /ˈʧildrən/), two points are illustrated:

1. The singular and plural forms of the word base itself differ (as also happens in the archaic plural of *brother, brethren*), and

2. A choice must be made between taking /-ən/ and /-rən/ as the plural allomorph. In favour of /-ən/ is the recognition of this form already in *oxen* /ˈɔksən/, but in favour of /-rən/ is the consequent greater similarity of the singular and plural base forms /ʧaild/ and /ˈʧild-/. The choice may be fairly evenly balanced, and either analysis is legitimate, though clearly, in a description of English grammar one must be chosen.

Words like *sheep* in English must be regarded as having singular and plural forms with the same overt shape, since the same word shape appears in sentences like *the sheep is grazing* and *the sheep are grazing*. Such words are sometimes analysed as having a plural formative element like *cows, horses*, etc., but without overt shape; that is to say an analytic entity is introduced without exponents at other levels or in the material, written or spoken, in order to keep the words in question within the same grammatical structure pattern as the majority of comparable words. This procedure, which goes back to Pāṇini, involves the use of **zero** elements, the name given to analytic entities without actual or overt exponents; it is justified if the introduction of the zero element simplifies the resulting analysis by

204

aligning the structures of more words together. If all English noun plurals are to be regarded analytically as involving a specific plural formative morpheme, this treatment of words like *sheep, aircraft, deer*, etc. seems inevitable. Zero may be symbolized Ø, *sheep plural* being represented /ʃiːp/+Ø.

Pairs of words like *foot, feet* and *man, men* are more troublesome in morphemic analysis, but a study of the possible alternative treatments is instructive. It may be held that the plural-forming morpheme is represented in words like this not by a shape but by a process of changing /u/ to /iː/, /æ/ to /e/, etc. added to the base or singular form, or that the plural morpheme is represented by /iː/,/ e/, etc., the allomorph /f . . t/, /m . . n/, etc. being used in conjunction with it, as /ˈtʃild-/ is used in conjunction with /-rən/. Neither of these solutions is very attractive, as a process is not really something that can be added to something else, and discontinuous roots like /f . . t/ and infixed morphemes are not otherwise found as part of English morphology. Alternatively the plural formative can be said to have zero shape, as in the case of *sheep*, and that /fiːt/, /men/, etc. are the alternant morpheme shapes or allomorphs used before the plural morpheme represented by zero. Yet another solution is to regard forms like *men* as single morphs representing two morphemes, because of their grammatical comparability with forms like *dogs*.

These solutions are all based on a determination to preserve the bimorphemic structure of all English noun plurals. If this requirement is relaxed, words like *feet, mice, men*, and *geese* are monomorphemic and are associated with singular forms like *foot, mouse, man*, and *goose* by the relationship of vowel alternance. In some respects this is an attractive solution, though it involves the admission that grammatically comparable word forms may be dissimilar in morphemic composition. In this mode of analysis *sheep* and other English nouns having the same overt form in the singular and plural would be said also to have the same morphemic composition in both cases.

The analysis and classification of the different phonological shapes in which morphemes appear, or by which they are represented, both in individual languages and in languages in general, is often called **morphophonology** or more briefly **morphonology**; in America where phonology, considered as part of descriptive, synchronic linguistics, has relied on phonemic analysis (4·3·6–7), the term *morphophonemics* is used for this aspect of grammar.

5·4·3 *Bound and free morphemes: root and affix*

Morphemes may be classified in more than one dimension (in this book the term *morpheme* will generally be used in referring to the actual form or representative shape, unless the specific use of *allomorph* is necessary for clarity). Firstly, morphemes are **bound** and **free**.

A free morpheme is one that may constitute a word (free form) by itself; a bound morpheme is one that must appear with at least one other morpheme, bound or free, in a word. In English *cats*, *cat* is free, since *cat* is a word in its own right, and -*s* is bound, as it is not a word in its own right. Free morphemes therefore necessarily constitute monomorphemic words. It has been said of one or two languages, for example Vietnamese, that almost all the morphemes are free, that is to say that the word and morpheme almost coincide in exponency. But such languages are a special case, and for the great majority the terms *word*, *free morpheme*, and *bound morpheme* are all required. Polymorphemic words may consist wholly of free morphemes, being accorded word status on the ground of uninterruptability and unitary behaviour in sentences (5·3·1); they are often called compound words, and English *penknife*, *aircraft*, and *housework* are examples.

Secondly, morphemes may be divided into **roots** and **affixes**, the root being that part of a word structure which is left when all the affixes have been removed. Root morphemes may be bound or free, and are potentially unlimited in number in a language, as additions to vocabulary are in the main made by the acquisition of new roots either taken from foreign languages ('loan words', 8·1·7) or created for the purposes (like a number of trade names for products and the like). Affixes are bound morphemes; they are limited in number, though their numbers vary from language to language, and they may be exhaustively listed. Some affixes serve to differentiate the paradigm forms of variable words, containing a common root; others recur in the formation of a large number of polymorphemic words together with a large number of different root morphemes. All words may be said to contain a root morpheme, and therefore monomorphemic words may be said to comprise a single root. Some words contain more than one root, and the number of affixes in words in addition to the root, or roots, varies considerably in different languages.

In the English paradigm *cat, cats,* the form *cat* /kæt/ is the root and *-s* /-s/ an affix; in *try, tries, trying, tried,* the root is *try (trie-)* /trai/, and *-s* /-z/, *-ing* /-iŋ/, and *-d* /-d/ are affixes. In *loveliness, manliness, react, recover,* and *remove, love, man, act, cover,* and *move* are roots, and *-li-, -ness,* and *re-* are affixes. In these examples the roots exhibit only one form in terms of consonant and vowel structure; but variant forms, or allomorphs of roots may occur with different affixes. This is the case with the irregular plural form *children,* noticed above, and with a number of verbs, such as *sleep, slept* /sli:p/, /slep-/ + /-t/. Some verbs in many languages combine quite different forms as variants of their roots; compare English *go, went* /gou/, /wen/ + /-t/, with *walk, walked* /wɔ:k/, /wɔ:k/ + /-t/, and French *aller* /al-/ + /-e/ to go, *irai* /i-/ + /-r-/ + /-e/ (I) will go, *vont* /v-/ + /-ɔ̃/ (they) go, with *donner* /dɔn-/ + /-e/ to give, *donnerai* /dɔn-/ + /-ər-/ + /-e/ (I) will give, *donnent* /dɔn-/ + Ø (they) give. Such roots involving total variation among their allomorphs are sometimes called suppletive (6·6).

Roots and affixes may be of any structure and length, though affixes generally tend to be shorter than roots. The only relevant criterion for establishing a part or the whole of a word as a single root is the impossibility of dividing it further into constituent morphemes by matching its parts with the parts of other words in the language. The disyllabic English word *express* (noun or verb) may be compared with *press, impress,* and *expression,* etc., and its bimorphemic structure thereby established; but *bishop, turtle,* and *potato* admit no such division into further morphemes. Matching the *pot-* /pət-/of *potato* with *pot* /pɔt/ will not help, because the remainder *-ato* /-ˈeitou/ cannot be similarly matched with recurrent elements of other words. The abstraction of morphemes such as *goose-* /guz-/ and *logan-* /ˈlougən/ in *gooseberry* and *loganberry* is justified, by the occurrence of *-berry* /-bəri/, with a number of other clearly defined morphemes, such as *black, straw, dew (blackberry* /ˈblækbəri/, *strawberry* /ˈstrɔ:bəri/, *dewberry* /ˈdju:bəri/), as well as by itself as a complete word in the allomorphic form /ˈberi/.

Cross-linguistic appeals to equivalents or earlier forms in other languages are wholly irrelevant to this sort of question in synchronic analysis. The trimorphemic status of the Ancient Greek word ἐπίσκοπος /epískopos/ overseer, guardian, is irrelevant to the monomorphemic status of its derivatives in several modern European languages, English *bishop*, French *évêque* /evɛk/, German *Bischof* /ˈbiʃoːf/, Hungarian *püspök* /pyʃpøk/, etc. This is just one illustration of the difference between diachronic etymological studies and synchronic descriptive studies, and of the need, not always observed in the past, to avoid diachronic considerations in what should be strictly synchronic analysis.

A particular relation holds between the root and the affixes in languages subject to vowel harmony, a feature of word structure characterizing Turkish, Hungarian, Finnish, and a number of other languages (4·4·2). In such languages it is the vowel or vowels of the root that determine the vowel qualities of the suffixes. Examples of this have already been given in the section just referred to in Hungarian and Turkish; in Finnish one may compare *puu* /puː/ tree, partitive case form *puuta* /puːta/, and *pyy* /pyː/ partridge, partitive case form *pyytä* /pyːtæ/. The relation between phonology and morphology in the analysis of word structures like this differs according to whether the phonology is phonemic or prosodic. The exponents of the root and affix respectively would be located in the phoneme sequences /puː/ and /pyː/, and /ta/ and /tæ/; the distinction between /a/ and /æ/ being maintained in the structural analysis of these morpheme shapes because it is phonemic elsewhere in the language, according to the general practice of overall, monosystemic, phonemic analysis (4·4·3). In a prosodic analysis of these words the back and front features characterizing the vowel harmony might be abstracted as part of the word and allocated to the root morpheme in each example, the partitive case morpheme showing only one allomorph *-ta*, *a* representing a vowel phonematic unit of open quality. The root morphemes in the partitive case forms *puuta* /puːta/ and *pyytä* /pyːtæ/ might be represented as

```
w----------       y----------
l, o ---    and   l, o---
 p   ɪ             p   ɪ
```

with *p* and *ɪ* being phonematic consonant and vowel units, *ɪ* being a close vowel, and w and y representing word prosodies of back and front quality respectively, o an initial syllable (and also root) prosody of lip-rounding, and l a syllable prosody of length.

The distinction between root and affix is not the same as that between bound and free morpheme, except that affixes are always bound within the word. Roots may be bound or free, and the relative proportions of the two types vary between different languages. In English the majority of root shapes are themselves free forms, that is words in their own right. Bound roots are relatively few, but some are found, such as *-ceive*, *-tain*, and *-cur*, in *receive*, *retain*, *recur*, etc. These bound root morphemes are established by comparing series of words such as *receive*, *recapture*, *redeem*, *recover*, *recur*, *retain*, *deceive*, *detain*, *contain*, *conceive*, and *concur*. A few English roots have bound and free variants, such as *sleep* and *slep-* /sliːp/ and /slep-/, and *child* and *child-* /tʃaɪld/ and /ˈtʃild-/ (or *childr-* /ˈtʃildr-/ with *-en* /-ən/, as the plural affix morpheme instead of *-ren* /-rən/).

In some other languages root morphemes are very frequently bound. In Latin the root morphemes of verbs are almost always bound forms not having the same shape as any member of the verb paradigms; thus the root of the Latin verb /amoː/ I love, is /am-/, and this does not constitute by itself any complete word form in the paradigm of /amoː/; similarly the root of the verb /regoː/ I rule, appears in the variant forms, both bound, /reg-/ and /reːc-/ (/reːk-/), as in /regere/ to rule, and /reːctus/ (/reːktus/) ruled. Many Latin noun roots are bound: /domin-/ in /dominus/, /dominum/, etc., master (the different forms represent different cases of the noun, 6·5·1), /puell-/ in /puella/, /puellam/, etc., girl; but some are free: /consul/ represents both the nominative singular case form of the word /consul/ consul, and the root of the other case forms, /consulem/, etc.

In some languages roots are not only bound forms, but are often represented by sequences that would be impossible as complete word structures; Japanese and Swahili root forms often end in a consonant, although the words in these languages in almost all cases end in a vowel (or, in Japanese, in /-ŋ/ the syllabic nasal, 4·3·4, p. 120). Thus Japanese /kas-/ to lend, appears as root in the verb forms /kasu/ lend, lends, /kasi/ lending, /kase/ lend!, etc.; Swahili /imb-/ to sing, appears in /waimba/ they sing, /hawaimbi/ they do not sing, /hawata-imba/ they will not sing, etc., /wa-/, /ha-/, /ta-/, /-a/, and /-i/ being some of the numerous affixes used in the verbal forms of the language.

Affix is a useful general term for the recurrent formative morphemes of words other than roots, but affixes may be divided formally into three major positional classes according to the position they occupy in relation to the root morpheme: *prefix*, *infix*, and *suffix*. Prefixes and suffixes may be readily illustrated from English (indeed, examples of them have already appeared from a number of languages in this section); *re-*, *de-*, *con-*, *per-*, and *pre-*, as in *receive*, *remove*, *deceive*, *deranged*, *conceive*, *contain*, *perceive*, *perform*, *preconceive*, *preempt*, are all prefixes, and they always precede the root or other prefixes in English words; the plural formatives *-s* (/-s/, /-z/, /-iz/), *-en* (/-ən/), etc., are suffixes, and so are the verb paradigm affixes *-ing* (/-iŋ/), *-t* (/-t/), *-d*, *-ed* (/-t/, /-d/, /-id/), etc. (*slept, walked, called, wanted*). The regular forms of French and Latin verb paradigms involve suffixation, but German, Ancient Greek, and Sanskrit make use of prefixation in their verb paradigms as well (German *machen* /ˈmaxen/ to make, to do, *gemacht* /geˈmaxt/ made; Greek λύω /lúːoː/ I loose, ἔλυσα /élu:sa/ I loosed; Sanskrit *bhavāmi* /bhava:mi/ I am, *abhavam* /abhavam/ I was.

Infixes are affixes that appear within the consonant and vowel sequences of root forms; they occupy fixed positions that are statable by reference to the consonants and vowels. Infixes are less commonly met with, and are not found in English apart from one mode of analysis of plurals like *feet, men* (5·4·2). Infixes are found in Cambodian, a language of South-east Asia (/deːk/ to sleep, /dɔmneːk/ sleep), in Sundanese (/gɣlis/ to be pretty, /gumɣlis/ to be vain), and in Yurok, an American-Indian language of California (/sepolah/ field, /segepolah/ fields; /kemoʔl/ he steals, /kegemoʔl/ he is a thief). Arabic is particularly marked as a language by its large number of what are traditionally called 'triliteral roots', roots represented by a sequence of three consonants, from which different paradigm forms of variable words are made by the addition of one or more morphemes, represented discontinuously by prefixes, infixes, and suffixes, to the roots. Thus /k-t-b/ to write: /yiktib/ he writes, /tiktib/ she writes, /ʔaktib/ I write, /katab/ he wrote, /katabit/ she wrote, /katabt/ I wrote. This type of word formation is not confined to Arabic, but Arabic provides a notable example of it in a fairly well-known group of closely related languages and dialects.

Polymorphemic words need not contain only one root morpheme though they must contain at least one. Two or more roots (i.e. morphemes able to constitute the roots of one-root words) may co-occur in a single word, with or without affixes; such words are often called compound words. They are exemplified in English by *aircraft* (root+root), *pickpocket* (root+root), *broadcaster* (root+root +affix), etc. The unitary behaviour of such forms in sentences and their uninterruptability (cp. p. 194) are the grounds for ascribing single word status to them, although the component roots may all constitute free forms as well. Compound words may include one or more bound roots, as in *ethnobotany* (*ethno-botan-y*, root+root +affix), wherein neither root morpheme is a free form. German is often said to have a particular propensity for forming long compound words containing several roots (e.g. *Kriegsfreiwilliger* /ˈkriːksfrai- viliger/ volunteer for active service (*Krieg-s-frei-will-ig-er*, root+affix +root+root+affix+affix), *Kriegsverpflegungsamt* /ˈkriːksfɛrpfleː- guŋsʔamt/ commissariat department (*Krieg-s-ver-pfleg-ung-s-amt*, root+affix+affix+root+affix+affix+root)). Other languages, as the English translations of these two examples show, tend to prefer word groups rather than compound words of such length. Classical Latin writers are said to have disapproved stylistically of an excess of compound words.

So far, the discussion has been concerned with word form differ-ences which can be readily described in terms of additions of bound forms to roots. However, there are some word form differences that do not lend themselves readily to such an analysis. English noun plurals involving vowel alternation, such as *man, men, foot, feet*, have already been mentioned; and verb paradigms that include such forms as *fight, fought* /fait/, /fɔːt/, *take, took* /teik/, /tuk/, are of this type as well. In German comparable forms are found, such as *finden* /ˈfinden/ to find, *find* /fint/ find!, *fand* /fant/ (he) found, *essen* /ˈʔesen/ to eat, *iss* /ʔis/ eat!, *ass* /ʔas/ (he) ate. In both languages these non-additive variations in word form are exceptional (though quite numerous), belonging mainly to classes of words that exhibit additive paradigm variations like *boy, boys, bake, baked, sagen* /ˈzaːgen/ to say, *sag* /zaːk/ say!, *sagte* /ˈzaːkte/ (he) said. But in some languages

211

alternations in the consonant or vowel structure of root forms without any overt additions are regular parts of paradigm variations. In Sundanese two forms of verb roots are used both as grammatically different words and as bases for affixation, and in many verbs these are related by the alternation of non-nasal and nasal consonants at the same point of articulation (e.g. /batʃa/, /matʃa/ to read; /pikʏn/ /mikʏn/ to give, /tendʒo/, /nendʒo/ to see).

Some linguists have insisted that all such formations must be analysed in terms of the addition of morphemes, and in English the uses of zero morpheme shapes, infixes and allomorphs consisting of vowel changes, have already been noticed in such attempts (5·4·2). It is always possible to describe any difference between word forms as the result of the addition of something; but it may be urged that in many cases the apparent consistency of such a description is bought at too high a price in divergence from the actual forms of the language as spoken.

Alternatively, apparently non-additive variations may be explained directly in terms of processes, not processes as something 'added' to another form. On these lines, one form of the paradigm, either arbitrarily or because it is grammatically parallel to an unaffixed root elsewhere in the language, is taken as basic (i.e. *take* is basic because it matches *bake* (past tense form *baked*); different forms of the paradigms are then described as the result of processes, vowel change, nasalization, etc. applied to the root form. (*Process* in this use is a descriptive term; it has nothing to do with historical processes in time or with changes in the forms of the language through the years.)

Process terminology can be generalized more easily than additive terminology, since affixation itself can be regarded quite reasonably as one process, among several others, to which the roots of many words are subject. It is then legitimate to regard *men* and *mice* as the monomorphemic forms resulting from the process of vowel change applied to the basic forms *man* and *mouse* (the change of written letter *s* to *c* in *mice* has no bearing on the final consonant in the spoken forms which is /s/ in both word forms), and to say that *boys* and *rats* are bimorphemic as a result of addition.

A particular type of grammatical formation, whereby a part or the whole of a root form is repeated in the same word, is found in a number of languages to varying extents; this is known as **reduplica-**

tion and is describable either as a process or as an addition. Ancient Greek provides a well-known illustration of partial reduplication. The perfect tense forms of most types of verbs in Greek are formed, together with certain suffixes, by prefixing to the root a syllable comprising the initial consonant of the root followed by the vowel /e/; thus λύω /lúːoː/ I loose, λέλυκα /léluka/ I have loosed; πιστεύω /pistéuoː/ I trust, πεπίστευκα /pepísteuka/ I have trusted (this is in no way a complete statement of the rules governing reduplication in Greek; the details are not relevant here). This type of formation is carried further in some languages. In Malay, Sundanese, and other Malayopolynesian languages, the reduplication of entire word forms is a regular means of forming noun plurals (it also serves other grammatical purposes); thus Malay /kapal/ ship, /kapalkapal/ ships; Sundanese /sirym/ ant, /sirymsirym/ ants.

The means principally exploited by languages to differentiate the paradigm forms of variable words, and the different modes of word formation in general, constitute one important factor in the classification of languages into various types (see 8·2·5).

It will have been noticed that in the establishment of the morpheme as a unit of grammatical analysis and description, as with the word as a formal unit, and in the discussion of the ways in which morphemes may be further classified as roots and affixes, no reference has been made to semantics; nor have any assumptions about meanings been made, except for the general one, fundamental to all linguistic analysis, that the material from the various languages dealt with was all meaningful, that is, genuine utterance or parts of genuine utterance. Grammatical elements, like grammatical classes and grammatical categories which will be treated in the next chapter, can be established by formal criteria alone; and if they are to be maximally useful and reliable for their purpose, they must be so established.

5·5 THE SEMANTIC STATUS OF WORDS AND MORPHEMES

Both words and morphemes may bear fairly easily definable meanings or ranges of meanings. Words occurring as complete sentences necessarily do when so functioning. Within a sentence they have their meaning describable primarily by reference to the contribution they

213

make to the total meaning or situational function of the sentence as a whole. By comparing the uses of words alone and as parts of larger sentences, statements about their semantic function can be made, to form part of the material of dictionaries. Irrespective of their grammatical functions and classes, some words are, as it were, more self-contained than others in the matter of semantic description and more easily given a semantic gloss in a dictionary; those whose use is deeply embedded in some peculiar aspect of the culture of the speakers are likely to require more detailed description in terms of contexts of situation (1·4·3) for their full meaning to be made clear.

Likewise some, but by no means all, bound morphemes, though by definition never occurring alone as a complete word or sentence, do show fairly definite semantic correlations with features of the external world, and can be conveniently labelled by reference to them. Terms like *plural formative*, that have already been used in this chapter, exemplify this usage. Where such labelling is at all possible, it is often helpful and it would be perverse not to use it; but it adds nothing to the formal status of the morphemes, as units of grammatical structure, and no such meaning is required for the identification of a morpheme. English *-ceive* and *-ing*, to mention only two, would be virtually impossible to gloss in isolation, apart from the word forms wherein they occur, but their morphemic status is clearly established by the formal comparison of word shapes.

The statement of any types or ranges of meaning apparently borne by particular morphemes in a language is an important part of the total description of it; but it can only usefully be done after the morphemes have already been established and classified in purely formal terms.

CHAPTERS 5, 6, AND 7, BIBLIOGRAPHY

1. F. B. AGARD, 'Structural sketch of Rumanian', *Lang.* 34 (1958), part 3, section 2.

2. W. S. ALLEN, *Phonetics in Ancient India*, London, 1953.

3. ——, *Sandhi*, The Hague, 1962.

4. E. O. ASHTON, *Swahili grammar*, London, 1944.

5. C. E. BAZELL, *Linguistic form*, Istanbul, 1953.

6. ——, 'Meaning and the morpheme', *Word* 18 (1962), 132–42.

7. J. T. BENDOR-SAMUEL, 'The verbal piece in Jebero', *Word* 17 (1961), supplement.

8. B. BLOCH, 'Studies in Colloquial Japanese', 1, *JAOS* 66 (1946), 97–109; 2, *Lang.* 22 (1946), 200–48; 3, *JAOS* 66 (1946), 304–15; 4, *Lang.* 26 (1950), 86–125.

9. ——, 'English verb inflection', *Lang.* 23 (1947), 399–418.

10. L. BLOOMFIELD, *Language*, London, 1935.

11. ——, *Eastern Ojibwa*, Ann Arbor, 1958.

12. E. BOURCIEZ, *Eléments de linguistique romane*, fourth edition, Paris, 1946.

13. M. BRAUN, *Grundzüge der slavischen Sprachen*, Göttingen, 1947.

14. R. G. A. DE BRAY, *A guide to the Slavonic languages*, London, 1951.

15. C. D. BUCK, *Comparative grammar of Greek and Latin*, Chicago, 1933.

16. N. CHOMSKY, *Syntactic structures*, The Hague, 1957.

17. S. EINARSSON, *Icelandic*, Baltimore, 1949.

18. W. D. ELCOCK, *The Romance languages*, London, 1960.

19. C. N. E. ELIOT, *Finnish grammar*, Oxford, 1890.

20. M. B. EMENEAU, *Studies in Vietnamese (Annamese) grammar*, Berkeley, 1951.

21. W. J. ENTWISTLE and W. A. MORISON, *Russian and the Slavonic languages*, London, 1949.

5 GRAMMAR: GRAMMATICAL ELEMENTS

22. J. R. FIRTH, 'Synopsis of linguistic theory 1930–55', *Studies in linguistic analysis*, special publication of the Philological Society, Oxford, 1957, 1–32.

23. C. C. FRIES, *The structure of English*, New York, 1952.

24. H. A. GLEASON, *Introduction to descriptive linguistics*, second edition, New York, 1961.

25. W. HAAS, 'Zero in linguistic analysis', *Studies in linguistic analysis*, special publication of the Philological Society, Oxford, 1957, 33–53.

26. ——, 'Linguistic structures', *Word* 16 (1960), 251–76.

27. M. A. K. HALLIDAY, 'Categories of the theory of grammar', *Word* 17 (1961), 241–92.

28. E. HAMP, 'Morphophonemes of the Keltic mutations', *Lang.* 27 (1951), 230–47.

29. ——, *A glossary of American technical linguistic usage 1925–50*, Utrecht, 1958.

30. Z. S. HARRIS, *Methods in structural linguistics*, Chicago, 1951.

31. ——, 'Discourse analysis', *Lang.* 28 (1952), 1–30.

32. ——, 'Co-occurrence and transformation in linguistic structure', *Lang.* 33 (1957), 283–340.

33. A. A. HILL, *Introduction to linguistic structures*, New York, 1958.

34. L. HJELMSLEV, *Les principes de grammaire générale*, Copenhagen, 1928.

35. ——, *La categorie des cas*, Aarhus, 1935.

36. ——, 'La structure morphologique', *Actes du 5me congrès internationale des linguistes* (1939), 66–93.

37. C. F. HOCKETT, 'Two models of grammatical description', *Word* 10 (1954), 210–34.

38. ——, *A manual of phonology*, Indiana University publications in anthropology and linguistics 11, 1955.

39. ——, *A course in modern linguistics*, New York, 1958.

40. H. HOIJER, 'The cultural implications of some Navaho linguistic categories', *Lang.* 27 (1951), 111–20.

41. ——, 'The relation of language to culture', *Anthropology today*, ed. A. L. Kroeber, Chicago, 1953, 554–73.

42. —— (editor), *Language in culture*, Chicago, 1955.

43. P. J. HONEY, 'Word classes in Vietnamese', *BSOAS* 18 (1956), 534–544.

44. H. P. HOUGHTON, *An introduction to the Basque language*, Leyden, 1961.

45. R. JAKOBSON, 'Beitrag zur allgemeinen Kasuslehre', *TCLP* 6 (1936), 240–88.

46. O. JESPERSEN, *The philosophy of grammar*, London, 1924.

47. R. B. LEES, review of Chomsky, *Syntactic structures*, *Lang*. 33 (1957), 375–408.

48. ——, *The grammar of English nominalizations*, Bloomington, 1960.

49. R. E. LONGACRE, 'String constituent analysis', *Lang*. 36 (1960), 63–88.

50. A. A. MCDONELL, *A Sanskrit grammar for beginners*, London, 1911.

51. B. MALINOWSKI, *Coral gardens and their magic*, London, 1935.

52. A. MEILLET, *Linguistique historique et linguistique générale* (1), Paris, 1948.

53. G. B. MILNER, *Fijian grammar*, Suva, 1957.

54. T. F. MITCHELL, *Introduction to colloquial Egyptian Arabic*, London, 1956.

55. J. MORRIS-JONES, *Elementary Welsh grammar*, Oxford, 1922.

56. J. C. NESFIELD, *Outline of English grammar*, London, 1910.

57. E. A. NIDA, *Morphology*, second edition, Ann Arbor, 1949.

58. ——, *Syntax*, Glendale, 1946.

59. F. R. PALMER, 'Linguistic hierarchy', *Lingua* 7 (1958), 225–41.

60. K. L. PIKE, *Tone languages*, Ann Arbor, 1948.

61. ——, 'A problem in morphology-syntax division', *Acta linguistica* 5 (1945–9), 125–38.

62. R. H. ROBINS, *Ancient and mediaeval grammatical theory in Europe*, London, 1951.

63. ——, *The Yurok language*, Berkeley, 1958.

64. ——, 'Some considerations on the status of grammar in linguistics', *Archivum linguisticum* 11 (1959), 91–114.

65. ——, 'In defence of WP', *TPS* 1959, 116–44.

66. ——, 'Nominal and verbal derivation in Sundanese', *Lingua* 8 (1959), 337–69.

67. E. SAPIR, *Language*, New York, 1921.

68. —— and M. SWADESH, *Nootka texts*, Philadelphia, 1939.

69. A. SAUVAGEOT, *Esquisse de la langue finnoise*, Paris, 1949.

70. R. K. SPRIGG, 'Junction in spoken Burmese', *Studies in linguistic analysis*, special publication of the Philological Society, Oxford, 1957, 104–38.

71. E. H. STURTEVANT, *The pronunciation of Greek and Latin*, Philadelphia, 1940.

72. H. SWEET, *New English grammar*, Oxford, 1892.

73. G. L. TRAGER and H. L. SMITH, *Outline of English Structure*, Studies in linguistics, occasional paper 3, Norman, Oklahoma, 1951.

74. H. VOGT, *Esquisse d'une grammaire du georgien moderne*, Oslo, 1936.

75. I. C. WARD, 'Tone in West African languages', *Proceedings of the third international congress of phonetic sciences*, 1938, 383–8.

76. R. S. WELLS, 'Immediate constituents', *Lang.* 23 (1947), 81–117.

77. B. L. WHORF, *Four articles on metalinguistics*, Washington, 1950.

78. ——, *Language, thought, and reality: selected writings of Benjamin Lee Whorf*, edited by J. B. Carroll, New York, 1956.

79. R. O. WINSTEDT, *Malay grammar*, Oxford, 1927.

80. D. S. WORTH, 'Transform analysis of Russian instrumental constructions', *Word* 14 (1958), 247–90.

81. J. WRIGHT, *A grammar of the dialect of Windhill in the West Riding of Yorkshire*, English Dialect Society, London, 1892.

Grammatical analysis and description, the subject of Chapters 5, 6, and 7, is covered in a number of general books. All the books referred to in the general bibliography appearing after Chapter 1 have chapters devoted to grammatical topics. Additionally, attention may be drawn to the following: Hjelmslev, 34; Nida, 57 and 58.

In the older European tradition, Jespersen, 46, is still an important contribution by an important writer.

BIBLIOGRAPHY FOR CHAPTERS 5, 6 AND 7

It must be remembered that not all the questions raised in these books, and in other writings referred to in the notes, are answered in the same way. Somewhat different theories and different interpretations of theory apply in grammar as in the other levels of analysis. This does not mean that any one of the writers is 'right' and the others 'wrong' in some particular matter.

ADDENDA

82. E. Bach, *An introduction to transformational grammars*, New York, 1964.

83. B. Elson and V. Pickett, *An introduction to morphology and syntax*, Summer Institute of Linguistics, 1962.

84. Z. S. Harris, *String analysis of sentence structure*, The Hague, 1962.

85. J. Atkinson, *Finnish grammar*, Helsinki, 1956.

86. H. Fromm and M. Sadeniemi, *Finnisches Elementarbuch*, Heidelberg, 1956.

87. N. Chomsky, *Current issues in linguistic theory*, The Hague, 1964.

88. ——, *Aspects of the theory of syntax*, Cambridge, Mass., 1965.

89. M. Bierwisch, *Grammatick des deutschen Verbs*, Berlin, 1963.

90. H. A. Gleason, *Linguistics and English grammar*, New York, 1965.

91. M. Joos, *The English verb: form and meanings*, Madison, 1964.

92. F. R. Palmer, *A linguistic study of the English verb*, London, 1965.

p. 180. The explicitly 'generative' approach to grammar has been the subject of much recent attention in America, since the publication of Chomsky, 16. The ultimate effects of this on grammatical work have still to be seen.

p. 182. Sanskrit is a special case among languages no longer spoken as a medium of regular communication. The excellence of the ancient Indian treatises on its pronunciation, which together with successions of commentaries have been preserved in continuous study in the learned tradition of India, make available far more comprehensive, detailed, and accurate knowledge of Sanskrit phonetics than is the case with any other dead language. For details, Allen, 2.

p. 183. cp. Nesfield, 56, 5; H. Sweet, 72, volume 1, 49–52.

p. 186. On the relation between the grammatical and phonological levels, Allen, *TPS* 1956, 145; Palmer, 59; Haas, 25; Halliday, 27.

On the total exclusion of grammatical factors from phonological analysis, cp. note to p. 148, above.

p. 187. Representation versus inclusion as the relation between grammatical and phonological elements is discussed in Hockett, 38, 15; cp. Harris, 30, chapter 12.

Definitions of the morpheme involving its necessary possession of a semantic meaning, Bloomfield, 10, 161; Hockett, 39, 123. On the irrelevance of semantic meaning to grammatical units as grammatical units, Trager and Smith, 73, 53; Robins, 64; Bazell, 6.

On the widest, Firthian, interpretation of *meaning* (cp. note to p. 28, above), the grammatical level and the elements that constitute it provide part of the total meaning of the utterance. In this sense grammar is meaningful at its own level, but so is phonology; by Firth's theory of linguistic analysis, all linguistic activity is meaningful, and the whole of linguistic analysis is the analysis of meaning. This general approach to language has no relevance to the distinction of grammar and phonology by the first being 'meaningful' in a sense in which the latter is not.

p. 190. On the use of the word as a basic grammatical unit, Robins, 65.

p. 191. The extension of linguistic analysis beyond the sentence and so beyond the confines of grammar as normally understood is discussed by Harris, 31. Collocational relations ($2 \cdot 4 \cdot 2$) between individual words are relevant not merely to words within a sentence, but also to words in different sentences that form a single utterance sequence on a single topic.

p. 192. Some of the relations between linguistics and logic are briefly noticed below, 9·2.

p. 193. Malinowski, 51, volume 2, 11; Sapir, 67, 32–6.

p. 194. On the word as a minimum free form, Bloomfield, 10, 177–81. An earlier type of definition may be seen in Meillet, 52, 30: 'The association of a given meaning to a given group of sounds susceptible to a given grammatical use.'

p. 195. Rumanian, Agard, 1.

p. 196. An exception to the statement about the unemphatic pronouns in French is found in the official formula *je soussigné certifie* /ʒə susiɲe sɛrtifi/ I the undersigned certify. This is a survival from an earlier stage in the language when these pronoun forms enjoyed greater freedom of position in sentences.

On 'weak forms', cp. note to p. 126. English -*s* is also discussed by Bloomfield, 10, 178–9.

p. 198. The possibility of one and no more than one full stress is often adduced as an additional mark of word unity in English (e.g. Bloomfield, 10, 182). But leaving aside the possibility of some double-stressed English words, according to Jones (cp. note to p. 146 above), stress is, in general, a potential criterion only, as words are never all given one fully stressed syllable in continuous speech, though each, with a few exceptions, can be, under specific circumstances of emphasis or the like.

p. 199. Congruence of levels, Firth, 22, 29.

p. 201. On sandhi in Sanskrit, MacDonell, 50, chapter 2; Allen, 3.

Tone-sandhi, Pike, 60.

Welsh mutations, Morris-Jones, 55, 35–7. Further study of this feature in Celtic languages in Hamp, 28.

Sandhi features of word shape variation in sentences are collectively handled as prosodies of word junction in prosodic descriptions (cp. Sprigg, 70).

p. 203. The term *allolog* has sometimes been used (e.g. Trager and Smith, 73, 59) for the 'strong' and 'weak' variant forms of the same lexical word; but as such variations are freer in their occurrence than are different allomorphs of a single morpheme, less use has been made of *allolog*.

p. 204. Zero elements, elements posited in a structure at a particular place, but without overt shape or exponents at another level, are also used in phonology. Thus in the interests of structural regularity, syllables of phonetic composition [VC] could be analysed as /CVC/ the first C element being a zero unit (cp. also note to p. 148). On zero in linguistic analysis, Bloomfield, 10, 209. Haas, 25, suggests certain rules for the use of zero elements. His proposals are not followed by everyone, but manifestly the excessive use of this device weakens one's total analysis, and probably means that a thorough re-analysis is required, to eliminate some of the apparently irregular structures that occasion it.

p. 206. On American uses of the word *phonology*, Hamp, 29. On morphophonemics, see further Hockett, 39, 271–300.

Vietnamese, Emeneau, 20, 2.

pp. 208–9. Finnish, Eliot, 19. The Finnish examples given here to illustrate morphemic analysis in terms of prosodic phonology involve considerable simplification. A number of other features relevant to a grammatical and phonological analysis of Finnish, whether on a prosodic or on a phonemic basis, are omitted. In particular, two phonetically front vowels, /i/ and /e/ do not wholly participate in the vowel harmony applicable to the other front vowels. Details in Eliot, op. cit., and Sauvageot, 69.

Japanese, Bloch, 8.

Swahili, Ashton, 4.

p. 210. The rules of formation of the regular English past tense forms may be stated in a manner similar to those governing the formation of regular noun plurals: verb roots ending in a voiceless consonant other than /t/ suffix /-t/; those ending in voiced consonants other than /d/ and in vowels suffix /-d/; those ending in /t/ or /d/ suffix /-id/ (*hissed* /hist/; *fanned* /fænd/; *tried* /traid/; *carted* /'ka:tid/; *traded* /'treidid/).

The regular distribution of /-s/, /-z/, and /-iz/ in verb forms is the same as that of the regular allomorphs of the noun plural morpheme (*gets* /gets/; *holds* /houldz/; *goes* /gouz/; *twitches* /'twitʃiz/).

English verb forms are analysed in Bloch, 9.

Sundanese, Robins, 66.

Yurok, Robins, 63.

Arabic, Mitchell, 54.

p. 212. 'Two models of grammatical description' involving respectively 'items and arrangements' and 'items and processes' are compared on somewhat similar lines by Hockett, 37.

p. 214. Traditionally the word is the unit of lexical entry in dictionaries. Some linguists today enter morphemes as the lexical units instead, stating the words built with them as part of the information to be given on each morpheme. The general principles of lexicography are not materially affected.

In a word entry dictionary, variable words must be listed by their root form, unless a particular member of the paradigm is arbitrarily chosen as the dictionary entry form, as the nominative singular forms of nouns and the first person singular present indicative active forms of verbs are traditionally chosen for this purpose in Latin and Ancient Greek. It may be maintained that such a dictionary should additionally list the bound affixes as well, with the relevant grammatical information and such semantic statements as can be made about each in isolation; but these morphemes, being limited in number, unlike root morphemes, will probably have been dealt with in appropriate places in the grammar.

6

Grammar: grammatical classes,
structures, and categories

6·1 SYNTACTIC RELATIONS

Sentences can be shown to be series of words (and printed sentences
in roman orthography are obviously so), and grammar is concerned
with the analysis of the structures and regular patterns of sentences.
In taking the word as a basic grammatical unit one may say that the
heart of grammar is that part which deals with the patterned interrelations of words in the sentences of a language, and with the means
of analysing them and stating them systematically. This is the traditional province of syntax, and it may reasonably be claimed that
syntax is the most important part of grammar. It is unfortunate that
sentence structure has until recently received less attention than word
structure, the province of morphology, and that it is sometimes badly
neglected in the teaching of languages. Languages vary in the amount
of word form variation that is found in them. Latin, Ancient Greek,
and Sanskrit have a good deal; so do Arabic and many American-
Indian languages. English has much less, and languages with few or
no paradigms of variable words, such as Chinese and some of the
languages of South-east Asia, show hardly any. The confusion of
grammar with morphology alone leads to the absurd statements still
heard such as 'English has less grammar than Latin', and that
'Chinese has no grammar'. If a language had no grammar, no
systematic ordering of its words in sentences, it could never be learned
by a native speaker or by a foreigner, nor could two people understand one another in it. Indeed, a language without grammar is a
contradiction in terms.

What does emerge from a comparison of different types of language is that the relative weight borne by morphology and syntax in governing the forms and patterns of sentences may vary from language to language, and that the role of morphological word form variation in paradigms may be very much reduced or even non-existent, but the syntactic classification and ordering of words in sentences are essential components of the grammar of every language.

The fact that English sentences can be of the type *the men eat*, but not of the type †*men the eat* reveals one essential basis of syntax, namely that words, even when they are collocationally appropriate (2·4·2), cannot be put together in just any order; in addition to grammatical acceptability and intelligibility, the total meaning of a sentence may depend in part simply on word order, as in the English pair of sentences *the tigers killed the hunter* and *the hunter killed the tigers*.

Syntactic relations are fundamentally very simple ones, and fall into three classes, **positional** relations, relations of **co-occurrence**, and relations of **substitutability**. The first of these are overt relations, observable as the word order of sentences; the other two are covert, not revealed by the observation of sentences alone, but by the comparison of ordered series of sentences with one another.

By relations of **co-occurrence** one means that words of different sets or classes may permit, or require, the occurrence of a word of another set or class to form a sentence or a particular part of a sentence. Thus in English words of the class *man, horse*, etc. may be followed by words of the class of *eat, live*, etc. in short sentences, and usually are so followed, though it is a fallacy to say that all proper sentences must be of this type. Response sentences may often be of other types, and a good many of the one-word sentences of many languages are response sentences (e.g. *Who are you? Travellers*, cp. 6·3·1). Words of the class *man, horse*, etc. may be preceded by words of the class *good, strong*, etc., and also by the words *the* and *a*. But *the* and *a* require the presence of a word of either the *man* class or the *good* class if they are to precede a member of the *eat, breathe, live* class. Here at once one sees that the positional order of elements is brought into play; *the* both presupposes *good* etc. or *horse* etc. (*the good are honoured, the horse eats*), and presupposes it in a fixed relative position. *The strong horse* is the only permitted order of these three words when they are all to precede *eats, works*, etc. as a complete sentence or as the first part of one. Further examples of presupposition or obligatory co-occurrence are the relations uniting Latin words like /in/ and /ad/ to a following word of the class /dominum/ master, /urbem/ city, etc., or to an equivalent group of words: /ad dominum/ to the master, /in urbem/ into the city.

The third relation, **substitutability**, has already been mentioned in the illustration of classes or sets of words substitutable for each other grammatically in the same sentence structures; but additionally groups of more than one word, contiguous or discontiguous in a sentence, may be jointly substitutable grammatically for a single word of a particular set. In English the group *the man* is substitutable for *man*, but not for *the*, in *man lives, man wants little*, etc.; and *strong man* is substitutable for *man* in *the man drank it all*, etc. In *yesterday he came, came* could be used in place of *yesterday . . . came*, but *yesterday* could not (*he came* is a sentence, but not †*yesterday he*).

The substitutability of word groups for single words according to certain statable principles in a language shows that sentences are not merely strings of words, but, except for the shortest sentences, they are hierarchically ordered in terms of interrelated groups. This is basic to the understanding by the hearer and the analysis by the linguist of longer sentences, and must be considered in more detail below.

6·2   WORD CLASSES

Words may be brought into **word classes** in a language, and sentences may be analysed grammatically by considerations separate from those of word form and morphological structure. In languages like Chinese or Vietnamese, wherein most or all of the words are invariable, the whole grammatical analysis must be carried out formally in these terms.

However, in most languages, to a greater or lesser extent, many words are differentiated formally into sets or classes by paradigmatic variations in word forms. In English one finds classes of the type *horse, horses, maintain, maintains, maintaining, maintained*, and *hot, hotter, hottest*, as well as strictly limited classes of words, such as *I, me, we, us,* and *he, him, they, them.* Similar classes with more complex paradigms are found in German and Latin, among other languages (paradigms of hundreds of different word forms built on a single root morpheme are common in quite a large number of languages).

Generally speaking paradigmatically differentiated classes coincide in membership with classes of words syntactically differentiated by the types of relationship illustrated in the preceding section. The centrality of syntax in grammar, even in languages having a high degree of morphological complexity in its word form paradigms is shown by two facts.

1. Where there is a conflict between syntactic and morphological classification, syntax is almost always accorded precedence. English *pretty, hot,* and *big* are paradigmatically alike (*prettier, prettiest,* etc.); *beautiful, temperate,* and *sizeable* are invariable (the adverb formative *-ly,* as in *beautifully,* etc., is not considered here as part of the paradigm of *beautiful,* any more than *lover* is considered part of the paradigm of *love*; these two different sorts of word formations will be considered in 6·5·5). But both sets of words are treated as members of one class, usually called adjectives, because syntactically their relations with nouns (words like *horse, house,* etc.) and words of other classes in sentences are the same; *pretty tree* and *beautiful tree, big house* and *sizeable house,* and *hotter climate* and *more temperate climate,* are all examples of the same English construction or syntactic grouping of words whereby adjective+noun or adverb+adjective+noun forms groups substitutable for single nouns in all or most places in sentence structures. Thus one can say in English *this is a tree, this is a pretty tree, this is a beautiful tree, this is a prettier tree,* and *this is a more beautiful tree,* and likewise *this is the prettiest tree, this is the tree,* and *this is the most beautiful tree.* Within some of these sentences the groups *more beautiful* and *most beautiful* illustrate another relation of substitutability, between adverb+adjective groups and single adjectives.

Within the noun and verb classes in English it is their identity of syntactic relations with other words in sentences that leads one to group the morphologically diverse pairs *man, men* with *horse, horses,* and *sing, sang, sung* with *chant, chanted* (*he sang the song and chanted the psalm; the song was sung and the psalm was chanted*). Recognition of these morphological differences is made as a subclassification

226

within the larger, syntactically based, word class: variable and invariable adjectives, 'strong' and 'weak' verbs (traditional terms for English (and German) verbs forming different tenses with vowel alterations and suffixation respectively).

2. Among the invariable words of a language different word classes must often be set up or recognized, where their syntactic behaviour shows regular differences. Thus among English invariables some words (e.g. *at, with, from*) precede nouns to form groups substitutable for adverbs (words like *quickly, then, often*, etc.); thus *he came with speed, he came quickly; we will discuss it at supper, we will discuss it then; he comes from London, he comes often*). These words are usually called prepositions, and are distinguished as such by this syntactic function. It is not their only function; sentences 'ending with a preposition', though frowned on by pedants, are very common; *where have you come from?* is commoner than *from where have you come?*, and *what are you at?* and *what are you up to?* have no alternative forms at all.

Other invariable words in English precede word groups that could otherwise constitute complete sentences, and produce groups substitutable for a single adverb: *he will have it if he sees it, he will have it then; he came home because he felt ill, he came home soon.*

In the substitutions of words by which word classes are formally established, there is no need for the pairs of sentences to have the same or similar meanings; some of the pairs given above are very much alike in meaning, others are not. The important thing is that the word group can occur in most or all of the formal environments or structural places in which single words of a given class can occur.

In the grammatical analysis of languages words are assigned to **word classes** on the formal basis of **syntactic behaviour**, supplemented and reinforced by differences of **morphological paradigms,** so that every word in a language is a member of a word class. Word class analysis has long been familiar in Europe under the title *parts of speech*, and since medieval times grammarians have operated with nine word classes or parts of speech: noun, verb, pronoun, adjective, adverb, preposition, conjunction, article, and interjection. Difficulties have arisen with such a scheme because the various classes were not always clearly defined in formal terms; though for the most part they could be justified formally in Latin and Ancient Greek, in which

227

languages they were first worked out, several of them were rather hazily defined in terms of types of meaning or philosophical abstractions (verbs being said to stand for actions or for being acted on, and nouns for things or persons). Because such extra-linguistic criteria were taken as the basis of this word classing (though it could originally have been quite well grounded on formal criteria), these word classes were applied to the material of other languages without regard for their suitability in terms of the actual morphological paradigms and syntactic relations found therein, and it was assumed that their alleged meaning content guaranteed their presence in any language worthy of the name.

In formal grammar, the number and nature of the word classes of a language must be worked out as the analysis proceeds, not assumed in advance, nor settled by reference to the grammatical class of the nearest translation equivalent of a word in English, Latin, or some other language. Traditional terms are useful as labels for formal classes, where they seem appropriate through some observed similarity of grammatical function with word classes already so named in other languages. The labelling of word classes by such names as *noun* and *verb* may be justified by a similarity of the meanings of some of its members with those of members of the classes called nouns and verbs in another language. Thus by the fact that persons and static objects are generally referred to by words of one particular formal class in a given language (whatever semantic functions other members of that class may fulfil), the label *noun* is applied to all the words formally assigned to that class. But when such labels, or any others, are given to word classes, it must be remembered that they add nothing to the formal grammatical description of the classes, or to their definitions, or to the assignment of words to them. The definition of a class, and its membership, can only arise from the criteria used to establish it in the first place.

In some languages, for example Chinese, prepositions do not stand out as a distinct class, and the nearest translation equivalents of several English prepositions, in so far as they may be found, exhibit the characteristics of the general class of verbs. In Japanese and some other languages the translation equivalents of many English adjectives also belong, as a subclass, to the class of verbs. This is often misexpressed by saying that 'Japanese adjectives contain the verb "to

228

be" '; thus /u'ma wa ha'jai/ the horse is quick, /u'ma wa 'hajakatta/ the horse was quick (the accent mark on Japanese examples indicates a syllable in certain words made prominent, not by stress, but by having a higher pitch than the following syllable).

The most general word class distinction in languages seems to be that between the classes designated nominal and verbal. Even in Nootka, a language of the North-west Pacific coast of America, wherein it is said that all root morphemes may be indifferently nominal or verbal, the distinction appears in some of the affixes that form words of different grammatical functions, noun-like and verb-like respectively.

As many classes are set up as words of different formal behaviour are found. This means that some words in many languages, especially words in frequent use, have to be classified under more than one head. The English classes noun, verb, and adjective are required respectively for words like *death*, *pursue*, and *malicious*, each of which belongs to one class only. Words like *work* belong both to the noun and verb classes (*he works well, his work is good, their works are good*); such words may be treated as separate entries in a dictionary, since the grammatical distinctions between two word classes are just as clear between the two uses of the word form *work* as they are between two word forms only functioning as noun and verb respectively (2·3). Words like *mature* belong to the verb and the adjective classes (*the scheme is maturing, this is a mature garden*). Words like *choice* belong to the adjective and noun classes (*choicest flowers, you may take your choice*). The English classes of preposition, adverb, and conjunction are required for words like *at*, *with*, and *from*, *soon*, *seldom*, and *prettily*, and *if*, *when*, and *because*, respectively, each group having its own syntactic functions in the language. But words like *before* and *after* belong to all three classes: preposition in *he came before tea* (cp. *he came at tea-time*), adverb in *he had come before* (cp. *he had come often*), and conjunction in *he came before we expected him* (cp. *he came when we expected him*).

The English word *round* belongs to five classes: noun in *one round is enough*, verb in *you round the bend too quickly*, adjective in *a round tower*, adverb in *he came round*, and preposition in *he wandered round the town*. Naturally, languages with less morphological word form variation admit of multiple-class membership more readily than

229

languages wherein several of the distinct word classes are characterized by separate morphological paradigms.

Word classes may be **open** or **closed** in membership; all languages have open classes, and most have some closed ones as well. An open class is one whose membership is in principle unlimited, varying from time to time and between one speaker and another. Most loan words (words taken in from foreign languages, 8·1·7) and newly created words go into open classes. Closed classes contain a fixed and usually small number of member words, which are the same for all the speakers of the language, or the dialect, and which do not lose or add members without a structural alteration in the grammar of the language as a whole. In English, nouns, adjectives, adverbs, and verbs are open classes; pronouns, prepositions, and conjunctions are closed classes, although prepositional phrases (word groups substitutable for prepositions, like *in the neighbourhood of*, grammatically substitutable for *near* or *at*) are open. In some languages the nearest equivalents of the English pronouns are members of an open class, and treated as a subclass of the nouns; Malay, in which the forms of personal address and reference are quite numerous and vary according to the degree of intimacy and the relative status of speakers, is such a language.

Some linguists prefer not to speak of *word classes* with reference to variable words. They use instead the term *stem class* (*stem* represents that part which is common to all the forms of the paradigm of the class; it may be coextensive with the root, as in English *love* or Latin /am-/ to love, or it may comprise the root and one or more affixes, as in English *lovely*, Latin /ama:bil-/ lovely). They argue that the individual forms of a paradigm are not alike morphologically or syntactically, but the stems, that are constant throughout, are. *Word class*, as used in this book, and as generally used, groups together all the word forms in any paradigm as collectively equivalent in grammatical function to all those of another paradigm of the same word class, and each separate form as grammatically equivalent to its corresponding form in the paradigms of other words of the same class. The choice between these two modes of statement may not be very important, provided one makes clear how one uses one's chosen terms.

6·3 IMMEDIATE CONSTITUENTS

6·3·1 *General principles: basic syntactic structures*

Among the fundamental relations between words in sentences constituting the material of grammar, the relation of group substitutability has been mentioned as the basis for the understanding and analysis of the longer sentences in languages.

Sentences are not merely strings of words in an acceptable order and 'making sense'; they are structured into successive components, consisting of groups of words, contiguous or discontiguous, and of single words. These groups and single words are called **constituents**, and when they are considered as part of the successive unravelling of a sentence, they are known as its **immediate constituents**. Immediate constituent analysis is basic to syntax, and is one of the means whereby native speakers form and understand longer sentences. It can be shown that each of the longer sentences of a language (and these are in the majority) is structured in the same way as one of a relatively small number of irreducibly short sentences, called **basic sentence types**. The ways in which the longer sentences are built up from, and conversely analysed into, short basic sentence patterns may be called expansions. This characteristic of language helps to account for one of the most important, and on the face of it astonishing, facts about language, that one can immediately understand sentences that one has never heard or read before in one's own language, provided only that the words in it are already familiar or may be interpreted from the rest of the sentence in its context. This ability implies the mastery of the basic patterns of sentence structures and of the regular means by which these patterns are expanded.

Examples from English will illustrate and clarify these terms and procedures. Sentences like *John spoke, run!, do you see?, where is it?* may be taken, on this scheme of analysis, as examples of basic sentence structures, in terms of which almost all longer sentences in English can be structurally analysed. In *John saw Mary* and *does Jennifer like cheese?*, *saw Mary* and *like cheese* (each being verb and noun respectively in class membership) appear in a position in which a single verb could appear (*John spoke, does Jennifer cook?*). The constituents can be discontinuous; in *tomorrow we leave*, *tomorrow*

231

. . . *leave* replaces a single verb, e.g. *leave, go,* etc., in sentences like *we leave.*

In longer sentences like *old father Thames keeps rolling along,* one sees successive immediate constituents. For *old father* (adjective+ noun) could be substituted *old* or *father* (adjective or noun) alone, and for *old father Thames* could be substituted a single noun, *water, John,* etc., or an article+noun group like *the river* (itself an expansion of a single noun constituent); for *keeps rolling along,* could be substituted *keeps rolling,* and for *keeps rolling* could be substituted *flows, runs,* etc. (single verbs). The immediate constituent structure of the sentence can be set out like this:

each lower bracket uniting a successive pair of immediate constituents.

The patterns common to large numbers of the sentences of a language may be called its **favourite sentence types**; and a basic syntactic structure is the simplest form of any favourite sentence type, from which innumerable longer sentences can be built up by series of expansions at various structural places.

Sentences are, however, found in all languages, that do not conform to and are not reducible to one of the basic syntactic structures. Some such sentences may be frequent in utterances, but as types they underlie very few expanded structures or longer sentences. Sentences of this sort may be referred to as **non-favourite**, or **minority pattern**, sentences. They fall into two main classes:

1. Those that are not referable to a longer sentence, of which they may always form a part, are structurally independent of a previous sentence, and may initiate a discourse or conversation. Sentences of this sort are often exclamatory: *John! hello! bother! drat! gracious!* Some are expandable in certain directions: *poor old John! hello there! drat that noise! good gracious me!* Others may be gnomic, such as *the more the merrier, easy come easy go.* Sentences of this latter type are lexically restricted in most cases, and little or no variation

of their particular word content is normally permitted in them; in consequence they are hardly at all productive.

2. Sentences that are referable to longer sentences containing the same word or sequence of words. These are often non-initial in a discourse, and constitute responses to a previous utterance, particularly a question: (*where do you live?*) *in Ashford*, (*what's that stuff?*) *porridge*. But they need not be. Sentences like *here!*, *hands up!*, *all right*, *fifteen all* (in tennis scoring), *fourpence a pound*, *jolly well done* can all be said (or written) and understood irrespective of previous utterance, in an appropriate situation.

What distinguishes them all from those of the first class is that each may be replaced in the situation by a longer and more explicit sentence (of a favourite type) serving the same purpose, and of which they may form a part: *we live in Ashford, that stuff is porridge, the score is fifteen all, these cost* (or *the price is*) *fourpence a pound, that was jolly well done*. A natural way of making clear the meaning of a non-favourite sentence of the second class to a child or foreign speaker who had not understood it would be to use such a longer, more explicit, sentence in its place. It is for this reason that such short sentences are often called 'incomplete' or 'elliptical', and explained grammatically in terms of other elements being 'understood'. Sentences like this, though referable to sentences of a basic syntactic structure, cannot, as they stand, be said to represent one.

Non-favourite sentences of class 1 have no such referability to a longer sentence in which they may be incorporated. Their meaning must be explained directly by reference to the situation, or indirectly by a paraphrase.

It will have been noticed that the favourite sentences so far cited all include a verb form, and a large number of sentences in all languages are expansions of a noun verb structure, either as a basic structure, as in English or German, or as a first expansion of a single verb sentence as in Latin, where verb forms such as /ve:ni:/ I came, and /vi:di:/ I saw, constitute complete sentences. The syntactically basic position of the verb in sentence structures led antiquity and some modern scholars to the mistaken view that all proper sentences must contain a verb, and that those without one are in some way defective or elliptical. This view was reinforced by the primacy of noun+verb sentence structures as the forms of logical propositions in

233

the dominant logic of the Aristotelian system, which through the period of antiquity and the Middle Ages in Europe exercised a profound, though extraneous, influence on the development of grammatical theory. The mistake arose through the confusion of a favourite sentence type with the supposedly only admissible sentence type.

In some languages a favourite, productive, sentence type is found beside those containing a verb, namely a noun + noun or a noun + adjective structure, with no verb required to complete it. This type, which is sometimes labelled equational, is found in Russian (/ˈɛtə ˈkatjə/ this is Katya), in Hungarian (*a rózsa szép virág* /ɔ roːʒɔ seːp viraːg/ the rose is a beautiful flower), and in Yurok (/wok nelet/ this is my sister). Sentences of this sort are found in Latin (/beaːtus ille/ blessed is he), but they are rare and in this language belong to the class of non-favourite sentence types.

The principal criterion for the grouping of words into constituents is their **cohesion**, that is to say the possibility of syntactic substitution of a single word for the whole group while preserving the rest of the sentence structure intact. It must be remembered that one is concerned here with words as members of word classes, not as individual lexical items; the examples already given must in all cases be interpreted in this light. Groups of words considered as members of word classes related to each other in syntactic structures have been called **colligations**, to be distinguished from collocations (2·4·2), which refer to groups of words considered as individual lexical items irrespective of their grammatical classes or relations.

6·3·2 *Endocentric and exocentric: subordinate and coordinate*

Words cohere into groups or constructions of two main types, **endocentric** and **exocentric** constructions; the distinguishing criterion is whether the group in question is syntactically equivalent or approaching equivalence to one or more of its component words or successively smaller constituents, or not. The former type are endocentric, the latter exocentric.

Exocentric construction types are fewer in number than endocentric types in languages, and exocentric constructions are fewer in number in most sentences; but the basic irreducible sentence patterns, if of more than one word, are necessarily exocentric, or they would not be irreducible. In the examples of English so far given in this section, most of the constituents have been endocentric except for the basic sentence structures themselves. Other typical English exocentric constructions are preposition followed by noun or noun group, *towards London, from the country*, etc., and conjunction followed by clause group, *if we had the money, because it is no good*, etc. These groups of words function in the same way as single adverbs, but not in the same way as any of their component words or groups, and are therefore not substitutable with any of their components.

Apparently corresponding sentences may be syntactically different in these respects in different languages. The English basic sentence type represented by *John walked, I ran*, etc. is exocentric, because neither a single noun, nor a single verb has the same syntactic possibilities as the group noun+verb; but in Italian, *Giovanni camminava* /dʒo'vanni kammi'nava/ John was walking, and *io correva* /'io kor'reva/ I was running, are non-basic endocentric constructions since single verb forms, *camminava, correva*, etc., can stand alone as complete sentences and are syntactically similar to those consisting of noun or pronoun followed by a verb. One might make a typological distinction between languages like French, English, and German, wherein a favourite sentence type is minimally represented by an exocentric noun or pronoun plus verb group, and those like Latin, Italian, and Spanish, in which the favourite sentence type could be taken as a single verb form.

English sentences consisting of a single verb or an expansion thereof, and equivalent to an exocentric favourite type do occur, but only contextually bound as response sentences (6·3·1) in the special situation of immediate reply to a question: *what did he do all day? Walked*; *where have you been? Climbing over Scafell*. Imperative sentences of a single verb, *run!* etc., which are basic in their type as being irreducible and self-sufficient, are different grammatically in employing different forms of the verb paradigm and in having different possibilities of expansion.

Endocentric groups are either **subordinative** or **coordinative** according to whether they are syntactically comparable to only one word or smaller component group within them, or to more than one. Thus *men and women* (noun conjunction noun) is coordinative, since it

235

could be replaced by either *men* or *women*, and *men* and *women* are coordinate; but *clever boys* (adjective noun) is subordinative, since it could be replaced by *boys*, but not in all syntactic relations by *clever*. The schematic subdivision of constructions can therefore be represented:

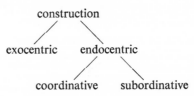

The word or group sharing the syntactic functions of the whole of a subordinative construction is called the **head**, and the other components are **subordinate**. Thus in English adjective noun groups, the noun is head and the adjective subordinate. In adverb adjective groups the adjective is head and the adverb subordinate, since in general the group is equivalent to a single adjective but not to a single adverb; in *reasonably clever boys*, *boys* is head and *reasonably clever* is subordinate, and within this latter group *clever* is head and *reasonably* is subordinate.

The following two fairly long sentences illustrate all the distinctions just mentioned, and provide examples of analysis into successive immediate constituents:

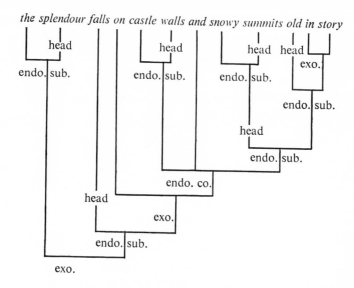

6·3·3 *Word order and syntactic structure*

Word order, the overt grammatical relation referred to above (6·1), is important not so much for itself as for its serving, in varying degrees from one language to another, as the mark or exponent of syntactic relationships within constructions. Sometimes word classes may be in part defined by positional criteria relative to other words, as is the case with prepositions, but even so the syntactic relevance of their position lies in their obligatory occupancy of it when forming part of a particular syntactic structure.

Languages vary according to the weight put on word order as a mark of syntactic construction and immediate constituency. English makes more use of it in this way than did Latin of the classical period. Languages also vary in the relative order used to mark specific syntactic relations. With a few exceptions for individual words and word groups (*princess royal, court martial*), English regularly puts adjectives before the nouns to which they are subordinated in endocentric constructions, as does German; in consequence of this, in English noun+noun groups, such as *government control, university teacher,* and the two groups from the examples given above,

237

(*old*) *father Thames* and *castle walls*, it is the final noun that is regarded as the head of the construction, by virtue of its occupying the position of the head in adjective+noun constructions (coordinate noun+noun groups are distinguished by a coordinating conjunction between at least one of the nouns: *men, women, and children*). French adopts the opposite word order for the most part with noun+adjective endocentric groups, though some of the commonest adjectives regularly precede their head nouns, and a few precede or follow with different meanings *homme brave* /ɔm bra:v/ brave man; (*brave homme* /bra:v ɔm/ good (type of) man). In French noun+noun groups it is the first noun that is regarded as the head of the construction: *l'affaire Dreyfus* /lafɛ:r drɛfys/ the Dreyfus affair.

Some languages go further than this in making word order a general mark of syntactic subordination. Japanese, for example, regularly adopts the order of subordinate before head; so that adjectives precede nouns in endocentric constructions, adverbs precede verbs, and nouns and pronouns precede verbs when forming part of their expansion, and subordinate word groups all precede the heads to which they are subordinated (e.g. /watakusi no ˈmita hito/ the man whom I saw (literally '(the) I-saw man').

One notices also the special syntactic function of certain words in some languages in closing endocentric constructions; thus in English adjective+noun groups are in theory indefinitely extensible by the addition of adjectives (*black dog, big black dog, great big black dog*, etc.), but the words *a, the, this, that, my, your, his, their*, and some others exclude further expansion of these constructions by preceding subordinate words. Only *all* and *both* can be endocentrically preposed to constructions closed in this way (*both my big black dogs*, etc.); constructions like *each of my big dogs, two of my big dogs*, etc. are of a different syntactic form, with *each* and *two* as heads and the following groups introduced by *of* subordinate to them, as with *each of them*, which is syntactically comparable with *each* (*each of them was guilty, each was guilty*).

6·3·4 *Cross-cutting of immediate constituents and word boundaries*

In most cases, with the majority of languages, it is found that a satisfactory immediate constituent analysis leads to single words as the ultimate constituents of the sentence structure, and this is part of the justification for operating with words as basic units of grammatical description and as the elements of syntax. However, sentences are found in which the most obvious immediate constituent analysis cuts across the word boundaries between bound morphemes within words. A well known example is the English possessive *'s* suffix in sentences, already referred to (5·3·1), like the *Warden of New College's lodgings*, which would be analysed

being equivalent to *the lodgings of the Warden of New Colleg?*.

A similar cross-cutting appears in Japanese; the bound form /-ra¹sii/ (is) like, may be added to nouns (/kodomo/ child, /kodomo-ra¹sii/ like a child) and to groups constituted by noun and postposition (postpositions being words similar grammatically to prepositions in English, but following, instead of preceding, the nouns with which they are syntactically linked). In /kodomo nora¹sii/ like a child's (/kodomo no/ child's, of a child), the constituent analysis would be

In Latin and Ancient Greek the forms generally known as enclitics sometimes involve cross-cutting. Though listed as words in dictionaries, forms like Latin /que/ (and) must be regarded formally as part of the word to which they are added; they can never occur initially in a sentence nor be separated by pause from the word they follow; and phonologically the word plus /que/ was treated as a single word for accentual purposes. A Latin sentence like

/de: provincia:que reve:nit/ and he came back from the province, would be structured

In a language in which cross-cutting of word boundaries by immediate constituent analysis was at all frequent in sentence structures, the word would be correspondingly less useful as a basic unit of grammar, and a description wholly in terms of morphemes, with less weight on the distinction of morphology and syntax within grammar, would be more appropriate. But it may be surmised that such languages are relatively few, and where this sort of cross-cutting is confined to a small part of the system and to few actual sentences, it scarcely justifies the abandonment of a framework of grammatical analysis eminently satisfactory in other respects.

6·3·5 *Comparison with traditional practice*

It will be observed that the processes of immediate constituent analysis illustrated here, by which the longest and most complex sentences can be reduced by analysis to successive expansions of one of a few simple basic sentence structures, bear some resemblance to the traditional processes of 'parsing and analysis' of school grammars. As has been emphasized throughout, however, and this is one of the main features of modern linguistic analysis, no attention has been paid to the individual meanings, discoverable or assumed, of the words or word groups in the sentences under examination, but only to their syntactic relations with one another as members of grammatical constructions. In particular, the formal categories of *head* and *subordinate* must not be confused with the semantic categories of *important* and *less important*. It is true that the head word of an endocentric construction is often the most important one therein in relation to the whole sentence, though it is not easy to lay down criteria for assessing this sort of relative importance; and in some sentences it would appear that the formally subordinate word is the most vital semantically, as in *contagious persons must be isolated*, wherein the essential word *contagious* is formally subordinate to the relatively less significant *persons*.

6·4 TRANSFORMATIONAL ANALYSIS

The account of syntactic structure analysis given above summarizes what was, until recently, generally regarded as the proper approach to this aspect of linguistics, once it was seen that formal observable criteria were all-important as the means to the investigation and description of languages, and the earlier rather haphazard reliance on a mixture of semantic and quasi-philosophical criteria, as well as some more strictly formal ones, was abandoned. Descriptive accounts of the syntax of individual languages and writings on the theory and practice of syntactic analysis differed mainly in the interpretation and application of accepted principles. In recent years, however, an analytic concept has been put forward, in part supplementary to, and in part replacing, the analysis of sentences in terms of basic sentence types and expansions. This is called **transformation**, and **transformational syntax** is particularly associated with the two linguists who pioneered its development, Chomsky and Harris.

At the present time the full value and the place of transformation cannot be definitely assessed, either as part of the theory of grammar or as an analytical procedure, but henceforward any serious consideration of language in general and the structural analysis of sentences in languages must take it into account. Transformation has been hailed as a break with tradition, though it is rather a break with the fairly recently established tradition of immediate constituent analysis than with the European tradition of grammatical statement. Traditional grammar, in the sense of schoolroom grammar and textbook presentation of languages, has always been aware of the usefulness of transformational techniques in describing the formation of certain syntactic constructions in a number of languages; and along with any other devices that came conveniently to hand it has always made use of them, when it seemed a convenient method of arriving at a particular syntactic structure, as, for example, when in Latin grammar rules are given for forming the clauses of reported speech (*oratio obliqua*) from the sentences of direct or quoted speech (*oratio recta*). Where the new approach to this aspect of grammatical

241

description differs from the older uses is in the rigorously formal terms in which it is set out and elaborated, and in the weight attached to it in the description and analysis of grammatical structures.

Essentially, transformation is a method of stating how the structures of many sentences in languages can be generated or explained formally as the result of specific transformations applied to certain basic sentence structures. These basic sentence types or structures are not necessarily basic or minimal from the point of view of immediate constituent analysis, and transformational syntax presupposes a certain amount of 'phrase structure' grammar of the immediate constituent type to provide the basis of the 'kernel' from which transformations start.

The original presentation of transformational syntax was made with reference to English, and English has so far received the most attention in the development of this branch of syntactic analysis. As an example of this approach to syntax, formally marked passive sentences of the type *the war was started by Hitler* are given a different treatment in transformational analysis from that which they would receive in immediate constituent analysis. In immediate constituency the sentence just cited may be simply regarded as the result of successive expansions of a basic sentence structure as represented by *John worked* or *war began*. Transformationally the sentence is said to have been produced by a specific transformation, formally describable in the changes in sentence form that result, applied to an underlying primary or kernel sentence *Hitler started the war*. The point is that generalizing from the example just given one can say that in English, subject to certain statable exceptions, from sentences of the structure $NP_1 V_t NP_2$ (where NP = noun or nominal group and V_t = a verb that admits the form *was . . . (was eaten, was seen,* etc.)), a lexically corresponding sentence of the form $NP_2 V_p$ *by* NP_1 (where V_p = verb groups *is, was, are, were,* etc., *eaten, seen,* etc.), can be produced by applying the transformational processes of word order change, word form change, and the addition of *by*. Since this procedure can be applied, with a few statable exceptions, to all such English sentences, irrespective of their lexical composition, it may be made into a rule for explaining part of the formation of English sentences of a certain structure. Moreover, the collocational compatibilities (2·4·2) between the particular words of any sentence and its

242

transform are likely to be substantially the same. *John eats spinach* and *spinach is eaten by John* are both acceptable, but *spinach eats John* and *John is eaten by spinach* are not acceptable in normal contexts.

Among the exceptions that must be stated, at least one verb, *marry*, does not admit of passive transformation in ways corresponding to its commonest active uses; *Jane was married by John* can only be used in the situation of John performing the ceremony of marrying Jane to someone else. As a class, active sentences involving pronominal back reference to NP_1, such as *Jones lost his umbrella*, do not transform into passive sentences with the same persons and objects referred to, and some sentences of this class scarcely admit of this transformation; *Jones first felt his headache after tea* is an example of such a sentence not admitting passive transformation.

The exceptions once stated, as they can be, transformation can be used to account for the syntactic structure of this large and frequent class of passive sentences in English, and similar rules can be worked out for arriving at passive sentences from active ones in several languages in which categories labelled in this way are applicable.

In English it also appears that transformation reduces the number of basic sentence types required, since the two interrogative forms like *is John ready?* and *what do you want?* can be shown to be formally arrived at by a succession of transformations applied to sentences like *John is ready* and *you want it*. This can most readily be illustrated with sentences involving verbal groups like *can see*. Kernel sentence *John can see the train* yields by application of the first interrogative transformation *can John see the train?*, and by application of the second interrogative transformation to this latter sentence, either *who can see the train?* or *what can John see?*

In many cases the syntax of longer sentences can be satisfactorily explained either in established immediate constituent terms or in transformational terms, and often jointly by the application of both methods; these are not mutually opposed, and as both can be carried out on strictly formal lines, they may each be employed on different parts of the syntactic analysis of a single language. Certain apparent ambiguities that are left in immediate constituent analysis unaided may be cleared up by transformational statement. The intuitively 'different' sentence types represented by *the war was started by Hitler* and *the war was started by 1939*, which yield an identical immediate constituent analysis

are distinguished transformationally, in that only one is an immediate transform of *Hitler started the war*, the other being the result of a second transformation by deletion of the original NP_1 from such a sentence as *Hitler started the war by 1939*.

A similar transformational distinction of structures that are identical in immediate constituency is seen in the traditional 'subjective' and 'objective genitives': *the child thrives on the care of his mother* (transformed from *his mother cares for him*); *he was driven on by love of power* (transformed from *he loved power*).

Sentences of the second class of minority pattern types (6·3·1) known traditionally as 'elliptical' can be conveniently handled by transformational analysis, as being produced from the longer, favourite type, sentence to which they may be referred, by means of one or more transformations involving the deletion or dropping of one or more of the elements present in the phrase structure stage, or in one of the intervening transformational stages, from which the given sentence is formed.

The procedures of grammatical description are not necessarily bound to try to parallel the procedures, in so far as they can be discovered or inferred, by which speakers frame and listeners understand the sentences of their language. But it may be suspected that in the resolution of apparent ambiguities in what is heard a conscious or subconscious transformational analysis often takes place as part of the process of comprehension, just as processes comparable to immediate constituent analysis may be employed in the comprehension of long sentences.

Transformational syntactic analysis has been set out by Chomsky within a general scheme of grammatical statement in which little use is made of the distinction between syntax and morphology in the way these are distinguished in the account of grammar outlined here, and syntax is made to cover all syntagmatic relations between elements of grammatical structures whether they be bound morphemes or separate words. This does not appear to be essential to the method, and one can envisage transformational analysis being worked out and applied within any formally satisfactory framework of grammatical structure.

The theory of transformational syntax and transformational techniques of grammatical analysis seem likely to play an increasing part in grammatical theory and grammatical expositions. One has seen that the approach is not wholly a new one when looked at against the background of the European tradition of practical language teaching. It is, however, as reviewers of its first presentations were quick to point out, a radical departure from the hitherto all-embracing immediate constituent type of analysis; it has still to be more fully worked out and refined, and tested in application to languages of all types, before all its potentialities become known, and before an elementary general account of linguistics can present it as a completely integrated part of grammatical theory.

6·5   GRAMMATICAL CATEGORIES

6·5·1 *Number, gender, case*

Just as different names are given as useful labels to formally defined word classes, different names or labels are also given to the types of formal relationship between words and word groups such as have been outlined above. Terms of this sort such as *subordination, coordination, endocentric construction*, and *exocentric construction* have already been instanced and explained; and such classifications are often subdivided according to the word classes involved. Thus the relation between subordinate adjective and head (or superordinate) noun is often called qualification or modification, a semantically derived label taken from a frequent, though by no means universal, function of adjectives in such constructions. Again it must be stressed that these terms are no more than labels, and can add nothing to the formal grammatical status of the elements and relationships involved.

These labels and other similar ones referred to in previous sections are the **grammatical categories** of a language. The term is sometimes taken as including the word classes, and is sometimes distinguished from them, the exact range of its application being unimportant provided clarity and consistency are maintained in any grammatical description or exposition of theory. But *grammatical category* covers more than the groupings already discussed, and, indeed, it is most familiar in applications that have not yet been dealt with in this chapter.

This has been deliberate; attention has been concentrated upon syntactic inter-word relations both in dealing with word classification and the structural analysis of sentences. These sorts of relationship, which virtually comprise the whole of the formal grammar of some languages (6·1), are the heart of all grammar and its indispensable condition. The relegation of syntax to a late and sometimes rather insignificant place in the description of a language or the setting out of grammatical theory is almost disastrous.

Nevertheless, in the majority of languages, and to varying degrees, just as paradigm differences in word forms parallel and supplement syntactic differences in the establishment of word classes, so syntactic relationships between members of word classes are accompanied by specific morphological forms in some or all of the variable words involved. Such syntactic requirements are the basis of the splitting up of the total set of forms of variable words into several different categories (exemplified by the traditional categories of number, gender, tense, person, case, etc.). Some examples will make this clear. Leaving aside the possessive suffix -*'s*, English nouns exhibit two grammatically different forms, which vary together with variation between verb forms consisting of root and root plus /-s/, /-z/, and /-iz/ (*man eats*, *men eat*) in the basic exocentric noun+verb sentence pattern. These two forms of nouns and the verb forms required with each are labelled *singular* and *plural*, and together form in English the category of **number**. In French the nearest corresponding category applies to nouns and verbs much as in English, except that there is more extensive variation in the verb forms, but in addition adjectives and the article *le* /lə/ the (singular) and *les* /le/ the (plural), show variations in number according to the number of the noun with which they are syntactically associated. English adjectives appear in the same form whatever the number of the associated noun, but in French one finds *le cheval royal* /lə ʃəval rwajal/ the royal horse, *les chevaux royaux* /le ʃəvo rwajo/ the royal horses (in

246

French these differences in word form are more marked orthographically than in speech, as they are in general maintained by the final letters of the spelled words, which often have no corresponding difference in pronunciation (thus *le parc royal* /lə park rwajal/ the royal park, *les parcs royaux* /le park rwajo/ the royal parks)). In English only one pair of adjectival words varies in number in this way, *this* and *that*, *these* and *those* (*this man, that man, these men, those men*).

Distinctions in grammatical number between singular and plural are the commonest representation of this type of category, but some languages formally distinguish three numbers, called singular, dual, and plural (the dual forms being used with reference to two items). Ancient Greek, Sanskrit, and Old Slavic all have three formally distinct numbers; a few have four, singular, dual, trial or 'paucal' (when three or a small number is referred to), and plural. Fijian is one such language, in which four numbers find formal expression in the pronouns.

The word forms of the article and the adjectives of English and those of French illustrate another difference in grammatical categories between the two languages. The English noun form variations are covered by the one category of number. French adjectives and the article require another category, with much less semantic correlation, usually called gender, to account for the forms exhibited by these words in sentences. English adjectives and the English word *the* do not vary according to the grammatical subdivision of the nouns with which they are syntactically associated (the occurrence of the forms /ðə/ and /ði/, /ðə ˈmæn, ði ˈɔks/, is controlled entirely by whether the following word begins, as pronounced, with a consonant or a vowel, and is therefore a matter of phonology).

In French, as in a number of other languages, nouns are divided into two classes according to the forms of the article and adjectives that are required with them; these two divisions of the category of **gender** are called masculine and feminine. Thus one finds *beau cadeau* /bo kado/ fine gift, *le cadeau est beau* /lə kado ɛ bo/ the gift is fine, but *belle maison* /bɛl mɛzɔ̃/ fine house, *la maison est belle* /la mɛzɔ̃ ɛ bɛl/ the house is fine.

Gender in English is a category with more restricted overt exponency or marking. Nouns may be divided into three main gender

247

subclasses according to whether they require *himself*, *herself*, or *itself* in sentences like *the boy hurt himself*, *the girl hurt herself*, and *the snake hurt itself*. Membership of these gender classes also governs the lexical relationship of anaphora or back reference which may hold across sentence boundaries. *Boy*, *girl*, and *snake* are referred to by *he*, *she*, and *it*, respectively. The choice of pronominal forms in back reference is governed by the gender of the noun originally used in other languages in which the category appears. In French the pre-verbal unemphatic pronoun referring to *cadeau* is *il* /il/; referring to *maison* it is *elle* /ɛl/. It may be noted that in English gender distinctions only apply with the singular number category, all plural noun forms requiring *themselves* in the sentence type quoted above (*the boys* (or *girls* or *snakes*) *hurt themselves*), and being referred to by *they*.

A few identical word forms are lexically distinguished in French by the gender to which they belong: *le poêle* /lə pwɑ:l/ the stove, *la poêle* /la pwɑ:l/ the frying pan, *le pendule* /lə pɑ̃dyl/ the pendulum, *la pendule* /la pɑ̃dyl/ the clock.

German is more complex in the categories required to account for all the differences between the word forms of the article, adjectives, and nouns in sentences. Number (singular and plural) operates much as in French, except that adjectives following verbs like *sein* /zain/ to be, show no variation in form (6·5·2); gender is similar, but three subclasses of noun are involved, called masculine, feminine, and neuter, and, as in English, no gender differences are found with the plural number category. In addition to these a category called **case** is required, whereby specific syntactic relations between nouns (and nominal groups) and other sentence constituents demand specific forms of the words involved. In English and French, nouns and adjectives do not vary in form according to their syntactic relation with a verb or other words in sentences. In German one finds the forms of words in the exocentric noun+verb construction different from those in an endocentric verb+noun one: *ein guter Mann liebt Gott* /ˈain ˈgu:ter ˈman ˈli:pt ˈgɔt/ a good man loves God, *eine gute Frau liebt Gott* /ˈaine ˈgu:te ˈfrau ˈli:pt ˈgɔt/ a good woman loves God, but *Gott liebt einen guten Mann* /ˈgɔt ˈli:pt ˈainen ˈgu:ten ˈman/ God loves a good man, *Gott liebt eine gute Frau* /ˈgɔt ˈli:pt ˈaine ˈgu:te ˈfrau/ God loves a good woman. In a subordinating noun+noun construction one finds *die Liebe eines guten Mannes* /di: ˡli:be ˀaines ˡguːten ˡmanes/ the love of a good man, and with a preposition such as *mit* /mit/ with, *mit einem guten Manne* /mit ˀainem ˡguːten ˡmane/ with a good man.

The category of case, involving different forms of nouns, pronouns, adjectives, and some other classes of words, is prominent in the grammar of Latin, with six different cases, Ancient Greek, with five, and Sanskrit, with eight, among many languages exhibiting this category. Some languages carry it to great lengths; Finnish, for example, has as many as fifteen formally different cases in nouns, each with its own syntactic function.

German adjectives involve yet another formal difference; the forms of the adjective in certain genders and cases differ according to whether the adjective is preceded by the definite article (or some other words) or not. This category is sometimes called **determination**: thus *der arme Mann ist hier* /deːr ˡˀarme ˡman ˀist ˡhiːr/ the poor man is here, but *ein armer Mann ist hier* /ˀain ˡˀarmer ˡman ˀist ˡhiːr/ a poor man is here.

6·5·2 *Concord and government*

The control over the forms of variable words exercised by certain syntactic groupings may be divided into two main types: concord (or agreement) and government (or rection). **Concord** may be defined as the requirement that the forms of two or more words of specific word classes that stand in specific syntactic relationship with one another shall also be characterized by the same paradigmatically marked category (or categories).

English nouns and verbs in sentences of the type *man eats* and *men eat* exhibit concord of number, in that both noun and verb in this construction must be either singular or plural. In the examples given in the preceding section, French noun+adjective constructions showed concord of gender and number, and similar constructions in German showed concord of gender, number, and case. Some languages of Africa have a highly developed concord system, whereby nouns, verbs, and adjectives show category correspondences within sentences, marked by prefixes. In the Swahili sentence /mti ule umekufa/ that tree is dead (tree that-one it-is-dead), the prefix /u-/ in the second and third words shows concord with the noun /mti/, whose concord category is itself indicated by the prefix /m-/.

Concord of category between pronoun and verb is seen in English in what is usually called person, as well as in number; *I*, *you*, *we*, and *they* are followed by *eat*; *he*, *she*, and *it* (like all singular nouns and nominal groups) are followed by *eats*; and with one verb, *to be*, *I*, *you*, and *he*, *she*, *it* are distinguished by threefold verbal concord: *I am*, *you are*, *he is*. In many other languages the category of person as a concord category between pronouns and verb forms is more extensive in its manifestation. The pronouns requiring different forms of verbs with which they are related are referred to as first person, second person, and third person. In some languages there is concord between pronouns and nouns, marked by affixes in the noun forms (often loosely called 'possessives'); Hungarian has pronominal suffixes: *az én házam* or *házam* /ɔz e:n ha:zɔm/ or /ha:zɔm/ my house, *a te házad* or *házad* /ɔ tɛ ha:zɔd/ or /ha:zɔd/ your (singular) house, *(a) ház* /(ɔ) ha:z/ (the) house (*én* I, *te* you (singular)).

Though concord may often be expressed by phonologically similar forms in different words, as in Latin /bona fe:mina/ good woman (feminine), /bonus hortus/ good garden (masculine), this is only contingent; the primary fact is that corresponding forms are required in words syntactically related in particular ways; Latin /bonus hortus/ (masculine), /bona humus/ good ground (feminine), and /bonus nauta/ good sailor (masculine), are all marked by concord of gender in the same syntactic relationship, though the word forms are different. As was seen in English, it is the concord with verb forms that united the word forms *boys* and *men*, *boy* and *man*, respectively, as grammatically equivalent.

In endocentric constructions in which concord of categories is involved, the category of the head word normally determines the categories of subordinate word in concord with it. In the examples of noun and adjective groups given above, the gender, number and case of the noun determined those of the adjectives and articles. Nouns belong to a specific gender in those languages where the category is relevant; adjectives have forms for all genders, the form used depending on the gender of the noun; the case in which the noun appears depends on its syntactic relations with other parts of the sentence.

It can be seen that the concord patterns of different languages are not necessarily the same, even when the syntactic constructions involved and the sentence translations appear to correspond. French and German make more use of concord than does English; Latin and Greek make more use of it than French and German. Sometimes corresponding constructions in different languages show a quite different concord requirement; in several languages adjectives and nouns are related in sentences in two principal types of constructions, endocentric or 'modifying', and exocentric, or 'predicative' (in English, *good man* and *the man is good*, respectively). In French (as in Spanish and Italian) adjective and noun in both types of construction 'agree', are in concord, in number and gender (*le garçon est beau* /lə garsɔ̃ ɛ bo/ the boy is beautiful, *beau garçon* /bo garsɔ̃/ beautiful boy (masculine), *la fille est belle* /la fiːj ɛ bɛl/ the girl is beautiful, *belle fille* /bɛl fiːj/ beautiful girl (feminine). In German the endocentric construction alone shows concord of number and gender (*guter Mann* /ˈguːter ˈman/ good man (masculine), *gute Frau* /ˈguːte ˈfrau/ good woman (feminine), but *der Mann ist gut* /deːr ˈman ʔist ˈguːt/ the man is good, *die Frau ist gut* /diː ˈfrau ʔist ˈguːt/ the woman is good, *die Frauen sind gut* /diː ˈfrauen zint ˈguːt/ the women are good (plural). In Hungarian the concord pattern is the reverse of that in German. Adjectives in endocentric constructions are invariable as regards number (gender is not an applicable category in this language) *a szép könyv* /ɔ seːp køɲv/ (singular) the beautiful book, *a szép könyvek* /ɔ seːp køɲvɛk/ (plural) the beautiful books, but *a könyv szép* /ɔ køɲv seːp/ the book is beautiful (equational construction, 6·3·1, p. 234), *a könyvek szépek* /ɔ køɲvɛk seːpɛk/ the books are beautiful. In English no concord between adjective and noun (except with *this, that, these, those*) is found in either type of construction.

The other type of syntactic control over word form, **government** or rection, may be defined as the requirement that one word of a particular class in a given syntactic construction with another word of a particular class shall exhibit the form of a specific category. Common examples are prepositions, which in languages like German and Latin require the noun associated with them to be in a specific case form. Latin /ad/ to, requires or governs an accusative case (/ad montem/ to the mountain); /deː/ down, from, requires or

251

governs an ablative case (the case names are of ancient origin and traditional in use; /de: monte/ from the mountain). In a more general sense words, like prepositions, that regularly presuppose the presence of another word of a particular class in a specific relation with them in sentences are said to govern the whole word; the two uses are combined when it is said that a particular preposition governs a noun in the accusative case.

Prepositions may govern different cases, and sometimes the same preposition governs more than one case, either indifferently or with a difference of meaning. In Latin, /ad/ and /de:/ govern, respectively, only the accusative and ablative cases; /in/ governs the accusative case to mean 'into', /in urbem/ into the city, and the ablative case to mean '(placed) in', /in urbe/ in the city. In German *von* /fɔn/ of, governs the dative case, *von dem Manne* /fɔn de:m ˈmane/ of the man; *statt* /ʃtat/ instead of, governs the genitive, *statt des Mannes* /ʃtat dɛs ˈmanes/ instead of the man; *gegen* /ˈge:gen/ against, governs the accusative, *gegen den Mann* /ˈge:gen de:n ˈman/ against the man; *längs* /lɛŋs/ along, governs the dative and genitive indifferently, *längs dem Flusse* /lɛŋs de:m ˈfluse/, or *längs des Flusses* /lɛŋs dɛs ˈfluses/ along the river; *an* /ʔan/ governs the dative to mean 'at' or 'in', *an der Türe* /ʔan de:r ˈty:re/ at the door, and the accusative to mean 'to', *an die Türe* /ʔan di: ˈty:re/ to the door.

In English, government as the term has been used here, applies only to pronouns among the variable words. Prepositions and verbs govern particular forms of the paradigms of pronouns according to their syntactic relation with them: *to me, to us, I helped him, he helped me, we came, save us!*, etc. On these grounds some linguists say that the category of case applies in English, but only to pronouns. Languages with case differentiation in nouns and other words often distinguish two cases of the noun as employed in the two commonest constructions with the verb of a sentence, as exemplified in Latin /fi:lius patrem amat/ (nominative accusative) the son loves the father, and /fi:lium pater amat/ (accusative nominative) the father loves the son. In Latin these are two types of endocentric construction (cp. /pater vi:vit/ the father lives, /vi:vit/ he lives), the one applicable to almost all verbs, the other, with the accusative, applicable to some only, though a large number. In Icelandic the exocentric and endocentric noun and verb constructions are marked by different case forms; *faðirinn elskar soninn* /faðirinn elskar soninn/ the father loves the son (nominative accusative), *sonurinn elskar föðurinn* /sonyrinn elskar føðyrinn/ the son loves the father (nominative accusative). The exocentric status of the nominative verb construction is due to the fact that in Icelandic, as in English and German, noun (or pronoun) and verb constitute a minimal basic sentence type (e.g. *hann rennur* /hann rennyr/ he runs, cp. 6·3·2). In both languages, these two uses of the noun in relation to a verb are often called subject and object respectively; the terms are legitimate if they are applied to relationships established formally in the language and not confused with the subjects and predicates of Aristotelian logic.

A different type of government is found in Hungarian; a noun in the accusative case in construction with a verb requires a different form of the verb according to whether it is preceded or not by the article. Thus one finds *látok* /la:tok/ I see, *embert látok* /ɛmbɛrt la:tok/ I see a man, *látom az embert* /la:tom ɔz ɛmbɛrt/ I see the man. These distinctions in verb form, which are separate from the other formal categories such as person and number, are usually called subjective and objective respectively.

6·5·3 *Subject, predicate, object*

The terms *subject*, *predicate*, and *object*, which often appear in grammatical descriptions, are a good example of the need carefully to distinguish formal linguistic categories from apparently similar ones in other disciplines also concerned with languages. Logical subjects and predicates are components of propositions (and hence of sentences regarded logically as their expression), and are distinguished by the part they play in traditional logic according to the rules of inference. Sometimes a further distinction is drawn between the logical subject and the psychological subject; the psychological subject is said to be the word or words referring to what is already known to the hearer, while the psychological predicate is that part of a sentence which tells him something new about it. Subject is also said to be that part of a sentence referring to an actor, one who does something, and object is said to be the part referring to that which undergoes or is the goal of the action.

If any or all of these terms are used as labels in formal grammar, the parts of sentences to which they are applied must be formally identifiable by reference to the shape and function of the words in them, and they must be defined separately for each language in which they are used. There is no need to employ these terms, or any other specific terms, unless they prove suitable labels to attach to categories established in a language as the most efficient means of stating the formal relationships of one word with another in sentence structures.

These terms have been variously applied in different languages, with equal validity. In English and German the term *subject* may be applied to the noun, or equivalent word or word group, found in the minimal basic exocentric sentence type represented in English by *John works*. In Latin the same term must be defined by reference to the concord of person and number that is found between one noun (or pronoun or corresponding word group) in the nominative case and the verb, and not between the verb and any other noun; word order is irrelevant. One may instance sentences like /pater fi:lium amat/ the father loves the son, /patrem fi:lius amat/ the son loves the father, /pater fi:lio:s amat/ the father loves the sons, and /patre:s fi:lius amat/ the son loves the fathers, in which /pater/ and /fi:lius/ are throughout seen to stand in the relationship labelled subject to the verb by their being in the nominative case and in concord of number with the verb /amat/.

When subject has been satisfactorily defined in a language, predicate may be used to refer to the rest of the sentence apart from the subject; this is often useful, as a fundamental division into two immediate constituents frequently divides the subject part and the predicate part of a sentence.

Similar criteria to those used in Latin may also be applied to the identification of the subject element in sentences in German, and to a lesser extent in French and English; but in these languages word order is a relevant factor as well, and in English the concord between the noun and verb is much less in evidence. *John saw Mary* and *Mary saw John* are distinguished as different sentences, with different words as subject by word order alone, a situation that could not occur in Latin.

Object may be partly defined in some languages by reference to the case of a noun in the sentence, and partly by reference to word order in languages like English. In the Latin sentences quoted above, /fi:lium/, /patrem/, and /fi:lio:s/ are so identified as object nouns; /patre:s/ as a word form is ambiguous, since it represents both accusative and nominative cases; it is identifiable as object in the sentence quoted by its absence of concord with the singular verb; in the two English sentences in the preceding paragraph, *Mary* and *John*, occupying postverbal position would be objects in the first and second, respectively. Object is, however, often most satisfactorily defined by reference to transformational identity in pairs of lexically equivalent sentences, active and passive respectively (6·4); /pater fi:lium amat/, /fi:lius a: patre ama:tur/ the son is loved by the father, and in English *John saw Mary, Mary was seen by John*. This also makes it possible to distinguish the relationship between the verb and following noun phrase in sentences like *he died last week* and Latin /vi:xit septua:ginta: anno:s/ he lived seventy years, where no passive transformation is possible, from that between verbs and object nouns.

It must not be assumed that subjects and predicates will be formally identifiable in all sentences of a language. In most sentences of the imperatival type, represented in English by *run! catch him!* etc., no such subject noun or pronoun is present. Traditional logicians regarded subject and predicate as essential components of all fully fledged sentences, as they were primarily interested in propositions expressed by sentences of a particular form. The correspondence, in many sentence structures, of what is formally identifiable as a grammatical subject of the sentence with the logical subject of a proposition, and with a psychological subject, is not surprising, but it is not necessary, nor is it invariable. Much confusion results from attempts to work logical and psychological abstractions into what should be the formal analysis of sentences, and from trying to force every type of sentence into a frame that allows for such elements to be always present, or, if obviously not present, then 'understood'.

6·5·4 *Morphology in relation to syntax*

The preceding sections have shown some of the ways in which languages may employ morphological differences in the paradigms of variable words to mark and distinguish syntactic relationships. The

255

extent of this use, as well as the different forms it takes, varies from language to language. Languages wherein morphological word form variation of this sort is almost or wholly non-existent have already been mentioned, the various Chinese languages and Vietnamese being among them. Among other languages, English uses relatively little morphological word form variation, German uses more, and Latin, Ancient Greek, and Sanskrit considerably more; and some American-Indian languages and some of the languages spoken in the Caucasus, such as Georgian, are morphologically very complex. This does not mean that such languages are more complicated grammatically as entire systems of communication, or even that they are harder to learn or describe; it simply means that more of the essential grammatical distinctions of the language are maintained wholly or partly by the means of exponents in the morphological structure of words, instead of, or in addition to, word class membership, word order, stress and intonation grouping, and other devices.

To some extent greater reliance on overt morphological forms as markers of syntactic relations may be matched by less use of word order, the overt relation between words (6·1), for these purposes. This is not universal; some languages combine morphological complexity with a fairly rigid order of words in sentences of different syntactic types. But in general one may say that Chinese and English lay more weight on word order than does Ancient Greek, and as between Latin and one of its descendents, modern French (8·1·1), one notes the change from complex morphology and fairly free word order to simpler morphology (especially in noun forms) and syntactically determined word orders. As a result of the Latin situation, word order was available in that language as a mark or exponent of categories at other levels than the grammatical (emphasis, contrast, etc.), and was freely so used in classical literature for stylistic effects by the great masters of the language, both in prose and poetry.

6·5·5 *Inflection and derivation*

Morphological differences in word forms are grammatically relevant and are classified under various headings and categories by virtue of the different syntactic constructions they enable words to fulfil in sentences and the different syntactic relations they help to mark.

These differences, both additive ones, resulting from affixation of some sort, and those involving processes like vowel and consonant alternations and the like, may be divided into two main types, with some marginal members between the two. These two types are known as **inflection** and **derivation**. The morphologically marked categories referred to in this chapter so far have all been inflectional ones, and this type, though not necessarily more numerous than the categories of derivational formations, is more central to the grammatical system of a language and to the marking of syntactic relations within sentences.

Broadly speaking **inflectional** formations or alternations (5·4·2) are those which uniquely determine and restrict the grammatical functioning of the resultant word form, whereas **derivational** formations produce a form substantially the same for grammatical purposes as a root form or as a simpler or more basic underlying form (this purely synchronic use of *derivation* must be sharply distinguished from the use of the same word in historical linguistics, 8·1·1).

Some examples will make clear the distinction between these two types of morphological formation. English noun plural formatives, of whatever morphological nature, produce words that cannot occur in certain positions or environments in sentences in which the singular (root or basic form, 5·4·3) can occur; conversely these plural forms can occur in positions and environments from which singular forms are excluded. Thus (*the*) *horses* may occur before *eat*, *sleep*, *are working*, etc., in a simple sentence, but not (*the*) *horse*, and this latter may appear before *eats*, *sleeps*, *is working*, etc., where (*the*) *horses* would not be found. These formations, therefore, and the category of number in English nouns (and likewise in that part of the English verb paradigms where it is formally marked) are inflectional. The very small number of unpaired noun forms in English that are only used as grammatical plurals, such as *cattle* (*the cattle are grazing*), and for which no singular paradigm member is found, are not sufficient to affect the descriptive status of English noun plurals as a whole.

The cases of languages like Latin, German, and Sanskrit, to mention only a few, are inflectional formations. Each case has its own syntactic function, or range of syntactic functions, and though some overlapping or sharing of functions between two or more cases

257

is found, the total syntactic range of use of each case is different from those of all the other cases in the language. Similar considerations place gender in adjectives and person in verbs among the inflections in the languages surveyed in preceding sections of this chapter.

Of necessity, inflectional formations, since they are syntactically restrictive, fall into those categories that serve to mark and distinguish different syntactic constructions and the different types of immediate constituent in sentences.

Derivational formations, by definition, do not directly involve the word in syntactic relations with other constituents of sentences in the way that inflectional formations do. Their grammatical relevance lies principally in the word class that results from their use; members of word classes that result from derivation have the same grammatical status, inflectional paradigms, and syntactic functions as do underived or simple members of the class. Such formations are, for this reason, best classified according to the class or classes of underlying form (which may itself be a root or already derived form) to which they may be applied, and the class or classes of the resultant words. As a first binary division one may distinguish **class-maintaining** derivations, which produce a derived form of the same class as the underlying form, and **class-changing** derivations, which produce a derived form of another class. Some derivational affixes or derivational processes may produce several different derivational formations on different underlying forms.

Both these types may be illustrated from English. -*hood* is a class-maintaining derivational suffix, in that it may be added to certain nouns (*nation, man*, etc.), so producing words which are syntactically and for further morphological formations equivalent to simple, underived nouns: *nationhood, manhood*, etc. The word *manhoods* (as in Shakespeare's 'hold their manhoods cheap') may be analysed:

man	–	*hood*	–	*s.*
root		derivational suffix		inflectional suffix

-*er*, in words like *runner, lover*, etc., is a class-changing derivational suffix, since added to verbs it produces a form which syntactically and for further morphological formations is equivalent to a simple, underived noun. *Runner* and *lover* inflect for plural number (*runners, lovers*) and function syntactically just as nouns like *boy* and *girl* do.

258

The suffix appearing in the written forms *-ly* and *-li-* shows at least three different derivational functions with different underlying words: class-changing in forming adverbs from adjectives (*quick, quickly*), class-changing in forming adjectives from nouns (*man, manly*), and class-maintaining in deriving adjectives from simple adjectives (*good, goodly, kind, kindly*; *kindly* is a member of two derived classes, adjective and adverb: *a kindly act, she acted kindly*; *-ly* derived adjectives do not admit subsequent adverb derivation with *-ly*, there being no words like †*kindlily*).

Several derivational formations may occur together in a single word, and though there are practical limits to the length of words in a language, it is impossible to determine in advance the exact limits of tolerance to word length of this type. In part it is a matter of style, context, and personal predilection; technical writing readily tolerates complex word forms like *redehumidification*, which in non-technical English might be rendered into several words, such as 'removing dampness over again'.

English *manliness* shows two successive class-changing derivations; one use of *-ly* (*-li-*) produces adjectives from nouns (*friendly, leisurely*, etc.), and *-ness* produces nouns from adjectives. Thus *manliness* may be represented

man – li   –   ness
noun → adjective → noun

Modernization illustrates a different pair of class-changing derivations:

modern – iz   –   ation
adjective → verb → noun

English prefixes are all derivational, and examples are found of their use both as class-maintaining and as class-changing derivations:

form, noun and verb, *reform*, noun and verb,
determine, verb, *predetermine*, verb,
new, adjective, *renew*, verb,
prison, noun, *imprison*, verb.

Cambodian provides examples of derivational infixes:

/de:k/, verb, to sleep, /dɔmne:k/, noun, sleep,
/saɤm/, verb, to be wet, /sɔmnaɤm/, humidity.

259

The distinctions between the two different types of derivation and between derivation and inflection are matters wholly to be decided by reference to the formal classes of the forms involved in the language. It may happen that a derivational formation in one language and an inflectional one in another have very similar meanings or semantic correlations; but this is of no concern to the establishment of their grammatical status. In English the category of number has been seen to be inflectional; in Japanese the formation of words, mainly pronominal ones, referring to more than one entity (/kore/ this, /ko'rera/ these, /sore/ that, /so'rera/ those) leaves the resultant words syntactically equivalent to unaffixed forms, there being no category of number in Japanese verbs, so that these formations must be classed as derivational.

As with other classifications, especially binary ones, marginal cases arise. Some formations in a language produce words that are syntactically equivalent to simpler or underlying forms in all but a few positional environments. Thus in English and Latin the comparative and superlative forms of adjectives (*hotter, hottest,* /calidior/, /calidissimus/) behave like the corresponding positive forms (*hot day, hotter day, it is hot today,* etc.), except that they can each occur in a particular type of construction from which the others are excluded: *it is hotter today than yesterday, this is the hottest day of all*; /hæc aqua calidior est quam illa/ this water is hotter than that, /fac aquam quam calidissimam/ make the water as hot as you can! Whether the category of grading in adjectives in these and similar languages should be regarded as derivational or inflectional depends on the relative weight given to the sameness of most of the uses of the words concerned as against the differences of a few particular uses.

Inflections are much more regular and general in their forms and occurrences than derivations. Almost all nouns in English have singular and plural forms, and verbs almost all distinguish a paradigm of syntactically different forms like *try, tries, trying, tried,* and in almost all cases speakers of a single dialect, and often of a number of dialects agree on the forms of these paradigms. But the possibility of using particular derivational affixes or other formations varies with the lexically different members of one class, and may well vary from person to person; in English one finds *boyhood, girlhood, nationhood,* etc., but not †*animalhood* or †*planthood* (though, of course, it is always possible that such words could be formed and used by someone and then catch on; it is noticeable how the derivational suffix *-wise*, as in *likewise, otherwise*, has in a certain style of speech spread to several nouns, as in *prestigewise, profitwise*); in deriving a noun from *comical*, one might hesitate between *comicality* and *comicalness*, with one person preferring the one and another the other while in other respects speaking the same sort of English.

As a general rule, where inflections and derivations involving affixes appear in the same word, the inflections appear on the rim of the word rather than inside it, i.e. as initial prefix or final suffix. This is shown in English words like *runners* and *nationalizing*, where the final suffix in each word, *-s* and *-ing*, is inflectional and the rest derivational. But this is not invariably the case, and is not part of the definition of inflection as against derivation; in Welsh the derivational *-os* and *-ach* follow the inflectional plural suffixes in *merchetos* /merxetɔs/ little girls:

merch   –   *et*   –   *os*
(girl   plural   diminutive)

and *dynionach* /dɪnjɔnɑx/ puny men:

dyn   –   *ion*   –   *ach*
(man   plural   diminutive).

The term *stem* is often used specifically to refer to that part of an inflected word less its inflections; stems may therefore be the same in form as roots, or they may consist of root morphemes together with one or more derivational affixes.

6·5·6 *Grammatical functions of stress and pitch features*

So far in this chapter grammatical word formations have been exemplified in the main by the affixation and the application of processes of alternation to the consonant and vowel content of words. This has been done for convenience of explanation and with the needs of persons coming newly to the subject in mind. Also these are the word form variations wherein orthographic spellings most accurately represent differences in the spoken words. But segmental consonant and vowel elements do not exhaust the phonologically relevant features of which speech in any language is made up; and stress and pitch are just as fit to serve as the markers or exponents

261

of grammatical categories and of syntactic relations as are segmentally represented morphemes, morphological alternations of vowels and consonants, and the order of words in a sentence. Grammatically, it makes no difference how a category or relationship is marked, any more than the phonological differences between the affixation of /-iz/ to /hɔːs/ in *horses* and the vowel change of /æ/ to /e/ in *men* affected the grammatical function of the forms as plural nouns.

In strictly logical presentation, as opposed to the convenience of exposition, it would be desirable not to treat the phenomena of stress and pitch, when they serve as grammatical markers, in a separate section as is being done here, but to use them as illustrations along with others all through. It must be emphasized that there is nothing strange about these features, nor about what are called the tone languages, which make use of pitch features in ways unlike the practice of most European languages. It is indeed unfortunate that such linguistic phenomena tend to be regarded as something rather esoteric; this is due, no doubt, in part to the facts that the use of pitch differences as lexical tones on individual words plays only a small part in some European languages and none at all in most, that pitch differences have seldom been adequately represented in orthographies, and that the ability to perceive and differentiate the pitch phenomena of utterances in foreign languages requires training and a particular ability sometimes developed later than other phonetic sophistication.

Stress features, as well as being an essential part of utterances, may be shown to play a specific part in some grammatical processes in English. English pairs of noun and verb distinguished by different stress placements, sometimes together with vowel differences consequential on the non-occurrence of short /ə/ in stressed syllables, have been noticed already (*import* /ˈimpɔːt/ and /imˈpɔːt/, *convict* /ˈkɔnvikt/ and /kənˈvikt/, 3·5·3, 4·3·4). In such word pairs it is possible to take the verb form as basic and to treat the stress shift backwards as one of the means whereby nouns are derived from verbs in English, along with suffixes like *-ment* (*establishment*), *-tion* (*imagination*), etc. Though historically the relative antiquity of the noun or the verb may vary in different word pairs, synchronically it is a matter of choice which class is treated as basic for grammatical description of the working of this (or any other) formative process.

262

In English endocentric nominal groups, forms that are orthographically identical, but semantically different and in transformational terms (6·4) differently generated, are often distinguished by different placement of the full stress. *French teacher*, for example, when equivalent to *a teacher who is French*, falls into the pattern with the final (head) noun fully stressed, as in *big book*, *good teacher*, *government control*, *French cooking*, etc., in normal speech when contrast stress or emphatic stress is not present; when the phrase is equivalent to *a teacher of French*, and is a transform of (*someone*) *teaches French*, it falls into the pattern in which the first (subordinate) word is fully stressed, as in *sheep farmer*, *Latin lesson*, etc.

Intonation in English may distinguish the immediate constituent structure of otherwise identical spoken sequences. *Tell me what you are doing on Sunday*, when *on Sunday* is immediately subordinate to *are doing* ('*tell me your Sunday activities*'), would ordinarily be uttered with a single Tune I, the final fall occurring on *Sunday* (4·3·7). If *on Sunday* is immediately subordinate to *tell me* ('*tell me on Sunday what you are doing*'), this may be marked by a falling sequence on *doing*, followed by a higher pitch on *on* before the final fall.

Among tone languages, that is to say languages wherein pitch differences are a property of individual words as lexical items, and not simply part of sentence intonation, as in English, tonal phenomena may serve, alone or with other features, as exponents of grammatical relations and categories. For example, it is reported that in Mixteco, a language of Mexico, the form /ka²anna/ with the tone sequence mid low high exhibits the category of future tense ('I shall talk'), but with the sequence high low high that of present tense ('I talk'). In Igbo, a language of West Africa, the three words /ofɛ de ɔkə/ with a tone sequence high high low mid mid constitute a complete sentence 'the soup is hot', but with the sequence high high mid mid mid form an endocentric nominal group 'hot soup'.

Some linguists treat the pitch sequences of English intonation as morphemes consisting of or represented by successive pitch phonemes (cp. 4·3·7, p. 152); and those who consider that all morphological formations must be stated in terms of additive morphemes (5·4·3, p. 212) treat grammatically relevant stress patterns as morphemes in their own right, the term *superfix* being used for such 'suprasegmental morphemes'. Alternatively, in a language like English, morpheme shape variation including different stress placements must be recognized. The morphemes in the spoken language corresponding to *legal* are represented by /ˈliːgl/ as a free form (complete word), and by /liːˈgæl-/ before /-iti/ in *legality*.

It is equally open to prosodic phonology to treat word and word group prosodies as exponents of grammatical categories and relations, but the phonetic exponents of the prosodies themselves need not be confined to the phonetic features of stress and pitch (4·4).

6·5·7 *Morpheme and category*

It should be clear from the preceding sections that **grammatical category** and **morpheme** are quite different concepts. The relations between them vary according to the type of language; and these relations are one basis for the typological classification of languages (8·2·5). The morphemic composition of words is decided by comparing them with other partially similar words; the number of grammatical categories involved in a word is decided by the number of separate derivational formations and syntactic relations that are or may be marked in sentences by its morphological form. A single morpheme may mark several such categories at once, or each category may be marked by a separate morpheme. One may compare the Latin inflectional suffix /-oːs/ in /libroːs/ books, wherein the categories labelled *plural number* and *accusative case* are both marked by the morphologically indivisible /-oːs/, with the comparable Hungarian word *könyveket* /køɲvɛkɛt/ books, wherein -ek- and -et serially mark plural number and accusative case (cp. *könyvet* /køɲvɛt/ accusative singular, and *könyvek* /køɲvɛk/ nominative plural (the nominative case in this language lacking an overt morphemic mark)).

In the Ancient Greek adjective form ἀνδρεῖος /andreîos/ brave, one may recognize a morpheme /-os/ by which three grammatical categories are indicated: masculine gender, by concord with masculine nouns, nominative case, by syntactic relationship with the main verb of the sentence, and singular number by concord with a noun and with the verb also marked by singular number. This is sometimes called the **cumulation** of categories, and may be contrasted with the serial representation illustrated in the Hungarian word above and with a Turkish word like *odalarımdan* /odalarumdan/ from my rooms, in which each morpheme marks a separate category:

oda –	*lar* –	*ım* –	*dan*
noun	plural	first person	ablative case

Languages in which this one-one morpheme and category correspondence predominates are called agglutinative languages, and the serial juxtaposition of morphemes is called agglutination.

The opposite process to cumulation is the **discontinuous** representation of a single category by two disjoined morphemes. This is seen in German words like *gebrochen* /geˈbroxen/ broken, in which the category of past participle (traditional term) is marked by the prefix *ge-* together with the suffix *-en*, morpheme shapes able to serve independently as exponents of categories in other parts of the German grammatical system.

6·6 SUBCLASSES AND IRREGULARITIES

As has been seen, grammar is concerned with the discovery, analysis, and statement of the regular patterns found in the word forms and the sentence structures of languages. It is these regularities that enable the linguist to class sentences together as examples of various syntactic structures and as being made up of various constructions, and to group words together in word classes whose members behave alike syntactically, and, if variable words, reveal similar paradigms of grammatically different forms. But the term *word class* is not as simple as may be at first suggested by the inevitable omission of detail in the preceding outline account of the ways in which words are classified grammatically. In most languages **subclasses** appear within several of the classes by the application of narrower criteria. Some such subclasses have already been mentioned above in other contexts.

The distinction between what are called **transitive** and **intransitive** verbs, made in the grammatical description of many languages, essentially depends on a syntactic distinction between those verbs that may construct with a second noun (i.e. other than the subject noun) under certain conditions, such as the noun exhibiting a particular case form or standing in a particular position in the sentence, or the whole sentence admitting the possibility of transformation into a passive (6·4), and those verbs which may not so construct. Hitherto the distinction has, like other grammatical distinctions, been expressed in quasi-semantic terms, but in fact it has always rested on a difference of syntactic possibilities between two subclasses of verbs. The weakness of semantic definitions is well illustrated here: *hit*, in *I hit you* is syntactically a transitive verb, and is often chosen as an example because the action referred to may plausibly be said to 'pass across' via my fist from me to you; but *hear* in *I hear you* is involved in exactly the same syntactic relations with the two pronouns, and is regarded as a transitive verb, though in this case, the 'action', if any action is in fact referred to, is the other way round; and who does what, and to whom in the situation referred to by the syntactically similar verb in *I love you*? Such questions, not being answerable in terms of the forms, positions, and relations of words in sentences, are irrelevant to grammatical analysis and classification.

In several languages, of which Malay and Japanese are examples, the translation equivalents of many adjectives in European languages are best regarded formally as a subclass of intransitive verbs.

Within the English noun class an important distinction must be recognized between what may be labelled countable (or bounded) nouns and mass (uncountable or unbounded) nouns, though there is considerable overlapping since many nouns belong to both subclasses. This formal distinction is most clearly marked syntactically: countable nouns may only be preceded by /səm/, *some* unstressed, when in the plural form, while mass nouns may be preceded by /səm/ in their singular form as well. One may contrast *some flour* (mass) and *some flowers* (countable); the use of *some* in its stressed form /ˈsʌm ˈflauə/ (i.e. an extraordinary flower) is a quite separate one, though orthographic representation fails to mark the distinction between them.

Wheat and *oats*, though denoting very similar 'things' in the world, belong grammatically to the mass and countable subclasses of noun respectively. Apart from the criterion chosen as the principal defining one, a number of other distinctions are observable in the use of these two subclasses of nouns. Mass nouns need not be preceded by *a* or *the* when standing otherwise alone at the beginning of a sentence (*flour makes bread*, but *a flower produces seeds*). When mass nouns

266

are preceded by *a* or *the* or a number word, they usually have the specific meaning 'species, or sort, of the substance or thing', and longer sentences with such words actually present are more usual in such contexts (*this district produces two (sorts of) metal(s), iron and copper; a (species of) wheat has been developed that ripens early*). As is often the case with major grammatical divisions, a difference of generic or class meaning may roughly be correlated with the formal distinction; mass nouns tend to refer to unbounded continua, shapeless substances, extents, and the like (*water, time, thought (=thinking), soup, sand, wheat, metal, silver*; hence the label), and countable nouns tend to be used of spatially or temporally discrete or formed objects and the like (*flower, bridge, house, idea, thought (=idea), season, boy*). But, as is the invariable rule in grammatical analysis, these semantic correlations, though of great significance in a total description of a language, cannot satisfactorily be used as criteria in the first place. Class meanings are not always easily identifiable, and do not always agree with the formally distinguishing features: *oats, pebbles, beans,* and *peas* are plural countable nouns; *wheat, shingle, millet,* and *rice* are mass nouns.

Among the invariable words of a language, subclassification, like the original classification, is carried out in syntactic terms alone. A distinction has already been noticed among the prepositions of several languages (6·5·2) according to the case of the noun or pronoun that each governs. In Vietnamese four subclasses of particles have been set up, according to their positional occurrence in sentences: initial particle, medial particle, final particle, and polytopic particle (unrestricted in place).

English adjectives may be positionally subclassified according to the relative order, or most frequent relative order, in which they occur in groups before nouns. *Big black dog* is more likely than *black big dog*, and *little old lady* than *old little lady*. This is not to say that a series of prenominal adjectives is always fixed in its relative order of words in English, but many English adjectives do occupy specific positions relative to each other, and still more have a preferred, though not invariable position, and this can be used as a criterion of subclassification.

Morphological differences account for a good deal of subclassing of the variable words in a language. English adjectives divide, with some marginal members of both subclasses, into variable adjectives, having forms ending in -*er* and -*est* (*prettier*, *prettiest*), and those forming semantically and grammatically comparable groups with *more* and *most* (*more beautiful*, *most beautiful*). Morphological differences among the paradigms of syntactically equivalent forms are the basis of the separate conjugations and declensions of verbs and nouns in Latin, Ancient Greek, and Sanskrit, and of the distinction between the 'weak' and 'strong' verbs of English and German, these latter being further divisible according to the type of vowel alternation involved (e.g. *sing, sang, sung*; *ring, rang, rung*; *take, took, taken*; *shake, shook, shaken*).

When, however, all these subclassifications have been made, it is almost always found that certain words cannot be accounted for wholly by assignment to any group, but must be described individually. These are the 'irregular' words. Ideally, perhaps, it might be supposed that the whole of a language should be such as to be brought within the compass of rules and classes, as far as the grammatical level is concerned; but for one reason or another no such language has ever been found, and within them all some words appear that exhibit forms outside the regular patterns, and some words differ syntactically in particular ways from the majority of members of the class to which they have been assigned.

Traditional grammar paid a great deal of attention to **morphological irregularities** and listed those words that displayed anomalous paradigms (irregular verbs, irregular noun plurals, etc.), but **syntactic irregularities** are just as noticeable, and should be described equally carefully. In both cases their establishment is the same, logically subsequent to the description of the regular forms. Irregularities may lie in the morphological alternations or affixations serving as exponents of a particular category (as in the English noun plurals *oxen, children, feet*) or in the use of more than one root in the same paradigm (as in *good, better, best*, or *go, went, gone*); these latter are called **suppletives**.

Another morphological irregularity appears in the absence of certain paradigmatic forms, for which comparable forms are found in other paradigms of the same class. The English noun *cattle*, established as plural by sentences like *the cattle are sick*, has no corresponding singular form, and the singular nouns *plenty* and *neglect* have no plural forms; the Latin verb /quatio:/ I shake, has no past tense form corresponding to /concussi:/ I shook, the past tense form of /concutio:/ I shake. Such words are called **defective** in respect of the paradigm forms not represented. This has nothing to do with lexical meanings. A single horned domestic animal and successive conditions of plenty or acts of neglect are all possible concepts, and so is the process of shaking referred to in the past. *Gluts, negligences,* and /concussi:/ all exist as words; it just happens that certain paradigms are formally incomplete.

Syntactically irregular words are those which behave differently from the majority of the words belonging to the class, or subclass, to which they are most readily assigned. The English words *afraid, asleep,* and some others behave in many respects as adjectives (*he is afraid, he is asleep,*`*he is happy, he is afraid of losing his money, he is fearful of losing his money*). But they cannot occur in prenominal position; one finds *the child is afraid* and *a child afraid of water cannot learn to swim,* but not †*an afraid child,* nor †*an asleep child,* though *a fearful child, a timid child,* and *a sleepy child* are found. The adjective *mere,* on the other hand, can only occur prenominally; *mere folly,* but not †*this folly is mere.* A few English words, best regarded as nouns, are of very limited syntactic distribution, being found only in a small number of constructions and with limited collocation therein; such are *sake* and *stead,* as in *for the sake of, for my sake, for his sake, for the king's sake, in his stead, in my stead, stand him in good stead,* etc. (notice that *instead* has come to be written as one word, *instead of me,* etc., and that this type of phrase has largely replaced *in my stead,* etc. in spoken English).

Obviously the fewer irregularities there are the simpler in that respect will be the grammatical description of a language, and it clearly behoves an investigator to bring as much as he can of the morphology and syntax under general rules that will adequately account for them, without neglecting or rejecting any word form or sentence form that constitutes a genuine part of the material of the language. Sometimes a choice between alternative methods of statement will have to be made. Is a subclass of English verbs ending in -*ind* /-aind/ to be set up, with a past tense form ending in -*ound* /-aund/ as part of the regular paradigm of that subclass (*bind, find, grind, wind* /waind/)? In this case *mind, minded* will be irregular within the

269

subclass. Or are the strong verbs of this group simply to be set among the irregular verbs, leaving *mind*, and any others like it (*rind* as a verb may be accepted by some speakers), simply as regular verbs without further comment? The former treatment adds one subclass to the verbal system, but within it the anomalous forms are fewer; the latter reduces the amount of subdivision among the whole word class, but leaves a larger number of verbs to be just listed as irregular.

It might reasonably be expected that, as languages develop, irregularities would gradually be eliminated in the interests of minimal effort in learning and in communication. This process does occur. Newly created and borrowed words (8·1·7) in a language nearly all follow the regular or most frequent patterns of the words in the class to which they are assigned in use. The comparison of Ancient Greek with Modern Greek shows that there were more subclasses and irregularities in the paradigms in antiquity than there are today; and several English strong verbs (minority type) have been replaced by a corresponding weak (majority type) form (*helped* has replaced *holp* and *holpen*, and *snowed* has replaced *snew*). This is the process known in historical linguistics as analogy or analogical formation (8·1·8).

On the other hand, a reverse process sometimes appears in the development of languages, though this is less easily accounted for. The suppletive verbs meaning 'to go' in most of the Romance languages (e.g. French *aller* /ale/ to go, *vais* /vɛ/ (I) go, *irai* /ire/ (I) shall go; Italian *andare* /anˈdare/ to go, *va* /va/ (he) goes, *andiamo* /andiˈamo/ (we) go) have developed from four separate Latin verbs each of which showed a complete paradigm: /ambulaːre/ to walk, /iːre/ to go, /vaːdere/ to go, /adnaːre/ to approach (by swimming),[1] all except /iːre/ being, in fact, regularly inflected verbs.

---

1. The original colloquial Latin verb from which Italian *andare* and the forms having the same root have descended is still a matter of dispute, and an alternative origin in an assumed verb /ambitaːre/ to walk around, has been suggested. The origin of *aller* in /ambulaːre/ has also been called in question, though no better alternative has found acceptance. These etymological questions do not affect the topic discussed in this section.

p. 224. On response sentences as opposed to free or opening sentences cp. Fries, 23, chapter 3.

p. 225. Further on substitution in syntax, Bazell, 5, 64–7.

p. 228. On the development of the traditional system of word classes, Robins, 62, chapters 1 and 2. The major differences between the system established in antiquity and that of traditional grammar were: 1. The adjective was treated as a subclass of nouns (cp. the expressions *noun substantive* and *noun adjective*); 2. The participle was regarded as a word class in its own right and not as part of the verbal paradigm; 3. The Greek article had no counterpart in Latin.

p. 229. Nootka, Sapir and Swadesh, 68.

It would also be possible to set up additional and separate word classes of words like *work*, combining the morphological and syntactic characteristics of both nouns and verbs, but in view of the numbers of other such combinations (noun and adjective, verb and adjective, etc.) that would, in consistency, have to be set up likewise, this procedure would not in general serve a useful purpose.

p. 230. Stem class, Bazell, 5, 76.

p. 234. Colligation, Firth, 22, 13–14.

Endocentric and exocentric constructions, Bloomfield, 10, 194–6. For a detailed examination of immediate constituent analysis, with examples from a number of languages, Wells, 76, 81–117. See also Gleason, 24, chapter 10.

p. 237. The serious student should not be content with merely following the immediate constituent analysis set out in the diagrams. He should examine the criteria by which each part is justified and construct similar diagrams of other sentences for himself. If he has any command of other languages, he should translate these or other English sentences into one or more of them, and compare the immediate constituent structuring, which need not be at all the same. A liking for taking the mechanisms of languages to pieces in this sort of way is what distinguishes the linguist from those who are content just to speak and understand languages.

Hockett, 39, 185, 195–6, treats the verb + noun constructions of English *saw Mary, visit Bill, reads books*, etc., as exocentric, on the ground that the total construction does not resemble either the noun or the verb in its ranges of syntactic occurrence. This seems a doubtful decision; *reads books* can be matched with *reads* in *he reads at home, he reads books at home, he reads a lot, he reads books a lot, on holiday he just reads, on holiday he just reads books*, etc.; cp. *he likes reading* and *he likes reading books.* Presumably the argument in favour of exocentricity turns on the impossibility in most cases of this sort of construction of adding a further noun in the way that further adjectives can be added to endocentric adjective noun constructions like *old man* (*nice old man*, etc.). But this also applies to many types of construction reckoned as endocentric, such as those beginning with *the* or *a*, to which further articles cannot be added.

The decision rests, as so often, on the weighing of criteria against one another. For the student of linguistics, understanding the argument is more important than the particular decision reached, though, of course, in the description of a language a decision must be made one way or the other and justified on the evidence.

Immediate constituents are generally found to be binary in structure (consisting of two parts), though some coordinate constituents may contain more than two divisions immediately below them in size, as in the examples on pp. 236-7. This point is discussed further by Wells, 76.

A rather different approach to this type of analysis, called string constituent analysis, has been suggested. See Longacre, 49.

p. 240. Japanese example from Wells, 76; further examples and discussion in Robins, 65.

Word accent in Ancient Greek was one of pitch, by which one syllable in the word was higher and so more prominent than the others. The nature of the Latin accent is not certainly known, but both stress and pitch features may have been involved. Further, Buck, 15, 161–7; Sturtevant, 71, chapter 7.

The 'enclitics' referred to by Bloomfield, 10, 187, include 'weak forms' like English /-z/ in *John's ready*; but these are in all cases variant word forms, beside which non-enclitic forms are always available without alteration of the grammatical form of the sentence (*John is ready*).

Pike, 61, mentions a language in which phonological and grammatical criteria seem to conflict in the matter of word delimitation; comment, Robins, 65, 142–3.

Bloomfield, 10, 221–2, carries immediate constituent analysis within word boundaries.

pp. 240-1. The confusion of syntactic constituency and semantic importance mars Jespersen's earlier adumbration of this type of analysis, in 46, 96–7.

p. 245. On transformation in grammar, Chomsky, 16; Harris, 32.

It is to be noted that the aims envisaged are somewhat different in these two writers. Chomsky is concerned with grammatical theory as the theory of how grammatical (as opposed to ungrammatical) sentences are generated or produced in a language, and which will, in consequence, permit the generation of all grammatically acceptable sentences and exclude those that are unacceptable (16, 13). Harris is more concerned

272

with grammatical theory from the point of view of the analysis and description of sentences already uttered.

An additional feature of Chomsky's treatment of language and that of those who follow his principles is that phonology, instead of being regarded as separate from grammar in the narrow sense, comes after the syntactic statements as a further set of rules by which the actual phonetic form of the utterance is generated from the previously generated string of grammatical elements.

The following further items may be consulted:

Gleason, 24, chapter 12 (note that a chapter on transformation only appears in the second edition of this book); Lees, 47; Lees, 48; Worth, 80.

But Chomsky, 16, should be read first; in its chapter 7 examples of different transformations applied to English are given. The account given in section 6·4 of the present book is necessarily over-simplified.

p. 247, Old Slavic, de Bray, 14, 1–24.

Fijian, Milner, 53.

p. 248. Further subdivisions of English gender distinctions can be made with certain words. *Dog, horse*, and many nouns standing for domestic animals can be followed by *himself* or *itself*, and be referred to by *he* as well as by *it*; similarly *mare* can have *herself* and *her* as well as *itself* and *it*.

p. 249. Swahili, Ashton, 4, 10–11.

p. 250. Icelandic, Einarsson, 17.

The labels *actor* and *action* for the two principal constituents of noun verb sentence structures are Bloomfield's (10, 172). As labels they are no more exact than *subject* and *predicate*, and in many sentences, dealing with situations in which actions, as ordinarily understood, are not involved, they are less appropriate.

p. 254. Where syntactically governed differences in word forms are available in English, as with the pronouns, word order may be freer. Hill, 33, 261, cites the contrasting sentences *two loves have I* and *two loves have me*, in which subject and object are distinguished by the pronominal forms alone; but neither sentence is really typical of normal spoken English.

p. 259. An example of the derivational processes of a language formally analysed on the lines described here may be seen in Robins, 66.

p. 261. Rim position of inflections, Bazell, 5, 69–70.

p. 263. The examples on these pages do not, of course, exhaust the functions of stress differences in such word groups.

Mixteco examples from Pike, 60, 23.

Igbo examples, Ward, 75, 385.

Further similar examples, Pike, 60, 22–4.

Stress superfixes in English, Trager and Smith, 73, 56–7; Hill, 33, 102–5.

English intonation morphemes, Trager and Smith, 73, 56–7; Hill, 33, 105–14. Morphemes of this sort are not, of course, confined within the boundaries of single words.

p. 264. An example of prosodies serving as exponents of grammatical categories is referred to in the note to p. 167, above.

p. 267. Vietnamese word classes, Honey, 43.

p. 269. English *mere* is also irregular morphologically: *merest* is found (*the merest stupidity*), but not †*merer*, in current English.

p. 270. For the two possible sources of *andare*, see Bourciez, 12, §209, and W. D. Elcock, 18, 127.

ADDENDA

p. 237. On string constituent analysis (referred to at end of note) see further Harries, 84, and Elson and Pickett, 83 (comprehensive and elementary).

p. 245. Bach, 82, is one of the first relatively elementary and general introductions to transformational and generative grammar. It sets out a progressive account of this recent development in linguistics, with examples and problems for students to tackle drawn from several languages.

See further Chomsky, 87 and 88; Bierwisch, 89; Gleason, 90.

Chomsky, 88, presents a version of transformational grammar different in a number of important respects from that set out in *Syntactic structures* and in publications deriving from it. In particular, several features of grammatical structure earlier assigned wholly to transformational rules (e.g. passive) are now incorporated in the phrase structure component of language description, and the distinction between kernel and non-kernel sentences is correspondingly rendered less significant.

7

Grammar: grammatical
semantics

7·1 SEMANTIC CORRELATIONS

This chapter recapitulates certain topics raised in Chapter 5, and considers them further in the light of what has been said subsequently. The question was raised of the relationship of grammatical analysis and grammatical theory to the semantic level of language, or to meaning as it is ordinarily understood. It was argued that grammatical analysis does not have to depend on semantic statements, and that the units of grammar (words and morphemes) and the categories by which their forms and syntactic relations with one another are described do not require or justify an explanation couched in terms of meanings allegedly expressed by them all (5·1·4, 5·5). In the account of the theory and the procedures of formal grammatical analysis it has been shown that meanings are not needed as criteria, and that their use can only hinder a systematic treatment of the material; stress has been laid on the avoidance of recourse to such considerations and on the necessity of concentrating on the observable data gained by the inspection and comparison of word forms and sentence patterns.

It may, however, be asked whether the linguist, in dealing with the grammatical aspect of languages, is interested in the meanings or semantic categories that appear, at least, to be closely associated with many of the elements, structures, and categories that form the basis of grammatical description. The proper answer is that the linguist is vitally concerned with these matters; although theories of meaning and the techniques available for the analysis and statement

275

of meaning still require further elaboration and systematization, it is certainly part of the task of grammatical description to attempt a statement of the types of semantic function ascribable in varying degrees to grammatical elements and categories. This is quite a different thing from relying on such statements as a means to establish and define the elements and categories in the first place.

Traditional grammar was well aware of the need for the semantic description of the uses to which grammatical elements and categories were put; and with the thorough knowledge that long continued study of the classical languages produced, its practitioners were able to make detailed, accurate, and subtle analyses of this sort. The objection to the treatment of meaning by traditional grammarians is not that they concerned themselves with it, which grammarians should do, but that lacking a full and explicit realization of the basis of grammatical analysis they approached it the wrong way round. The analysis of meaning is not yet, and perhaps never will be, in a position of comparable precision and exactitude to that now enjoyed by grammar and phonology. The semantic aspect of language is very much the province of the linguist, but it is just this aspect that takes him to the borders of his discipline where he may make use of the methods and findings of other sciences concerned with man, since it is by its semantic functions that language is connected with and useful in human life in general and the world at large. Inevitably, therefore, the linguist cannot exert the same objective control over the theory and methods of semantic statement as he can, and must, over the formal intralinguistic activities of discovering and analysing the elements and structures of phonology and grammar.

Therefore, if one starts grammatical analysis by relying on semantic criteria, and to the extent to which one does so rely (for traditional grammar was never wholly semantically based, but drew on a mixture, usually unacknowledged, of different types of criteria), one will be beginning from the less secure and systematizable side of the subject, and the resultant statement will be that much less systematic and reliable. Moreover, if grammatical categories and structures are worked out on the basis of alleged or actual meanings, any subsequent statement of their semantic correlations or content must be narrowly circular and so uninformative.

Two facts stand out. Firstly, a purely formal theory of grammar and purely formal methods of grammatical analysis are possible, and constitute a consistent and secure basis for grammar. Secondly, the elements, categories, and structures of grammar do correlate in varying degrees with more or less definitely statable semantic categories and types of meaning. Having established the formal grammatical system of a language, one should proceed to the investigation and statement of all such semantic correlations as can be satisfactorily worked out. The objection to traditional grammar in this respect is not so much that it did the wrong thing, as that it went about it in the wrong way, without an orderly appreciation of the principles involved.

One may begin by again considering the semantic status of words. Manifestly, meanings can be stated of the words of a language, as the existence of dictionaries makes obvious, and it is clear that most words do serve as individual semantic units of some sort. But it has been shown that the status of the word as a unit of grammar, and in some cases as a phonological unit, is established quite independently of any considerations of meanings (5·3·1, 5·3·2); therefore no semantic content can be assumed in advance, since nothing can be demanded by right of an element that was not first put in it by the type of criteria used in establishing it. Broadly speaking, the more frequently a word is used as a complete utterance, a one word sentence (and availability for such use was seen to be one of the criteria of word status), the more readily will its meaning be individually statable. This is the basis of the old, and usually rather indeterminate, distinction between what were called the 'full' words and the 'form' words, or 'empty' words (words like *raspberry* on the one hand, and words like *of* on the other), the latter sort of words being used almost only as components of larger sentences. This distinction, though resting on observed facts, is far too imprecise to be really useful, and within the 'form' words of a language, syntactic analysis of the type illustrated in the preceding chapter is likely to reveal a number of grammatically distinct classes.

The bound morpheme, just because it is bound, is likely to be a much less semantically isolatable unit, and confusion only results from attempts, that are still frequent, to define the morpheme as a minimal unit of semantic meaning. As has been seen (5·4), bound morphemes, as grammatical units, are the product of the comparison of ordered

277

sets of partially similar word forms, and no requirement or consideration of a specific and individual meaning enters into their formal establishment. One can, of course, say that a morpheme, bound or free, is the minimal element capable of bearing an individual meaning, and call it a minimal potentially meaningful unit; but such a criterion cannot be used with any approach to rigour in working out the morphemic structure of words; it comes down to little more than the assertion that utterances are only uttered because they are meaningful, and that the linguist does his best to attach parts of the semantic analysis that he carries out on utterances to the smallest analytic elements therein established that he can use for this purpose. He can do a lot in this way with words, and a fair amount with individual morphemes. But it is a question to be answered empirically to what extent independently statable meanings can be usefully ascribed to bound morphemes in isolation; and it must be borne in mind that the isolation of a bound form is an activity of the analyst, not of the speaker of the language.

In many cases separate meanings and translations can be ascribed fairly precisely to root morphemes, although they are bound, if the words built on them are themselves semantically associated. In Latin the root /terr-/, in /terreo:/ I frighten, /terror/ fear, etc., can be semantically circumscribed and a meaning, 'fear', 'fearfulness', and the like, assigned to it by itself. But roots of the type -ceive and -cur in English, already noticed as bound components of words such as *receive, perceive, concur, recur,* etc., can hardly be said to have any specific semantic function of their own by themselves and apart from the various words in which they appear. To say they have the meaning that is common to the word meanings of all the words of which they form a part is virtually to say nothing of their meaning, or at least to say nothing useful; nor is such a statement required for their establishment as bound root morphemes, or implied by the criteria used therein.

7·2   MEANINGS OF GRAMMATICAL CATEGORIES

Affixes vary greatly in the degree to which their presence in a word correlates with a definite semantic function ascribable to the word as a whole. This is particularly the position with those inflectional affixes that mark grammatical categories and with some derivational formatives. Where there is any sort of correlation, even though a very partial one, a semantic label attached to the affix and the category marked by it may be useful; and categories such as number, divided into singular and plural, and tense (past, present, future, etc.) have been so used in the preceding two chapters, and are well known in grammatical writings; there is no point in rejecting them, provided it is realized that they are no more than useful designations for parts of the grammatical systems of certain languages; they are not universal, or necessary, and their use adds nothing to the actual delimitation and formal definition of the morphemes and categories concerned.

Semantic correlations of formally established categories may vary from tolerable closeness to extreme indeterminacy. Between the category of **number** and the actual singularity and plurality in what is referred to there is a fairly close correlation in most languages in which number may be used to label a formal category of grammar. It may be observed that within the category there is a tendency for the dual (specific word forms associated with two objects, persons, or the like) to be merged with the plural; the dual forms cease to be used and in situations in which they would have been used the corresponding plural forms come to be used instead. The gradual replacement of the dual by plural forms was already beginning in Ancient Greek, and only singular and plural numbers are formally distinguished in Modern Greek, as too in all but two of the modern Slavic languages. Dual is therefore a lexical, not a grammatical category in most European languages today; two persons or things can be so designated, and duality can be referred to, but doing so does not involve the sentence in any concord patterns other than would be involved for reference to three, or four, or any number greater than one.

One cannot assume that the semantic correlations of similarly labelled categories in grammar will be the same from language to language. Some sort of translation similarity over at least part of both their uses must be the basis for matching the categories, and the morphemes marking them, of one language with those of another, and the justification for the use of the same label for them both. It is for reasons of translation that one matches the English noun suffixes /-s/, /-z/, /-iz/ (and the other less common variants) with the /-ər/

suffix, and any variants of it, in Norwegian, with the /-i/ suffix and any variants in Italian, with /-k/, /-ək/, /-ok/, /-ɛk/, and /-øk/ of Hungarian, and with the /-lar/ and /-ler/ of Turkish. The semantic function of number in English and in many European languages is, with minor exceptions, very much the same; that is to say, in similar situations, the same sort of factors in the actual environment governs the use of nouns, and other words in concord with them, in one form rather than the other. But the category of number in Hungarian, and several other languages in different parts of the world correlates with a somewhat different semantic distinction, between definite and indefinite number, so that the same form of the noun and of the verb in concord with it that is used for referring to one entity is also used when a specific numeral word accompanies the noun; thus in Hungarian *könyv van* /kønv vən/ there is a book, *könyvek vannak* /kønvɛk vənnək/ there are books, *két könyv van* /keːt kønv vən/ there are two books.

The category of number, though a very widespread one among languages, is in no way universal. Presumably, every language is able to refer to plurality as opposed to singularity, but there is no more need for this to involve a specific grammatical formation in words or concordial relations in sentences than there is for duality to be referred to in this way. The Chinese can distinguish more than one from one as easily as anyone else, but plural in Chinese is simply a lexical category; in addition to the numeral words themselves, words whose translation equivalent in isolation would be 'several' are employed in endocentric constructions with nouns when it is necessary to specify more than a single item, and this lexical addition to the sentence has no grammatical effect on any other part of it.

While the investigation of the ranges of meaning of grammatical categories is a very proper part of the grammatical description of a language, even the most favourable category for this purpose must be formally established first, and in doubtful cases appeal to form alone can be decisive. One and more than one are reasonably clear concepts, and languages like English correlate singular and plural noun forms with them fairly closely. But collections can be viewed either way, and a field of rolling grain is one or a myriad according to one's point of view, and it is no part of the linguist's task to decide between the two. But one definitely assigns the nouns *wheat, barley*, and *corn* to the singular number, and *oats* to the plural, by observing the concord required with a following present tense verb: *wheat grows well here, oats grow well here.*

Some other formal categories are less closely correlatable with extralinguistic categories and features in contexts of situation. The category of **gender** in languages such as French, Italian, and German bears some relation to actual sex differences, in that in denoting male and female animate beings, masculine and feminine nouns are generally used. But in French, in which only two genders are formally distinguished, masculine and feminine, inanimate beings and abstractions must be referred to by nouns of one of the two genders, with the same concord requirements with the rest of the sentence, and in these nouns and the words in concord with them, the semantic reference of the specific gender is non-existent. The position in languages like German, Ancient Greek, and Russian, in which three genders are formally distinguished, masculine, feminine, and neuter, is not essentially different, as inanimates and abstractions are referred to by nouns of all three gender classes. Moreover, in all these languages what are called 'anomalous' genders are found, animates whose sex is known being referred to by nouns of a non-corresponding gender. In French *bête* /bɛ:t/ beast, simpleton, is feminine in gender whatever the sex of the animal or person referred to, and *sentinelle* /sãntinɛl/ guard, sentry, is also feminine, though its reference is most often to a male being. *Souris* /suri/ mouse, is always feminine in gender, and specifically to indicate a male or female mouse one must add an adjective, *souris mâle* /suri mɑ:l/ male mouse, *souris femelle* /suri fəmɛl/ female mouse. In German a number of nouns are neuter in gender that refer to persons: *Mädchen* /mɛ:tçen/ girl, *Fräulein* /ˈfrɔylain/ young lady, etc. Likewise, in Ancient Greek, τέκνον /téknon/ and βρέφος /brépʰos/, both meaning 'child', are neuter in gender, irrespective of the sex of the child referred to.

In English, in which gender is a category with much less formal marking in sentences, one notices a few words denoting inanimates that regularly construct with *herself* in sentences of the type cited in 6·5·1, and are referred back to by *she*; *ship* is the best known of such words, but in a certain style of speaking a number of other words such as *car* and *bicycle* are assigned to the same class. One may notice that whereas *baby* may be referred to by *it*, where the sex is unknown, the word *cousin*, in which the sex distinction is equally unmarked (contrast *brother* and *sister*, and French *cousin* /kuzɛ̃/ male cousin, *cousine* /kuzin/ female cousin), may never be referred to in this way.

A slightly different formal distinction with a similar partial semantic correlation is seen in some languages in the categories of **animate** and **inanimate**, nouns belonging to one of the two category classes and requiring correspondingly different concord forms or grammatical arrangements in sentences. Here too anomalies are noticeable. Ojibwa, one of the Algonkian languages of North America, exhibits this category distinction, and one sees such nouns as /aːkim/ snow-shoe, /ekkikk/ kettle, and /essap/ net, with manifestly inanimate referents, belonging formally to the animate gender.

Case in nouns and pronouns and tense in verbs are two formal categories to which a great deal of attention has been paid in the search for ways of stating and systematizing the semantic ranges applicable to the different members of each. Their formal status as grammatical categories is not in doubt. In many, but by no means all, languages, including several familiar European ones, and the classical languages, Greek, Latin, and Sanskrit, nouns and pronouns (and adjectives in concord with them) exhibit regular paradigms of morphologically different forms in different syntactic relations with other words, and verbs exhibit regularly different sets of forms through which the distinction of other categories, such as person and number, are wholly or partly maintained.

From the time of classical antiquity, the different cases have been labelled by reference to some semantic characteristics, and these labels are still with us in the traditional terms: *nominative, vocative, accusative, genitive, dative*, and *ablative*. In most of them, these names refer quite well to one of the semantic functions of the case forms designated by them. As examples the ablative case (Latin /ablaːtus/ carried away) is used when motion away from is indicated (/ab urbe discessit/ he departed from the city), but this by no means exhausts the sorts of situation in which constructions requiring the ablative case are used. In German the dative case is used when giving is involved (*er gab mir ein buch* /ʔeːr ˈgaːp mir ʔain ˈbuːx/ he gave me (dative) a book), but it is also used after the preposition *aus* (*aus der Mode* /ʔaus dɛr ˈmoːdə/ out of fashion). From antiquity also attempts have been repeatedly made to identify a common component of semantic function, underlying and observable in all the various uses to which each different case form is used in all the constructions in which it is found. An elementary book, such as this, cannot go into the details of this work, but the following facts stand out: important light is shed by investigations of this sort on the means of expression and semantic distinctions available to languages that give them their wonderful flexibility; many of the different uses of a single case form can be shown to rest on a common feature distinguishing the meaning correlation of the case from that of other cases; but it has yet to be shown indisputably that all the semantic functions of a single case form are reasonably to be linked to a common element of meaning or relation with the situations in which the forms are used; and the formal identification of the cases in different languages depends, not on semantic investigations of this sort, but upon morphological differences in word forms correlating with different syntactic constructions. Finally it must be remembered that a case in one language cannot be identified in its semantic range with a similarly labelled case in another. Similarity of some of its semantic functions must be the basis for the use of a common label, but one can go no further than that, and it is obvious that between languages in which there are different numbers of formally distinct cases, correspondences are bound to be very inexact and to involve much overlapping of function.

It has already been seen that, while it is reasonable to assert that everything can ultimately be expressed in every living language as the need arises, languages differ in the ways in which they divide up and lexically categorize the world of human experience, so that translation can seldom be satisfactorily carried out on a word for word basis (1·3·2, 2·4·3). Some things are more easily talked about in some languages than in others. This applies equally to the semantic categories linked in varying degrees to the obligatory formal grammatical categories and syntactic relations in languages.

The absence of a formal grammatical category of number in Chinese has been mentioned already; and many languages are without a formal category resembling the cases of German and Latin; this does not mean that they are less (or more) efficient as the means of communication about the world at large and the world of the speaker's cultures; it merely means that they operate in different ways and by different means. In this lies part of the interest of linguistic studies.

The category of **tense** in verb forms is familiar in European languages. The semantic ranges covered by the different forms are mainly on two axes, time relations and what are usually called aspectual difference of completion, incompletion, continuation, and momentariness. In Latin and Ancient Greek the different tense forms combine semantic differentiations of the two axes together; one may contrast the Latin imperfect and perfect, and the Greek imperfect, perfect, and aorist. In Russian the aspectual differences of imperfective and perfective are prominently marked by differences in verb forms separately from the marking of formal differences correlated with time differences; in languages like this the former sets of differences are usually called aspects or aspectual forms, and the latter tenses.

In English and German only two one-word tense forms are found in the verbal paradigms (other differences in the single-word forms being referable to the categories of person and number): *write, wrote, begin, began, describe, described*; *schreibt* /ʃraipt/ (he) writes, *schrieb* /ʃriːp/ (he) wrote, *sagt* /zaːkt/ (he) says, *sagte* /ˈzaːkte/ (he) said. Compound verbal expressions, consisting of a member of the verb paradigm and one or more of what are often called auxiliaries, are very common in these languages, and fulfil some of the semantic functions of the single-word tense forms of other languages (*will write, was writing, would have been writing*, etc.). The forms of several of these auxiliaries resemble the forms of the verbs *be, have,* and *will* in English, and *werden* /ˈveːrden/ to become, and *haben* /ˈhaːben/ to have, to which they are etymologically connected; but it is a mistake to identify the auxiliaries with these independent verbs descriptively, as their syntax is quite different.

Though tense is a familiar category of the verb in European languages, there is no universal necessity for it, or for any category semantically associated with time distinctions, in the morphological structure of the verb forms in a language. Malay and Yurok are two languages in which no formal category of tense can be abstracted from the morphological paradigms of the verbs. Time and aspect relations, when not already clear from the situation, are indicated by adverbs and particles forming part of the immediate endocentric expansion of the verbs. Similar functions are performed in Chinese, where word paradigms in the ordinary sense are not found, by various members of the word class of particle.

Studies in the semantic analysis of the different tense forms of verbs in languages where these form part of the morphological system are often very revealing, as they can only be undertaken by means of extensive and minute semantic analysis of large numbers of sentences systematically compared with one another both formally and in their functions in contexts of situation. One may search for common semantic components underlying apparently diverse uses of the same tense form, in the same way that a semantic unity underlying different uses is sought for the case forms of languages; but in all such investigations it must be kept in mind that the unity of each case or tense form (or set of tense forms in the different person and number categories) can be based solely on their morphological and syntactic identification, and while a semantic unity among the different uses of each may be looked for, it cannot be regarded as necessarily there for the finding or in any way guaranteed by the grammatical unity of the forms themselves.

In many languages pronominal words are organized into a system of three terms, or **persons**, as they are called, referring to the speaker (first person), the person addressed (second person), and the person referred to but not addressed (third person); different forms for each person category are often found, distinguished as singular and plural in the category of number, with a semantic correlation similar to that seen with number in nouns. In many European languages the category of person, like that of number, is a grammatical one, requiring concord with the forms of the verb with which it stands in specific relations. This is not universal; in Japanese, for example, verb forms do not vary according to the person category of the pronoun, and the category of person in such a language may be regarded as a lexical, rather than as a grammatical one.

In several European languages some uses of pronouns reveal a divergence between number and person as formally marked categories and the actual number and relationship of those involved. Standard English has only one form of the second person pronoun, *you* irrespective of number, and one concord form of verbs associated with it (*you are a fool, you are all fools*). Some dialects of English, in the north of England and elsewhere have separate forms for singular and plural second person pronouns, with different forms of verbs in concord with them. These pronominal forms are etymologically connected with the forms *thou* and *thee*, familiar in this use in Biblical English, e.g. /ˈðaː ˈaːt/ you (singular) are, /ða ˈnoəz vari ˈwiːl/ you (singular) know very well. These specifically singular forms with singular concord in the verbs are, however, only used in situations of familiarity and intimacy: in other circumstances only one form, corresponding to the plural in intimate use, is used, as in standard English. A similar situation is found in French, where in normal discourse, *vous* /vu/ functions indifferently in addressing one or several persons; among close friends, members of the family, and the like, *vous* is used as a plural and the specifically singular form is *tu* /ty/. There is a French verb *tutoyer* /tytwaje/ made up from two of the forms of the singular second person pronoun, *tu* and *toi*, meaning 'to speak familiarly to'.

In German and Italian formally distinct second person pronouns with second person concord forms of verbs are confined to familiar discourse. In other situations otherwise used in reference to third persons, with third person verbal concord are used; in Italian the usual third pronominal forms are *lei* /ˈlɛi/ otherwise used for 'she', and *loro* /ˈloro/ singular and plural respectively. In German *Sie* /ziː/ otherwise used as third person plural pronoun, is used for both numbers as a second person form, with plural concord in the verb (in writing the second person use of *Sie* is distinguished by an initial capital letter); *sind sie fertig?* /zint ziː ˈfɛrtiç/ are they ready?, *sind Sie fertig?* are you (singular or plural) ready?; familiarly *bist du fertig?* /bist duː ˈfɛrtiç/ singular, *seid ihr fertig?* /zait ʔiːr ˈfɛrtiç/ plural.

The precise limits of familiarity within which the familiar second person forms are used naturally vary from language to language and from community to community, with individual differences of use between persons within communities. The formal distinction maintained by the languages is clear enough, and the detailed semantic examination of the contrasting forms involves setting up contexts of situation for each language and each community, with factors other than the actual numbers of those addressed brought into relation with the forms of utterance (cp. 1·4·3).

A different anomaly in relation to number in pronouns is seen in what is often called the 'editorial *we*'. It occurs in fewer utterances than the forms mentioned above, but its use is a widespread convention in European and other languages. It consists in the use of what in other contexts is the first person pronoun referring to more than one person, by a writer when he is referring to himself. Somewhat similar is the use of the 'royal *we*'; in strictly ceremonial circumstances reigning sovereigns in some countries (of which Great Britain is one) use what are otherwise first person plural pronouns in reference to themselves in their official or constitutional capacity.

Relations of deference and social gradation are part of the relevant context determining the use of specific forms of pronouns within the personal categories in some languages. Different words correlating with different relations of social status between speakers are used in a number of languages; Malay (in which pronominal words are a less clearly delimited word class than in many other languages), Japanese, Tamil, and some other languages of southern India are examples.

While a formal distinction of three persons is the commonest type of pronominal system, systems of four persons are found in some of the Algonkian languages of North America. Four distinctions are made in the category of person in pronominal forms and in the forms of verbs and nouns syntactically related. The semantic reference of the fourth person is to a person or object distinct from one already referred to by a third person form. This further distinction is called **obviation**, and the fourth person forms distinguished in this sort of language are called obviative. Thus in Ojibwa, /nuwa:pema: aw enini/ I-see that man (third person); /uwa:pema:n eniw eninuwan/ he-sees that man (obviative).

Some languages show a formal distinction in pronominal forms between inclusive and exclusive plurals. Thus Ojibwa /ni:nuwi/ we (he and I), /ki:nuwi/ we (you, he, and I), Fijian /keimami/ we (they and I), /da/ we (you, plural, and I). The personal inflexions of verbs may include similar differentiation of inclusion and exclusion.

Of course English and any other language can make explicit the inclusive or exclusive use of plural pronominal forms, but this must

287

be done by circumlocution (*he and I*, *but not you*, etc.), and is not part of the semantic correlation of an obligatory formal grammatical category. A language can express anything required of it; they differ in the sort of situational features compulsorily brought to notice by the grammatical system (cp. in this respect the different treatment of singularity and plurality in nouns as between English and Chinese).

7·3   CLASS MEANINGS AND STRUCTURAL MEANINGS

Beside the semantic correlations of formal grammatical categories, one finds similar correlations with different word classes and with sentence structures and syntactic constructions. Such correlations are familiar, because traditional grammar often made improper use of them to define word classes, or 'parts of speech', in semantic terms. The theoretical and practical objections to this sort of procedure in grammar have already been mentioned (5·1·2, 5·1·4); but the statement of the sorts of meanings, semantic functions, or ways of referring to features and entities of situations, ascribable to members of formally differentiated word classes, after these have been established, is a relevant part of a complete grammatical description of a language.

Nouns are used to refer to discrete things, persons, and abstractions; and verbs are used to refer to processes and activities. From this arises the possibility of matching many of the nouns and verbs of one language with those of other languages (6·2). But the semantic correlations are never complete, and in the nature of things cannot be always clear-cut in their applications. They play no part in the formal establishment and definition of word classes within a language. In assigning words to word classes, the linguist need not worry whether dying, being silent (cp. German *schweigen* /ˈʃvaigen/, Latin /ˈtace:re/ to be silent), and bisecting, in geometry, are actions or processes, nor with whether they are 'conceived' as such by native speakers, or whether brightness, sunset, electron, and geometrical point are things. The formal status of the words concerned is not in doubt and is not settled by considerations like these. Their place, in so far as the linguist can deal with them, is in the subsequent analysis of the various semantic uses to which members of different word classes are put.

In the same way the linguist distinguishes sentence forms or structures (declarative or indicative *John goes home*, interrogative *are you going home?*, imperative *go home!*, etc.) from the situational functions of utterances, such as giving information, eliciting information, and inducing or preventing action by others. Each of the three sentence structures exemplified above from English and represented by formal differences in many languages, correlates regularly with one of the situational functions just mentioned; but it is not hard to show that any sentence form can fulfil any function. Interrogative word order, with a particular intonation in sentences like *am I tired!* and 'rhetorical questions' like *is it not better to suffer in silence?* serve to make emphatic statements to the effect that one is tired and that it is better to suffer in silence. *I want to know the time* is in most contexts a means of eliciting information, like *what is the time?*, rather than a statement of one's feelings. *You will go home now* may be as much a command as a formally imperatival sentence *go home!* and in instruction manuals and the like, sentences like *to disconnect the water supply turn the main tap clockwise*, though formally imperatival, are more in the nature of informative statements (the borders between these situational functions are bound to be hazy, and the simplified illustrations given here scarcely begin to exemplify the numerous and diverse types of language functions in human society).

Endocentric adjective+noun constructions often do indicate some modification of the semantic reference of the noun, by further specification; *red flower* has a narrower range of application than *flower* does. But *a probable event* does not denote a particular sort of event in the way that *a dangerous event* or *a nocturnal event* does, and the sorts of specification indicated in the latter two examples are not the same. Knowing a language means knowing all the formal structures available for sentence formation and the different semantic functions to which they may, in various situations and with various lexical collocations (2·4·2), be applied.

Such facts, when looked at clearly, are very obvious; it was the long subordination of linguistics to logic, both in theory and methods, that prevented their proper realization in earlier days.

7·4 METHODOLOGICAL IMPLICATIONS

The object of grammatical analysis is to explain the forms of sentences and the forms of the words in them by referring them to appropriate structures, classes, and grammatical categories. No matter how the formal criteria are drawn up and ordered, hard cases and borderline examples are likely to appear. But as has been seen in earlier discussions of such cases, the ultimate decision turns on the balancing of one set of observations against another; and the decision can be defended, and challenged, by appealing to the same sets of publicly observable phenomena (the sort of data that the empirical sciences purport to deal with, and consisting, in the case of linguistics, of the shapes and patterns of meaningful utterances).

Traditional classifications relying, or apparently relying, on notional criteria and types of semantic meanings are of no help in difficult cases, as definite answers to the relevant questions cannot be given. The assignment of the English word *sake* to the noun class, as an irregular member (6·6), was based on observations of the ways in which it can be used syntactically in sentences. The appropriateness of such decisions may be challenged, but the observations on which they are based are manifest to everyone alike. To the question *is a sake a thing?* or *how do you conceive of a sake?* either no answer can be given, or a mere guess, incapable of rigorous formulation and likely to vary from one person to another.

Are *tomorrow* and *yesterday* nouns or adverbs, or members of both classes? Formally they must certainly be classed among the English nouns; they can be pluralized and preceded by adjectives and can occupy positions in sentences occupied by other nouns: *all our yesterdays, we face a gloomy tomorrow, tomorrow is Sunday*. But since they can also occupy sentence places otherwise occupied by adverbs, and from which most nouns would be excluded, it would seem that the words in question must either be assigned to both classes, as must a number of English words anyway (6·2), or they must be grouped together as a syntactically differentiated subclass of nouns (*he came yesterday*, but *he came on Wednesday*; *tomorrow they will be here*, but *in the morning they will be here*).

The argument is carried on, and its conclusions can be tested, by examining and comparing actual and possible English sentences. To attempt to decide questions like this by asking whether the words primarily refer to 'things', or qualify 'verbal ideas', is to condemn them to insolubility. In so far as native speakers, by what is sometimes called *sentiment linguistique* or a sort of intuition, consistently want to group certain forms together without quite being able consistently to say why, this is probably due in most cases, as with the intuition of word unity mentioned above (5·3·1), to a subconscious awareness of relevant formal criteria. Speakers' intuitions are a valuable, indeed an invaluable, aid in linguistic research, but only as pointers to lines of investigation, and not as the ultimate justification for decisions.

The linguist should not stop short at the formal analysis of the grammar of a language, but should seek out the sorts of meanings associated with the classes and categories he has set up to describe it. He should discover the extent to which form classes and meaning classes are closely or loosely correlated in different parts of the system, and note the sorts of semantic distinctions that are emphasized in this way by association with the obligatory features of word forms and constructions in the language. Grammatically emphasized ranges of meanings may in part be responsible for the different ways in which human beings envisage, categorize, and think about the world of their experience. Such linguistic or metalinguistic speculations are very far from advanced; they must depend on the detailed analyses of the grammatical systems of a large number of languages being carried out; and if they are to escape from circular and uninformative argumentation, they must start from purely formal descriptions.

Grammatical theory and grammatical practice should not ignore meanings, but the semantic aspect of grammar can only be fruitful if undertaken after, and on the basis of, a comprehensive and meticulous formal analysis.

p. 277. On full words and form words, Sweet, 72, 22–4.

p. 278. On the relations between grammatical units and meanings, Chomsky, 16, chapter 9.

p. 279. Among the Slavic languages, the dual survives in Slovenian (spoken in North-west Yugoslavia) and in Lusatian (spoken on the upper reaches of the river Spree in East Germany); see de Bray, 14.

p. 280. A sort of pluralizing suffix /-mən/ is suffixed to some North Chinese words, notably the pronominal forms, /wo³/ I, /ni³/ you (singular), and /ta¹/ he, she, (/wo³mən/ we, /ni³mən/ you (plural), /ta¹mən/ they), and a few others (/rən²mən/ men; /ʃye²ʃəŋ¹mən/ students). This has no effect on the word forms of the rest of the sentence. The superscript numerals refer to the different tones of Chinese syllables (3·5·4, 4.3·5); ¹ indicates a high level tone, ² a rising tone, ³ a falling and rising or a low rising tone, and ⁴ (not exemplified here) a falling tone; /mən/ is an example of a syllable called 'toneless'; its actual pitch is determined by the tone of the preceding syllable.

The distinction between grammatical and lexical categories in languages is discussed by Hjelmslev, 36.

p. 281. In the weaker relations of back reference across sentence boundaries (cp. 6·5·1), 'anomalous' neuter nouns referring to animates are often taken up with the pronoun whose gender correlates with the sex of the being referred to, particularly in informal speech. Thus German *Mädchen* may be taken up by *sie* as well as by *es*, and French *sentinelle* by *il* as well as by *elle*.

p. 282. Ojibwa, Bloomfield, 11.

The term *accusative case* is probably the result of an ancient mistranslation of the Greek αἰτιατικὴ πτῶσις /aitia:tikè: ptô:sis/ meaning 'causal case', as being the case in which the objects of transitive verbs are put, many of them referring to things or persons whereon are directed the actions denoted by verbs. But the verb αἰτιάομαι /aitiá:omai/ meant 'I accuse' as well as 'I allege as a cause', and from this the translation of the related αἰτιατική (πτῶσις) into the Latin /(ca:sus) accu:sa:ti:vus/ arose.

p. 283. The search for common or basic meanings of the cases in Latin, Russian, and other languages has been taken as far as it can be in such works as Hjelmslev, 35, and Jakobson, 45.

p. 284. On aspect as a grammatical category in Russian, Braun, 13, 95–125; Entwistle and Morison, 21, 106–9. On the English verbal categories, Joos, 91; Palmer, 92.

Malay, Winstedt, 79. Yurok, Robins, 63.

p. 286. Wright, 81, 144, 178–80.

There is also the French verb *vouvoyer* /vuvwaje/ to use *vous* in addressing one person; cp. German *duzen* /ˈduːtsen/ to use *du*, and *siezen* /ˈziːtsen/ to use *Sie*, in addressing a second person.

p. 287. Singular and plural number are distinguished in English in the pronominal forms *yourself* (singular) and *yourselves* (plural): *you saw it yourself* and *you saw it yourselves*; so, too, the 'editorial *we*' is sometimes followed by *ourself* instead of *ourselves*.

p. 288. The category of person in verbs, with concord with what is generally called the subject, is familiar in European languages, but bipersonal verb forms, with two separate and distinctive personal categories are quite common (e.g. Swahili /nilimwona/ I saw him, /aliniona/ he saw me, /mlituona/ you (plural) saw us, /tuliwaona/ we saw you (plural); Yurok /koʔmoyotʃek'/ I hear you (singular), /koʔmoyotʃ'o/ I hear you (plural), /koʔmoyosek'/ I hear him, /koʔmoyopaʔ/ you (singular and plural) hear me). Bipersonal verb forms are found in Basque (Houghton, 44), Georgian (Vogt, 74), and in a number of American-Indian languages, among others. An isolated bipersonal form appears in Hungarian verbs, involving the first and second person singular persons only, *látlak* /laːtlɔk/ I see you, *szeretlek* /sɛrɛtlɛk/ I love you, etc. (roots *lát-* and *szeret-*). Bipersonal verb forms with distinction of inclusive and exclusive plurals are exemplified in Ojibwa and in Jebero, a language of Peru (Bendor-Samuel, 7).

p. 291. Speculation on the lines suggested in the final paragraphs of this Chapter forms a main part of the Whorf hypothesis (cp. note to p. 71, above), whose main principle is that the way in which one thinks is in part conditioned by the way one's language structure enables one most easily to think, and that in consequence different languages induce different ways of envisaging the world of experience. Considerations of this sort, in protest against the naïve view that all of mankind live in 'the same world', full of 'the same things', to which each language merely attaches different labels, are at least as old as Sapir in linguistics, but were forcefully put forward later by B. L. Whorf, who contrasted the world view of the Hopi (an American-Indian people), for which he held their language partly responsible, with that of 'standard average European', conditioned by centuries of Aristotelian logic, itself cradled in the language structures of Ancient Greek and Latin.

Whorf's case has sometimes been overstated to the effect that one can only think on the lines laid down by the structure of one's language, and has in consequence not escaped criticism; but he was asserting no more than that certain ways of thinking about the world are made easier than others by the sentence structures of particular languages and the sorts of semantic functions most associated with its obligatory grammatical categories and word classes.

See further: Whorf, 77; 78; Hoijer, 40, 41, 42.

8

Linguistic comparison

8·1 HISTORICALLY ORIENTATED COMPARISON OF LANGUAGES (COMPARATIVE AND HISTORICAL LINGUISTICS)

8·1·1 *The material*

Comparisons of one sort or another between different languages are as old as the study of languages. This is inevitable, since any acquaintance with or interest in one or more languages other than one's own provokes the comparison of various parts or aspects of these languages from some point of view. Often this has been naïve and trivial, as when foreign languages were examined with a view to finding deficiencies and marks of inferiority when compared with a language enjoying high prestige like Ancient Greek, Latin, or Hebrew.

In general linguistics today **comparative** studies form an important part of the subject and of our understanding of the working and development of languages the world over. In particular, two types of linguistic comparison have come to be recognized, working on rather different principles and with different ends in view. It is desirable that the bases and methods of these two types should be clearly understood, as inconsistencies and confusions have not always been avoided, in a field in which, if satisfactory conclusions are to be reached, clarity of thought is essential.

One type of linguistic comparison, probably the one best known to the general public, is historically orientated comparison, which can strictly be designated **comparative and historical linguistics**, and is widely known as 'comparative philology' (cp. 1·1·3). This branch of linguistic studies rather dominated the field during the nineteenth century in Europe, partly as a result of the stimulus derived from the discovery of Sanskrit, the ancient classical language of India, by Western scholars and the demonstration at the end of the eighteenth century of the indisputable historical connection of this language with Latin, Greek, and German. In British universities chairs of Comparative Philology antedated by many years established posts in general linguistics, and the term *comparative philology* is still sometimes used to refer generally to all branches of the systematic study of language. General linguistics, indeed, to some extent developed as comparative and historical studies aroused wider interests in the nature of languages and the means whereby they could be analysed.

The linguistic evidence, the facts on which comparative and historical studies are based, is in part very obvious. Word forms in languages are in the great majority of cases only conventionally linked with their referents or with their whole semantic functions; this has been expressed by speaking of the essentially arbitrary nature of linguistic forms. Onomatopoeic forms, whose sound sequences suggest or vaguely imitate within the phonological system of the language noises characteristic of what the forms refer to, are well known linguistic phenomena (*cuckoo, ding-dong, ting-a-ling-a-ling, cockadoodledoo*, German *Bimbam* /ˈbimbam/ noise of bells, *Kikeriki* /kikeriˈki/ noise of cocks crowing, etc.), but their relative numbers in any vocabulary are extremely limited. Other semantic associations with certain word forms are found; several English words ending with *-ump* have connotations of thickness, bulk, heaviness, and the like (*clump, hump, dump, thump*, etc., cp. 1·3·2). Such factors play some part in the determination of the word forms of all languages, so far as is known, but they leave untouched the greater part of their word stocks.

One is at once struck by the fact that among different languages greater or smaller numbers of words, in which onomatopoeia and sound symbolism are scarcely adduceable as relevant, and whose meanings are related or similar, exhibit manifest similarities of phonetic form (the limits of the application of the terms *related* and *similar* in this connection cannot be definitively circumscribed, but they are sufficiently clear in most cases, and borderline or doubtful examples can be left out of account as evidence).

Some samples from European languages will illustrate this:

MEANING	ENGLISH	GERMAN	FRENCH	ITALIAN	SPANISH
'hand'	hand	Hand	main	mano	mano
	/hænd/	/hant/	/mɛ̃/	/'mano/	/'mano/
'life'	life	Leben	vie	vita	vida
	/laif/	/'le:ben/	/vi/	/'vita/	/'vida/
'summer'	summer	Sommer	été	estate	estio
	/'sʌmə/	/'zɔmer/	/ete/	/e'state/	/es'tio/
'give'	give	geben	donner	donare	donar
	/giv/	/'geben/	/dɔne/	/do'nare/	/do'nar/

It will be seen from these examples that English and German constitute one group, and French, Italian, and Spanish another group, in which these word forms of similar meanings show obvious similarities with one another, but not between languages of the different groups.

One may now consider the following examples:

MEANING	ENGLISH	GERMAN	FRENCH	ITALIAN	SPANISH
'foot'	foot	Fuss	pied	piede	pie
	/fut/	/fu:s/	/pje/	/pi'ɛde/	/pi'e/
'two'	two	zwei	deux	due	dos
	/tu:/	/tsvai/	/dø/	/'due/	/dos/
'three'	three	drei	trois	tre	tres
	/θri:/	/drai/	/trwa/	/tre/	/tres/
'me'	me	mich	moi	me	me
	/mi:/	/miç/	/mwa/	/me/	/me/

In these word forms it is clear that, while the similarities within the two groups of languages mentioned above are closer, a general similarity in at least some part of each word unites all five languages into a larger group in terms of this evidence.

The immediately apparent basis for this sort of lexical comparison is similarity of word forms, but further examination reveals that similarity is only a special case of **systematic and regular correspondences** between component sound segments in semantically related words. Single pairs of similarly sounding words of the same sort of meaning are of no significance unsupported by others, and can be found between almost any two languages. The significance of Italian *piede* and English *foot* is not so much the similarity between /p/ and /f/, as the fact that the correspondence is matched by such further pairs as *padre* /padre/ and *father*, *pesce*/'peʃʃe/ and *fish*, and that /d/

and /t/ correspond in *due* and *two*, *dieci* /diˈɛci/ ten and *ten*, and other pairs; and the same thing applies to all the other examples quoted. Examples of such correspondences become cumulatively weightier as their number multiplies.

When the series of words exhibiting correspondences of this sort between languages is set out and examined, it is found that they are far too numerous to be plausibly explained away as coincidental (as single unsupported examples could be), and that they are each confined to certain groups of languages. Languages can be grouped together on the evidence of these correspondences; some groups, such as the one that includes English and German, and the one that includes French, Italian, and Spanish, show a larger number of words related in this way, but include smaller numbers of languages, while other groups, such as one that includes in itself all the members of the two smaller groups just mentioned, and some more such groups, show fewer correspondences holding between word forms of the different included groups, but cover a much wider range of languages.

Since the particular correspondences and similarities by which languages may be grouped in this way are not universal as between all languages, nor reasonably regarded as coincidental, an explanation is required and comparative and historical linguistics is an explanatory discipline. Some word-form similarities, though less readily correspondences of dissimilar sounds, can be explained as the result of word borrowing, the taking over of words from foreign languages into a language as the result of contacts with their speakers (8·1·7). While no type of meaning can be ruled out from representation by a borrowed word, and loan words, as they are called, cover all ranges of semantic functions, it is scarcely likely that a considerable number of words in several languages, covering meanings virtually essential to any language, should all be borrowed from a single source. The other, and the only plausible, explanation is that the different word forms related by one or more correspondences of phonetic composition are the result, after varying intervals of time, of the gradual divergence of the languages involved from an earlier linguistic situation in which their predecessors in time constituted something like a single language (itself, of course, like all languages, an abstraction and no doubt divided by isoglosses into regional dialects, 2·1·1, 2·2).

297

This is what is meant by saying that, historically, a language is **derived** from an earlier language, and that particular words in it are **derived** from particular earlier words.

This explanation, as well as accounting for the phenomena, describes a situation that one knows from other evidence to occur. The group of languages exemplified above with French, Italian, and Spanish, and actually comprising in addition Portuguese, Rumanian, Catalan (spoken in part of Spain), Provençal (spoken in part of southern France), and some others, and commonly called the **Romance languages**, is especially illustrative in this connection. It is known historically that the areas covered by these languages in Europe were for some centuries occupied by the Romans, beginning in the first century B.C., and formed the most Romanized part of the Roman Empire (in much of the eastern half Greek was in use as the official language). In these areas spoken Latin, or Vulgar Latin, as it is often called to distinguish it from the literary language studied as 'Latin' then as now, soon became established as the language of the governors, the language of large scale trading, the law, defence, administration, and social advancement, with the prestige of classical literary, Latin, as the language of culture and education, behind it. So much did Latin displace the earlier languages of a great part of these provinces of the empire, that it survived the breakdown of it in the west and the inroads of barbarian invaders.

The gradual and continuous development of spoken Latin in these regions through successive stages into the present-day mutually unintelligible Romance languages can be traced in varying degrees of detail with the aid of inscriptions and old texts. Languages are constantly changing, though imperceptibly at any time, except in the matter of vocabulary content, which can change very rapidly. Differences of pronunciation and grammar become noticeable when recorded forms of a language of some centuries ago are examined and compared with examples of the language today, or, more generally, when the recorded forms of different stages of the language of a continuing speech community are compared and contrasted (e.g. the English of King Alfred's time (Old English), the English of Chaucer's time (Middle English), the English of Shakespeare's time, and the English of the present day).

Where the social unity of a speech community is maintained, the general need for mutual intercourse prevents these changes from diverging too widely so as to produce mutually unintelligible forms of speech, and the changes, though they may be great, tend to be fairly uniform, with regional differences marking dialect areas rather than language divisions, and this must have been the situation during the years when the Roman Empire was more or less intact. Once the unity of speech communities is broken, and linguistic contacts between regions become few, nothing prevents the stream of changes from widening the differences between the types of speech in different areas and, in the course of time, producing separate languages.

Linguistic divergences resulting from geographical separation may be seen elsewhere. The Dutch of the early settlers in South Africa developed differently from the Dutch of Holland, and Afrikaans, as the development of Dutch in South Africa is called, is now reckoned a different language from Netherlands Dutch. Between the English of North America, Australia, and New Zealand, and between these and British English (and their various dialects) definite differences are observable in phonetics, grammar, and vocabulary; and the same is true of the Spanish of Central and South America and that of Spain, and between the Portuguese of Brazil and that of Portugal. But in all these the differences have not gone beyond the stage of dialectal differences, and contemporary conditions are almost certain to prevent them widening outside the limits of mutual intelligibility.

The fact of continuous, though gradual, change in languages at every level, phonetic, phonological, grammatical, and lexical, is indisputable; indeed, the assumption, for the purposes of description, of a stage of a language at which no change is recognized as occurring is strictly speaking in the nature of a fictional abstraction (1·1·2).

The causes of this continuous process of change are as yet not fully understood, but two sets of factors may be distinguished, external influences and internal processes. External causes of linguistic change are the contacts between the speakers of different languages, of the sort that occur when a foreign language is imposed on a people by conquest or by political or cultural domination, or when cultural and other factors produce a high degree of bilingualism between adjacent speech areas. Under such conditions speakers who acquire a second language in adulthood will inevitably bring into their use of it, phonetic, grammatical, and some lexical habits of their own first language. This is what is loosely known as 'speaking with an accent', and in the course of time such habits, passed on from generation to generation, become standardized and acceptable. In some cases, as in parts of Spanish-speaking South America, the effects of an originally spoken language on the form of Spanish now spoken by many speakers are still noticeable and have persisted long after that original tongue ceased to be spoken. Such linguistic phenomena are often called the effects of linguistic substrates or of substrate languages. External factors of one sort or another have been held responsible for many of the differences in languages that take place when an original language is diffused over wide areas displacing languages spoken there before, as happened with the spread of Latin over much of the western half of the Roman Empire and of English, Spanish, and Portuguese over large areas of the world in more modern times.

Internal causes of linguistic changes lie in the nature of the transmission of speech habits from one generation to another. Apart from all external influences, gradual changes appear to be inevitable, and in the processes some general tendencies are found repeatedly at work in various times and areas. Examples of these at the phonetic level are the change of aspirated plosives into fricatives (as in Ancient Greek θέλω /tʰélo:/ I wish, Modern Greek θέλω /ˈθelo/), the voicing of intervocalic plosives (Latin /(via) stra:ta/ made-up road, Italian *strada* /ˈstrada/ street), Latin /se: cu: rus/ untroubled, Spanish *seguro* /seˈguro/ secure, and the changing of velar plosives before front vowels to affricates or alveolar fricatives (Latin /centum/ (Latin /c/ was a voiceless velar plosive), Italian *cento* /ˈtʃento/, French *cent* /sɑ̃/ hundred). Sometimes shifts in the whole mode of articulating certain classes of sounds, for example the change from unaspirated to aspirated plosives, take place in a certain area during a certain period. At another level, changes take place in grammar, for example in a gradual shift from a syntax relying on inflectional word forms to one relying on word order in the marking of structural relations.

A chain of internal changes may sometimes be seen to operate in the phonological and grammatical history of a language. The development in words of a strong stress on a non-final syllable may cause the articulation of the consonants and vowels of the final syllables to become gradually less distinct; this in turn renders these final syllables less effective as the carriers or exponents of grammatical categories and the indicators of syntactic relationships. These relationships as a consequence gradually come to be marked by other means, such as additional words in the sentence or a grammatically determined word order. Some inflections, such as the cases of nouns, are replaced by word groups or relative position in relation to other words in the sentence. Along with this process, the development of the new methods of marking grammatical relations renders inflectional differences in the final syllables of words less important and so more easily abandoned. Some such chain of causally connected changes may be seen at work in the gradual passage of spoken Latin to modern French.

Various causal explanations of this sort of change over the course of generations have been put forward. The great diversity of the sorts of changes at all levels that have occurred in different areas and at different times rule out any simple or general explanation in terms of a single cause. Whatever the causes, continuous changes in the forms and systems of languages are a universal linguistic feature, and provide the material for the historical study of sets of languages. Historical linguistics may in a sense be said to be a special case of this sort of comparative linguistics, in that one is comparing the forms exhibited by temporally successive stages of the language of a continuing speech community.

8·1·2 *Semantic changes*

Part of the change that takes place in the history of all languages consists of change in the meanings or semantic functions of some of the words in their vocabularies, considered as the continuing lexical content of successive stages of the language. The study of **semantic change**, as it is called, though of less immediate concern in comparative linguistics, is very relevant to the historical study of languages.

The conditions of life of individuals in society, their artefacts, customs, forms of organization, and the like are constantly changing; and consequently the referents of many words in languages and the situations in which they are employed are equally liable to change in the course of time. New products often require new designations, and some words pass out of current vocabulary as the particular sorts

301

of objects or ways of behaving to which they refer become obsolete. One need only think in English of the former specialized vocabulary, now largely vanished, relating to obsolete sports such as falconry, and of the vastly increased vocabulary relating to the mechanical sciences and technological developments that characterize the language at the present time.

In the course of time many words, as they are used in sentences, change in regard to the sorts of features in situations to which they refer, or in the ways in which they refer to them. These changes are very numerous and diverse, and it will not be necessary to do more than notice some of the most obvious. Some words come to be used and understood with somewhat different connotations (part of their total situational meaning) after a lapse of time. In part these changes may be correlated with social changes. One may revealingly compare the account given of the meaning of *enthusiasm* in Dr. Johnson's English dictionary, published in the eighteenth century, with that to be found in the *Oxford English Dictionary* today.

Some words have their contextual application reduced in scope. Thus *meat* is now used to refer to butcher's meat, i.e. flesh food, though in the time of the translation of the Authorized Version of the Bible it meant food in general, as it still does in the fixed collocation *meat and drink*; this semantic survival may be compared with the survival, in certain collocations, of some older lexical forms not otherwise current in English today (2·4·2). Similarly *gobbet*, formerly used to mean 'piece' (of meat, bread, etc.), is now almost exclusively used to refer to short passages in texts set for comment in examination papers. Middle English (c. 1400) *dēor* /deːr/ beast, animal, has become *deer*, now denoting one species of animal. Some words change their principal reference; in parts of the western Roman Empire the Latin word /testa/ tile, also skull, came to be used with general reference to the head (whence French *tête* /tɛt/ and Italian *testa* /ˈtɛsta/ head). Some words widen the range of their application or meaning, when they come to be used in contexts in which they were previously not used or with reference to elements of the contexts with which they were previously not connected. Middle English *brid* /brid/ also spelled *bird* /bird/ meaning 'young bird', has become modern English *bird*, now used with reference to all birds irrespective of age. Proper names of persons noted in connection with some product or way of behaviour widen their meaning to cover the class thus designated; *Rolls* and *Royce*, the names of two motor manufacturers have produced the word Rolls-Royce, designating a type of car; similarly *he looks like a quisling* (= traitor, Quisling being a leader of the Norwegian Nazi party at the time of the German invasion in 1940). Some words increase their class membership in this process: *boycott* is both a noun and a verb, and is derived from the name of a Captain Boycott, an Irish land agent of the nineteenth century, subjected to the process. A very extensive type of semantic widening consists in metaphorical uses, wherein on the basis of some similarity in the meanings a word is used in different sorts of context and in reference to different sorts of features, usually of a more abstract nature, than was once the case. Metaphorical extension of meaning, already mentioned in 2·3, is too well known to require exemplification.

Sometimes changes in material culture directly cause some extensions of meaning. Thus in recent years *jet*, in addition to its meaning of 'forcibly ejected stream of liquid, gas, etc.' and 'the nozzle through which it is ejected', has come to be used in reference to a jet propelled aircraft (i.e. one whose propulsion is derived from a jet of vapour of some kind). Similarly *nuclear*, in addition to 'central' now has the meaning 'referring to explosions involving the fragmentation of certain chemical atoms, and to armaments based thereon'.

The importance of the field of words associated together in a language at any time with reference to a range of semantic functions has already been mentioned as an important factor in determining and analysing the meaning of many words in languages (2·4·3). So the meanings of some words may be affected by changes in the composition and in the meanings of the associated field, over the language as a whole or in particular usages. To take a trivial example, if in the terminology of examination grading a mark of fair, good, or excellent was awarded to all candidates who passed, but after a certain date this grading was replaced by one of four terms: fair, good, excellent, first class, it is obvious that, in this specialized field, the meanings of the three original terms, particularly that of *excellent*, will be somewhat lowered and contracted. The appearance in English after the Norman Conquest of the words of French origin (given in their modern orthographic form): *veal*, *beef*, *mutton*, and *pork*, caused a contraction in the semantic range of the English words corresponding to modern English *calf*, *ox*, *sheep*, and *pig* or *hog*, in that these were no longer employed in normal discourse to refer to the meat derived from these creatures, and their use in collocation with words like *flesh*, *meat*, etc. became less widespread.

8·1·3 *The Indo-european family*

The observed and attested facts of historical changes in many of the word forms of the Romance languages and some other groups both confirm the inferences that must be drawn to explain the systematic correspondences of phonetic composition in words of similar or related meanings in these languages, and give reason to assume similar developments as lying behind other groups of languages brought together by their exhibiting comparable sets of correspondences, but of whose earlier common descent nothing is directly known.

The group represented earlier by examples from English and German is called the Germanic languages, and to it belong, besides English and German, Swedish, Danish, Norwegian, Icelandic, Dutch, and some other living languages, as well as the extinct Gothic language, which is preserved in Bible translations from the fourth century A.D. In addition to Romance and Germanic, other languages are grouped on the same sort of evidence: into the Indo-iranian languages, comprising Iranian (Persian) and Avestan (extinct), Hindi, Bengali, Marathi, and several other languages of northern India, together with Sanskrit which stands in a somewhat similar relation to them as Latin does to the Romance languages; into the Celtic languages, including Scots Gaelic, Irish, Welsh, and Breton (spoken in parts of Brittany); and into the Balto-Slavic languages, subdivided into the Baltic group, Lithuanian and Lettish, and the Slavic group, including Russian, Polish, Slovak, Serbo-croat, Bulgarian, and some others, together with Old Slavic, an early written language now extinct apart from its use in some religious services. Latin, from which the Romance languages developed, was itself the principal member of the Italic group.

All of these groups, and a number of other languages not immediately members of groups comparable to those given above such as Greek (Ancient and Modern) and Armenian, exhibit correspondences linking them all together, though less closely than within each constituent group. These more wide-ranging correspondences were illustrated above with the words for 'foot', 'two', 'three', and 'me'. On the basis of correspondences like these, and by the same arguments, all these languages are grouped into a larger family, usually called **Indo-european** (abbreviated to I-E), from the geographical distribution of most of its members.

The I-E languages may be inferred to have diverged in stages roughly represented by the groups or subfamilies from a once more homogeneous and mutually intelligible language area. In some details the membership and constitution of the family is still uncertain. In particular the position of Hittite, an ancient language of the Near East attested in cuneiform inscriptions, in relation to the others is still disputed. That it is connected with the I-E family is now quite definite, but scholars differ as to whether it is an I-E language or a representative of a collateral branch forming with I-E a yet more inclusive Indo-hittite family. This question need not be pursued further here, and the term *Indo-european* (I-E) will be used throughout.

I-E is the largest family into which the languages of most of Europe and some other areas can be grouped by the application of comparative methods with any degree of reliability. The relatively unitary state assumed to lie historically behind the family is in no general sense an 'original language', still less 'the original language'; it is merely as far back as one can at present go by comparative and historical inference. Whatever date may be ascribed to the relatively unitary state of I-E as a language in a speech community (and c. 3000 B.C. has been suggested), aeons of linguistic history lie behind it. The peculiarity of I-E lies in the fact that it sets a limit on scholarly inference, not in anything special about the language or its speakers. In particular, language, a culturally acquired set of habits, must not be confused with race, an inherited set of physical characteristics. The diffusion and disperson of the I-E languages over most of Europe and North India was doubtless due to an early dispersion of population; but languages also spread by superimposition on existing communities, replacing their former languages, as in the case of the diffusion of Latin over much of the western part of the Roman Empire. The diffusion of a language over a wider area is not the same as, nor a necessary ground for inferring, the parallel diffusion of a racial type. At the present time the membership of a language in the I-E family has nothing to do with the membership of its speakers in any racial group. One must insist on this, as the confounding of race and language has been an error of scholarship in the past, and has been perverted into false arguments in support of the dogmas of political racialism in all too recent history.

8·1·4 *Other language families*

So far attention has been concentrated upon the I-E family. This is not by any means the only family of languages that may be set up by the methods of comparative and historical linguistics on the basis of systematic correspondences of word forms. Such linguistic studies developed mainly around the I-E family, and this family has had more attention devoted to it than any other. Rather as within the I-E family the Romance group of languages may be regarded as a specially privileged field for comparative and historical work, in that records of the 'parent language', colloquial Latin, are available, so the I-E family as a whole is a particularly favourable area for this sort of study, for a number of reasons. Among these are: 1. There is more detailed knowledge available of the continuous history of the I-E speech communities than is generally available with the other families; 2. Three of the major classical languages of the world, Ancient Greek, Latin, and Sanskrit, are I-E languages, and they have been the objects of unbroken and minute scholarship from antiquity to the present day in the west or in India; and 3. There is a mass of inscriptional and manuscript records of successive stages in the development of many of the I-E languages; this enables the history of these languages to be documented, and the forms of dead languages to be brought into the material from which systematic correspondences are abstracted, and the more material available there is, the more secure and informative are the correspondences taken from it.

The I-E family covers most of Europe and North India; and as a result of the European expansion by land and overseas in the modern world I-E languages predominate in North and South America (English, Spanish, and Portuguese), and in Australasia (English), while Russian, as the official language of the Soviet Union, is widely spoken over Asiatic Russia; and the I-E language family is represented all over the world today through the internationally current languages of trade, English, French, and Spanish.

Other language families have been set up on the same basis as I-E, systematic correspondences in the phonetic composition of words of similar or related meaning. In Europe much of the territory not covered by I-E languages is occupied by members of the Finno-ugrian family, represented by Lappish, Finnish, Estonian, and Hungarian in Europe, and by a number of related languages in central and east Russia, a family possibly though not certainly connected historically with the Altaic family, which includes Turkish, Tartar, and Uzbeg, and a number of other languages of Asiatic Russia stretching as far north as Siberia. Two non-I-E families that contain classical languages and a long tradition of literary culture are the Sino-tibetan family, which includes the numerous Chinese languages and dialects, Tibetan, and Thai (Siamese), and the Hamito-semitic family, represented by classical Arabic and the Arabic languages and dialects of the Middle East and North African coast, and by Ancient and Modern Hebrew and other related languages; in Europe this family is represented by Maltese, a language derived from Arabic as a result of medieval Arabic settlement on the island.

Many of the languages of central and southern India belong to the Dravidian family (Tamil, Telugu, etc.), and the Malayo-polynesian family includes many of the languages spoken in the Malay peninsula, Indonesia, and the neighbouring islands (Malay, Sundanese, Javanese, Indonesian, etc.); as the result of early migration, Malagasy, the language of Madagascar, also belongs to this family.

All these families contain languages which have for centuries been literate, and in them extant written records, inscriptions, and manuscripts, provide evidence of the forms of earlier stages of some of the member languages, as is the case on a larger scale with I-E. But some families have been established simply by reference to systematic correspondences in contemporary languages, as they are represented by languages spoken in parts of the world where before the coming

307

of Europeans literacy was virtually unknown. Obviously the difficulties of operating in such areas are usually greater, and there is
mostly a corresponding lack of reliable earlier history of the peoples,
such as is available as supplementary information in I-E and other
families with long literate member languages. Among these families
are the Bantu languages, including Swahili, a language widely used
in much of East Africa, and many other South African languages, and
two language families of North America, Athabascan and Algonkian,
the former stretching with intermissions from north-western Canada
to the southern states of the U.S.A., the latter concentrated in the
central and eastern plains area of Canada and the U.S.A. and in New
England, but also represented by isolated languages in the western
states, Blackfoot (Montana, and Alberta, Canada), and Wiyot and
Yurok (California).

The families mentioned above by no means exhaust those that can
be and have been set up satisfactorily on comparative and historical
lines. But the principles and methods are the same, and no very
useful purpose would be served in an introductory survey by the
listing of these families and their member languages. In principle, all
languages could probably be assigned to a family together with other
languages given adequate information; but in fact, and especially in
the case of languages of which historical records do not survive, very
many are not certainly known to be affiliated to any family, and are
likely to remain thus isolated. In Europe the Basque language,
spoken in a group of dialects on either side of the Franco-Spanish
frontier in the eastern Pyrenees, is one such language, even though
written records survive from some centuries ago. This language,
which exhibits some grammatical features not otherwise found to any
great extent in European languages, has been the object of extensive
study (among others, Prince Louis Napoleon, later Emperor of
France 1852–71, wrote a grammar of Basque), and while tentative
efforts have been made to include it in the Caucasian family (Georgian
and others), despite its geographical remoteness, nothing can be said
with any certainty about its historical connections.

8·1·5 *The representation of correspondences*

A brief account has already been given of the sort of evidence on
which the history and development of language families is based. Of

course not all the words in any language can be related in the ways described to words in other languages. Even in the smaller and more closely knit groups within I-E, such as the Romance languages, there are numbers of words appearing uniquely in each individual language without certain cognates elsewhere; and the stock of words represented in languages of more than one subgroup and so regarded as of common origin within I-E is quite small; but the words concerned appear from their meanings unlikely all to be the result of later borrowings (number words, names of parts of the body, etc.), and it is on these that the existence and linguistic history of the I-E family is established.

As has been said, the significance of sound correspondences between the words of different languages lies in their appearance in series. A set of such correspondences that is well known is the basis for what is generally called Grimm's Law, by which a regular relationship can be stated between consonants of particular articulatory types in the Germanic languages and in languages of other branches of I-E. The full statement of all the correspondences in the different languages concerned would be a lengthy procedure; the following pairs of words come under and illustrate them:

Voiceless plosive and fricative (or continuant) in:

Latin	/pater/	father	English	/ˈfaːðə/
	/tenuis/	thin		/θin/
	/cornu:/	horn		/hɔːn/

Voiced and voiceless plosive in:

Latin	/duo/	two	English	/tu:/
	/ed-/	to eat		/i:t/
	/ager/	field	acre	/ˈeikə/

Voiced aspirated and voiced unaspirated plosives in:

Sanskrit	bhrātā	/bhra:ta:/	brother	English	/ˈbrʌðə/
	vidhavā	/vidhava:/	widow		/ˈwidou/

The correspondences are between sound segments, not letters, though in dead languages the written letters may be the only evidence for the existence, in the words concerned, of the sounds; and the attested correspondences of sound segments in the different languages in which they appear in the words may for convenience be summarily represented by a single symbol, usually prefixed by an

309

asterisk, to distinguish it from the representation of an actual sound in a particular language, and referred to as a 'starred letter'. Thus *p represents the series Sanskrit /p/ (*pitā* /pita:/, father), Latin /p/ (/pater/), Ancient Greek /p/ (πατήρ /paté:r/), English /f/ (/ˈfɑ:ðə/), German /f/ (*Vater* /ˈfa:ter/), and so on in the other I-E languages; and in the same way *e represents the series Sanskrit /a/ (*asti* /asti/ is), Ancient Greek /e/ (ἐστί /estí/), Latin /e/ (/est/), etc.

When the same procedure is applied to several segments in the series of words compared in this way and showing regular correspondences of this sort, the series of related words may be jointly represented by a sequence of starred letters to give what is called a 'starred form', usually representing what appears to be common among the several languages concerned either to the root of the words, or, if any of them are variable words, to a similarly related series of bound affixial elements. Thus *septm* represents the sound correspondences in Sanskrit *sapta* /sapta/, Latin /septem/, Ancient Greek ἑπτά /heptá/, German *sieben* /ˈzi:ben/, English /ˈsevən/, etc., and *-nti* represents those in the third person plural forms of present tense paradigms of verbs in such words as Sanskrit *bharanti* /bharanti/ (they) carry, Greek φέρουσι /pʰérousi/ (Doric dialect φέροντι /pʰéronti/), Latin /ferunt/, and Gothic *baírand* /ˈbɛrand/.

It must be stressed that starred word forms can be set up from series of actual attested words because the sound correspondences found between them are paralleled by the same correspondences in the same languages in other word series. Not every vowel and consonant in each member of a series of related words can necessarily be brought into a set of correspondences; but where a number of segments in each of the words can be so related, the starred form is constructed to summarize these related segments.

A single articulatory category of sound does not necessarily correspond to the same category of sound in another language, and one sound in one language may correspond to different sounds in different environments in another. Latin /qu/ is matched in Ancient Greek by /p/ before /a/ and /o/, and other consonants (/sequor/ ἕπομαι /hépomai/[1] (I) follow), and by /t/ before front vowels (/quis/ τίς /tís/ who?). This reinforces the point made above (8·1·1), that while

---

1. Only the roots of these words are historically related.

similarities in the forms of words in different languages are the starting point in the establishment of historical relationships, it is upon regular correspondences that a fully documented language family rests, similarity of phonetic category being only a special and obvious case of correspondence.

8 · 1 · 6 *The neogrammarian thesis*

The need for strict regularity in the admission of sound correspondences between the words of different languages in comparative and historical linguistics was the principle emphasized by a group of German scholars in the latter half of the nineteenth century. The name is a translation of *Junggrammatiker*, a nickname given to those who first insisted on this principle, as if they were a sort of political party, and from them what is called the **neogrammarian** hypothesis or theory has, in a modified form, become part of the accepted theory of comparative and historical linguistics.

As first formulated the hypothesis was that 'sound laws' were without exceptions; that is to say, within certain geographical limits and between certain dates a change of one sound in a language to another would affect in the same way all words containing the sound in the same phonetic environment of other sounds. It was soon seen that geographical and temporal limits in matters like this are hazy and indeterminate; one is dealing not with things, but with changes in certain human habits, the ways men pronounce particular words. These changes cannot be expected to affect all words simultaneously, and on the borders between languages or dialects, some words may be subject to the change while others escape it or are affected by a different change.

The value of the hypothesis is not in the hypostatization of some sort of iron law operating blindly on languages in the course of time, but as a working principle. The linguist must not rest content with a series of sound correspondences between the words of two or more languages without being able to account for apparent exceptions, words which appear to contradict his statement of them. Broadly speaking four types of explanation may be called for:

1. Words apparently belonging to a correspondence series are historically unrelated. Thus Latin /die:s/ day, and the English word

311

day, though similar in their initial consonants, and in their meanings, are not regarded as the results of divergence from a single word form, as the correspondences that regularly appear in such word pairs are Latin /d/ and English /t/ (/duo/ *two*; /ed-/ *eat*; /decem/ *ten*, etc., part of the more general correspondence system known as Grimm's Law (8·1·5)).

2. The rules by which the correspondences were stated were not drawn up strictly enough and must be modified by a number of subsidiary and more exact statements to account for all word series properly falling within their scope. For example the correspondence of voiceless plosive and fricative does not apply when the sounds concerned follow a fricative in the word: Latin /tenuis/, English *thin* /θin/, but Latin /sta-/, English *stand*, Latin /est/, German *ist* /ʔist/. Another important modification to Grimm's Law is known as Verner's Law, from the name of the scholar who first worked it out; within the correspondences known under the general title of Grimm's Law some medial consonants show different correspondences according to the position of the accented (stressed or high pitched) syllable of the word in the early period of I-E unity.

3. The apparently exceptional word is a loan word, that entered the language at a period subsequent to the operation of the sound change responsible for the particular form the correspondence takes.

4. The operation of the sound change in the particular word or words concerned has been prevented or reversed, or a different change has taken place, under the influence of analogy.

These last two factors are of great importance both in comparative and historical linguistics and in the history and development of every language, and must be considered in turn.

8·1·7 *Loan words*

Wherever there are culture contacts of any sort between the speakers of different languages, and this means virtually everywhere, speakers will make use of words from other languages to refer to things, processes, and ways of behaviour, organization, or thinking, for which words or phrases were not available or convenient in their own language hitherto. Some of the foreign words so used by individual speakers pass into general currency in the language, being altered in pronunciation in the process in the direction of the sounds and phonological patterns of the language acquiring them. These are known, by a rather inappropriate metaphor, as **loan words**. They are most obviously exemplified in the words for foreign products; the words for coffee, tea, and tobacco, in English and in most European languages are all loans, from Arabic, Chinese, and an American-Indian language respectively, languages of the regions from which, or through which, these products were first imported into Europe.

Any prolonged cultural contact, especially with speakers of a language who enjoy political power or prestige in any sphere, leads to a considerable amount of borrowing of vocabulary from that language in the spheres concerned. One may instance the large influx of words of French origin into English after the Norman Conquest and the establishment of Norman rule in England, the borrowing of Greek words for terms in the sciences, arts, and philosophy into Latin as a result of Greek prestige in these fields in the ancient world, the similar borrowing of numbers of Sanskrit words into the non-I-E languages of India, and the later passage of a great deal of English vocabulary into all the languages of India during the period of English rule, especially in fields directly associated with it, such as government, railways, industrial development, etc. A noticeable linguistic result of the British development and popularization of organized sport in the nineteenth century and after is seen in the large number of sporting terms in European and other languages that are of British origin (e.g. French *le starter*/ lə sta:(r)tœ:r/ the starter (of a race, etc.), *le football* /lə futbɔl/ football, German *das Kricketspiel* /das ˈkriketʃpi:l/ cricket, Italian *lo sport* /lo spɔrt/ sport, etc.). Apart from any other evidence, the strong representation of loan words from a single language in the vocabulary of one or more languages in an area is firm evidence of culture contacts of some sort.

Manifestly the term *loan word* is only used sensibly in relation to a language assumed to be already in independent existence. One cannot regard the vocabulary of French that has been in continual use from Roman times, while the linguistic changes constituting the passage of Latin to French were taking place, as loan words from Latin, since French is simply the form taken by Latin in a certain part of Europe. Languages are in a continuous state of change, and loans must be considered as those words which were not in the

313

vocabulary at one period and are in it at a subsequent one, without having been made up from the existing lexical stock of the language or invented as entirely new creations, as, for example, certain names for products are (*kodak*, etc.). Loans are, in fact, entering a language all the time, but their frequency and sources are temporarily affected by political or other factors leading to close cultural contacts of one sort or another.

Loans entering a language after a sound change has ceased to operate are not affected by it; conversely, loans entering before or during its operation will be affected in the same way as any other words containing the sound segments subject to the change. Apparent exceptions to sound correspondence may be the results of subsequent borrowing. Thus English *dental* does not exhibit the /t/ /d/ correspondence with Latin /dent-/, tooth, because it is a loan from Latin (cp. French *dental* /dãtal/) subsequent to the period in which the sound changes involved in the Grimm's Law correspondences were at work (the /d/ /t/ and /t/ /θ/ correspondence is seen between Latin /dent-/ and English *tooth*: cp. Gothic *tunþus* /ˈtunθus/). French loan words with /iː/ that entered the English language soon after the Norman conquest participated in the change of /iː/ to /ai/ mentioned earlier (4·1); French *ligne* /liːɲ/ became *line* /lain/, just as Old English *hwīt* /hwiːt/ became *white* /wait/ but the later loan *machine* /məˈʃiːn/ still has the same type of vowel sound as in French.

Normally loan words are assimilated to the phonetic sound classes and the phonological patterns of the borrowing language, the original consonants and vowels being replaced by consonants and vowels as close to them as are available; thereafter, synchronically as opposed to historically, they are no longer recognizable by their form as loans. However, in certain cases words continue to be recognized and treated as foreign in origin, and attempts are made to pronounce them as such. English *coupon* and *restaurant* when pronounced with a final nasalized vowel, and *rouge* and *garage*, when pronounced with final /ʒ/, which does not occur finally except in a few loans, are examples of this, and so is the Italian *lo sport*; and the names of foreign persons and places, unless so well known as to be almost international linguistic property, are usually treated in this way also. This does not mean that they are pronounced in the same way as they are in the languages from which they have been taken (except by a few specially gifted or trained persons), but it does mean that they continue to be uttered with sounds or sequences of sounds not found in the bulk of the vocabulary of the borrowing language. There is a tendency for doublets of such words to appear, assimilated and unassimilated, depending on the attitude or background of the speaker; /ˈrestərənt/ is heard as well as /ˈrestərɔ̃ː/, and /ˈgærɑːdʒ/ or /ˈgærɪdʒ/ as well as /ˈgærɑːʒ/.

A special sort of loan word is found in many languages, loans taken directly from the vocabulary of dead languages that have attained the status of classics. Since the Renaissance all European languages have quarried in Latin and Greek for scientific, literary, artistic, philosophical, and learned vocabulary generally, freely pro - ducing from Latin and Greek morphemes words that have no necessary correspondent in Ancient Greek or Latin (*microorganism*, *reinvestment*, etc.). Greek and Latin morphemes are often mixed in one word (*naturalism*, *monolingual*), though hitherto there has been some reluctance over the coining of neologisms with Latin or Greek morphemes and morphemes of other languages together in a single word. This process is, however, increasing, and is freely used in technological vocabulary (*speedometer*, *megaton*). Elsewhere, Sanskrit morphemes provide a similar source of loan neologisms in a number of Indian languages, and Chinese morphemes are formed into a number of polymorphemic Japanese words without counterparts in the stages of Chinese languages from which the component morphemes were taken. In such cases a large number of actual loan words has often been present in the language from the same sources from which the morphemes are taken for new creation, as the result of direct or indirect contacts, but in some European languages the post-Renaissance process of creating learned vocabulary from classical sources was independent of any large stock of loans of Latin origin from a Romance language.

8·1·8 *Analogy*

The other factor that may account for divergences from the strict application of regular sound changes is **analogy**, a universal process in the history of languages.

It is only by virtue of regularities of word form and sentence

315

structure that languages can operate at all as means of communication; nevertheless in all known languages a number of exceptions to the general patterns are found, the so-called irregular forms. Western antiquity was well aware of the two contrasting features of regularity and irregularity in the word forms of the languages they were interested in (Latin and Ancient Greek, in the main), and referred to them as analogy and anomaly respectively, different scholars stressing one or the other as a dominant feature.

In so far as any universal trend can be properly discerned in the grammatical development of languages, it would seem that it lies in the direction of replacing irregular forms by more regular ones (although contrary instances are also found, 6·6). When the early history of mankind is considered, it may be surmised that, in the small speech communities that must have existed in sparsely populated areas without much wide intercourse or permanent contacts outside, irregularities would be far more tolerable than in a language serving ever wider spheres of communication. At the other extreme one finds the fewest irregularities in deliberately created artificial languages, like Esperanto, and in some of the trade jargons or Creole languages that arose out of the needs of intercourse between peoples of greatly different linguistic and cultural backgrounds.

In its widest sense analogy is at work in every utterance and understanding of a sentence not hitherto heard by either party, and in the similar use of forms of variable word paradigms that have not so far occurred with a particular root in the experience of a particular speaker.

The replacement of an irregular or suppletive form by a new form modelled on the forms of the majority of members of the class to which the word in question belongs is the work of analogic creation. Individual examples of this are repeatedly found in the speech of children and foreign speakers with incomplete command of a language; 'seed' /si:d/ and 'hitted' /ˈhitid/, as mistaken past tense forms of see and hit, are analogical creations. Often such forms are corrected by others and never pass beyond a stage in the acquisition of the language by individuals; but, for reasons not wholly understood, some such individual variations persist and are adopted by others in widening circles until they come to be accepted beside and ultimately to replace the older forms. The virtual supercession of kine by cows as the plural of *cow* is an example of successful analogical creation, and so are the more modern regular, 'weak', past tense forms *helped, climbed*, and *snowed*, for the earlier *holp, clomb*, and *snew*. A few contrary examples of analogy are found in which word forms belonging to regular, majority, patterns are remodelled on the analogy of minority patterns. *Rang* and *rung* as past tense and past participle forms of the verb *ring* are the result of analogy on such patterns as *sing, sang, sung*, as the earlier corresponding Old English verb *hringan* /ˈhriŋgan/ followed the weak past tense formation. But almost every new word that enters the vocabulary of a language, either as a fresh creation (*television*) or as a loan word from abroad (*tomato, rumba*), if it is assigned to a class of variable words, follows by analogy the patterns of the majority of regular words in the class.

There is, however, in the very regularity of sound changes on which the neogrammarians insisted, a constant source of grammatical irregularities. Such changes working on every example of a sound in the same phonetic environment in the same way, irrespective of its place in a grammatical paradigm, may serve to generate paradigmatic irregularities. At a certain period in English /w/ disappeared before a back rounded vowel in words like *sword*, pronounced /sɔːd/; this was prevented from happening or the change was reversed in *swore* /swɔː/, by association with the other members of the paradigm, *swear, swears, swearing*, in which the /w/ was not affected anyway. At an early stage in Ancient Greek intervocalic /s/ had ceased to be pronounced, but it was retained in past tense verb forms like ἔλυσα /élu:sa/ (I) loosed, under the analogic influence of forms like ἔπεμψα /épempsa/ (I) sent (root /pemp-/), in which it was not subject to loss, since it was not intervocalic.

The contrary and conflicting tendencies in the historical development of languages represented by phonetic change and analogy have been summarized by Sturtevant: 'Phonetic laws are regular but produce irregularities. Analogic creation is irregular but produces regularity.'

8·1·9 *Historical inferences*

After reviewing the processes that govern the changes taking place in languages in the course of centuries, one is now in a position to review the historical inferences that may legitimately be made in the light of the linguistic evidence. Since the systematic correspondences that form the basis of comparative and historical linguistics can only be explained on the assumption of a once closer relationship between the earlier stages of the languages that exhibit them, they may, in conjunction with what is known about the sources and dates of loan words, throw great light on the history of the languages and the linguistic communities concerned.

A recent development in this branch of linguistics has been the attempt to quantify linguistic divergence from a common source and linguistic relationship based on it, and to calculate from the numbers of cognate (systematically related) words in them the period of time since the effective separation of two languages. This is known as **lexicostatistics** or **glottochronology**, and operates on the assumption that the rate of change that involves the replacement of one word by a different one (i.e. other than the word form resulting from gradual phonetic changes in the earlier word) in relation to the same range of semantic functions in the everyday basic vocabulary of languages is, in the absence of sudden cultural upheavals, relatively constant; around twenty per cent for every thousand years has been suggested. It is argued that on this basis one can infer the length of time two cognate languages have been separated and also determine the relative closeness of relationship between a number of cognate languages in one historical family.

At the present time a definitive statement of the effectiveness and reliability of glottochronology cannot be made. There have been trouble and disagreements about the sort of referential meanings that constitute a basic vocabulary likely to be common to languages spoken in different parts of the world and by speakers whose cultures are very different. Checks in the controlled fields of languages whose historical connections are known already, as in the I-E family, have been made. It has been found that applied to the Romance languages within I-E the method gives a picture of the relative closeness of the relationships between the member languages that accords with what is known of their histories and geographical positions, though some adjustment is needed to bring the inferred dates in line with the historically known or probable times of separation; a similar picture of the relationships and chronologies of the Germanic languages has been obtained by glottochronological methods, which is claimed to agree well with recent historical and archaeological findings.

When the methods have been confirmed further and certain theoretical and practical problems have been settled and difficulties overcome, glottochronology is likely to be of considerable assistance in the historical investigation of language families in parts of the world in which there is a lack of detailed early historical knowledge and of adequate (or indeed any) written records.

It is important not to go beyond the legitimate historical deductions from the linguistic evidence. Languages are not peoples, they are simply the speech habits of peoples; and the history of languages is part of the material of the history of peoples, but no more. The evidence of the systematic correspondences of word forms must not be misinterpreted, as is often done in the case of the 'starred forms' that are set up to summarize them. Such misinterpretation is rather encouraged by the misleading title 'reconstruction' which is given to these forms and the general process by which they are established.

Basically 'starred forms' are abbreviations of the correspondences exhibited between phonetic components of series of words of similar or related meanings in different languages, that may be matched by like series of words in the languages. The fact that these forms can be set up within a group of languages indicates a historical relationship of divergence from a more closely related state between the languages, but the 'starred forms' themselves are simply formulae summarizing the attested correspondences. The great French philologist Meillet put the matter succinctly: 'Comparison provides a system of relationships on which one can base the history of a family of languages; it does not furnish a real language.'

The 'starred forms', or misdesignated 'reconstructions', give reasons for assuming the existence of an earlier relatively unitary stage of I-E (or any other family established in this way), the so-called Ursprache, or parent language; but they do not constitute it, or represent word forms in it or in any language. The evidence for the earlier existence of an Ursprache is not the same as bits of the Ursprache itself.

The letters of writing systems of actual languages, however inadequate they may be as phonological representations, can be referred to the sound units of the languages at a given time, and the words of actual languages may be represented in transcriptions as analysable into the units of phonological systems. But it cannot be assumed that all the letters of the 'starred forms' in I-E necessarily represent the phonemes, or phonological units of any sort, of the phonological system of the I-E language itself. Bloomfield's suggestion that the formulaic summary of systematic correspondences is also 'a kind of phonemic diagram of the ancestral form' must be regarded as a desirable possibility, a limiting case of the formulae in some especially favoured language groups, rather than as a necessary consequence of the way in which the formulae are actually arrived at.

Certainly the choice of letters or symbols used in the representation of these forms is guided by the aim of indicating the earliest phonetic shapes that can be ascribed to members of the word series involved, on the basis of the forms actually attested. As it is known that in the Germanic languages earlier b, d, and g changed under Grimm's Law to p, t, and k (subsequently to undergo further changes in some of the languages), one represents the initial consonantal element of the formula summarizing the correspondences of Latin /duo/, Ancient Greek δύο /duo/, Sanskrit $dv\bar{a}$ /dwaː/, English *two* /tuː/, German *zwei* /tsvai/, etc. with a d, rather than with a t or some other letter. But these forms, in so far as they can be said to give any information about the early pronunciation of the words, simply reach back as far as is possible on the available evidence to what may reasonably be considered as the earliest pronounced forms we have any right to assume. Essentially they are formulae summarizing correspondences, but as these correspondences are historically significant, the letters in them, instead of being no more than arbitrary symbols, are chosen to indicate as much as can be inferred about the early history of the words concerned.

The difference between 'starred forms' that summarize the evidence for I-E and the word forms of an actual once-existing I-E language may be made clearer by considering the position of these essentially different linguistic entities within the most controlled field of comparative and historical linguistics that we have, namely the Romance languages, in which we have copious correspondence series, historical knowledge of the communities, and actual material preserved from the earlier unitary language.

The formulae set up on the basis of corresponding word forms in present-day Romance languages do in many instances coincide with an actual word form in Latin, in so far as its spelling may be used to infer its pronunciation; but in others this is not so. From the series Italian *capo* /ˈkapo/ head, Spanish *cabo* /ˈkabo/ end, French *chef* /ʃɛf/ chief, etc., one would not be led to set up the formula **caput*, as there is no evidence of a final /t/ in any of the cognate words of this series in the languages today; but written records make clear that the Latin word for head was /caput/. Apart from the local languages of Sardinia, no present-day Romance language preserves the Latin /k/ before front vowels. Latin had words like /decem/ ten, /cervus/ stag, and /cælum/(later /ceːlum/) sky, and it is known that in these and all other words /c/ was a velar plosive. Sardinian still has a /k/ sound in the words /dik/, /ˈkerbu/, /ˈkelu/; in the other Romance languages the sound has long since passed to an affricate or a fricative (Italian *dieci* /diˈɛtʃi/, *cervo* /ˈtʃɛrvo/, *cielo* /ˈtʃɛlo/; Spanish *diez* /dieθ/, *ciervo* /ˈθjervo/, *cielo* /ˈθjelo/; French *dix* /dis/, *cerf* /sɛrf/, *ciel* /sjɛl/). Alone among the existing Romance languages, Sardinian happens to preserve evidence on which one might use a *k* letter in the 'starred forms' set up for series of words like this in comparative Romance.

With possibilities such as these of discrepancies between the actual forms of the earlier unitary language and the formulae that arise from the existing evidence, one perceives the need to be very wary indeed of assuming that the formulae set up for I-E as a whole, where the time gap is much longer, the linguistic divergences much greater, and the attested forms of corresponding series of words much more varied, represent any sort of actual word form in an actual, though no longer extant, language.

For the same sort of reasons, one must beware of interpreting the 'family tree' representation of linguistic families too literally. Leaving out Hittite and many of the smaller languages, one can diagram the I-E family in this way:

with all but Armenian, Albanian, and Greek followed by further major language branches:

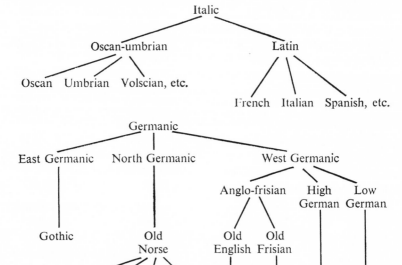

If dialectal differences within the modern languages are included, these appear at the bottom of the tree:

This suggests that dialects are the most recent linguistic development, as of course some are, but the lack of easy communications between scattered and scanty groups of people in ancient and prehistoric times must have favoured greater dialectal variation, of which we shall never have any record. I-E itself, as the earliest stage of the I-E languages that we are able to infer (not 'reconstruct'), though unitary as a language, must have been cut up by numerous dialect divisions, some of the differences between the major language groups within it being the results of a gradual widening of such divisions. Many different languages of the I-E family developing in this way from dialects within it must have disappeared without trace, as Gothic in the East Germanic group might have done; we are just aware of some such vanished I-E languages, such as Phrygian, from external historical records, and a few inscriptions.

Languages do not live, beget children, and die, as people do, for whom the genealogical tree diagram was originally designed (though terms like *parent language* and *daughter* or *sister languages* suggest that they do). In particular, languages do not separate sharply, at a given time, as might be implied by the tree diagrams; during periods of contact adjacent dialects may continue to influence each other to a considerable extent while in other respects the differences between them are widening.

Though tree diagrams read downwards from the top do bear correspondences with the changes that have taken place in a developing language family in the course of time, they should properly be read upwards as a diagram of how the linguist is able, on the evidence available to him, to set about grouping together different languages in historically connected sets of families.

The differences between the actual I-E attested and existing languages, and the 'starred forms' which are the summaries of our evidence for it, indicate that arguments on the geographical area and culture of the speakers of unitary I-E must be treated with great reserve. Attempts have been made to infer something of the habitat and way of life of the speakers of the Ursprache by reference to the meanings of the words represented in several of the major groups within I-E and therefore almost certainly present in the language in its unitary period.

Arguments for one area or another have turned on the likelihood of the words in several I-E languages for particular minerals, useful or cultivated plants, domestic animals or those used as food, etc. being derived from words forming part of the vocabulary of the inferred unitary language. This aspect of comparative and historical linguistics is sometimes given the title of **linguistic palaeontology**. It cannot claim more than probable conclusions. A common meaning for all attested members of a series of cognate words is no guarantee that an earlier common 'ancestor' form had the same meaning. Meanings are not labels carried around by words and remaining unchanged through time, but are simply what may be abstracted as common to the various uses of them in sentences uttered in situations as meaningful discourse (1·4). We have no sentences of a language whose existence is just inferred, and no way of hoping to get any. Moreover, one notices that some obviously related words have different referents in different languages; /faːgus/ in Latin means 'beech tree', φηγός /pʰeːgós/ in Ancient Greek refers to a species of oak tree; where time differences are greater and culturally relevant factors in situations more divergent, more extensive semantic differences must be allowed for. But if the inherent limitations are recognized, some light may be shed on certain features of the possible way of life of the earliest speakers of I-E languages whose existence we may infer; and on this basis some scholars have argued that the unitary I-E language, or group of dialects, was spoken around 3000 B.C. by a people living in an area of South Asia north of the Black Sea and Caucasus mountains, with some use of domestic animals and with a patriarchal social order.

The comparative and historical study of languages dominated the whole field of linguistics in Europe for nearly a century, and today it remains for many the most fascinating branch of the subject. This is partly due to the feeling that from linguistic evidence by linguistic inference we are enabled to pierce the veil of ignorance that shuts us off from so much of our own prehistory, and by similar methods to penetrate the prehistory of other peoples speaking languages of different families. It is necessary to proceed from the linguistic to the extralinguistic with great circumspection; but quite apart from such applications of this part of linguistic studies, the detailed investigations of the history of different languages, of the spread of languages over new territories and the replacement of one language by another among groups of people, of linguistic diversification in conditions of isolation and of linguistic unification in conditions of proximity and social intercourse, of the changes in word forms, of the acquisition of loan words, and of the operations of analogy, all serve to bring before our eyes the ways in which 'time and chance' and changing conditions, internal and external, work out their effects on the languages of mankind.

8·2   TYPOLOGICAL COMPARISON

8·2·1   *General principles*

Historically orientated linguistic comparison, comparative and historical linguistics, or comparative philology, is probably the best known form of the comparative study of languages, and, indeed, of linguistic studies generally, to many people, both because of its traditional place in classical studies in European universities and because of the exciting prospects it offers of throwing light on some of the darker places in mankind's earlier history. It is, however, possible to compare languages, systematically to study them in relation to each other, simply by reference to any significant general features of form or structural organization that they share at any level of analysis. Such comparisons group languages together by their jointly exhibiting features of some sort in common, other than those features which are exhibited in common by all languages and so form part of the nature of language itself. Comparison of languages on this basis is usually distinguished from the comparison described in the preceding sections of this chapter by the title of **typological comparison**.

In the European linguistic tradition, typological comparison had attracted attention in the seventeenth and eighteenth centuries, whereas comparative and historical linguistics really began its period of marked progress in the nineteenth century. Some would claim that as part of general linguistics typological comparison is a more strictly linguistic activity, in that it does not concern itself with any extralinguistic matters such as cultural history, population movements, and the like, which may be brought into comparative and historical linguistics to supplement purely linguistic facts.

Comparative and historical linguistics, as was seen, bases its comparisons on the correspondences between the forms of words of similar or related meanings. Its material is individual lexical items in different languages. Typological comparison is based on general features of the systems and structures of languages, and thus forms part of the wider process of classification of any observed phenomena according to revealed similarities of form and structure. Its linguistic groups are set up irrespective of historical language families, and may in part agree with them or cut across their boundaries.

325

The nature and function of human language imposes limits on the forms it may take. Every natural language is primarily a spoken medium of communication, and the forms of written languages, though not identical or to be equated with their spoken counterparts, are obviously controlled and to be understood by reference to the essential spoken nature of language. These limitations may be seen on either side of language, where it is linked to the extralinguistic world (1·3·2). Phonetically, the physiology of the human vocal organs sets limits on the types of sounds that can be produced, and the physiology of the ear and of the perceptual centres of the brain sets limits on the degree to which sounds as used in continuous discourse may be acoustically similar and yet serve efficiently as phonologically distinctive units and features. Speech consists of serial events occurring in time, and the signalling devices in languages must, therefore, be such as can be manifested by means of a series of sounds and sound features, just as in writing they are manifested in linear successions of letters, syllable signs, or characters.

On the other side, any language must be adequate for the communication needs of its speakers. The distinctive sound differences must be combinable in a sufficiently diverse number of separate word and morpheme forms to provide for an adequate word stock or lexicon; and the phonic (and graphic) resources of a language must be organized into a sufficiently flexible and productive grammatical system to produce sentences of the different types and patterns required for communication, readily understandable by other speakers of the same language. The double structuring of all languages in phonological and grammatical systems is the means whereby the physiologically limited possibilities of sound production and recognition can be made to serve the unlimited demands that languages have to meet in fulfilling the diverse and ever changing needs of speech communities.

Within these limits of speech production and speech requirements, languages differ in the ways in which they fulfil their purposes; and these differences may be observed at every level of language and linguistic analysis. Languages are typologically classified according to the similarities of form they exhibit with other languages at any level or levels. This type of linguistic comparison is best explained by illustrations from the main levels in which similarities of formal constitution are exhibited. Some of the classifications so produced have already been noticed implicitly in earlier chapters in which the different features and categories were mentioned.

8·2·2 *Phonetic typology*

At the phonetic level it is an obvious fact, readily noticed by those acquainted with more than one language, that some groups of languages make use of similar ranges of sounds, while others differ more widely from them in the types of sound they employ. Often enough languages sharing a number of the major sound features of one's own language are regarded as easy to speak, and those differing more widely are felt to be hard to speak, since they require the learning of a greater number of different phonetic habits than do the former. The main articulatory positions, bilabial, dental or alveolar, and velar, and the main articulatory processes, voice and voicelessness, plosion and friction, oral and nasal release, and some others, are employed in all, or in almost all, languages, but within these limits very marked phonetic differences are found. This is part of the difficulty of learning to speak foreign languages and the reason why most people who do, do so 'with an accent'.

Standard English does not make any distinctive use of glottalized or ejective consonants. Cockney speakers often have glottalized stops intervocalically (*copper* /ˈkɔpˀə/, *ripper* /ˈripˀə/), and make frequent use of medial glottal stops in positions where speakers of standard English have /p/, /t/, or /k/ (*what bad luck* /ˈwɔˀ ˈbæd ˈlʌˀ/). But several languages in different parts of the world make regular and systematic use of glottalized consonants just as English does of voiced consonants. Languages may be grouped into classes on the basis of shared phonetic features or types of articulation that play an important part in their phonological systems while being only represented to a limited extent or altogether lacking in others.

Features like glottalization appear in languages spoken in several different parts of the world, and frequently cut right across linguistic families established by the methods of comparative and historical linguistics. It has been noticed that languages that occupy geographically contiguous areas, whether they are related or not in descent, often share common phonetic characteristics. Three instances may be cited. Glottalized, or ejective, consonants, of limited or insignificant use in most European languages, are very prominent in the phonetics of several languages of the Caucasus area; among these are Georgian, Armenian, and Ossetic, languages spoken in contiguous regions, but belonging to different families, Armenian and Ossetic being I-E languages, and Georgian one of the members of the Caucasian family. In many languages of India, both the I-E languages descended from Sanskrit in the north and the genetically distinct Dravidian languages of the south, a series of retroflex consonants is found, articulated with the tongue tip curled back towards the roof of the mouth (3·3·4), and phonologically distinct from consonants articulated with dental closure or friction. This mode of articulation, prominent in many Indian languages of two separate genetic families, is only sporadically represented (e.g. in Scandinavia), except for the *r* sounds of some English dialects, in other I-E languages. Within Europe and the I-E family, the feature of distinctive front rounded vowels, familiar in French (*lune* /lyn/ moon, *peu* /pø/ little, *bœuf* /bœf/ beef), is found in neighbouring German, Dutch, Swedish, Norwegian, and Danish, all Germanic languages, but not in English, nor in the Romance languages Italian, Spanish, or Portuguese. Facts such as these have been explained in part as the result of the spreading of phonetic habits across genetic family boundaries as a result of population movements and the effects of bilingualism. Similar regional resemblances in features of grammatical organization have also been found.

8·2·3 *Phonological typology*

Perhaps of more significance are typological classifications based not primarily upon the presence in languages of particular phonetic features, but on the different ways in which the sounds and sound features of languages are organized into phonological systems and syllable structures. Such classifications have been made on a number of different dimensions.

The distinction between tone languages and the non-tonal languages, according to the functions assigned in them to differences of voice pitch, though not as clear-cut as is sometimes supposed, represents a major typological classification that has already been referred to (3·5·4). Within the tone languages a distinction may be made between those whose tones, phonologically considered, may be analysed in terms of different and contrasting levels (as in several tone languages of Africa) and those wherein rising and falling tones must be recognized as forming part of the tone system itself (as in the Chinese languages, 4·3·5). Further classifications may be made on the basis of the different numbers of tones involved and on the different uses to which they are put (cp. 6·5·6).

One of the more noticeable differences between languages lies in the different types of syllable structures permitted (4·3·4). While syllables of the type CV are found in every known language, English and German are distinguished from many others by the degree of consonant clustering allowed in syllable initial and syllable final position, and Fijian is a language notable for the simplicity of its syllable structures in terms of consonant and vowel elements occurring in the two positions and for its paucity of consonantal clusters. The possibilities of syllable structures in different languages may be arranged on a scale, with those languages that permit the greatest degree of syllabic complexity at one end, those with the least at the other. Languages then fall into relative places on the scale and may be grouped into classes on this basis accordingly; but as these classifying differences are on a more or less continuous scale, the number of different classes and the dividing lines between them have to be decided arbitrarily. On such a scale, some of the Caucasian languages would come near one end, with the greatest degree of syllabic complexity, English and German fairly up towards this end, and Japanese and some of the Oceanic languages at the other end with very simple syllable structures.

Syllabic structure classification relates to the syntagmatic dimension of phonology. Languages also differ in the paradigmatic dimension according to the composition of their phonological systems in terms of distinctive consonant and vowel elements, and may be grouped into classes accordingly. A scalar classification may be made according to the relative numbers of distinctive consonants and vowels, though this classification will be somewhat variable, as it is often possible to analyse the sounds of a language into more than one satisfactory phonological system (4·3·3, 4·3·4). Languages have also been classified according to the interrelations of their consonant

329

and vowel elements considered as distinct phonemes. This sort of classification was pioneered by Trubetzkoy. One may, for example, distinguish languages with vowel systems organized in two principal dimensions, open and close, and front and back, with lip spreading accompanying front vowels and lip rounding accompanying back vowels (Italian and Spanish), and languages making independent use of the three dimensions, open and close, front and back, and lip spreading and lip rounding (French, German, Turkish). Consonant systems may similarly be classified according to the number of articulatory places and processes characterizing the greater part of each system. English plosive and nasal consonants fall into a three-place and three-process system, bilabial, alveolar, velar, and voiceless, voiced, nasal:

/p/	/t/	/k/
/b/	/d/	/g/
/m/	/n/	/ŋ/

If the rectangle is extended, e.g. by including the affricates /ʧ/ and /ʤ/ in the alveolar column, it is no longer possible to fill out all the places, as there are no bilabial or velar affricates in English.

Ancient Greek had a three-place and four-process system, bilabial, dental, velar, and unaspirated, aspirated, voiced, nasal:

/p/	/t/	/k/
/pʰ/	/tʰ/	/kʰ/
/b/	/d/	/g/
/m/	/n/	[ŋ]

In terms of distinctive consonant units, or phonemes, the Greek system has a gap in the velar column, as [ŋ] was a positional variant of /n/ (an allophone of /n/), occurring before a velar consonant (written with the γ letter in the Greek alphabet).

In terms of prosodic phonology, languages may be classified according to the predominant role played by particular types of prosodic feature. Prosodic phonology being a relatively recent development in linguistics, detailed work in this field remains to be done, but languages such as Irish, Russian, and a number of other Slavic languages, in which prosodies of palatalization and velarization (Y and W) play a prominent part in the distinction of lexical items and different members of grammatical paradigms, suggest the lines on which such classifications could well be made.

8·2·4 *Grammatical typology*

At the grammatical level, languages may be classified according to the predominant characteristics of their grammatical systems. In one such dimension, Chinese and several languages of South-east Asia stand at one extreme, in relying almost entirely on word order and word class membership as the markers of syntactic relationships and sentence structures, and are in contrast with languages like Latin and Ancient Greek, wherein word order is relatively insignificant grammatically and syntactic relationships and sentence structures are mostly marked by the morphological categories of concord and government (6·5·2) exhibited by the word forms of different word classes. On this dimension, English, French, and German lie somewhere in the middle between the two extremes, with English further towards the Chinese end of the scale than the other two, and French further towards it than German. Within the languages relying heavily on categories of concord and government (Latin, Ancient Greek, Sanskrit, Swahili, etc.) further classifications may be made according to the types of categories involved (case, gender, number, tense; etc.) and the relative weight placed upon each. Languages vary according to the relative weight of grammatical categories formally concentrated on words of different grammatical classes (6·2); but it appears to be a general feature of languages with morphologically marked grammatical categories that the verb classes carry more morphologically marked categories than the noun classes. Abaza, a Caucasian language, has been cited as an extreme case of a verb-centred language in which the verb form represents in itself a sort of small-scale model of the structure of the whole sentence, of which it forms the syntactic centre.

8·2·5 *Structural typology*

In dealing with the typological classification of languages, the best known procedure has so far been left unmentioned. This is the three-fold division of languages into the **isolating** or 'analytic', **agglutinative,** and **fusional** or 'inflecting' types, and it goes back to von

Humboldt, a linguist and ethnographer of the late eighteenth and early nineteenth centuries. Von Humboldt put forward this tripartite division as a means of classifying languages as total systems of communication, but it is more strictly a classification of the word structures of languages and of the way in which phonological structures and grammatical structures are related in word forms. Features of isolation, agglutination, and fusion are usually to be found in most languages, though in different proportions, and as a mode of typological classification the three types are best regarded as directions towards which languages approach with greater or lesser purity. If the three types were arranged as a triangle, each language could be placed at some approximate point therein after a statistical analysis of its word-structure patterns.

English is in fact a fairly mixed type of language in respect of the three types, and each can be illustrated from English. Invariable words, such as prepositions, conjunctions, and many adverbs, are isolating in type; they exhibit no formal paradigms, in many cases they are monomorphemic (e.g. *since*, *from*, *as*, *when*, *seldom*, *now*), and their grammatical status and class membership are entirely determined by their syntactic relations with the rest of the sentences in which they appear, without formal mark of these appearing in their own word structure. Morphologically complex words in which individual grammatical categories may be fairly easily assigned to morphemes strung together serially in the structure of the word form exemplify the process of agglutination; *illegalities* /i-li:g-ˈæl-iti-z/, *ungodliness* /ʌn-ˈgɔd-li-nis/, *unavoidably* /ʌn-əˈvɔid-əbl-i/, and *stabilizers* /ˈsteibil-aiz-ə-z/, are examples from English of agglutinative word structures. Words in which several grammatical categories are marked by word forms in which it is difficult, if not impossible, to assign each category to a specific and serially identifiable morphemic section are instances of fusional word structure (the term *inflecting*, or *inflectional*, is the older and traditional name for the typological class here called fusional; but this latter term is preferable in view of the quite separate use of *inflection* as the designation of a type of morphological formation, 6·5·5). English noun plurals like *men*, *mice*, *geese*, and *women* are inflectional in structure as against the grammatically equivalent agglutinative forms like *cars*, *houses*, and *cats*. It may be noticed that the specifically inflectional structures of

English words are in the minority subclasses and irregular forms of the word classes concerned. Regular morphological structures in English are usually agglutinative.

While pure exemplars of any of the three types of word form structure throughout a language are very rare among the languages of the world, some languages make use of one type of word formation to a predominant extent, and are consequently classified as isolating, agglutinative, or fusional languages. Chinese and several of the languages of South-east Asia, Vietnamese being perhaps the purest example of the type, are classified as isolating. In them bound morphemes are rare, and words containing more than a single morpheme are not thereby grammatically different in other respects from monomorphemic words. Because the boundaries of syllables and morphemes in these languages largely coincide, though they belong to different levels of analysis, these languages are sometimes rather loosely referred to as 'monosyllabic'. Words in such languages are assigned to word classes on the basis of different syntactic functions, but they do not exhibit any marks of such functions or class membership in their forms or morphemic structures.

This typological classification of Chinese and some other languages is a separate one from that given in the previous section; the previous classification was based on the predominant syntactic characteristics of languages, while the present classification relates to characteristics of word structure; but the two characteristics of languages of the Chinese type are generally associated with each other, since a language devoid of morphological markers of syntactic relations must rely more on positional order for such purposes.

Turkish, Sundanese, and Japanese are among typically agglutinative languages of the world, with Turkish generally considered the purest example of such a language. But it must be insisted that languages of this type are only alike of necessity in respect of word structure. The grammars of Turkish, Sundanese, and Japanese are very different in other respects, and the grammatical categories carried by the morphologically complex words in them are in great part quite unlike each other's.

The classical languages, Latin, Ancient Greek, and Sanskrit, are the most obvious examples of fusional types. Latin /amo:/ (I) love, is morphologically divisible into two morphemes, root /am-/ and

333

suffix /-oː/; but this suffix, though morphologically not further divisible, marks five separate categories, each syntactically relevant in different ways to other words in sentences in which the form may occur (and in varying degrees correlatable with separate semantic functions): singular number, first person, present tense, indicative mood, and active voice. Likewise the morphologically indivisible /-us/ of /magnus/ great, marks nominative case, masculine gender, and singular number. The monomorphemic /iː/ go!, cumulatively comprises five grammatical components, verb class root, singular number, second person, imperative mood, active voice.

The last few paragraphs may be compared with section 6·5·7, above, where the same sorts of features in languages were considered from a different point of view.

A fourth class of language or of word structure characteristic of some languages is sometimes introduced, under the title **polysynthetic** or **incorporating**. Eskimo and some American-Indian languages have been called incorporating or polysynthetic, as their word forms are said to be very long and morphologically complex, and to contain numerous bound morphemes the translations of which would be represented by separate words in more familiar languages. This fourth class of language types, however, is of little use in linguistic typology. Languages falling within it only differ from the agglutinative and fusional types by carrying these processes to extremes and uniting within single grammatical words what in most other languages one would find spread out among several words. This fourth type introduces no qualitatively new feature of word structure; it only multiplies the numbers of bound morphemes within its words. The muddled nature of this type is well illustrated by the amusingly circular definition in the *Shorter Oxford English Dictionary*: 'polysynthetic: characterized by combining several words of a sentence into one word.'

The threefold Humboldtian typological classification was rather looked down on by linguists during the later nineteenth and early twentieth centuries. Meillet referred to it as 'too well known', and regarded the grouping together of languages on such a basis as no more than academic play. There were probably two main reasons for this rather contemptuous dismissal. In the first place, classifications based on the relation between the phonological and the grammatical structure of words can only be scientifically worth while if these rest on a sound phonological and formal grammatical analysis, the techniques for which only developed fully during the present century. In the second place, as has been seen, comparative and historical linguistics and the grouping together of languages into historically related families were the dominant aims of nineteenth century linguistics, and it is clear that Humboldtian typological classification is very unreliable as a guide to genetic relations.

Certain preponderating characteristics of word structure are found in many of the languages of some genetic families; in many of the Bantu languages sets of prefixes, marking grammatical concord between the words of different word classes in the sentence and constituting a sort of gender system, are a notable feature; but a recent classification of these languages includes within the family, on the basis of inherited lexical items from a common unitary source, several languages wherein the prefix system is very much reduced in scope or even unrepresented.

Within the I-E family many different degrees of the fusional structural type are found, from highly fusional Latin, Ancient Greek, and Sanskrit, to languages like English in which features of isolation and agglutination are quite prominent. Examples have already been given of the diffusion across the boundaries of separate genetically based families, of certain general phonetic characteristics.

Typological and historical comparison, and classifications based on them, should be kept distinct; they serve different ends and employ different sorts of criteria differently orientated. In the I-E field this has generally been the practice, but in some less well documented language areas of the world a loose amalgam of quite disparate criteria has sometimes been used to bind together intended genetic families.

Considered simply as a means of classifying languages, typological criteria are a valuable aid in carrying this out objectively, and they reveal the several different ways in which, within the limitations imposed on it by its nature and purposes, language manifests itself in different speech communities. Within typological comparison, the Humboldtian tripartite division, properly understood, may be said to be a more significant system of classification than some others, in as much as it involves at once two of the most central levels of linguistic structure and linguistic analysis, phonology and grammar. Among linguists of the present century, Sapir notably gave prominence to this sort of classification, and linguistic typology occupies a central position in his brilliant book *Language*, published in 1921. He here set out a more detailed scheme of classification, employing criteria in addition to those of the type used by von Humboldt, but working fundamentally on the same lines. This line of linguistic classification has most recently been taken up again by Greenberg. Working in strictly formal terms throughout, he takes a number of different but related features of phonological and grammatical word structuring (agglutination, fusion, prefixation, suffixation, etc.), and quantitatively compares the parts they play in different languages. Languages are then classified into types on the basis of a combination of these quantified characteristics.

8·2·6 *Historical changes in structural typology*

When historically related languages of different periods are compared and contrasted in respect of their structural characteristics, it is seen that in the course of time changes in their formal composition take place, altering some of their most prominent structural features and entailing a reassessment of their typological classing. Attempts at finding some order and correlation with extralinguistic developments in these matters have exercised scholars' minds. In particular it was felt that the dominant structural features of language must somehow be related to the level of civilization of its speakers. Notions of 'complexity' and 'simplicity' have played a prominent part in this sort of speculation; but it is hard to see how such attributes of languages can ever be objectively established. A 'complex' language may mean no more than one showing a considerable number of features unfamiliar in the linguistic experience and native language of the learner. All that one can say with certainty is that every normal person is able to master his own language in childhood and thereafter finds it 'easy' and 'natural' to use and understand, and that, when properly investigated, every language in the world is immensely complex in its organization. It has been found that every structural type of language can coexist with any level of civilization or cultural development. Only in the matter of actual vocabulary, as against phonetic composition, phonological systems, and grammatical systems, do languages directly reflect the cultural environment of their speakers. Sapir strikingly summarized this: 'When it comes to linguistic form, Plato walks with the Macedonian swineherd, and Confucius with the head-hunting savage of Assam.'

It need not be suggested that analytic, agglutinative, or fusional types of word structure are either more or less complex than each other when placed in the total context of the grammatical and phonological organization of the language. More is involved than the relations between the phonological and grammatical structure of words, central as this is as a means of typological classification. But there do seem to be signs of certain trends operating over long periods in one direction or another, though not necessarily irreversibly.

When Latin is compared with the present-day Romance languages, and Old English with Modern English, a general movement towards a more isolating type of structure seems to emerge, with fewer morphologically marked grammatical categories and less extensive variations within those that there are, and more reliance on word order as an exponent of syntactic relations. In the Romance languages, one can observe in Old French a language at a stage between the two types represented by Latin and by Modern French: two morphologically differentiated case forms are found in nouns, survivors of the Latin nominative and accusative respectively, with different syntactic functions, and the order of words in sentences, though less free grammatically than in Latin is freer than the word order of comparable sentences in modern French. A similar trend is apparent in other language groups in Europe, and it has been suggested that the present isolating form exhibited by the Chinese languages is the product of a gradual development away from fusional type of structure, small parts of which can be inferred from the study of existing word forms and those attested from earlier periods of the language.

One must also notice, however, that despite the general overall trend towards more isolating types of structure in European languages, some of the Romance languages exhibit a partial tendency in the direction of agglutination within limited word classes and in particular categories. The French grouping together of unemphatic personal pronoun and verb forms has already been considered (5·3·1).

337

Traditionally these structures are regarded as consisting of several separate words, and there are reasonable grounds for treating the pronominal forms as words, though rather marginal in word status in view of their limitations of positional occurrence in relation to each other and to the verb. If the relative solidarity and inflexibility of these pronoun verb groups are emphasized, they could be compared to single loosely jointed word-like complexes, incorporating a number of elements represented in other languages, and (historically) in Latin, from which the forms themselves are derived, by pronominal and other words positionally much freer in their occurrence in sentences. One may instance a sentence like *il ne m'y en a pas donné* /il nə mi ɑ̃n a pa dɔne/ he has not given me any of them there, in which the relative order of each of the word units is fixed, and which permits no further interpolation of other words between most of them.

Orthographic conventions of word spacing and hyphenation are not to be regarded as infallible guides to the establishment of word divisions in formal grammar, but one notes the practice in French of hyphenating unemphatic pronouns occurring in post-verbal position (e.g. *donnez-le-moi* /dɔne-lə-mwa/ give it to me!), and in Italian of joining post-verbal pronominal elements to the verb as bound forms (e.g. *vogliamo andarcene* /voʎˈʎamo anˈdartʃene/ we want to go away, cp. *ce ne andiamo* /tʃe ne andiˈamo/ we are going away).

8·2·7 *Semantic typology*

Besides comparisons of formal structuring in languages of the sort that have been discussed so far, languages differ in systematically describable ways in their lexical composition, and may be classified on this basis.

Every language must be or become adequate to the needs and environments of its speakers at any time, and vocabularies therefore vary from place to place and from time to time in their relative richness or poverty of lexical items in different semantic fields or ranges. There are several different words for distinct types and conditions of snow in Eskimo and Lapp, whereas English and many other European languages, to whose speakers snow is not an all-pervasive climatic and topographical feature, make do with one, further specifying its nature with additional words if necessary. Some Arabic dialects have been said to distinguish a large number of separate words for different types of camel, and for camels in different states of health and the like, and the use of a generic word for 'camel' without further specification is said to be rare. This has given rise to the absurd suggestion that such people are incapable of abstraction to the extent of visualizing a camel apart from one or more specific attributes.

Aside from the specialization of vocabulary in different semantic fields according to the cultural and environmental needs of different speakers, which is only to be expected, languages differ in their formation of parts of their vocabulary dealing with particular subjects. Kinship term systems, for example, are generally built around the lexical differentiation of three fundamental human family relations, filiation, consanguinity, and spouseship; but they may vary from the type represented in English, in which different words are used primarily to distinguish the sex of kin relations (the English words *spouse*, *sib*, and *parent* (in the singular) are rare), a process carried further in French and German (*cousin* /kuzɛ̃/ male cousin, *cousine* /kuzin/ female cousin; likewise *Vetter* /ˈfɛter/, *Base* /ˈbaːze/) to languages that distinguish lexically between members of kin who are older or younger than the speaker or other point of reference, often with less lexical distinction of sex or degree of consanguinity. Thus in Malay /adeʔ/ is used for 'younger brother' or 'younger sister', /abaŋ/ for 'elder brother' or 'male cousin', /kakaʔ/ for 'elder sister' or 'female cousin', /bapa/ for 'father' or 'uncle', and /ˈləmaʔ/ for 'mother' or 'aunt'; this involves a lexical focusing of attention on a distinction not inherently marked in the principal kinship terms of English. Of course further distinctions can be made in any language, but different ones are central to these sections of the vocabularies in different languages. Other kinship term systems distinguish lexically relationships for which in English no single word is available (e.g. Latin /maːtertera/ maternal aunt, /aːmita/ paternal aunt; /avunculus/ maternal uncle, /patruus/ paternal uncle). A type of kinship terminology is found in some languages which provides separate words for such relations as brother and sister according to the sex of the speaker or other person taken as the point of reference (e.g. Yurok

/nelet/ my sister (woman speaking), /neweyetʃ/ my sister (man speaking); /neleyˀ/ my brother (woman speaking), /nepa:/ my brother (man speaking).[1]

Lexical systems, whether of kinship terms or of any other semantic range, are not the same thing as systems of interpersonal relations, such as kinship systems forming a part of the social life of peoples, and differences between lexical systems do not necessarily imply differences of behaviour in the fields so designated, though some correlations are found, such as enforced respect for age differences together with lexical distinction of them in kinship terms.

Comparison of the lexical systems of languages is often undertaken as part of a more general comparative study of different social systems and different cultures. A more centrally linguistic classification of vocabulary types may be made by reference to the different preponderant characteristics of the words themselves. Ullmann has applied a number of criteria in this approach to lexical typology, in particular the extent to which languages employ specific as against generic words (already noticed in specific contexts above), and the relative frequency of what may be called motivated and unmotivated words. By the former, the specification of detail by lexically different words is contrasted with the normal use of words of more general meaning, further specification being supplied by other words in collocation or left inferable from the context (German *arbeiten* /ˈˀarbaiten/ to work, *bearbeiten* /beˈˀarbaiten/ to produce by working, and *brechen* /ˈbreçen/ to break, *zerbrechen* /tsɛrˈbreçen/ to shatter in pieces, are contrasted with the French words *travailler* /travaje/ to work, and *casser* /kase/ to break). By the latter, vocabularies are compared in the extent to which the morphemic structures of their words reveal any correlation with their specific meanings by association with other items of the vocabulary. Thus German *Handschuh* /ˈhantʃu:/ glove, and *Schlittschuh* /ˈʃlitʃu:/ skate, are compared with the monomorphemic French words *gant* /gɑ̃/ and *patin* /patɛ̃/; and *hineingehen* /hiˈnainge:en/ to enter, and *hinausgehen* /hiˈnausge:en/ to go out, with *entrer* /ɑ̃tre/ and *sortir* /sɔrti:r/. In a general lexical comparison of French, German, and English, based on these and some other similar criteria, French and German appear

---

1. The Yurok roots /-let/, /-weyetʃ/, /-leyˀ/, and /-pa:/ are all bound morphemes.

as relatively extreme opposites, with English occupying a somewhat central position.

8·2·8 *Summary*

Unlike historically orientated comparison, which is directed towards the single goal of genetic relationship, and based on the systematic comparison of the forms of words of similar or related meanings, the typological comparison of languages, as it will have been seen, may be based upon numerous separate and different criteria; and languages will often form groups of different membership according to the criteria of classification selected. The examples of this sort of classification that have been given in the preceding sections are illustrative, and not in any way exhaustive. Enough has been given to show the ways in which the different languages of the world may be gathered into classes by sharing some features in common, other than those features necessarily shared by every language. The more far reaching and deeply embedded in the structures and systems of the languages at various levels are the features that are made the basis of a classification, the more solid and significant will be the resulting typological grouping. But in every case, the study and working out of such classifications brings into prominence the various ways in which the universal human faculty of language may operate, in fulfilling the purposes of communication between speakers within the physiological limitations and the cultural and environmental requirements that are imposed on it.

CHAPTER 8, BIBLIOGRAPHY

1. W. S. ALLEN, 'Relationship in comparative linguistics', *TPS* 1953, 52–108.

2. ——, 'Structure and system in Abaza', *TPS* 1956, 127–76.

3. W. W. ARNDT, 'The performance of glottochronology in Germanic', *Lang.* 35 (1959), 180–92.

4. C. E. BAZELL, 'Syntactic relations and linguistic typology', *Cahiers F. de Saussure* 8 (1949), 5–20.

5. ——, *Linguistic typology*, London, 1958.

6. L. BLOOMFIELD, *Language*, London, 1935.

7. F. BOAS, 'The classification of American Indian languages', *Lang.* 5 (1929), 1–7.

8. L. L. BONAPARTE, *Observations sur la basque*, Paris, 1877.

9. E. BOURCIEZ, *Eléments de linguistique romane*, fourth edition, Paris, 1946.

10. R. G. A. DE BRAY, *A guide to the Slavonic languages*, London, 1951.

11. M. BRÉAL, *Essai sur la sémantique*, fourth edition, Paris, 1908 (also available in an English translation by H. Cust, London, 1900).

12. V. BRØNDAL, *Substrat et emprunt en roman et en germanique*, Copenhagen, 1948.

13. L. F. BROSNAHAN, *The sounds of language*, Cambridge, 1961.

14. C. D. BUCK, *Comparative grammar of Greek and Latin*, Chicago, 1933.

15. ——, 'Some questions of Practice in the notation of reconstructed I-E forms', *Lang.* 2 (1926), 99–107.

16. T. BURROW, *The Sanskrit language*, London, 1955.

17. A. CAMPBELL, *Old English grammar*, Oxford, 1959.

18. C. D. CHRETIEN, 'The mathematical models of glottochronology', *Lang.* 38 (1962), 11–37.

19. A. DARMESTETER, *La vie des mots*, twelfth edition, Paris, 1918.

20. W. D. ELCOCK, *The Romance languages*, London, 1960.

21. M. B. EMENEAU, 'India as a linguistic area', *Lang.* 32 (1956), 3–16.

22. W. J. ENTWISTLE and W. A. MORISON, *Russian and the Slavonic languages*, London, 1949.

23. L. FOULET, *Petite syntaxe de l'ancien français*, Paris, 1930.

24. J. FOURQUET, *Les mutations consonantiques du germanique*, Paris, 1948.

25. H. A. GLEASON, *Introduction to descriptive linguistics*, second edition, New York, 1961.

26. J. H. GREENBERG, 'A quantitative approach to the morphological typology of language', *Method and perspective in anthropology*, edited by R. F. Spencer, Minneapolis, 1954, 192–220.

27. M. GUTHRIE, *The classification of the Bantu languages*, London, 1948.

28. A. G. HAUDRICOURT and A. G. JUILLAND, *Essai pour une histoire structurale du phonétisme français*, Paris, 1949.

29. A. A. HILL, 'A note on primitive languages', *IJAL* 18 (1952), 172–7.

30. ——, *Introduction to linguistic structures*, New York, 1958.

31. C. F. HOCKETT, *A manual of phonology*, Indian University publications in anthropology and linguistics, 11, 1955.

32. ——, *A course in modern linguistics*, New York, 1958.

33. H. M. HOENIGSWALD, *Language change and linguistic reconstruction*, Chicago, 1960.

34. H. P. HOUGHTON, *An introduction to the Basque language*, Leyden, 1961.

35. T. HUDSON-WILLIAMS, *A short introduction to the study of comparative grammar*, Cardiff, 1935.

36. W. VON HUMBOLDT, *Ueber die Verschiedenheit des menschlichen Sprachbaues*, Berlin, 1836 (reprinted Darmstadt, 1949).

37. D. H. HYMES, 'Lexicostatistics so far', *Current anthropology* 1 (1960), 3–43.

38. I. IORDAN, *Introduction to Romance linguistics* (translated by J. Orr), London, 1937.

39. B. KARLGREN, 'Le proto-chinois, langue flexionelle', *Journal asiatique* 15 (1920), 205–32.

40. A. L. KROEBER, 'Romance history and glottochronology', *Lang.* 34 (1958), 454–7.

41. W. P. LEHMANN, *Historical linguistics*, New York, 1962.

42. H. LEWIS and H. PEDERSEN, *A concise comparative Celtic grammar*, Göttingen, 1937.

43. A. MARTINET, 'La double articulation linguistique', *TCLC* 5 (1949), 30–7.

44. ——, *Economie des changements phonétiques*, Berne, 1955.

45. A. MEILLET, *La méthode comparative en linguistique historique*, Oslo, 1925.

46. ——, *Introduction à l'étude comparative des langues indo-européennes*, eighth edition, Paris, 1937.

47. ——, *Linguistique historique et linguistique générale* (1) and 2, Paris, 1948 and 1938.

48. ——, *Les caractères généraux des langues germaniques*, seventh edition, Paris, 1949.

49. C. MEINHOF, *Grundzüge einer vergleichenden Grammatik der Bantusprachen*, Berlin, 1906.

50. S. ÖHMAN, 'Theories of the "linguistic field"', *Word* 9 (1953), 123–134.

51. C. OSGOOD (editor), *Linguistic structures of native America*, New York, 1946.

52. L. R. PALMER, *An introduction to modern linguistics*, London, 1936.

53. H. PEDERSEN, *Linguistic science in the nineteenth century* (translated by J. W. Spargo), Cambridge, Mass., 1931 (republished as *The discovery of language*, Bloomington, 1962).

54. R. PRIEBSCH and W. E. COLLINSON, *The German language*, London, 1934.

55. E. PULGRAM, 'Proto-Indo-European, reality and reconstruction', *Lang.* 35 (1959), 421–6.

56. E. SAPIR, *Language*, New York, 1921.

57. F. DE SAUSSURE, *Cours de linguistique générale*, fourth edition, Paris, 1949.

58. E. H. STURTEVANT, *The pronunciation of Greek and Latin*, Philadelphia, 1940.

59. ——, An introduction to linguistic science, Yale, 1947.

60. ——, 'The Indo-hittite hypothesis' (reprinted), *Lang.* 38 (1962), 105–10.

61. L. TESNIÈRE, *Eléments de syntaxe structurale*, Paris, 1959.

62. P. THIEME, *Die Heimat der indogermanischen Gemeinsprache*, Wiesbaden, 1954.

63. N. S. TRUBETZKOY, *Principes de phonologie* (translated by J. Cantineau), Paris, 1949.

64. S. ULLMANN, 'Descriptive semantics and linguistic typology', *Word* 9 (1953), 225–40.

65. ——, *The principles of semantics*, second edition, Glasgow and Oxford, 1951.

66. J. VENDRYES, *Le langage*, Paris, 1921.

67. C. F. VOEGELIN, 'Models for cross-genetic comparisons', *Papers from the symposium on American-Indian languages*, Berkeley, 1954, 27–45.

68. A. WALDE and J. POKORNY, *Vergleichendes Wörterbuch der indogermanischen Sprachen*, Berlin and Leipzig, 1927—32.

69. U. WEINREICH, *Languages in contact*, Publications of the Linguistic Circle of New York 1, 1953.

70. J. and E. M. WRIGHT, *An elementary grammar of Middle English*, second edition, Oxford, 1928.

A large body of literature on comparative and historical linguistics is available, as a result of its long study over the past century and a half in Europe and America. Much of this is more advanced and technical than is required for the needs of the student beginning his acquaintance with the field of linguistics as a whole; but a number of general introductions to the principles and methods are to be recommended:

de Saussure	57, part 3	Sturtevant	59, chapters 7–15
Vendryes	66, 349–66	Gleason	25, chapters 27–8
Palmer	52, chapters 3–5	Hockett	32, chapters 41–61
Sapir	56, chapters 7 and 8	Lehmann	41
Bloomfield	6, chapters 18–27		

Elementary treatments with special reference to the Indo-european family are available in Hudson-Williams, 35; Buck, 14; Meillet, 45 and 46.

A number of excellent articles by Meillet on comparative and historical linguistics, as well as on other linguistic topics, are collected together in 47.

A more advanced treatment, examining the subject from the point of view of one of the schools of contemporary linguistic theory, is to be found in Hoenigswald, 33.

An enjoyably written history of comparative and historical linguistics in the nineteenth century and up to the 1920's is available in Pedersen, 53. This book also sets out some of the theoretical principles very lucidly.

In the titles and usage of a few of the writings cited, it should be noted that *comparative grammar* is equivalent to *comparative and historical linguistics*, and that *Indogermanisch* (English Indogermanic) is equivalent to *Indo-european* (Buck, 14, 1).

ADDENDUM

71.   J. H. GREENBERG, "The Languages of Africa" *IJAL* 29.1 (1963), part 2.

p. 295. Sir William Jones, of the old East India Company, first enunciated the historical connection of Sanskrit with Latin, Ancient Greek, and German, in 1786 (Pedersen, 53, 17–19).

On the arbitrary nature of words in relation to their semantic functions, de Saussure, 57, 100–2.

p. 298. On Old English and Middle English, Campbell, 17; Wright, 70.

p. 300. On linguistic substrates, Brøndal, 12; Weinreich, 69.

p. 301. Among the causes adduced to account for phonetic changes have been climate, which has not been substantiated scientifically, and alleged 'ease of articulation' or 'economy of effort'. While this does clearly account for some changes, and in particular for the reduction or abbreviation of the forms of frequently used words ('allegro forms' like *howd'yedo*, and *yes'm* for *yes madam*, as well as the 'weak forms' of languages like English), it is clearly quite insufficient as a single cause; otherwise phonetic changes would be much more alike and universal in different languages than they are. A genetic factor, involving the preference for particular processes of articulation as a result of inherited differences in the musculature and innervation systems of the vocal organs has recently been argued by Brosnahan, 13.

Many changes can be shown to be due to or facilitated by pressures that have arisen within the phonological systems of particular languages, or dialects, at certain periods; for example, to render four distinctive back rounded vowels. /ɒ/, /ɔ/, /o/, and /u/, more easily differentiated from one another, /u/, the closest, may gradually be fronted in articulation to /y/, to supplement its distinctive characteristics and to leave more room in the back for the others. On this aspect of linguistic change, see further Haudricourt and Juilland, 28; Martinet, 44.

On semantic change, Bloomfield, 6, chapter 24; Bréal, 11; Darmesteter, 19; Ullmann, 65.

p. 303. Changes in semantic fields, Ullmann, 65, chapters 3 and 4; Öhman, 50; Hoenigswald, 33, 38–9.

p. 304. Survey of the I-E family, Buck, 14, 3–4.

Romance languages, Bourciez, 9; Iordan, 38; Elcock, 20.
Germanic languages, Priebsch and Collinson, 54; Meillet, 48.
Indo-iranian languages, Burrow, 16.
Celtic languages, Lewis and Pedersen, 42.
Balto-slavic languages, Entwistle and Morison, 22; de Bray, 10.
On the position of Hittite, Sturtevant, 59, 158–63; 60.
Suggested date of unitary I-E, Buck, 142.

p. 306. General survey of languages and language families, Bloomfield, 6, chapter 4; chapter 18 contains examples of comparative and historical methods applied outside I-E.

p. 308. On the Bantu family, Meinhof, 49; Guthrie, 27.
On American-Indian languages, Osgood, 51.
Basque, Bonaparte, 8; Houghton, 34.

p. 309. Grimm's Law, Bloomfield, 6, 347–51; Buck, 14, 120–1; Hudson-Williams, 35, 29. Detailed study in Fourquet, 24.

p. 310. More details of correspondences in Buck, 14, with special reference to Ancient Greek and Latin. Full treatment in Walde and Pokorny, 68.

p. 311. Neogrammarians, Bloomfield, 6, 354–64; Pedersen, 53, 292–310; Iordan, 38, 15–24.

p. 312. Verner's Law, Bloomfield, 6, 357–9.

p. 315. On loan words, Bloomfield, 6, chapters 25–7.

The difference between loan words and inherited vocabulary is well illustrated by comparing the Norman French element in English vocabulary with the vocabulary inherited from Old English (before the Norman Conquest) and ultimately from the inferred common Germanic language. English at the present time contains a large body of words derived from Latin through Norman French, but it is counted a Germanic language in view of the earlier existence of the Germanic component in Old English, from which Modern English can be shown to have developed through Middle English by an unbroken series of gradual changes.

p. 316. On analogy and anomaly, see further 9·6.

p. 317. Analogical examples from English and Ancient Greek, Buck, 14, 46, 133; Sturtevant, 59, 109.

pp. 318–19. *Lexicostatistics* and *Glottochronology* are sometimes used interchangeably, but they have been distinguished: *lexicostatistics* to refer to the use of vocabulary statistics for historical inference, and *glottochronology* to refer to the study of the rate of change in languages for calculating the times of divergences in linguistic families.

See further: Hockett, 32, chapter 61; Gleason, 25, 450; Hymes, 37.

Applied to Romance, Kroeber, 40; applied to Germanic, Arndt, 3.

Theoretical as well as practical problems still remain to be overcome; see Chretien, 18.

p. 319. Meillet, 45, 15; Bloomfield, 6, 303.

p. 320. On the nature of the formulae, Buck, 15.

p. 321. On the phonetics of Latin, Sturtevant, 58.

Latin /k/ in relation to Romance, Pedersen, 53, 268–9.

See further, Pulgram, 55; Allen, 1. In this, Allen takes up an extreme position in regard to the whole of traditional comparative and historical linguistics, submitting its principles and methods to severe criticism.

p. 323. The theory of common characteristics resulting from the spreading of linguistic features 'in waves' over adjacent dialects within a family is called the 'Wellentheorie' (Bloomfield, 6, 317–18; Pedersen, 53, 313–18).

p. 324. Linguistic palaeontology, de Saussure, 57, 306–10; Bloomfield, 6, 319–20; Pedersen, 53, chapter 8.

South Asia, Buck, 14, 2. The geographical area has been the subject of much controversy. In a recent study P. Thieme, 62, argues in favour of northern Europe, in the region of the Vistula, Oder, and Elbe rivers.

p. 326. Double structuring of language, Martinet, 43.

p. 328. These common features of adjacent languages are discussed under the title *affinités phonologiques*, by Jakobson in *Actes du quatrième congrès international de linguistes*, 1936, 48–58, also printed in Trubetzkoy, 63, 351–65. Cp. Emeneau, 21.

p. 330. Phonological typologies, Trubetzkoy, 63, 93–245; Hockett, 31, chapter 2; Voegelin, 67.

A recent example of phonological classification of some Scottish dialects, J. C. Catford, *TPS* 1957, 107–17.

Suggested typological classification in prodosic terms, F. R. Palmer, *TPS* 1958, 119–43.

p. 331. Allen, 2 (see pp. 138–9).

On syntactic typology, Bazell, 4; L. Tesnière, 61, chapter 14 (the whole book, which is very long, though not written in strictly formal terms, is of considerable interest on questions of syntax); von Humboldt, 36, 114–26. Cp. Bazell, 5.

p. 334. The morphological division /magn-us/ is partly arbitrary. The paradigm can also be analysed on the basis of a division /magnu-s/, with different root allomorphs (/magnu-/, /magna-/, /magno-/, etc.), instead of the single form /magn-/ (cp. Hill, 30, 456). But the cumulation of several grammatical categories on a single affix is not affected. In a form like Latin /i:/ some of the cumulation could be avoided by the positing of zero morphemes serially representing certain of the grammatical categories, but this would not alter the general characterization of the language typologically.

pp. 334–5. 'Polysynthetic' languages, cp. Sapir, 56, 135–6.

Eskimo, M. Swadesh, 'South Greenlandic (Eskimo)', 51, 30–54; Hill, 30, appendix A.

Meillet, 47, II, 53, (I), 76–7; Guthrie, 27, 18–19. Typological similarity and genetic unity contrasted in Pedersen 53, 246–7.

p. 335. A confusion of the criteria employed in the two different processes of classification is, of course, quite another thing from arguing that in some parts of the world the lack of documentation and the nature of the evidence available may render a historically orientated comparative study unprofitable (cp. Boas, 7).

p. 336. Sapir's typology, 56, chapter 6; Greenberg, 26.

p. 337. Sapir, 56, 234.

On Old French, Foulet, 23.

Chinese, Karlgren, 39.

The conjoint pronominal forms of parts of the verbal paradigms of some of the Romance languages may be compared with the bipersonal verb forms referred to on p. 293, above. Bipersonal verb paradigms in some languages may have started in this way from the gradual 'petrifaction' of once free pronomial elements.

p. 340. Lexical typology, Ullmann, 64 (reference to Lapp, p. 232).

On mistaken inferences, Hill, 29.

ADDENDUM

p. 308. On language families in Africa, Greenberg, 71.

9

Wider perspectives

9·1 LINGUISTICS AND ANTHROPOLOGY

Some of the immediate connections between general linguistics and
other academic subjects were briefly mentioned in Chapter 1. After
an outline of the subject as it is taught and practised today, a further
review of some of its external relations in the scholarly world is
desirable as a conclusion.

The close bonds between linguistics, as the science of language,
and the other sciences devoted specifically to man were seen earlier,
in dealing with meaning, the link joining language to the rest of man's
world. In particular the association of linguistics and anthropology
has become very prominent in the recent and contemporary development of both these disciplines.

The use of the word *culture* as a technical term in anthropology has
already been mentioned (1·4·4), and a little reflection makes it clear
that language comes within the scope of anthropology, the study of
human culture in all its aspects; but the particular nature and special
characteristics of language justify its specific science, general linguistics. In the practice of the two disciplines it may be claimed that
some familiarity with the principles and methods of each is a very
desirable part of the equipment of a scholar in either.

It has already been said that languages are not mere collections of
labels or nomenclatures attached to preexisting bits and pieces of the
human world, but that each speech community lives in a somewhat
different world from that of others, and that these differences are
both realized in parts of their cultures and revealed and maintained
in parts of their languages (1·4·2, 2·4·3). Apart from the fact that

351

anthropological investigations into a culture remote from European influence may well require some command of the language of the community on the part of the investigator, many of the most significant details of a people's way of life are likely to be verbalized in certain key words belonging to different spheres (religion, ethics, kinship, social hierarchy, etc.), for which one-word translation equivalents are not readily available, and are certainly unlikely to be known to a speaker merely because he happens to be partially bilingual. Indeed, part of the linguist's task is to translate and explain the uses of such words in the language, by setting up suitable contexts of situation wherein the analysis of their semantic functions can be carried out $(1 \cdot 4 \cdot 3)$.

Anthropological investigation involves observation as well as enquiry, and it is clearly possible to arrive at some description of a people's culture without learning anything of their language, just as linguists who relegate semantics as lying outside their main preoccupation $(1 \cdot 3)$ can investigate the formal structuring of a language at the phonological and grammatical levels without regard to wider aspects of the culture of the speakers. But one may surmise that a description of a culture that has involved some acquaintance with the language or languages of that culture will be in certain important respects more penetrating and revealing, and that a description of a language by someone who has made use of some knowledge of the rest of the culture of its speakers will provide a more comprehensive account of the working of the language within the community as a symbolic communicative system. If the linguist wishes to include the level of semantics within his description, recourse to some cultural knowledge of the community may be a prerequisite if his statements of meaning are, in important spheres of the vocabulary, to rise above the superficially obvious and not to be confined to listing the nearest one-word translation renderings. On a more theoretical plane, the intimate connection between the subject-matters of the linguist and of the anthropologist implies that progress in the theory and methods of either is likely to serve correspondingly to advance understanding in the other.

The specific study of the interdisciplinary links, both theoretical and practical, between anthropology and linguistics has been called **ethnolinguistics.**

Closely related to many of the aspects of anthropology is the range of studies known as sociology. The precise nature of the distinction between social anthropology and sociology is a matter of debate, in which the linguist is not involved; here it will be sufficient to cite the view that anthropologists tend to concentrate on cultures remote from those of familiar European industrialized communities, with particular references to the form and organization of different cultures, while sociology is mainly focused on the social groups of European and Europeanized communities, and concerned with their formation and interaction.

The dialectal differences within a language involve, in many cases, not only regional variations, but class differentiations within and often transcending regional differences of speech (cp. 2·2·3). The differences of social status and social gradations, observed by persons within a society and evoking responses from them, and systematically described by sociologists, involve far more behavioural aspects than just habits of speech. But these are vital, as the nervousness of some socially insecure persons' speech evinces, and the linguist is uniquely qualified to describe and classify formally the speech features concerned, at all levels of linguistic description. Practically, as Bernard Shaw's Professor Higgins demonstrated, he can try to help people 'rise in the social scale', as far as the use of language is involved; he would, perhaps, be better employed trying to reduce the amount of deference accorded to the vocal manifestations of social rank, an aspect of many modern societies, which presumably does not add to the sum of human happiness, despite lip-service to equality in various guises.

The collaboration of the linguist and the anthropologist can be particularly close when the people whose language or culture is under investigation is remote from the well trodden paths of European civilization and European influence. The reasons are obvious; in the case of such communities, knowledge on the part of the rest of the world is scanty, and in relation to the work to be done investigators are few. The more reliable and systematic information each can provide, the greater will be our total knowledge both of the languages and the cultures of mankind. In familiar and long-studied parts of the world, the cultural backgrounds involved in the analysis and statement of meanings are in part well known and so taken for

353

granted, and have been the subject of diverse studies; conversely the languages of such communities, though no less intimately bound up with their way of life and culture, are more widely known and therefore less likely to be barriers to investigation, and serviceable accounts are available of them even if by modern linguistic standards some fall short of fully scientific descriptions.

It is in dealing with distant and primitive cultures, and with largely unknown and hitherto unstudied languages that the anthropologist and linguist can come closest together. Where workers are inevitably few, and the languages and peoples are many, our knowledge may depend on the reports and analyses of one or, at best, of a small number of scholars. The task is the more urgent at the present time, as in many rapidly developing parts of the world, isolated languages and dialects, spoken in small communities only, are rapidly passing into obsolescence and oblivion before the spread of major world languages in the path of modern communications, technical advances, and industrial and commercial development. Such is the situation in parts of South-east Asia and of Africa, but perhaps above all in North and South America, which present among their indigenous (Indian) populations a bewildering and fascinating array of languages, of widely different genetic stocks and typological classifications; some of these are still spoken by a hundred or even by less than a score of people, and they are likely to be lost without trace unless recorded in time and subjected to descriptive analyses at all levels.

Work among such languages, where there is a total absence of written records, and an almost total absence of prior scholarship, is known, appropriately, as **anthropological linguistics**. The importance of linguistic studies to the language teacher engaged in teaching languages of international importance is obvious; but the linguist's field is all language and every language, and he hopes to learn more about language itself, and about the relations between languages and between language and life, and to make progress in the development of linguistic theory and linguistic techniques, from every individual language he studies. To anyone not made purblind by the demand that all scholarship should be directed at materially profitable objectives, the many languages in peril of unrecorded extinction present a very special challenge.

Quite apart from the intrinsic value of the resultant descriptions,

354

recorded texts, and dictionaries, the methods necessitated by the situation of most of these languages have a particular value to linguistic science itself. The absence of written records, and usually of an indigenous writing system, means that the linguist must obtain his material entirely through informants, in most cases by visiting the communities in their own territories, 'in the field'.

Since the primary material of language is spoken utterance, the **informant**, as he or she is called, is a familiar and necessary part of the study of any living language, whatever its position in the world. The informant is not a teacher, nor a linguist; he is simply a native speaker of the language willing to help the linguist in his work. Work with informants may take place in isolation, when the informant visits the linguist, or in the field, when the linguist visits the informant. In either case the informant speaks as naturally as he can be induced to in response to the linguist's elicitations. These may and do take the form of individual words as lexical items, and of ordered series of words for phonetic description and phonological analysis and for the discovery of paradigms and paradigm classes (of the types *gate, fate, Kate, late, spate, date*; *gate, gape, gave*; *gate, goat, gout*; *gate, gates, walk, walks, walking, walked*, etc.), and of ordered series of sentences with controlled substitutions at various places for the discovery and analysis of syntactic structures and the formal patterns of sentences (*I see a dog, I see a cat, he sees a dog, he chases a cat*, etc.). Finally, informants may tell whole tales, personal histories, accounts of particular activities, and the like, uninfluenced by the promptings of the linguist (inevitably coloured at the outset by his own language background). Only after such relatively lengthy stretches have been subjected to phonological and grammatical analysis, can the linguist be certain that his description is more or less a complete statement of the systems and structures required for the language he is dealing with.

Work of this sort with informants is a very general part of all investigations of living languages; but with languages having a writing system and a written literature, and a tradition of scholarship, it is at all stages supplemented by the material provided from these sources and the work of previous scholars.

Informant work in the informant's own community has certain manifest advantages over work with one in isolation at home. There

355

are many personal variations in a language, and in any dialect of a language. An account may be deliberately, or inevitably, based on a single speaker acting as an informant, but the possibility of comparing one speaker's characteristics at every level with those of others of the same language or dialect results in a more representative statement. Language is rooted in social intercourse, not in isolated utterances to a foreigner. Certain features, constructions, intonation patterns, and stylistic variations arise in conversation and in the use of language in its normal settings; these are liable to be missed away from the speech community to which the informant belongs. The analysis of semantic functions, or meanings, of words and locutions of prime significance within the culture of the speakers must be facilitated by one's presence in the actual environment from which contexts of situation may be abstracted.

It is, therefore, in **field study** on the speaker's home territory that linguistic work with informants can achieve the fullest success; and anthropological linguistics, working on languages with no orthographies and few if any previous published accounts, both reveals the possibilities of modern linguistic methods and puts them to their severest test. Whatever is to be discovered and set down about the language, its transcription, its phonological and grammatical systems and structures, and the meanings of its lexical items must here be the unaided product of the linguist's own resources. In such matters as the devising of transcriptions, the isolation of words as formal units, and the establishment of grammatical categories and classes adequate to account for the patterns of utterance found in a language, the linguist, as has been seen, demands adherence to formal procedures based on observation, uninfluenced by traditional predilections. In a field situation, dealing with a language remote from the influences of European ways of thinking and European scholarship, the linguist is testing and refining his science in as pure an environment as its nature allows. The value of such a discipline to linguistics should need no stressing.

In the field situation the linguist is of necessity concerned with all aspects of a language. Not the least of these are oral texts, continuous stretches of speech other than responses to the linguist's direct elicitations. The importance of texts in the analysis and description of spoken languages has already been mentioned in this section. But

356

they have additional importance. Many texts, whatever their nature, are revealing of some part of the culture and traditions of the speakers. Traditional stories, songs, fables, myths, personal biographies and group histories, ritual utterances, accounts of activities and processes of production within the culture (utensils, weapons, food, etc.) are only some examples of the material that the linguist is in a unique position to be able to gather and analyse. Their significance may extend far beyond the confines of linguistics itself.

Many such traditional stories and the like exhibit aesthetic merits of their own; in communities at the preliterate stage, it is well known that oral literature often flourishes, and culturally determined forms of utterance are preserved from generation to generation in the memories both of ordinary people and among those officially or unofficially recognized within the culture as preeminently qualified to preserve, transmit, and create such artistic uses of language.

Stories and accounts of activities may, of course, be gathered bilingually from informants with a knowledge of the linguist's language or of a mutually understood 'trade language'; they may also be gathered through interpreters. But there is a constant risk of loss in such transmissions. It requires a high degree of linguistic sophistication and a deep knowledge of both languages to render the culturally vital elements of one speech community into the language of another. The linguist may profess or acquire such skills; he cannot assume that his informant will have them. In earlier days, among the pioneers of modern linguistics, texts were recorded by dictation from informants, with inevitable limitations, delays, and possible distortions arising from the need to pause repeatedly. Present-day linguists are privileged; modern science has provided them with tape recorders of great accuracy, many of which are constructed to work independently of mains electricity. With their aid the speech of communities whose language or particular dialect is soon to perish may be recorded and preserved for all time.

A recorded oral text needs a transcription and a translation, preferably accompanied by a description of the phonetics, phonology, and grammar of the language from which it is taken. Such accompaniments are the product of the trained linguist. The selection of representative and informative texts to provide something of a fair and balanced picture of the culture and way of life of the community

357

requires knowledge of the theory and techniques of anthropology. In the realm of anthropological linguistics we see the needs and the achievements of collaboration between these two disciplines of the study of man.

9·2   LINGUISTICS AND PHILOSOPHY

The study of language, and in particular the study of meaning and of the problems connected with it and the study of grammar, have been closely linked in western Europe with philosophical studies since the dawn of western scholarship in ancient Greece. Linguistic studies partly grew out of philosophic enquiries, and the association of the two subjects, after their distinctiveness was recognized, is manifest. On any view of philosophy and of its subdivisions, language remains the vehicle of logical discourse and inference. Propositions may be regarded as something different from sentences, but they must be expressed in sentences, and even the formulaic propositions of modern symbolic logic are ultimately explained by and reducible to sentences in actual languages. Metaphysical systems, whatever immanent or transcendent status may be accorded them, can only be communicated to others by the use of words in sentences constructed in a language known to the philosopher and his hearers or readers. No matter what view a philosopher takes of the nature and scope of philosophy, his explication and public elaboration of it is dependent on his use of language. This is true also of all sciences and enquiries, and is a reason for ascribing a central place to the study of language among the intellectual disciplines (1·2·1); but philosophy, not being an empirical science, claims no particular field of experience as its own, and concerns itself with the very general questions about human knowledge, perception, argumentation, and obligations, all matters dependent on language for their public communication and discussion.

At various times it has been claimed that some of the major features of systems of logic and metaphysics are partly determined by certain predominant features of the structure of the language used in the philosopher's community and recognized as the language in which philosophical discourse should be expressed. Some of the differences between the philosophies of the world have been referred to basic differences in the languages in which they were framed. Such speculations are a specialized application of the more general hypothesis of an intimate connection between the language of a community and the basic patterns of their thinking and their ordering of the world of experience (1·4·2, 2·4·3, 7·4, and note to page 291).

Especially since the work of Wittgenstein, the association of philosophy and some aspects of linguistics has increased. Among many philosophers today it is held that a good deal of what passed as metaphysical system building and statements about the nature of things in general was little more than an illegitimate projection of the rules by which philosophers and others were in the habit of constructing their sentences with which to talk about the world. On this view a considerable part of the philosopher's task is therapeutic, in showing how several apparently fundamental problems and philosophical puzzles are the results of language misused; when this misuse is pointed out, it is claimed, the question apparently raised or the proposition on which it is based, is shown to be strictly meaningless within philosophical discourse, and therefore a solution is neither possible nor necessary.

Such developments in philosophy would seem to imply, and many philosophers would agree, that philosophy today is primarily concerned with language. If this is so, he is obviously not concerned with it in the same way that the linguist is, as philosophy and linguistics are not the same. To circumscribe the field of language that is of concern to the philosopher is no part of anyone's task who does not represent philosophical studies, but in at least two respects the interests of the two subjects are divergent. The philosopher is concerned with particular aspects of the use and misuse of language for specific purposes or mistaken purposes; the linguist is concerned with all uses of the language and with the description and analysis of languages and language utterances of all types and at all levels. Moreover, the philosopher concerns himself with the uses of language for certain purposes that are common to many communities, and is not interested in the detailed differences between languages except when these are reflected in philosophically significant differences of use; the linguist is concerned with the details of each language for its own sake, and he evolves and evaluates linguistic theories primarily to deal with particular languages.

359

Recent developments have made it desirable that linguists and philosophers should know something of each other's work, if only because they tend to use statements and concepts in relation to language that properly fall within the purview of the other, without always realizing the theoretical implications of their use. The traditional reliance of linguists on the unexamined 'idea' theory of meaning and on philosophical notions as part of the definitions of fundamental categories and classes in grammar has already been referred to. Some philosophers, on the other hand, have appealed to grammatical terms in their treatment of philosophical questions. Bloomfield refers to a statement by Carnap to the effect that saying redness is a concept is just saying that *redness* is a noun. Nouns, as a particular part of speech or word class in the grammar of a language, are not self-evident entities, but have to be justified by the procedures of grammatical analysis; and although there are grounds for asserting that the noun–verb distinction is in one way or another a very general feature of languages, the definition of the noun class and the assignment of words to it in any language are matters for the linguistic analysis of each separately. Behind the use of *noun*, or of any other technical term in linguistic usage, there lies a body of relevant theory by which such words bear the technical meanings ascribed to them (cp. 6·2).

It is possible to say that the linguist's particular concern is with the formal structuring of the sentences of a language as sentences in a particular language, and that the philosopher is concerned with the logical structure and the inferential possibilities of the propositions they express irrespective of the grammar of any particular language. But propositions can only be expressed within the available range of sentence structures in some languages, and even the abstract formalized propositions of symbolic logic must ultimately be referred to the grammatical sentences of some natural language.

9·3   LINGUISTICS AND PSYCHOLOGY

Psychology as an independent science among sciences devoted to man is relatively recent. In the European tradition a good deal of the questions and subject-matter now referred to psychology was dealt with under the general heading of philosophy. Part of the maturity of psychology at the present time is seen in its assertion of its own specific field and its own methods of dealing with it, without being beholden to any system of philosophy in its work.

With this assertion of independence has come a considerable widening of the field claimed for psychology. It has been asserted that the psychologist is concerned with the discovery and formulation of general laws covering human behaviour. Earlier psychology was said to be primarily the study of mental states and events in human beings, though this did not commit the psychologist to the assertion that minds and mental entities existed in their own right as a separate order of being from human bodies and bodily events, and perhaps in a controlling relation to them. Questions on the status of mind versus body and the relations between the two components of human experience, mental events and bodily events, are controversial, and it is neither pertinent nor necessary for the linguist to intervene herein. On any view of their subject, presumably, psychologists would assert that what have been called subjective events (experiences and activities essentially private to the individual and as such experienced only by him, popularly called feelings, thoughts, and the like) are an important part of their field of study. It is here that a principal link is found between such studies and the study of language. Subjective events in human beings are, by definition, known only to him directly; but people's overt behaviour in publicly observable activities constitutes, deliberately or otherwise, evidence for such subjective personal events, and is confidently treated as such by other people, extrapolating from their own experience. A great part of this manifesting behaviour is speech utterance, or verbal activity. This is no less true because the relations between speech and these personal experiences are not simple or uniform. Straightforwardly one may seek to communicate one's feeling and thoughts to others; but one may also try to conceal them in a specialized use of lying (but it must be remembered that lying unilaterally presupposes truth telling; the liar's hope of successful deception rests on the credence given to speech as normally truthful). One's feelings and thoughts may unintentionally be revealed in what one says or the way one says it, without and even in spite of the set purpose of the speaker.

Such statements as these may seem to hark back to the old unsatisfactory definition of language as 'the communication of thought'.

There is, however, an important difference. Here one is not defining language, nor making a general assertion about its use and purpose; one is simply drawing attention to one of the uses (among many others) put upon language and expected of it by speakers and hearers.

More generally, the continuing and developing set of features and dispositions that one knows collectively as a man's individual personality, uniquely his and distinguishing him from others, and in part a reliable guide as regards his expected actions and reactions to external events and to other people, is largely made known, deliberately or unwillingly, by a man's speech habits. The study of these at all levels, and in relation to the speaker's dialect situation, regional and social, must be counted an essential part of the study of human personality.

A field wherein linguistics and psychology meet at the borders of their respective domains lies in the chains of causal connections within human beings linking experiences with speaking and writing, and hearing and reading with further behaviour. This interdisciplinary study has been entitled **psycholinguistics,** and within its range lie such topics as the use of language in concept formation, learning, abstraction, and kindred processes.

A more long-standing and traditional question within this field is that of the relation between language and thought, or speaking and thinking, and the extent to which the two can be separated and the extent to which language is necessary for thought. As with many questions worth examining, a short answer is not readily available. *Thought* and *thinking* are not simple terms, and such words, and their translations in other languages, are used in a variety of different contextual functions.

In one use *thought* and *thinking* are more or less similar in use to *care*. We speak of thoughtless actions, as, for example, stepping into a crowded motor road without looking ('He never thought of seeing if it was safe'). Many such spheres of application of words like *thought* involve trained and habitual responses to types of situation, failure in which is stigmatized as 'thoughtless', and which in the learning process are often accompanied by actual explicit thinking about the procedure to be adopted (as when children are taught how to cross busy roads). These words, however, are also used to refer to

362

the conscious and deliberate process by which an individual handles some pieces of information up to the determination of some action, the solving of some problem, or the arrival at some satisfactory conclusion. Between this type of 'full dress' thinking and trained careful behaviour there are doubtless many intermediate stages. Explicit thinking has been identified by some as subvocal speech activities, involving the same cerebral and muscular actions but on a very small scale; and Bloomfield wrote of '*talking to oneself* or *thinking*'. A great deal of thinking is just that, whether the unuttered sentences are fully rounded periods or disjointed note-like fragments, and in the privacy of one's own company such thinking may pass over the borders of silence into muttered or even fully articulated speech and back again as a train of argumentation proceeds. But one can operate similarly with imagined diagrams and pictures; no doubt the extent to which one can think in images differs from person to person. Most people can perform simple geometrical operations on imagined figures such as circles and triangles, though there is clearly an upper limit on the number of different lines that can be pictured at once. Such thinking may be interspersed with diagram drawing or figuring with the fingers. But 'thinking in words' is the commonest form of this explicit handling of information within oneself, and all thought is ultimately dependent on sentences for its communication to others or setting down on paper for subsequent personal use; if diagrams, actual or imagined, are used, their explanation and interpretation involves the use of language.

What should be borne in mind is that, in this type of situation, the thinking is not something apart from the language utterances in which it is expressed (uttered aloud or written down); as far as language is concerned in these private thinking processes, it is a form of monologue, or dialogue with oneself, usually silent but sometimes aloud.

In a more general sense, it is clear that the lexical composition of every language enshrines a vast collective way of forming, interpreting, and understanding the world in which the speakers live (1·4·2). Languages are the product of millennia of reflection and intuition handed from one generation to the next, and always developing, a process we must assume to have accompanied the earliest uses of language among mankind's most primitive ancestors. In particular places and periods of cultural advance, for example in the

Greek-speaking world during the last eight centuries or so B.C., one can see the language developing under the impact of the use forced on it by pioneers in various intellectual fields, wherein many of the concepts taken for granted in European cultures today were first made explicit.

It is open to suggestion that the semantic correlations found in varying degrees with many of the formal categories and structures of the grammars of different languages (Chapter 7) may have originated in various situational likenesses, real or assumed, but that these were variously blurred, diluted, or altered in subsequent periods by the extension of the categories and structures to formally associated words outside the original semantic spheres. Such speculations do no harm, provided it is remembered that they can be no more than speculations, and that in the analysis of any language, formal criteria alone are relevant to the establishment and definition of grammatical categories and classes.

Conversely, it is perfectly possible that the major formal patterns and classes in languages, by associating together different parts of the speaker's experience, have themselves taken a hand in the shaping of people's collective world pictures through the ages. The traffic between conceptualization and verbalization must be operating continuously in both directions.

9·4   LINGUISTICS AND LANGUAGE TEACHING; LINGUISTICS AND COMMUNICATIONS ENGINEERING

9·4·1 *Linguistics and language teaching*

The application of some of the results of general linguistic studies to the work of the language teacher and of the communications engineer were briefly noticed in an earlier chapter (1·2·2). At first sight these two subjects might seem strangely linked in a single section; but in relation to general linguistics, both essentially involve the application to specifically practical purposes of some of the findings of the study of language and the recognized subdivisions of this study.

The language teacher's aim in regard to a language is not the same as that of a descriptive linguist. The teacher is not simply concerned with its systematic and exhaustive description and analysis, but with facilitating the acquisition of a language other than their mother tongue by other people with the greatest ease and thoroughness. This both restricts the number of languages he is primarily concerned with, and determines the type of presentation he requires. Linguists describe and analyse many languages that will, for economic and practical reasons, never be taught to others, and may themselves be on the verge of extinction; indeed, this situation which renders a language utterly irrelevant to the teacher, may make it of especial interest to the general linguist (9·1). But it is to be hoped and believed that the techniques and methods of scientific linguistics, at every level of language analysis, will aid and improve the work of the language teacher. The teacher must present his material sometimes in a different order from that used in disinterested description, and has to vary his presentation according to the linguistic background of his pupils; there have to be somewhat differently constructed teaching grammars for students according to the principal typological differences of their own languages, since these to a large extent determine the chief difficulties in the path of learners and engender the sort of errors, in pronunciation and grammar, to which they are most prone. Considerations like this are extraneous to the work of the descriptive linguist as such; but his specialist knowledge should be a powerful aid in applied linguistics where these have to be taken into account.

Linguistic science as one knows it today has been stimulated and nourished all the time by the work of language teachers. They, and others who for purely practical purposes have mastered foreign languages, have provided linguists with a great deal of their material, and the problems and difficulties they encountered stimulated linguistic research along fruitful lines. The science of language owes much to the work of people who would never have claimed for themselves the title of general linguists. But it may be asserted that the teacher who understands and can make use of the methods of scientific linguistics will find the task of presenting a language to his pupils very much lightened and facilitated. In particular the intuitive feeling for correctness in a language on which teachers have often relied as a fruit of their long experience will be replaced by an objective and publicly communicable knowledge of its elements and structures, which can be systematically imparted to others.

Recent events in the world have attracted considerable attention to the needs and advantages of close collaboration between linguists as defined in the context of general linguistics and teachers of languages. The sudden requirements for numbers of persons to be rapidly trained in particular aspects and styles of languages spoken in operational areas in the second world war made a profound and progressive impact on linguistic work in Great Britain and America. The results of such work, produced under the pressures of an emergency for which little preparation had been made, have contributed greatly to the programmes of language teaching, and particularly to the teaching of English in many parts of the world today. Many linguists devote much of their time to the study and development of teaching methods and the improvement of teaching materials in the service of English as a foreign language.

In particular the linguist has contributed his experience in the use of native speakers as informants, being the sources of language material and a check on the adequacy of his own and his pupils' performance. His technical experience of the mechanical aids to linguistic work today, in particular recording apparatus, and of the controlled production and use of recorded material specially designed for and integrated into courses of language instruction, is one of the most important contributions he can bring to the work of language teachers.

9·4·2 Linguistics and communications engineering

The communications engineer is concerned with more than one type of process involving language material, the transmission of speech as such by wire and radio waves, and the conversion of linguistic signals, written messages, into some other medium, via Morse code and the like, or directly into sequences of electric impulses, their transmission, and reconversion into written messages. The technical problems of the apparatus involved in all this are scarcely within the competence of the linguist as a linguist, though persons equipped with a knowledge in these fields as well as in linguistics are of particular value in many of the aspects of this sort of work. But the linguist may be expected to contribute to the communications engineer's work in so far as the linguistic nature of the material to be transmitted is concerned. In the transmission of written messages, as long as the units serially transmitted are letters of a recognized alphabet, he has little of his own to offer; but in any form of telephony something is lost in the processes of transmission. In commercial telephones a great deal is lost, but the utility and efficiency of the instruments are virtually unaffected for the purpose they ordinarily serve. It is within the scope of the linguist's potential contribution to estimate the relative value of the different phonetic components in the sound waves that result from successive speech articulations; their localization into different bands of frequencies is part of this (cp. 3·4). Controlled experimentation, including the production of artificial speech sounds by the generation of sound waves at the frequencies mainly responsible for the distinctive differences between the sounds of languages (speech synthesis) helps to reveal the limits of tolerable loss at the different frequencies under the conditions in which the apparatus is used, and as a result the extent to which costly technical improvements in fidelity would be justified economically.

The opposite process to speech synthesis is the mechanical analysis of speech. A number of instruments are now available for this type of work. One, usually known as the sound spectrograph, produces a permanent visual record of the succession of sound features in speech, in the form of different concentrations of energy at different frequencies. Another working in a similar fashion produces a transitory visual representation of the sound sequences, and was first devised as an aid to the deaf, being known for that purpose as 'visible speech'. The use of these processes in advanced phonetic research within linguistics itself is obvious, but their potential practical utility in various aspects of communications work is no less clear.

An extension of communications engineering in the field of linguistics lies in attempts to develop the techniques of translation by computers ('machine translation'). Apparatus has been designed into which can be fed the sentences, edited if necessary in various ways, of one language; the machine processes these lexically and grammatically, and produces translations of them in another language. Such machines are already in existence, though their practical application in the replacement or supplementation of human translators is still largely in its infancy. This whole field requires a thorough knowledge of the apparatus and its uses and possibilities, and of the linguistic analysis, semantic, collocational, and grammatical, that is involved

367

in the processes of translation. Considerable efforts are being currently devoted to this work in Great Britain, Europe, the United States, and the Soviet Union.

9·5   LINGUISTICS AND LITERATURE

Linguistic studies and literary studies are clearly connected in certain respects as intellectual disciplines. In the history of linguistics in western Europe (9·6) literary criticism and literary scholarship, together with philosophical studies, constituted a main source of the systematic study of language.

There is a certain sense of rivalry and even at times of hostility expressed between literary pursuits and the study of language in linguistics today. This feeling, though one would think it wholly mistaken, may be attributed to the long dominance over linguistic work and the teaching and study of language exercised by almost exclusively literary considerations. This is mainly the result of the literary bias of education in Europe from the Renaissance onwards until the rise of natural science during recent years in educational esteem. (Whether this will itself be carried too far remains to be seen.)

The effects on the literary domination of language studies are seen in the concentration of attention on written language and on the styles of well known and highly respected authors. Grammatical rules and systems of grammar were drawn up on the basis of literary works and the types of sentence structures and word forms found therein. Within a language, the dialect of the literate and literary classes (usually also the socially dominant classes) was taken as representing a special standard of correctness, from which other dialects were uneducated deviations or debasements. This attitude, in fact, flies in the face of many palpable instances wherein at different linguistic levels nonstandard dialects preserve older features once more widely present in a language and now lost in standard speech; grammatically, the separate second person singular forms of the pronoun and the corresponding inflected forms of verb paradigms, as preserved in some northern dialects, and phonologically, postvocalic /r/ as found in West-country and Scottish dialects, are examples from English.

A further effect of the same literary approach to language study

368

was the relative neglect of phonetic studies, except by specialists, and of spoken utterance in general, except as part of the study of orthography; phonetics was treated in terms of 'the pronunciation of the letters', and was not as the independent study of spoken language in its own right. The great prestige and educational preeminence of Latin and Ancient Greek, languages almost wholly studied in their written forms, reinforced these tendencies.

Such a situation can hardly be said to obtain today, and though old prejudices die hard, and old ways of thought linger on, it is most desirable that linguists, in the light of their contemporary understanding of their subject, should consider the links it may have with the work of students of literature.

Linguistics, as the scientific study of language, necessarily covers all aspects and uses of language, and all styles. Literature comprises a number of particular uses and styles, and forms an important and valuable part of the linguistic material in the study of a particular language and in the study of mankind's use of the faculty of language. Moreover, once the bias towards written language is overcome, it may be seen that literature, considered as utterances that are regarded for one reason or another as worthy in their own right of preservation and as aesthetically valuable, is a form of language use present, so far as is known, in all cultures, literate and preliterate. **Oral literature** is as much a distinct component of cultures as is **written literature**; and in the absence of writing, it may be preserved by memory from one generation to another, and in many such communities certain individuals are charged with its preservation and its transmission to other similarly charged persons as their successors. Narratives, myths, ritual utterances, poems, and songs are prominent parts of oral literature, and their possession in entirety by certain persons involves feats of memory prodigious by the standards of people in literate communities, wherein such capacities have been largely lost as being no longer needed (cp. 9·1). Since all utterances are not in any sense rated as literature, linguistics comprehends within its field much more than the literary uses of language. On the other hand, the evaluation, appreciation, and criticism of literature of all sorts covers much more than the relative excellence of the author's or the tradition's exploitation of the resources available in the language. Linguistics and literary scholarship do not operate on the whole of the same field, or in the same way; but within the subject-matter of each it is reasonable to see some common ground and opportunities for profitable cooperation.

In all forms of literature, part of the aesthetic evaluation, whether of the author's skill or of the work itself, written or spoken, turns on the specific use made of the material employed, the phonetic, grammatical, and lexical constitution of the language (or a dialect thereof). The relative weight of this part of the literary merit of a composition differs according to the kind of work that is involved. To take a familiar field, in European literature poetry and oratorical prose are more dependent on the material of the language wherein they are composed than are prose narratives and histories; within poetry, what is called lyric poetry is much more dependent on the language itself than are epic and dramatic poetry. The degree to which the literary merit and character of any work depend on the material of the language, as against other extralinguistic factors, may be partly seen in the difficulties involved in its translation into another language. In all works of literature levels of language in addition to the semantic level are brought into play as aesthetically exploitable in their own right; but in certain types of poetry, known to be 'virtually untranslatable', the formal levels of language play a preponderant part in giving the work its literary form and literary excellence.

The literary artist, the orator, story-teller, dramatist, or poet, need not himself be a linguist or be explicitly concerned with the study of the structure of his own language. Art is the product of intuition; that is why it is personal and not communicable by sets of rules to other people. But any great artist's intuition works in and through the material in which he expresses himself, whether it be bronze or marble, paint, music, or a language. The nature of the material imposes its own limitations and conditions on the artist, and artistic genius consists in part in seizing on these inherent limitations and building in them and by means of them products that are recognized as of enduring merit. The linguist is not necessarily, or usually, an artist, any more than a literary artist is a linguist; but it is part of the linguist's task and competence, by the application of the specific methods of linguistics, to analyse the forms and patterns of languages, and so to make explicit some of the features of it that in varying degrees, according to the nature of the work, constitute the material

370

which the author must use and exploit in expressing himself to his public.

It is known that not all forms of literary composition flourish equally in all languages, even though the cultural conditions may in other respects be fairly similar. This is one cause of difficulty in translating literary works from one language into another. The correlation of such differences of literary styles in different languages with characteristics of the formal structures of the languages themselves suggests itself as a field to be worked jointly by literary critics and linguistic specialists, though, of course, such work alone will not exhaust the analysis and explanation of the differences of the literary styles peculiar to certain languages.

Certain such differences of style have long been recognized as partly due to linguistic differences. English poetry has been as a whole far less dependent on the use of rhyme than has French poetry, and in the classical periods of Greek and Latin literature rhyme in poetry was virtually unknown. These facts have been correlated with the differences between the stress based rhythms of English, in which stressed syllables contrast with unstressed syllables, and within these limits different degrees of stress operate, the quantitative rhythms of classical Greek and Latin, in which long syllables contrast with short, and the syllable unit rhythms of French, in which distinctions of stress and length are, by comparison with English and Latin, relatively slight.

The metres developed in Greek poetry were taken over by Latin poets of the classical age of Latin literature; but in doing so, those Latin authors recognized as the greatest masters of each style of poetry felt compelled to alter the rules of composition in some respects, despite the similar quantitative rhythms of the two languages. In particular, the elegiac couplet in the hands of Ovid, the greatest elegist of Latin literature, was subjected to very stringent rules governing the position of word boundaries in relation to the sequences of long and short syllables. The need for these, as against the more permissive patterns of Greek elegiac couplets, must reflect certain differences in the Latin language, considered as the material of poetry, compared with Greek, features of which the poet recognized as preeminent in his style became aware as vitally affecting his art. Such statements, valid as far as they go, have by now the crudity

371

of the obvious. As linguistics progresses in the analysis of features like stress and length, and the many concomitant characteristics of utterance as yet not fully investigated or understood, in the comparison from different points of view of the syllable structures of languages and of their word structures, and in the statement of their grammatical and collocational patterns, linguists may expect to be able to penetrate more deeply and move more delicately in making explicit the many components of languages that great authors and generations of composers of oral literature have unconsciously seized on and moulded into works of literary art.

In research of this sort, the linguist in applying his own methods to a specific body of linguistic material may be able to deepen the appreciation of different literary styles and of the artistic uses of language, both his own and that of other people. In a wider sense, this all forms part of one's penetration into the different cultures of the world and their sympathetic appreciation. Linguistic stylistics, as such applications of linguistics may be called, is as yet little developed. It is to be hoped that significant progress will reward the collaborative work of linguists and literary scholars, and that this will rank as not the least service of general linguistics to the world of learning.

9·6 OUTLINE OF THE HISTORY OF LINGUISTIC STUDIES IN WESTERN EUROPE

In a short survey of the subject, such as has been the purpose of this book, attention must necessarily be concentrated on it as it is taught, practised, and understood at the present time. General linguistics, as a separate academic subject and discipline is relatively modern. Several of the sciences look back to the nineteenth century or earlier for their attainment of the position and outlook characterizing their present condition. Linguistics, in its contemporary state, is very much the product of this century, and the child of the labours of European, American, and British scholars in the years 1900–50.

Nevertheless, every science and every branch of study is in part a development of what went on before, and in each age the workers in any field are in part determined in the directions they take by the work of their predecessors, if only, in extreme cases, in the terms and principles that they deliberately reject. Studies concerned with the nature, structure, and working of language, though on different lines, and with different ends in view, have been a feature of the intellectual activity of a number of civilizations, notably in ancient China, where particular attention was paid to lexicography, the construction of dictionaries, in ancient India, in the Greco-Roman world, and among the early Arabic scholars.

Of these, the linguistic work of Greece and of India are by far the most important in the history of linguistics in Europe and America today. In the study of language, as in so many other fields of the intellect, one can trace a continuous line of development, virtually from the beginnings in Greek thought of the fifth and subsequent centuries B.C. through its transmission by Rome, the Middle Ages, and the Renaissance, to the present day; and from the end of the eighteenth century, the quite remarkable work of the ancient Indian linguistic scholars and their successors became known to the West, and made a profound contribution to this branch of western learning. By contrast, the impact of Chinese linguistic scholarship, except within the field of Sinology itself, has been slight, and the linguistic work of the Arabs was itself a derivative of Western thinking, in particular of the philosophical writings of Aristotle.

In ancient Greece linguistics was not at first a separate branch of learning or enquiry, but it grew out of the wide fields of questioning that became known as φιλοσοφία /philosophía:/, a term that embraced numbers of topics that today would be assigned to separate disciplines, and cannot be simply equated with *philosophy* as this word is understood now. Early speculation on the nature of language turned largely on the degree to which it should be regarded as a 'natural' as opposed to a 'conventional' product of mankind. This dispute between the rival claims of nature, φύσις /phúsis/, and convention, νόμος /nómos/, formed part of a wider context of debate on the nature of human institutions. The Platonic dialogue devoted to linguistic questions, the *Cratylus*, gives its main attention to a discussion of the arguments in favour of each of the two opposing views.

This early debate conducted with almost exclusive reference to the Greek language, merged later in a more far-reaching controversy between the 'analogist' and 'anomalist' theories of language, to some extent championed respectively by the Aristotelian and Stoic

373

philosophical schools. The analogists emphasized the regularities of grammatical structures and word forms, and the parallels between grammatical forms and word meanings, as constituting the essence of language and the direction in which standards of correctness should be sought, and tended to take up a 'conventional' attitude towards language itself. The anomalists stressed the numerous irregular forms in grammatical paradigms, and 'anomalous' associations of plural number with singular entities, genders divorced from any sex reference, and the like, and leaned more to the 'naturalist' view of language, accepting its anomalies as they stood. This famous controversy would be of less historical importance, were it not for the fact that in its course the patterns of Greek grammar were first worked out and codified, subsequently to be taken over and applied to Latin by the Latin grammarians, and thence to form the basis of traditional grammatical theory and language teaching throughout Europe.

In the Alexandrian age, beginning towards the end of the fourth century B.C., a second conditioning factor in the development of Greek linguistic studies began to take effect, the literary criticism and exposition of earlier recognized classical authors. With the spread of Greek over wide areas of the Near and Middle East after the Macedonian conquests, the growing differences between the Greek of the classical authors, not only Homer, but those whose language was Attic (Athenian) Greek as well, and the colloquial Greek spoken by the general public, gave rise to critical studies of the grammatical forms used by the great writers and to attempts to preserve, especially on the part of analogists, the 'correct' Greek of Attic literature for literary purposes. Throughout Greco-Roman antiquity and the Middle Ages, language studies were very much under the control of these two subjects, philosophy and literary criticism, one or the other being successively, or in different schools, the dominant consideration.

Greek grammarians dealt with many of the topics that fall within the linguistic study of languages today, though they concerned themselves almost exclusively with their own language, and within it, with the dialects used in literature, particularly Homeric and Attic Greek. Phonetics, grammar, and the analysis of meanings were all treated, but by far the greatest attention was paid to grammar. Phonetic observations were made on the pronunciation values of the letters of the Greek alphabet and on the accent signs, some theory of the syllable as a structural unit was developed, and it was realized that in different environments the same letter sign could have different phonetic values; but no very penetrating analysis was made at this level, and certain features of the phonetics of the language, notably the distinction between voiced and voiceless articulation, escaped a correct description altogether.

Within grammar morphology held pride of place, and morphological description was built around the identification and definition of the word classes (parts of speech) of Greek. The first distinction recognized in this field was that of noun and verb, a distinction found in Plato, who based it on the logical distinction between subject and predicate. Subsequently Aristotle and the Stoics added further members to the system of word classes, and refined their defining criteria. The number was finally fixed at eight (noun, verb, pronoun, participle, adverb, preposition, conjunction, article) in the short Greek grammar of Dionysius Thrax, which dates from the first century B.C., and became recognized as a standard manual on the subject. Thrax's definitions, largely the product of earlier work, were in the main formally grounded on the morphological categories of the variable words. Thrax had nothing specific to say on syntax, and later writings on this aspect of grammar, such as the Greek syntax of Apollonius Dyscolus do not show anything like the same degree of formal analysis or systematic description.

In linguistic studies, in this context specifically in grammar, the Romans were content largely to model themselves on Greek patterns. Throughout the classical period of Latin literature linguistic studies on the Latin language were undertaken, and among others Julius Caesar interested himself in some questions of grammar. But the great age of the codification of Latin grammar came later, during the period of imperial decline and disruption. Among several grammarians of this period known to us, the most famous are Donatus and Priscian, especially the latter, whose comprehensive Latin grammar, written about A.D. 500, ran to eighteen volumes. Priscian models himself on Thrax and Apollonius. His word-class system is the same as theirs except that the article, a class not represented in Latin, is omitted and the number of classes made up by the addition of the interjection, a class whose members had earlier been included among the adverbs.

Priscian's work, of which some thousand manuscripts survive, became the standard textbook of Latin in subsequent centuries. Mediaeval scholars worked over it in successive commentaries, and its influence is plainly seen in the standard grammars of Latin in use today.

Medieval European linguistic scholarship continued the study of Latin grammar through the works of Priscian and Donatus and the commentaries written on them. Knowledge of Greek, and of much of Greek thought and literature, was temporarily lost in the West after the breaking up of the Roman Empire. Latin continued to enjoy immense prestige as the language of the Church, the language of classical literature, and the common language of educated discourse and scholarly writing throughout Europe. A particular flowering of medieval linguistics is seen in the production by several authors in the thirteenth and fourteenth centuries of what are called speculative grammars. In these writings the Priscianic framework of Latin grammar was integrated into a comprehensive scholastic theory of language, itself forming part of a scholastic philosophical system. These grammars represent the culmination of one line of scholastic thought, and though they are constructed round a theory of grammar not widely accepted today, they display some very interesting and revealing interpretations of the data of the Latin language.

The effects of the Renaissance on linguistic studies in Europe were firstly the rediscovery of Ancient Greek by the West and its incorporation into Western education and scholarship. The renewed study of the Greek language was accompanied by the grammatical study of Hebrew and Arabic, the first two non-I-E languages to be the objects of systematic European scholarship. Progressively thereafter, trade, exploration, colonization, and later missionary work brought Europeans into contact with the languages of different parts of their expanding world and with cultures very far removed from the traditions of Greco-Roman and Christian civilization. This continuous widening of European linguistic horizons was accompanied by a growth in linguistic interest in the vernacular, spoken, languages of Europe itself, as the hold of Latin on the world of scholarship relaxed and printing presses produced books in more and more European tongues.

At the end of the eighteenth century a new and highly important stream entered European linguistic scholarship. This came from the European colonization of India, and took two forms, the discovery of Sanskrit, the classical language of India, and of its indisputable relationship with the major language groups of Europe, and the transmission to the west of the Indian linguistic tradition itself, and in particular the work of Pāṇini on the Sanskrit language, the first translation of which appeared in Europe early in the nineteenth century. The effect of the discovery of Sanskrit and the stimulus it gave to comparative and historical linguistics during that century have already been mentioned (8·1·1). The Indian tradition of linguistic scholarship, devoted to the Sanskrit language, was of a very high order, and its influence on Western linguistics was profound, and is by no means over. Unlike the Greek and Latin grammarians and their medieval successors, Indian linguists exhibited great interest and masterly competence in the phonetic analysis and description of their speech; and the development of the phonetic and phonological levels of linguistic analysis in the last hundred years or so owes a great deal to their work.

Pāṇini is the best known of the Indian linguists. His date is uncertain, but around 600 B.C. or later has been suggested in the light of the evidence available. His Sanskrit grammar has been described by Bloomfield as 'one of the greatest monuments of human intelligence'. Unfortunately its very perfection of method renders it extremely obscure to the reader even with a knowledge of Sanskrit, and its elucidation to the general linguist as a standard model of description, despite numerous commentaries and translations, remains to be done. Its main characteristic is the startling economy with which the details of Sanskrit morphology are expressed in statements of rules, often of great brevity, in which no avoidable repetition of a previous statement is made at any subsequent point, though this compression has always been recognized as a source of difficulty to the student. Pāṇini's work clearly constitutes the culmination of much previous scholarship, and it was afterwards the subject of extensive commentaries. Its origin lay in the need felt to understand and preserve intact the language of the Vedic scriptures, but the world

377

of linguistics is fortunate that the interest of this line of Indian scholars went far beyond these immediate requirements.

The work of the Indian linguistic scholars is distinguished historically by two features, the excellence of their phonetic description of Sanskrit, both as regards its accuracy and the systematic terms in which they stated it, and their ability to carry formal analysis below the word in terms corresponding to the modern *morpheme*. Greco-Roman morphological analysis was set out in terms of paradigms of whole words grouped together by similarities of morphological composition, but the actual concept of the morpheme as a formal component of such words was never clearly explicated by scholars in Western antiquity. In part this accounts for the rather wild statements they made in etymologies, on the basis of which their work and that of their medieval successors have been rather unfairly judged as a whole.

Pāṇini is also to be credited with the device of zero in linguistic description, by which part of an apparently irregular set of morphological forms can, by positing an analytic entity without actual exponents as an element of their structure, be brought into line with the regular forms. This procedure has already been illustrated above (5·4·2).

In Europe general linguistics of the modern period largely grew out of nineteenth century comparative and historical studies, as scholars began to widen the scope of their interests. In America, there was the additional influence of anthropological studies, especially those dealing with American-Indian peoples, whose languages at once presented a field of great difficulty and great interest. In Britain, both these sources contributed, and were supplemented by the strong British interest in phonetics, that can be traced back for some centuries and was reinforced by the Indian tradition. At the end of the nineteenth and in the first half of the twentieth centuries Sweet and Jones were among the pioneers of modern phonetics, and the latter contributed to a considerable extent to the development of the phoneme theory.

Among others whose influence on the course of general linguistics in various parts of the world in this century has been profound, one must mention de Saussure, Trubetzkoy, and Meillet in Europe, Sapir and Bloomfield in America, and Firth in Britain. It was during their lifetimes and through their work that the essentially structural nature of language was made clear and structural theories at every level of description were developed to deal with it (2·1·2). Under the influence of scholars such as these also, linguistics achieved for the first time in its history the position of academic autonomy, a position not attained in Western antiquity, nor in the Middle Ages, nor, despite the excellence of their work, among the linguistic scholars of Pāṇinean India. The contemporary linguist is under an obligation to study every aspect and type of language unbeholden to the particular interests in language that other disciplines may have. Interdisciplinary cooperation between the linguist and all those whose subjects touch at any point on his are much to be encouraged and fostered; but the methods and terms employed by the linguist in making statements and framing analyses, at every level he recognizes, are designed and selected with one end only in view, their efficiency in dealing with the forms of language and the uses of language.

The purpose of this book has been to give a short introductory account and general survey of linguistics at the present time. The last fifty years have seen remarkable and encouraging growth both in the subject itself and in the scholarly interest taken in it in many parts of the world. Much work remains to be accomplished; new lines of thought open up, and new methods must be devised to follow them; and general linguistic theory must be always keeping pace with methodological progress. The languages of mankind in all their fascinating detail and with all their immense power among the human faculties still present a potentially limitless field for disciplined investigation and systematic study. It is altogether right that they should be the object of scholarly enthusiasm, controlled imagination, and great reverence.

CHAPTER 9, BIBLIOGRAPHY

1. D. ABERCROMBIE, 'Forgotten phoneticians', *TPS* 1948, 1–34.

2 W. S. ALLEN, *Phonetics in Ancient India*, London, 1953.

3. H. ARENS, *Sprachwissenschaft: der Gang ihrer Entwicklung von der Antike bis zur Gegenwart*, Freiburg, 1955.

4. S. K. BELVALKAR, *An account of the different existing systems of Sanskrit grammar*, Poona, 1915.

5. L. BLOOMFIELD, *Language*, London, 1935.

6. ——, 'Language or ideas?', *Lang.* 12 (1936), 89–95.

7. ——, *An outline guide for the practical study of foreign languages*, Baltimore, 1942.

8. A. D. BOOTH, L. BRANDWOOD, and J. P. CLEAVE, *Mechanical resolution of linguistic problems*, London, 1958.

9. C. BROCKELMANN, *Geschichte der arabischen Litteratur*, Weimar and Berlin, 1898–1902.

10. C. D. BUCK, *Comparative grammar of Greek and Latin*, Chicago, 1933.

11. J. B. CARROLL, *The study of language*, Cambridge, Mass., 1953.

12. E. DELAVENAY, *An introduction to machine translation*, London, 1960.

13. J. R. FIRTH, 'Wartime experiences in linguistic training', *Modern languages* 26 (1945), 38–46.

14. ——, 'The English school of phonetics', *TPS* 1946, 92–132.

15. ——, 'Modes of meaning', *Essays and studies* 1951, 118–49.

16. ——, 'Applications of general linguistics', *TPS* 1957, 1–14.

17. A. G. N. FLEW (editor), *Logic and language*, Oxford, 1951.

18. R. A. D. FORREST, *The Chinese language*, London, 1948.

19. A. C. GRAHAM, ' "Being" in Western philosophy compared with *shih/fei* and *yu/wu* in Chinese philosophy', *Asia major* 7 (1959), 79–112.

BIBLIOGRAPHY FOR CHAPTER 9

20. M. R. HAAS, *Tunica*, New York, 1941 (*Handbook of American Indian languages* 4).

21. ——, 'The linguist as a teacher of languages', *Lang.* 19 (1943), 203-8.

22. D. JONES, *Outline of English phonetics*, sixth edition, Cambridge, 1947.

23. A. L. KROEBER (editor), *Anthropology today*, Chicago, 1953.

24. W. P. LEHMANN, 'On earlier stages of the Indo-European nominal inflection', *Lang.* 34 (1958), 179-202.

25. W. N. LOCKE and A. D. BOOTH (editors), *Machine translation of languages*, New York, 1955.

26. F. MAUTHNER, *Beiträge zu einer Kritik der Sprache*, Leipzig, 1923.

27. C. MOHRMANN, A. SOMMERFELT, and J. WHATMOUGH, *Trends in European and American linguistics 1930-1960*, Utrecht, 1961.

28. E. A. NIDA, 'Field techniques', *IJAL* 13 (1947), 138-46.

29. ——, *Morphology*, second edition, Ann Arbor, 1949.

30. A. G OETTINGER, *Automatic language translation*, Cambridge, Mass., 1960.

31. C. K. OGDEN and I. A. RICHARDS, *The meaning of meaning*, eighth edition, London, 1946.

32. C. OSGOOD and T. A. SEBEOK (editors), *Psycholinguistics*, *IJAL* 20 (1954), number 4, supplement.

33. D. Y. PANOV, *Automatic translation*, London, 1960.

34. R. K. POTTER, G. A. KOPP, and H. C. GREEN, *Visible speech*, New York, 1947.

35. E. PULGRAM, *An introduction to the spectrography of speech*, The Hague, 1959.

36. R. H. ROBINS, *Ancient and mediaeval grammatical theory in Europe*, London, 1951.

37. ——, 'Dionysius Thrax and the Western grammatical tradition', *TPS* 1957, 67-106.

38. ——, 'Linguistics and anthropology', *Man* 59 (1959), 175-8.

39. E. SAPIR, *Language*, New York, 1921.

40. T. A. SEBEOK (editor), *Style in language*, London, 1960.

9 WIDER PERSPECTIVES

41. C. SHANNON and W. WEAVER, *The mathematical theory of communication*, Urbana, 1949.

42. H. SWEET, *Handbook of phonetics*, Oxford, 1877.

43. ——, *Primer of phonetics*, Oxford, 1890.

44. I. C. WARD, *Practical suggestions for the learning of an African language in the field*, London, 1937.

45. L. WITTGENSTEIN, *Tractatus logico-philosophicus*, London, 1922.

46. ——, *Philosophical investigations* (translated by G. E. M. Anscombe), Oxford, 1953.

ADDENDA

47. M. A. K. HALLIDAY, A. MCINTOSH and P. STREVENS. *The linguistic sciences and language teaching*, London, 1964.

48. M. LEROY, *Les grands courants de la linguistique moderne*, Brussels and Paris, 1963.

49. S. R. LEVIN, *Linguistic structures in poetry*, The Hague, 1962.

50. C. MOHRMANN, F. NORMAN, and A. SOMERFELT, *Trends in modern linguistics*, Utrecht, 1963.

51. S. ULLMANN, *Language and style*, Oxford, 1964.

52. R. E. LONGACRE, *Grammar discovery procedures: a field manual*, The Hague, 1964.

53. D. HYMES (editor), *Language in culture and society: a reader in linguistics and anthropology*, New York, 1964.

p. 352. Ethnolinguistics, Carroll, 11, chapter 4. Several of the topics surveyed in the present chapter are discussed in this valuable book. cp. Robins, 38.

On the distinction between social anthropology and sociology, Carroll, 11, 117.

p. 353. In addition to class dialects, the jargons of various special groups in society, such as criminals, prisoners, sailors, regular servicemen, certain schools, semi-secret associations, etc., are valuable material for linguistic analysis if the linguist can get at them reliably.

p. 354. On anthropological linguistics, Hoijer, 27, 110–27.

p. 356. As an example of what can be done when the linguist is of necessity limited to a single surviving speaker of a language, see Haas, 20.

On field work, Ward, 44; Bloomfield, 7; Nida, 28; 29; F. G. Lounsbury, 'Field methods and techniques in linguistics', Kroeber, 23, 401–16; Longacre, 52.

p. 359. Wittgenstein, 45; 46.

On the influence of languages on philosophy, Ogden and Richards, 31, 96–7; Mauthner, 26, volume 3, 4; with reference to Chinese, Graham, 19.

On the therapeutic tasks of philosophy, Flew, 17, chapters 1 and 2.

p. 360. Bloomfield, 6.

p. 361. On the range of psychology, Carroll, 11, 69; further discussion on linguistics and psychology, chapter 3.

p. 362. Psycholinguistics, 32.

p. 363. Bloomfield, 5, 28; cp. Carroll, 11, 74.

p. 364. On the early history of some grammatical categories, Buck, 10, 170; Lehmann, 24.

p. 366. On linguistics and the teaching of languages, Haas, 21; 'The application of linguistics to language teaching', Kroeber, 23, 807–18; Moulton in 27, 82–109; Firth, 13; 16.

p. 367. On communications engineering and linguistics, Carroll, 11, chapter 7.

'Visible speech', Potter, Kopp, and Green, 34; Pulgram, 35.

Communication theory, Shannon and Weaver, 41.

Machine translation, Locke and Booth, 25; Brandwood and Cleave, 8; Panov, 33; Delavenay, 12; Oettinger, 30.

p. 372. Linguistics and literature, Sapir, 39, chapter 11; Firth, 15; Sebeok, 40; Ullmann, 51.

9   WIDER PERSPECTIVES

p. 373. On the history of linguistics in Europe, Robins, 36; Arens, 3.
Chinese linguistic scholarship, Forrest, 18.
Arabic linguistic scholarship, Brockelmann, 9.
p. 375. Dionysius Thrax, Robins, 37.
p. 377. Bloomfield, 5, 11.
On Pāṇini and ancient Indian linguistic studies, Belvalkar, 4; Allen, 2.
p. 378. Phonetics in England ,Sweet, 42; 43; Jones, 22; Abercrombie, 1;
Firth, 14.

ADDENDA

p. 358. On linguistics and anthropology, Hymes, 53.
p. 366. On linguistics and the teaching of languages, Halliday, McIntosh
and Strevens, 47.
p. 372. On linguistics and literature, Levin, 49.
p. 379. On the recent history of linguistics, Mohrmann, 27 and 50;
Leroy, 48; Waterman, 54; Ivić, 55; Malmberg, 56.

384

Index

Page numbers in **boldface** refer to the
most important treatment of the topic.

385

INDEX